Mervyn Matthews

CLASS AND SOCIETY IN SOVIET RUSSIA

Walker and Company, New York

First published in the United States of America in
1972 by the Walker Publishing Company, Inc.

Published simultaneously in Canada by Fitzhenry &
Whiteside, Limited, Toronto

ISBN: 0–8027–0364–X

Library of Congress Catalog Card Number: 79–179615

Printed in Great Britain

To L.B.,
who showed me that despite everything
Russia is still in Europe

Contents

Preface

ANYONE who sits down to write something in the nature of a 'sociological' analysis of the Soviet Union must expect trouble. Even if he manages, after a long period of effort, to complete the manuscript, he can hope for little but criticism when it eventually appears, neatly printed and attractively bound.

The best historians of Russia, he knows, will be horrified by the lack of temporal profundity, and will take up their fountain pens to register an elegant, and probably justified, protest. Sociologists of happier lands, used to sifting through tons of gritty statistics, will think it absurd that this work has been attempted on so narrow a factual basis, and will spring to their typewriters to register that thought. Many powerful brains, should they bother to read the book at all, will regard it as further proof that sociology, as a discipline, doesn't exist. And although this is by no means an 'anti-Soviet' work, the writer can hardly expect a positive response from Mr Trapeznikov and other comrades in the Central Committee.

Only a strong element of enthusiasm – some might say foolhardiness – can prompt him to proceed in such circumstances. And, perhaps, the belief that something new and useful can be said after all. This is perhaps why I have been persuaded to continue. I would not have done so without the encouragement and help of many friends and colleagues. My thanks are due to Dr Marshall Shulman of the Russian Research Centre, Columbia University, for inviting me to spend three months in New York to work at the Institute and University Library. This was a most pleasant and valuable experience which enabled me to assemble data for several chapters.

A study of this kind must rest on materials which are the stuff of other disciplines, principally economics, politics, law, and education. I would certainly not lay claim to an adequate grasp of all of them. In an endeavour to reduce the number of errors I have asked some very able and eminent scholars to read and comment on those parts of the manuscript which come most within their purview. I have been exceptionally fortunate in this respect.

Mr J. Newth of Glasgow University kindly picked out a number of errors and omissions in the chapter on demography. Dr I. Lapenna of the London School of Economics advised me on weaknesses in my interpretation of Soviet ideology and social theory. Mr Michael Kaser of St Antony's College, Oxford, made several useful comments on the economic and planning aspects. Mr Harry Willets of St Antony's and Mr Everett Jacobs of Sheffield University helped me find a path through the maze of collective farm economics and law. Professor Leonard Schapiro of L.S.E., whose knowledge of the Party is scarcely surpassed outside Russia, read chapter 8, and I benefited from his very pertinent criticisms of it. Mr D. Hutchings of the Department of Education at Oxford and Mr J. Tomiac of London University have commented on some of the educational material. Mr Martin Dewhurst of Glasgow University promptly and carefully scanned nearly all of the manuscript, and it is much better as a result. Mr David Shapiro was kind enough to read it all through in its final form. I have done my best to incorporate most of the suggestions which were made into the text; pressure of time and certain constructional difficulties have not allowed me to use all of them. I could not, of course, ask everyone to read the whole manuscript, and any mistakes which remain are, in the standard phrase, entirely my own responsibility.

I am most grateful to the Nuffield Foundation for timely financial support which made it possible for me to visit libraries abroad and engage some research assistance at home. I must not omit to thank those of my colleagues at the Technological University of Surrey who facilitated my research, and provided some measure of protection from the fashionable view that a teacher should be firmly attached to his blackboard, and discouraged from wasting time writing books. Finally, I would like to express my gratitude to those scholars in the Soviet Union and abroad whose work I have used, or referred to, in the text. Without this body of material my study could never have been attempted.

Introduction

THE growth and structure of Soviet society are subjects of immense interest, not only to sociologists, but to all who concern themselves with Russia. It is fortunate that the circumstances of Soviet rule again allow Soviet scholars to investigate a few of the problems involved, and publish some of their findings.

The break in the tradition of sociological research in the USSR began in the late twenties, and lasted for three decades. The reasons for it need little explanation. Indigenous Russian sociology, though severely limited by the Bolsheviks, was nevertheless a productive discipline until the Stalinist clampdown of the late twenties and early thirties. Thereafter empirical work, even of a strongly 'Marxist' character, was banned, and the flow of official statistics – the stuff of generalization – ceased. Sociology may be considered to have been re-established only in 1958, when the Soviet Sociological Association was set up. The Soviet annual statistical handbooks had, however, begun to appear after 1956, and All-Union censuses were renewed in 1959. The nature of the Soviet state has, of course, always completely excluded first-hand field study by outsiders.

The sixties saw the publication of a body of work which has thrown much light on Soviet social structure and processes. The difficulties of study which remain are, however, by no means slight. It is unpleasant to begin on a negative note, yet they need to be set out at least once, for they make themselves felt at many points, and will in some measure shape our study. We are primarily concerned with the obstacles facing the Western scholar, though many of them hamper the Soviet investigator too.

They may be thought of as ideological and practical. The former spring from the premises on which official theories of Soviet society are based. This society, in the view of Lenin, would quickly come to differ fundamentally from the bourgeois

societies of the West. Private ownership of the means of production, which gave rise to class frictions and all manner of social
evils, would be abolished. The very nature of the individual
would change appreciably, social dissension would more or less
evaporate, and society as a whole would become 'homogeneous'.
Consequently lesser ills such as poverty, social privilege, crime
and religious belief (which Lenin equated with superstition)
would gradually vanish, like morose Cheshire cats.

It was only natural that the Soviet leadership, trained in an
authoritarian tradition, should always have tended to give undue
prominence to facts which seemed to support these ideas, and
conceal those which contradicted them too blatantly. A further
element of distortion is introduced by the fact that this leadership is strongly nationalistic. The authorities have an inbuilt
tendency to boast about Soviet (or Russian) successes and are
reluctant to disclose failures.

The practical difficulties of study are a direct consequence of
these inhibitions. The relative abundance of data on Soviet
achievements in a few economic and social activities is offset by
the total absence of information on less happy, or ideologically
suspect, phenomena. Let us take just one illustration. Central to
the study of society is an understanding of social stratification:
most sociologists like to think of society as an infinitely complicated hierarchy of groups of people which they usually term
'classes'. A great deal of the interest of sociology derives from
determining the size and nature of these bodies, the relationships
between them, and their hold on the individual. This is by no
means the only approach, but it is a popular one. Now one of the
most important stratification hierarchies is based on income.
Unfortunately, Soviet 'official' theory insists that all people who
are not peasants are members of a single 'working class', which
is relatively 'homogeneous'. The Soviet authorities allow little
information to be published on income distribution, presumably
because they fear that some kind of élite would be revealed and
their viewpoint invalidated. Any attempt to construct a hierarchy
or continuum of toilers on an income basis is therefore a very
difficult operation indeed. Yet it is absurd to lump nearly 200
million souls together in one social group.

Much information which seems to contradict the avowed

principle of social unity is withheld by the Soviet authorities, though we must add, in fairness, that in some cases it has just not been collected, or has proved too unreliable for use. Other lacunae are data on the more obvious social evils, the ruling group, most aspects of politics, certain kinds of social mobility, unemployment, nationalism, etc.

Our study is built on the islets of hard fact which have recently emerged from a barren sea. The most important source of sociological data at our disposal is the series of statistical handbooks which have appeared annually since 1956. For all their faults and shortcomings these collections are extremely useful. The same may be said of the 1959 and 1970 Censuses (though only the preliminary results of the second were available when the manuscript was completed). The third major source of information is the sociological data derived from social surveys, or 'concrete sociological investigations' as they are called in Russia. Finally, many revealing articles by responsible newspaper reporters now throw light on problems which would otherwise have gone uncharted. The results of the sociological investigations which have been published are evidently only a fraction of all that have been gathered: they are nevertheless of unusual interest and deserve an extra word of comment. Without them even the limited study we attempt here would have been impossible.

The areas which Soviet sociologists have been able to illuminate for us show up rather well in a count of their published writings. A recent bibliography of 830 titles of Soviet works on sociology (excluding criticism of the 'bourgeois' brands) which was compiled for private use shows the following distribution:

Topic	Number of titles
Social consciousness	130
General problems of sociological theory: sociology and philosophy	102
The sociology of labour	89
Population: demography: social hygiene	83
Social structure of society: classes and social strata	77
Methodology, methods and techniques of sociological investigation	55

In the pages which follow use has been made of works from the majority of these categories.

It is logical that we should begin with a review of the outstanding demographic features of Soviet society. Despite a continuing shortage of information on many central features of Soviet population history, the results of the January 1959 census provide enough data to make this a worthwhile operation. A graphic breakdown of the Soviet population by age group (the 'population pyramid') shows many deviations from what is regarded as 'normal' for an industrial society, and each of these abnormalities may be explained, up to a point, by the social history of the state. This is an intriguing exercise.

Next we move on to the question of Soviet social structure. We have already noted the proclivity of the sociological fraternity for seeing all but the most primitive societies in terms of classes which bear a hierarchical relationship to one another. The definition of 'class' is, however, an intricate topic. Western textbooks of sociological theory suggest a number of possible indices: apart from income there are occupation (which comes closest to the Marxist concept of relationship to the means of production), education, cultural background, and people's own opinion of their 'class' standing. A good definition of class would have to include all of these, and perhaps others. The indices would tend to show a marked degree of correlation with one another.

The most orthodox analysts of Soviet social structure dispense with most of these yardsticks, or perhaps it would be more exact to say that they have not yet adopted them. The official formula of classes contains only three major social groups – a working class, a peasantry and an intelligentsia – and most statistical information is tailored to fit this mould. Certain administrative and legal practices are also based on it. For these immediate reasons an examination of the 'official sociology', its development and validity, form the second and third chapters of the book.

In chapter 4 we turn to the problem of stratifying the Soviet 'working class', by income; chapter 5 covers stratification by occupation and education. The figures available on these topics vary considerably in adequacy, and it is often extremely difficult to correlate them, even when a high degree of correlation is probable. Nevertheless, taken together, the data do provide a sort of impressionistic image of the social structure, one which is perhaps an advance on what we had before. In each instance we have attempted to show, by means of time studies, how differences of income, occupation and education affect people's way of life. To do this has sometimes necessitated taking material from studies which were intended to illustrate other phenomena, or whose results have not been published in full. In cases such as these we have been careful to mention these drawbacks, and at the same time do as much justice as possible to the authors' original intentions. Occupation and education are the two indices by which the Soviet 'intelligentsia' is normally delineated, so this is the spot we have chosen to illustrate the more common definitions of the term. Of course, the intelligentsia is covered in the discussion of urban income and elsewhere.

The next chapter is devoted to the social structure of the Soviet village, with particular reference to the collective farm. There are irrefutable arguments for treating urban and rural society separately, not least because the *kolkhoz* is the last refuge of the peasantry. This is one of the spheres, incidentally, in which the findings of Soviet sociologists (as opposed to census and statistical returns) are particularly valuable. Next we go on to examine the problem of migration between town and country, which we describe as the drift from the land. In so far as the change from peasant to working-class status represents a move upwards, this may also be regarded as a form of social mobility in the USSR.

The second part of the book is devoted to three topics which are both important and of special interest to the author. (An advantage of writing a book is that one has some control over what goes into it.) The first of these is political sociology. The Soviet system of government is one which does not readily lend itself to analysis in depth, and the materials available have in most cases been worked through pretty thoroughly by students of politics, history and, of course, Kremlinology. For our own treatment we have tried to choose a few aspects which continue our study of social structure, yet have not, in our view, been explored thoroughly enough. These are selected numerical relationships between the Party and certain social groups, and the interesting problem of participation by the masses in officially approved, politically orientated activities. We hope by this means to add an important political perspective to our analysis of society, without repeating observations made by other Western observers. Some of the social survey results used here show, incidentally, an interesting degree of political dissent.

The second theme is education. We have singled out for examination the relationships between various kinds of institutions of learning and different social groups. One chapter deals with the social complexion of the middle and lower schools, and another treats the social origins of the student body. Apart from its intrinsic interest this throws further light on social mobility.

The last topic is the employment, or more exactly placement, of young people in full-time jobs. We shall be concerned with two major categories of work-seekers, those who have completed the general school, and graduates of higher and middle special educational institutions. In an industrialized society work-finding is a complicated process which seems to attract public attention only when things go wrong and unemployment is reported. We have set ourselves the task of explaining, as far as possible, how placement is handled in the Soviet Union, and tracing the social consequences of success and failure in this field.

The study of any society is interesting in so far as it tells us things that we did not know, or may have been disinclined to believe about it. This inevitably brings us to the problem of comparison, either in historical perspective, or between societies.

We may well ask how quickly Soviet society is changing, and how far it resembles, or differs from, American or British society.

These are matters which we shall touch on only indirectly. Our main concern will be to write about certain aspects of Soviet society in so far as they can be discerned in the years covered by our data. A comparative study of the same scope would mean moving to a completely different plane, and one which would doubtlessly be beyond the capabilities of a single writer. We have tried to make historical or inter-societal comparisons only when they seemed particularly accessible. For the same severely practical reasons we have not included much on ethnic distinctions; the sector of Soviet society which might be described as basically European in character has been our main concern.

One last matter remains to be considered: the premises which underly our approach. A society cannot be studied without making some prior selection of the facts available; the sociologist, like the historian, while trying not to prejudge the issues, must decide what the issues are.

In a recent essay on models of Soviet social development Dr Alex Inkeles, who has led the study of Soviet society for so many years, pointed out that students of Soviet society consciously or unconsciously use stereotypes or 'models' to help them in their analysis.[1] The three which he thought most helpful were the so-called 'totalitarian' model, in which the decisive factor is seen as a powerful state apparatus with a highly authoritarian government; the 'development' model, in which the momentum of change from an agricultural to an industrial status is considered to be the central motive force; and the 'industrial' model, in which the overriding factors are thought of as industrialization and urbanization. This is particularly useful when comparing Soviet society with that of the USA and West Europe. As Dr Inkeles pointed out, this by no means completes the list of possibilities: he went on to mention Mr Daniel Bell's ten models, and

1. *Survey*, July 1966. Dr Inkeles's writings are numerous and mostly well known. His article 'Social Stratification and Mobility in the Soviet Union', first published in 1950 and reprinted in *Social Change in Soviet Russia*, Cambridge, Mass., 1968, may be regarded as a landmark in the Western appreciation of Soviet social structure.

even suggested that a historical model, in which the traditional Tsarist elements predominated, might be the most apt.

Our own approach has been to try, as far as sources allow, to illustrate phenomena which currently attract the attention of sociologists in the study of any modern society. Our study should thus provide a fund of argument for proponents of many schools: we have not elected to choose between them. Our main aim has been to throw a sympathetic, and to our mind objective, light on the structure and development of a predominantly European society.

Part I
SOVIET SOCIAL STRUCTURE

I
The Demographic Background

THE study of any society, especially if that study is rather quantitative in nature, must begin with a survey of population structure. Demographic history inevitably leaves a clear imprint on social structure and development.

It is a basic premise of demography that the population of any large area responds to social stimuli in fairly well-defined ways, and develops in accordance with recognized patterns. Of course, it has to. Man, being a creature of flesh and blood, cannot transgress his own obvious biological and psychological limits.

The size and age and sex distribution of the population at present within the Soviet frontiers is partly a consequence of the voluntary procreativity of generations past, and partly the result of an infinity of extraneous events, from the unplanned birth of individual children (who have then begotten their own) to the death of millions by man-made calamity. This is only another way of saying that the specific traits of the Soviet population structure, like those of any other, can hardly be studied apart from the history of the land. But this presents particular difficulties.

Soviet demographic science, which is concerned with these problems, has had a very uneven career. Although the Soviet authorities have been, on the whole, fairly rigorous in their data collection, the amount they have published has varied considerably with time and political circumstance. Local censuses were organized as early as 1920 and 1922, and the peak of Soviet statistical endeavour was reached in the census of 1926, which appeared in 57 volumes. Since then we have been less lucky. The results of a census conducted in 1937 were suppressed completely and many of the compilers arrested. A few figures were released from the census returns of 1939, but this was itself a very imperfect undertaking. The questionnaire omitted, for example, any reference to large but unfortunate social groups

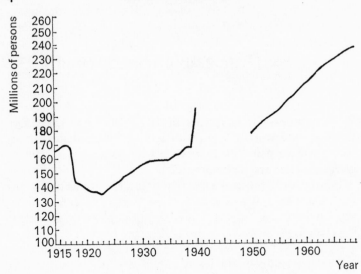

FIGURE I.   *Total population of Imperial Russia–USSR, 1914–69*

Sources:

1914–18: W. W. Eason, 'The Population of the USSR', Report to the Judiciary Committee of the House of Representatives of U.S. Congress, Washington, 1964, p. 31. Figures for 1914 to 1917 are given for territory of Imperial Russia.

1914–39: F. Lorimer, *The Population of the Soviet Union*, Geneva, 1946, pp. 30, 134–5, mostly hypothetical. After the graph had been composed Mr J. A. Newth of Glasgow kindly drew my attention to a set of figures for 1917–24 in E. Z. Volkov, *Dinamika narodonaselenia SSSR za 80 let*, Moscow-Leningrad, 1930. These follow the same basic pattern as those I have used, but are about 2 million lower.

1926 (17 December), 1939 (17 January): official All-Union Census returns, *Narodnoe khozyaistvo SSSR*, Moscow, 1956, p. 17.

1939 (17 September): P. G. Pod'yachikh, *Naselenie SSSR*, Moscow, 1961, p. 14.

1940 (1 January, estimate): *Narodnoe khozyaistvo SSSR v 1968*, Moscow, 1969, p. 7. This registers a discrepancy of no less than 2.4 million with the estimate given in *Narodnoe khozyaistvo SSSR*, Moscow, 1956.

1950 onwards: Estimates for 1 January from *Narodnoe khozyaistvo* of relevant years, with the exception of 1959 which gives the Census figure for 15 January, see *Itogi vsesoyuznoi perepisi naselenia 1959 goda*, *SSSR, svodny tom*, Moscow, 1962, p. 13. This volume will subsequently be referred to as *1959 Census Returns*.

like vagrants, the unemployed, or persons interned in the many labour camps. The global population figures, as published, may have contained inaccuracies of several million.

The questionnaires of the 1959 and 1970 censuses were, unfortunately, closely modelled on that of 1939, and the published results of the 1959 Census were not adequately correlated with one another. The statistical material at our disposal must therefore be supported by the careful estimates and projections of a number of Western scholars, if it is to be used to answer the broad questions which interest us.[1] A convenient way to begin is by looking at the size and growth of the population since November 1917. Then we can consider the demographic situation as it is today.

POPULATION GROWTH 1914-69

Figure 1 gives a rough idea of the growth of the total population of the Soviet state since its establishment, with account taken of the changing frontiers. The total figure has risen from a nominal 169 million in the Tsarist empire of 1914 (or about 142 million on post-1920 Soviet territory) to 241.7 million in January 1970. At the same time the rate of growth has decreased from a high of about 17 per thousand to 9.6 per thousand a year. This general trend is basically normal for an urbanizing and industrializing society. Figure 2, showing the birth-rates and death-rates (some official, some estimated, and some blatantly hypothetical), attempts to show how this has come about. The overall picture is of two falling curves which contain some surprise fluctuations. It would be no exaggeration to say that Soviet demographic history is amongst the most varied and interesting of modern times. A glance at the relatively smooth curves for America and Great Britain show how unfortunate the Soviet Union has been in this respect (Figure 3).

The First World War, the Revolution and Civil War

Soviet demographic history can be divided into a number of clearly defined periods, according to whether growth has been

1. At the time of writing only the preliminary results of the 1970 Census were available.

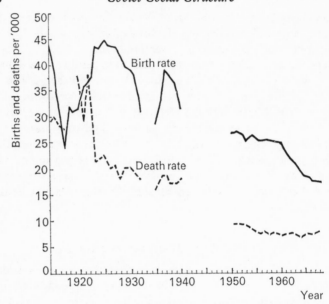

FIGURE 2.   *Birth- and Death-rates of Imperial Russia–USSR,*
1914–69

Sources:

Births: 1914–30, 1935, 1936: B.Ts. Urlanis, *Rozhdaemost' i prodolzhitelnost'*
zhizni v SSSR, Moscow, 1963, pp. 21–8.

   1931, 1932: W. W. Eason, op. cit. (Figure 1), p. 32. Eason provides figures
for the years 1920–23 which are slightly below Urlanis's.

   All other figures from *Narodnoe khozyaistvo SSSR*, (various years).

Deaths: 1914–17: Urlanis, op. cit., p. 84. Eason gives a figure of 25.3 for 1914.

   1920–32: Eason, op. cit., p. 32. Official figures from *Narodnoe khozyaistvo*
SSSR v 1964 covering 1926, 1928, put the death rate at 20.3 and 23.3
respectively.

   1935, 1936, 1940: Eason, op. cit., p. 32.

   1937–9: *Narodnoe khozyaistvo SSSR v 1964*, p. 34.

   Figures for 1950 onwards from *Narodnoe khozyaistvo SSSR* (various
years).

encouraged or inhibited. We have taken the population of the
Russian Empire at the outbreak of the 1914–18 war to be about
169 million. As may be seen from Figure 2, the period of marked
instability of birth- and death-rates which began with the outbreak of fighting went on until 1922–3, and corresponded with
some extremely agitated years in Soviet history. Let us take the
most relevant factors in turn.

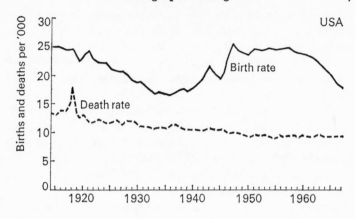

FIGURE 3. *Birth- and Death-rates of the USA and UK (England and Wales), 1914–67*

Sources:

United States: Vital Statistics of the United States, 1967, Volume II Mortality A, and Volume I Natality.

Figures for 1915–32 inclusive are based on the birth- and death-rates of those states which registered them.

England and Wales: U.K. Annual Abstract of Statistics, HMSO, London, 1953, 1968, and *U.K. Registrar General's Statistical Review of England and Wales*, HMSO, London, 1958 and 1967.

The engagement of the Russian Empire in the struggle against the Central Powers in the First World War began when the Tsar ordered complete mobilization of the Russian Army on 30 July 1914. The immediate impact of the war on demographic development was twofold: married recruits were separated from their wives, and some couples who were not separated probably decided that it would be better not to reproduce for the present. This led to a sharp fall in the birth-rate in the following year.[2]

Soon other demographic effects of the war began to make themselves felt, mostly in a logical and foreseeable manner. The struggle, of course, went disastrously for Russia. The military commanders demanded more and more men, so that the army, originally comprising 1.4 million souls, had absorbed a total of over fifteen million – well over a third of the total male population in the reproductive age-groups – by 1917.[3] This, together with other forms of disruption of social life, caused the number of children born annually to fall by a half.

The death rate went up alarmingly. Loss of life directly attributable to the war effort was enormous. Estimates vary, but Frank Lorimer, to whom we are indebted for one of the best Western studies of these years, suggested a round figure of two million soldiers' deaths alone. In addition to this, several hundred thousand civilians probably perished when they were caught up in military actions on the field of battle, and about 350,000 people died of typhus, typhoid, dysentery and cholera. Apart from the 'direct' deaths, military and civil, several categories of 'indirect' losses were inevitable. Firstly, there were the lost births – the children who would have been born if society had been untouched by this catastrophe. These, according to Lorimer, would have numbered up to 10 million. Secondly, we may presume that infant mortality rose steeply, for in wartime the amount of food and warmth available even for the new-born must diminish. Older people tended to die off more quickly, too. The three million Russians who were sent back from the front,

2. The figures on which this statement is based are B. Urlanis's, and they are only estimates. He does not associate them with any month. The same applies to the death-rate for these years.

3. M. T. Florinsky, *Russia, a History and an Interpretation*, New York, 1964, Vol. II, p. 1,353.

or repatriated from foreign jails because of sickness, may have died younger as a result of their experiences. Large numbers of Russians also emigrated during these years and in the early twenties.

The actual change in the size of the population over this period is still largely a matter of conjecture. Lorimer's figures, which we have used in the graph, showed an increase of only about a million against an expected 'normal' increase of about 12 million.[4] The Soviet figures published in the 1959 All-Union Census returns showed an increase of some four million between 1913 and 1917, which would mean that the loss was in the order of 8 million.

The loss of population to the new Soviet state did not, however, end with the war. The Treaty of Brest–Litovsk, signed on 3 March 1918, ceded to the Central Powers vast tracts of territory which had been part and parcel of the Tsarist domains since the days of Catherine the Great, and whose population numbered, before the war, over 26 million souls.[5] The war, and the terms on which it was concluded, were, then, wholly disastrous for the Soviet state in demographic terms.

The Russian Civil War is usually thought of as beginning in May 1918, when a legion of Czech soldiers who had been fighting on the Russian side refused to surrender their arms to the Soviet authorities in Penza, and became a centre of revolt. In the course of the next two and a half years bitter fighting took place throughout the country, including most of European Russia, Siberia, the Far East, and the South. The history of the Russian Civil War is complex and defies summarization. But the territory over which it was fought was vast, and a high proportion of the population was directly involved in it. As if this were not enough, the Bolsheviks inaugurated, in the areas under their control, the régime of 'War Communism', which entailed extremely repressive policies towards large sections of the peasantry, in particular the richer – and more efficient – *kulaks*. This caused considerable social disruption in the villages, and further restriction of food supplies to the towns. Annual agri-

4. He took the population of the area which was enclosed by the frontiers of the Soviet state.

5. *1959 Census Returns*, p. 13.

cultural output may have dropped by at least a third between 1917 and 1921.[6]

It is not surprising if, as B. Urlanis's data suggest, there was a continued depression of the birth-rate. His figures for the death-rate are too erratic to inspire much confidence, but it is not at all improbable that deaths were at certain times much higher than during the First World War. Civil war tends to have more negative effects on the demographic processes than foreign wars of similar magnitude. The total population of the country probably *fell* by nearly 7 million by 1921, despite the return of part of the old Imperial Army from abroad.[7]

The Civil War ended in the spring of 1921, and the policies of War Communism were effectively terminated at the Tenth Congress of the Party in March. The misfortunes of war and revolution were, however, followed by a widespread drought which affected the Volga area in 1921 and 1922, and brought famine and disease in its wake. Between 1920 and 1923 the losses from epidemics in the large towns of European Russia alone amounted to nearly two million souls and deaths from starvation must have been numerous.[8] This is the explanation for the alarming peak which W. Eason suggests for the death-rate around 1922.

Such, then, were the principal causes of the great fluctuations which characterized Soviet birth- and death-rates in the first five years of Soviet power. The total direct losses may have been in excess of 14 million, to which at least ten million lost births should be added.[9] Soviet society was born amid a demographic catastrophe.

The New Economic Policy and the First Five-Year Plans

The second period in the history of the Soviet population may be thought of as extending from the initiation of the moderate economic policies of NEP to the outbreak of the Second World War in June 1941. We would expect to find in the curves some reflec-

6. S. N. Prokopovicz, *Histoire économique de l'URSS*, Paris, 1952, p. 126.
7. W. W. Eason, op. cit., p. 31. These figures do not quite accord with those of S. N. Prokopovicz, op. cit., p. 41.
8. F. Lorimer, op. cit., p. 41.
9. F. Lorimer's figures for 1914–26, territory of the USSR, p. 41.

tion of such important social processes as accelerated industrialization, the collectivization of agriculture, and the great political
purges of the late thirties.

The total population rose from about 135 million in 1923 to a
reported 170 million on the eve of the territorial annexations
which began in September 1939. This included some territorial
expansion in Central Asia in the mid twenties. The rate of increase was by no means even. According to Lorimer's hypo-
theses, it averaged 2–3 million a year until about 1931, when it
virtually stopped: it resumed its upward course only in 1936.[10]
What happened to the birth- and death-rates during this four-
year halt is one of the central mysteries of Soviet demographic
history. It seems unlikely that it can be solved on the basis of the
materials at present available.

The mid twenties were a period of economic reconstruction
and comparative political quiescence amongst the masses, if not
in the top leadership. Soviet society was still largely rural – over
three quarters of the inhabitants lived outside the towns. A
rather high birth-rate is, of course, a known characteristic of the
pre-industrial stage of economic development. Peasants tend to
have more room to house children whose labour they need, and
they don't have to worry too much about educating them. And
it is possible that the boredom of village life causes them to
copulate more frequently. These relatively calm social conditions
probably explain the high and fairly steady birth rate. The figures
for the death-rate are too erratic to be safely commented upon.

Profound changes were, however, imminent, in both town and
country. By the middle of 1928 Stalin had taken over the reins of
power and was in a position to effect those modifications in the
economic and political functioning of the state which became
the essence of his rule. Stalin himself termed 1929 'the year of the
great change': it was then that forced industrialization and the
collectivization of agriculture began in earnest. These policies
implied a new and ruthless attitude towards the labour force and
the population at large.

The main burden of suffering was borne by the peasantry.

10. W. W. Eason's figures show the same movement, except that he reveals
a pause at about 147 million in 1926–7. If there was one, its causes are not
immediately apparent.

Collectivization began in the late autumn of 1929, and by 1935 over 80 per cent of all peasant households had been forced into collective farms. Nearly 50 per cent of them went in during 1930 alone. The process meant extensive disruption of village life. The peasants responded to coercion by killing off their cattle (which they would have had to hand over to the collective anyway), by sowing less, and generally working less efficiently. The immediate effect of collectivization was to reduce the amount of food produced, and it is hardly necessary to add that the shortages were not made good by increased imports. The variations in the supply of grain and livestock are shown in Table 1. Output of grain dropped considerably and scarcely

TABLE I. *Collectivization and Agricultural Output*

	1928	1929	1930	1931	1932	1933	1934	1935
Grain harvest, real (million tons)	73.3	71.7	83.5	69.5	69.6	68.4	67.6	75.0
Grain harvest, biological (million tons)	—	—	—	—	—	89.8	89.4	90.1
Cattle (million head)	70.5	67.1	52.5	47.9	40.7	38.4	42.4	49.3
Pigs	26.0	20.4	13.6	14.4	11.6	12.1	17.4	22.6
Sheep and goats	146.7	147.0	108.8	77.7	52.1	50.2	51.9	61.1

Sources:
Alec Nove, op. cit., p. 186, from *Sotsialisticheskoe stroitel'stvo*, 1936, pp. 342–3, 354; Moshkov, *Zernovaya problema v gody sploshnoi kollektivizatsii*, Moscow University, 1966, p. 226.

regained the immediate pre-collectivization level before the outbreak of war. The holdings of animals fell by a half or two thirds, though they picked up rather more quickly.[11] Not surprisingly, there ensued in 1932 and 1933 a famine which was particularly severe on the Volga, in the Ukraine and Kuban. The absence of a death-rate figure for those years lends credence to the presumption that the death-roll was very heavy.

No less important from the demographic point of view was the

11. Alec Nove, *An Economic History of the USSR*, London, 1969, pp. 185, 238.

treatment meted out to the kulaks, or so-called 'rich' peasants. Most of them were not rich at all by West European standards, yet they had suffered in the period of War Communism, and were to suffer again. The fate that awaited perhaps five million of them was deportation to labour camps or inhospitable parts of Siberia and Asiatic Russia. The cost of this operation measured in terms of separated families and premature death must have been enormous.

Industrialization, though less frightening, also affected population trends. The urban population rose from about 26 million, or 18 per cent of the total, at the end of 1926 to 56 million, or 33 per cent by the beginning of 1939. The number of workers and employees as a social group more than trebled.[12] The heavy influx of former peasants into the towns led to a fall in housing standards and over-crowding; Stalin's policies caused real wages to drop, and there was stagnation, if not a fall, in the overall standard of living. Finally, we must not forget that these were the years when the smaller age-groups of the post-1914 period were reaching marriageable age.

There can be little doubt that the explanation for the precipitous decline in the birth-rate in the early thirties is to be found in some combination of these many negative factors. It is difficult even to estimate figures for 1933 and 1934, but it is entirely possible that the birth-rate fell below the level of the Civil War days, and might well have reached its lowest point since 1917. The death-rate, which was unsteady but probably falling throughout the twenties, must, of course, have risen to equal the birth-rate, so as to account for the pause in population growth which we have noted.

By 1936, however, the birth-rate was evidently back to the 1931 level, and this, together with some stabilization in the death-rate, must have accounted for the fact that the population began to increase again. It seems very likely that this recovery reflected a return to some kind of normality. It was also to a significant extent due to the law of 27 June 1937, which made abortion illegal and divorce more difficult. The authorities (who had every reason to be alarmed at the demographic trends) must have been aware that abortion was reducing the birth-rate,

12. See the table on p. 35 for selected years.

especially as the practice had increased very considerably in frequency since the late twenties.[13]

The three years 1936–9 are often thought of as those of the Great Purge, which began in earnest in the summer of 1936. The danger which now emerged was mass arrest. The most conservative estimates put the number of incarcerations during this period at three million, though by the early forties up to twenty million persons may have been sent to labour camps for alleged political crimes.[14]

Such massive oppression could not but have a visible effect on population growth. In fact official Soviet sources admit to a fall of about eight per thousand in the birth-rate between 1937 and 1940, but claim that the death-rate was steady. Some of the fall may indeed have been a consequence of urbanization. B.Ts. Urlanis has suggested that the partial mobilization for the Russian–Finnish war which started in 1939, and rumours of a forthcoming conflict with Germany, were also relevant. The take-over of the Western borderlands, where the birth-rate was much lower, was, no doubt, a contributory factor. These arguments, however, are in themselves less than adequate, and Soviet demographers have so far left a great deal unstated.

The direct and indirect losses of population between the year of the Great Change and the war, including as they did deportation, arrest, famine and lost births, may have been in the region of ten million. Even Lorimer's cautious projections put them at five and a half.[15] The suppression of the 1937 and 1939 Census results suggests that unwelcome information on these matters had been gathered.

In the autumn of 1939 and summer of 1940 Soviet society received a boost of at least 20 million souls. The inhabitants of the Baltic Republics, Karelia, Western Poland, White Russia, Bessarabia and Northern Bukovina were acquired by the Molotov–Ribbentrop pact and uncomplicated invasion. This total was

13. B.Ts. Urlanis, op. cit., p. 27.
14. The classic treatment of this appalling problem is to be found in D. Dallin and B. I. Nicolaevsky, *Forced Labour in Soviet Russia*, London, 1947. See also S. Swianiewicz, *Forced Labour and Economic Development*, London, 1965.
15. Lorimer, op. cit., p. 134.

reduced by the migration during the war of three million or so Soviet citizens, old and new, who decided to take refuge in the West, and nearly a million and a half persons who returned to Polish governance in 1945. The overall gain was nevertheless tremendous.[16]

From the Second World War to the Present Day

The Soviet authorities have, to the best of our knowledge, published no information on demographic movements between 1940 and 1950. Their reticence (presuming that they have figures themselves) is understandable, for these ten years saw a demographic disaster greater than any of those which the Soviet people had suffered before. The Second World War, or the Great Patriotic War as the Russians call it, combined the evils of both civil and foreign war in that the battle was fought against a foreign enemy on Soviet soil. The greater part of European Russia was occupied at one time or another.

The extent of the Soviet losses became evident only in 1956, when the first official estimate for a quarter of a century of the population was published. This put the total population at the incredibly low figure of 200 million. The 1959 census showed that even this was an overstatement of two million or so. The direct losses for the decade were therefore in the region of 20 million, and the deficit of births at least equalled that figure. Western observers had tended to underestimate these losses by magnitudes of up to *twenty million*: Frank Lorimer, for example, had hypothesized male military deaths at 5,000,000, and total losses, including the deficit in births, at 22 million. N. S. Timasheff suggested the audacious figure of 37.5 million, but may still have been short of the mark.

The losses, as may be expected, did not affect all age-groups and both sexes equally. Males in the age-groups suitable for call-up bore the brunt of the catastrophe, though, as we shall see later, the womenfolk suffered as well. The shortages of food and fuel, a famine reported in the Volga region in 1947, and massive internments of people said to have collaborated with the Germans must have raised the death-rate for all ages even after

16. M. K. Roof and F. A. Leedy, 'Population Redistribution in the Soviet Union, 1939–56', *The Geographical Review*, Vol. XLIX, No. 2, April 1959.

hostilities had ceased. The birth-rate, as we have seen, showed some decline as early as 1939. We may presume that it reached its lowest point some time after the spring of 1942, and did not rise again significantly until 1945–6, when the postwar baby boom started. The age-breakdowns available in Soviet sources are too crude to allow the nadir to be determined with any degree of accuracy. But the fall in the numbers of children who attended school later makes it clear that the birth-rate must have gone down by at least half. Small wonder if this tragedy has left a deep imprint on the outlook of the Soviet leaders and masses alike.

TABLE 2. *Population of the USSR 1940–69*
(in millions; estimates for 1 January)

Year	Total population	Annual increase	Urban population	Annual increase	Rural population	Annual increase
1940	194.1	—	63.1	—	131.0	—
1950	178.5	—	69.4	—	109.1	—
1951	181.6	3.1	73.0	3.6	108.6	−0.5
1952	184.8	3.2	76.8	3.8	108.0	−0.6
1953	188.0	3.2	80.2	3.4	107.8	−0.2
1954	191.0	3.0	83.6	3.4	107.4	−0.4
1955	194.4	3.4	86.3	2.7	108.1	0.7
1956	197.9	3.5	88.2	1.9	109.7	1.6
1957	201.4	3.5	91.4	3.2	110.0	0.3
1958	204.9	3.5	95.6	4.2	109.3	−0.7
1959*	208.8	3.9	100.0	4.4	108.8	−0.5
1960	212.3	3.5	103.8	3.8	108.5	−0.3
1961	216.2	3.9	108.3	4.5	107.9	−0.6
1962	219.8	3.6	111.8	3.5	108.0	0.1
1963	223.2	3.4	115.1	3.3	108.1	0.1
1964	226.4	3.2	118.5	3.4	107.9	−0.2
1965	229.3	2.9	121.7	3.2	107.6	−0.3
1966	231.8	2.5	124.7	3.0	107.1	−0.5
1967	234.4	2.6	128.0	3.3	106.4	−0.7
1968	236.7	2.3	131.0	3.0	105.7	−0.7
1969	238.9	2.2	134.2	3.2	104.7	−1.0

*Census returns for 15 January.
Source:
Narodnoe khozyaistvo SSSR v 1968, p. 7. Annual increases calculated.

The fifties and sixties have been relatively calm years, demographically speaking. Some official data on population growth is reproduced in Table 2. From 1950 to about 1960 the total population rose steadily at a rate of about 17 per thousand a year. This might be described as fairly high for an industrial society, though the USA averaged 18.5 per thousand for the decade. The Soviet death-rate steadied at about 7 per thousand after 1956, the corresponding figure for the USA being just over 11. This rather reassuring state of affairs was partly the result of improvements in the medical services, and was partly due to the relative paucity of people in the upper age groups (i.e. those who had been involved in the First World War and the Revolution). There was a large proportion of the population in the reproductive age groups.

Since about 1960, however, another demographic problem has arisen. Throughout the 1950s the birth-rate tended to fall gently, perhaps as a concommitant of the continuing industrialization. Abortion, incidentally, was again legalized in November 1955, though this seems to have been prompted by political rather than demographic considerations. From 1960 the birth-rate began to sink quickly, and in seven years had dropped from 25 to 17.4 per thousand. The main reason for this was that the people born during the war years were now entering the reproductive period in their lives, and these people, as we have seen, were few in number. In the absence of factors prompting them to have much larger families, it was only natural that they should produce, between them, fewer children. Moreover, the death-rate, which had been unusually low, showed a tendency to rise, as the proportion of old people increased. These factors do much to explain the marked easing in the rate of growth of the population.

The problem is a serious one, given the present economic situation: natural resources, even if uneconomically used, are ample, and the Soviet Union still has much to gain from vigorous population growth. The highest growth rates, which reach high Asiatic levels, are registered amongst the ethnic groups of Central Asia and the Caucasus, who are culturally most backward. The overall slow-down is not something that can be easily checked. Although the people born after the war are now of marriageable age and may help to steady the fall in the birth-rate by having larger families, it will be at least two decades before parents born in wartime cease to affect it. Soviet demographers have expressed concern over this problem; that something of the sort would happen must have been evident, but even as late as 1963 they were optimistic enough to forecast a total population of about 250 million by the end of 1970. The January 1970 figure was only 241.7 million.[17]

THE SOVIET POPULATION PYRAMID, 1966

It is probably true to say that the demographer, like the sociologist, is interested in the past mainly in so far as it explains the present and overshadows the future. All the changes we have touched upon so far have left their mark on the age and sex characteristics of the Soviet population today. These may be shown fairly simply by means of a population pyramid. The number of people in successive age groups is shown by horizontal bars of various lengths, arranged one above the other with the highest (and numerically smallest) age groups at the top. Males may be placed on one side of a central axis and females on the other, to show regularity or imbalance. The pyramid 'grows' from underneath, as new children form new bars. Death flakes off the sides and summit.

Pyramids have certain characteristic shapes, according to the relationship between the birth-rate and the death-rate in each separate age-group. They vary from broad-based and concave structures produced by countries like India, where both birth and death rates are high, to fat beehive-like vessels, signifying bourgeois plenty, which are characteristic of states like Switzerland or Sweden. Here the base is narrow, betokening a low birth-rate, and there are comparatively few deaths until the upper age-groups. Population explosions and wars cause bulges and dents: immigration, emigration and territorial changes have rather similar effects.

The history of the Soviet population growth would lead us to expect an unusual population pyramid, and this is just what we find. Figure 4 shows the hypothetical age and sex distribution of the population of the USSR for 1966 which was prepared by an American demographer.[18] It is hypothetical because it is

17. *Narodnoe khozyaistvo*, 1963, p. 8, and *Pravda*, 19 April 1970.
18. J. W. Brackett, *New Directions in the Soviet Economy*, Government Printing Office, Washington D.C., 1966, p. 611.

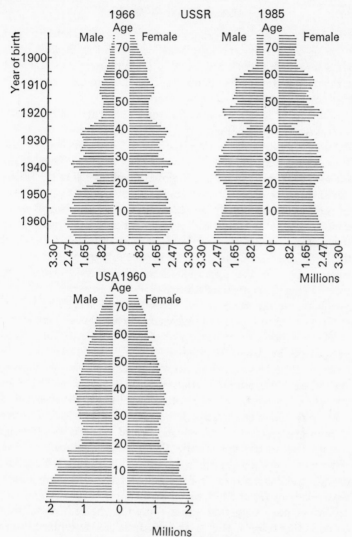

FIGURE 4. *Age Pyramids*

Sources:

J. W. Brackett, *New Directions in the Soviet Economy*, Government Printing
  Office, Washington D.C., 1966, p. 611, slightly simplified.
The full title used is 'Hypothetical Distribution of the Population of the
  USSR, by age and sex: 1966, 1985, 2000 and 2020'. The last two pyramids
  are not shown here. No explanation provided for the lateral scale.
  1960 U.S. Census Returns, table 156.

based only on five-year groups in the 1959 census returns, and because certain assumptions have had to be made about the years for which there are no birth or death figures. The degree of error is, however, probably not large, so the pyramid as it stands may serve as a basis for generalization.

The top of it is narrower than one would normally expect, with a heavier preponderance of females than purely biological considerations demand. Here we see the consequences of the First World War, the Revolution and the Civil War. The dent in the 45–50 age-groups reflects the corresponding fall in the birth-rate at this time. People who were between 40 and 55 years of age in 1966 were also mostly caught up in the Second World War, which accounts not only for the narrowness of the pyramid at that point, but also for the relative scarcity of males. The fall in the birth-rate in the early thirties is probably the reason for the smaller dent in the pyramid where the thirty-year-olds are located. The most striking feature of all is the enormous dent in births during the years of the Second World War. The fall-off in births after 1960 which we have already noted is also apparent.

There is not a great deal to be gained from a detailed comparison of the Soviet population structure with that of other lands, or from making prognostications about the future. Nevertheless, an American population pyramid is reproduced here for the sake of interest, together with a hypothetical distribution of the population of the USSR in the year 1985, by which time the irregularities caused by the Second World War will be affecting mainly the 35–45 age group. There are, of course, marked differences between the age pyramids of different ethnographic groups: the Baltic republics, for example, have older populations, with relatively fewer children, while the Central Asian Republics are, as we have suggested, much more like the underdeveloped lands in this respect. But these considerations lie rather beyond the scope of our study.

According to the 1959 census there was a shortage of nearly twenty million males in all age-groups above thirty-two. This imbalance between the sexes, though less striking than the losses, has had many unwelcome effects. It helps to explain the high proportion of women in the labour force: during the last three years these made up a full 50 per cent of all persons employed outside the collective farm sector.[19] In 1959 it seems that some 68 per cent of all women aged between 15 and 79 were in full- or part-time employment, and there was a rate of no less than 80 per cent for the 20–39 age groups.[20] Obviously, we cannot say that the employment of women in the Soviet economy should generally have been discouraged, or that their heavy involvement is solely a result of the shortage of males. The picture is far more complicated. Governmental encouragement, the manner in which the economy is organized, and perhaps tradition have played their part. Yet it does seem that in view of the other duties which devolve on the average Soviet woman – shopping under difficult conditions, housekeeping and child-care – the proportion of women workers is excessive.[21]

The lack of males has been particularly acute in the country-side. There is, of course, no immutable reason why the sex struc-ture should be the same in both sectors: in many rural societies there is a pronounced tendency for young male adults to migrate to the towns. A principal channel for migration from the Soviet village is, incidentally, military service, as many young peasants make for urban centres when they are demobbed. At the same time Soviet figures reveal excessive irregularity: the shortage of males above the age of forty is much more serious in the country-side than in the town. In 1959 57 per cent of the regular labour force in the collective farms was composed of women, though in the upper age groups the proportion must have been very much higher. There is reason to believe that the private sector of agri-culture is worked very largely by peasant women.[22]

The shortage of men in both town and country has of course had many other socially deleterious effects: family well-being has suffered, and many children have no doubt felt the lack of paternal advice. The burden on widowed mothers cannot be measured only in economic terms.

The loss of births to Soviet society has been one of the factors

19. *Narodnoe khozyaistvo SSSR v 1968*, p. 552.
20. N. T. Dodge, *Women in the Soviet Economy*, Baltimore, 1966, p. 38. The figure for the 15–79 age-group is based on his estimates.
21. See pp. 103 ff. and 175 ff. for details of women's time expenditures in urban conditions and in the collective farm respectively.
22. *1959 Census Returns*, p. 108.

prompting the Government to use the labour force more economically. The continued fall in the birth-rate, with the long-term shortage of labour which it implies, will probably ensure that the Government continues to try to improve its training and placement facilities, so as to make the best possible use of the people available.

THE NATIONALITIES

Soviet society is a mixture of many peoples. The 1959 census listed altogether 111 'nationalities' or ethnic groups: some 17,000 persons were not attributed to any.

About 80 per cent of the inhabitants of the USSR were Slavs, and the next most important group (containing about 10 per cent of the population) comprised the Turkic peoples. The remainder consisted of groups numbering from two and a half million down to a few hundred. The main determinants of an individual's nationality for official purposes seem to be the nationality of his or her parents (as entered in their internal passports), and his or her mother tongue. The individual may choose nationality within this framework when applying for a passport at the age of sixteen.

The manner by which all these nationalities became part and parcel of the Soviet state has been an object of study for many eminent historians. Absorption into Soviet society took place in one of three ways. Some peoples found themselves living on the territory of the Russian Federation after 1918, others were quickly affiliated to it in the consolidation drive of the early or middle twenties, and yet others were annexed by Soviet forces in 1939 or later.

The degree to which they have managed to preserve their cultural heritage against the pressures of Russification is a topic which is mainly of interest to anthropologists and ardent nationalists. Most outside observers agree that Russification of life in former non-Russian areas is proceeding apace. In the past it was backed up by transportation and the imprisonment of dissenters, but now quiet suppression of national languages, religion and certain national customs is more common. It is accepted Soviet practice to place Russians, or strongly Russified natives, in leading political and administrative positions in non-Russian localities.

How far, in effect, have the non-Russians been assimilated? Or, to phrase the question in slightly more manageable terms, what proportion of the Soviet population has, by and large, accepted those cultural and social norms which underly our study? One of our premises is that Soviet society is, despite all the political draperies, still basically European in nature and shares 'western' values. We may exclude the residue of the population – principally certain Asiatic and nomadic peoples – from our conclusions on class structure, social mobility, etc., as these concepts are hardly applicable to them in the same way as they are to the others.

The 1959 census provides enough data to allow us to make a very rough estimate.[23] Of a population of 208.8 million, 159.2 million were Russians, Ukrainians and White Russians: if we add the Balts, Jews, Moldavians, Poles, and some seven other groups of over 10,000 who may be regarded as being of traditionally 'European' culture, the figure rises to about 172.5 million (Table 3). Another category of a million and a half, who were of other nationalities but who regarded Russian as their native language, may safely be added.

This leaves us with the problem of those non-European peoples who have a highly developed culture of their own – the main ones being the urbanized Transcaucasians. If we allow, say, five million for this group, then the total rises to about 179 million, which was, in 1959, 86 per cent of the population. This means that, though Soviet society may be regarded as overwhelmingly Slav and European, the Asiatic element provides the leadership with a demographic basis for the claim that the Soviet Union is an Asiatic nation as well. And it may well be that the non-Russian – or perhaps non-Slav – peoples have to have two mutually exclusive sets of values: one which relates to their nationality, customs, and languages, and another which is standard Soviet.

The reader may well object that the problem of nationality in Soviet society cannot be treated in such an exceedingly superficial manner. We have every sympathy for that point of view. Nationalistic feeling, even among people of predominantly

23. *1959 Census Returns*, pp. 184–9, 226–31.

TABLE 3. *Slav and other Europe-orientated* Groups
in the USSR*

Nationality	Number
Russians	114,113,579
Ukrainians	37,252,930
White Russians	7,913,488
Lithuanians	2,326,094
Jews	2,267,814
Moldavians	2,214,139
Germans	1,619,655
Latvians	1,399,539
Poles	1,380,282
Estonians	988,616
Bulgarians	324,251
Greeks	309,308
Hungarians	154,738
Rumanians	106,366
Finns	92,717
Czechs	24,557
Slovaks	14,674

*Our understanding of this term is to be found in the text. Only groups over 10,000 included.

Source:
1959 Census Returns, pp. 184–8.

European culture, can be very great, and frictions correspondingly acute. Anyone who has lived in the Soviet Union can cite observed examples of anti-semitism, anti-Russianism, anti-Georgianism, to mention but three of the most common. Many people in most societies have their own likes and dislikes. And there is no denying that in certain instances the cohesion within national groups, or the fissures between them, can override the sort of class and group relationships which will be our main concern here. Sociological information on nationalism is, however, as yet very scarce, and facts will doubtless not be allowed to contradict the basic ideological formulation that the Soviet nationalities are merging happily together. The problem itself is extremely complex and not easily analysed. We have therefore reluctantly decided to exclude it from our study. The sociology of religion in the USSR, which often carries nationalist overtones, has also been omitted.

TOWNS AND VILLAGES

Sociological analysis must take some account of where people live. The main problem is not so much the geographical distribution of the population (though this cannot be ignored) as the kinds of community in which society is concentrated. A few words on Soviet urbanization and migration are in order within this context.

Any discussion of the former must begin with a definition of 'town'. Obviously, it is more than a large number of people living in close proximity. A small community, like a hamlet or a village, changes into a town when it frees itself from the primary tasks of food production, achieves a critical size and density of population, and becomes a centre for administration, trade or the production of goods. It must have a political or administrative unity of its own. By the time it has gone through this process it is profoundly different from an agricultural community, and its inhabitants have a different pattern of life.

But having said this much we are still faced with the practical problem of deciding at what point a village community in any given society makes the transformation. Size may often be the most important factor, but it may be outweighed by others. In an agricultural area one may find *villages* of several thousand inhabitants, while industrialized societies may boast *towns* of much smaller dimensions. The problem is easier to resolve in highly industrialized societies, where the appurtenances of urbanity are more elaborate and distinctive.

It will be sufficient for our purposes to take the Soviet administrative definitions which are based on the size of the settlement and the occupations of its inhabitants. These definitions vary from one union republic to another, and they have also changed over time. At present two basic types of urban settlement are recognized – the so-called 'workers' settlement' and the 'town' proper. Since 1958 communities in the RSFSR numbering more than three thousand inhabitants have been considered as workers' settlements, and those of more than twelve thousand inhabitants as towns, provided (in both cases) that more than 85 per cent of the population are engaged in non-agricultural pursuits. This seems fairly satisfactory. Units in the more backward republics, however, are smaller and more open to question: in the Central Asian Turkmen Republic, for example, urban settlements begin at 1,000 inhabitants, towns at 5,000, and the non-agricultural sector falls to 66 per cent. Furthermore, smaller settlements anywhere may be raised to urban status if special circumstances justify it. Fortunately the problem of these marginal kinds of settlements is not really serious, as only a tiny proportion of the population live in them.[24]

Urbanization in the USSR has been very rapid, but the rate has varied over time and place. In 1913, before the outbreak of the First World War, only 18 per cent of the population lived in the towns. The war at first caused rapid urban growth, but the period of War Communism which followed had the opposite effect, and the urban population went down to about 15 per cent of the total. Not only did the foreign and civil wars bear most heavily on urban inhabitants, but many people who had come to the towns in the preceding years moved out again to the country, firstly in the hope of receiving a piece of the newly sequestrated landlords' estates, and later in search of food. The up-turn took place, if we can judge from the figures published on Moscow and Leningrad, in 1921.[25] According to Soviet data the 1913 level of urbanization was regained by 1926, which we also know as the year of the first All-Union census. This reflected the easing of the food shortages and the encouragement given to urban development by Lenin's New Economic Policy. The era of the Five-Year plans was accompanied by massive drafts of able-bodied population from the countryside into the towns. These, combined with a system of internal passports and residence permits, were intended to ensure a considerable degree of government control over the whole process.[26] Between 1926 and January 1939 the urban population rose by nearly 30 million, while the rural population fell by 6.2 million. This was an incredible rate of advance by any standards. By the outbreak of war, with account taken of territorial acquisitions, about 32 per cent of all Soviet citizens were town-dwellers.

By 1950 the figure had risen to 39 per cent and until 1966 the

24. P. G. Pod'yachikh, *Naselenie SSSR*, Moscow, 1961, p. 69.
25. S. N. Prokopovicz, op. cit., p. 50.
26. These are questions which we return to in chapter 3.

proportion of the population living in urban settlements increased at the rate of about one per cent per year. Since then, to judge from official Soviet data, it has slowed down markedly. 1960 was a landmark in the history of Soviet urbanization, for by that year, according to official estimates, half of the population were living in towns. The 1970 Census figure was 56 per cent. This puts the Soviet Union well ahead of most underdeveloped countries, but still some way behind the most economically advanced: over 70 per cent of the American population are town-dwellers, while the figure for Great Britain is just under 80 per cent.

The development of urban centres in the USSR proceeds much as in the West, by natural growth of the urban population, immigration from the countryside, and administrative conversion of rural settlements into urban ones. Between the censuses of 1939 and 1959, for example, the natural growth of the urban population amounted to 8 million, about 25 million rural inhabitants moved to the towns, and rural settlements containing about 8 million inhabitants were recategorized as urban.[27]

This brings us to the question of how Soviet settlements are distributed by size. Is the average Soviet urbanite a small-town man or a large city dweller? And what about the villages?

A breakdown of the urban population of the USSR by size of settlement is provided in Table 4. By 1969 half of the urban population of the USSR lived in largish towns of 100,000 or more, while a third lived in medium-sized provincial towns of 10,000 to 100,000. Twenty million people, or 16 per cent of the urbanites, lived in 'settlements of an urban type', only a few of which were larger than small towns.

Not all Soviet towns have grown at the same rate, and various tendencies can be distinguished. The largest towns have tended to grow faster, so that an ever larger proportion of the urban

27. P. G. Pod'yachikh, op. cit., pp. 71–2. These figures do not quite fit the growth data in the official statistical handbooks, but there is no reason to suppose that the actual proportions are far wrong. In a recent article, 'Urbanization in Russia and the USSR, 1897–1966' (*The Annals of the Association of American Geographers*, Vol. 59, No. 4, December 1969), Robert A. Lewis and R. H. Rowland demonstrate that urbanization in the USSR seems to correlate closely with the 'traditional' factors of industrialization, transportation, accessibility and migration from the village.

TABLE 4. *Distribution of Soviet Urban Settlements by Size,*
1926, 1959, 1969

All types of urban settlement (population)	Number of residents (millions)			% Distribution of residents 1969	Increase 1926–69
	Dec. 1926	Jan. 1959	Jan. 1969		
less than 3,000	1.2	1.6	1.4	1.0	0.17
3,000–5,000	1.3	3.6	3.9	2.9	3.0
5,000–10,000	2.7	9.2	12.1	9.0	4.5
10,000–20,000	3.5	11.2	13.9	10.4	4.0
20,000–50,000	4.0	14.8	18.1	13.4	4.5
50,000–100,000	4.1	11.0	13.2	9.8	3.2
100,000–500,000	5.4	24.4	35.3	26.3	6.5
500,000 and over	4.1	24.2	36.3	27.0	8.9

Source:
Narodnoe khozyaistvo SSSR v 1968, p. 33, and calculated.

population has become concentrated in them. Between 1926 and 1969 the population living in the largest towns increased by a factor of nine, whilst the number of inhabitants of towns under the five-thousand mark only trebled. The number of people in the smallest settlements was almost static. In other words, the years of Soviet power have seen the widespread introduction of habits and customs associated with life in large urban communities.

The Soviet authorities generally take the view that the growth of towns can be controlled by the State for the good of society, and indeed the elaborate sets of residence restrictions have made this theoretically possible. A number of Soviet town planners have stipulated optimum sizes of from 200,000 to about 400,000 for Soviet towns. But in fact the attempts made from time to time to restrict the growth of the largest centres have been far from effective, and this suggests that Soviet towns, like most others, have potential of their own which is not easily braked by administrative order.

The inequalities of growth between towns of different sizes have inevitably had mixed social consequences. The advantages such as improved amenities attained in large conurbations have been offset by economic stagnation in middle-sized and especially small towns. In recent years this has made the latter more liable to harbour unemployment, while complaints about the inadequacy of their transport facilities, trade and communal services have been frequent. Their tardy development has, indeed, been recognized as a problem in its own right.[28]

Soviet rural settlements are, if anything, more difficult to generalize on than urban ones. They are much less standard in type, each reflecting the ethnographic peculiarities of its inhabitants. The 1959 Census stated that there were over 704,000 rural

TABLE 5. *Distribution of Rural Settlements by Size*

No. of inhabitants	*Total no. of rural settlements*	*Residents in them (in millions)*	*Villages of various kinds**	*Residents in them (in millions)*
Total	704,811	107.0	581,542	92.4
up to 5	212,076	0.6	185,792	0.6
6–10	71,617	0.5	51,325	0.3
11–25	69,675	1.2	47,324	0.8
26–50	67,410	2.5	54,791	2.1
51–100	80,924	5.9	68,920	5.0
101–200	76,402	11.0	65,130	9.4
201–500	74,762	23.7	63,206	20.0
501–1,000	31,763	22.1	27,023	18.8
1,001–2,000	14,218	19.3	12,587	17.2
2,001–3,000	3,482	8.4	3,172	7.7
3,001–5,000	1,807	6.7	1,684	6.3
Over 5,000	675	5.0	588	4.2

* See footnote 29.

Source:
1959 Census Returns, p. 38.

'settled places', of which some 581,000 were large villages or villages of the Russian type, Cossack villages, farmsteads of the Ukrainian or Baltic type, Central Asian and Caucasian settlements.[29] In addition five other kinds of tiny, solitary or seasonal settlement were listed. The distribution of rural population by size of settlement as revealed in that Census may be seen from Table 5.

28. D. G. Khodzhaev, *Puti razvitia malykh i srednikh gorodov*, Moscow, 1967; H. Chambre, 'Urbanisation et croissance économique en U.R.S.S.', *Économie appliquée*, No. 1, Jan.–March 1964, p. 4.

29. This is an attempt to translate *sela, derevni, khutora, kishlaki* and *auly*.

Urbanization has been accompanied by marked geographical shifts of population, mainly from the densely populated European areas into the towns of the East and South. This is, of course, a long-standing tradition. Migration eastwards has been strongly encouraged by the Soviet authorities on the grounds that there is a considerable discrepancy between the regional

TABLE 6. *Urban Growth in the USSR*

Economic Region	(*Average annual increase in %*)		
	1926–39*	*1939–59**	*1959–1966*†
North-west	6.03	0.80	3.01
West	1.25	2.26	3.74
Central	7.44	1.83	2.22
Volgo–Vyatsk	10.59	2.88	3.92
Central Black Soil	2.84	2.48	5.10
Volga	5.93	2.95	3.50
Belorussia	4.90	1.66	5.33
Moldavia	0.85	3.67	5.93
South-west	2.38	1.29	4.81
South	3.08	1.20	4.31
Donetsk–Dnepr	9.56	1.82	4.23
North Caucasus	3.56	2.31	4.36
Transcaucasus	5.36	2.73	3.49
Ural	10.32	4.02	2.73
West Siberia	10.22	4.10	2.84
East Siberia	11.17	3.72	3.56
Far East	12.43	2.95	3.14
Kazakhstan	11.27	4.37	5.56
Central Asia	4.70	3.55	5.70
All regions	6.46	2.45	3.64

*Centres of 15,000 and over.   †Centres of 50,000 and over. The authors provide careful methodological notes.
Source:
R. A. Lewis and R. H. Rowland, op. cit., pp. 784 and 789.

distribution of the population and the country's natural resources. Strategic considerations such as a fear of Western 'warmongering' and more recently the conflict with China have also prompted this policy.

Migratory movements are no less complex than demographic ones, but fortunately, with one exception, are not central to our study.[30] For this reason we may content ourselves with listing the principal movements of urban population between large geographical areas, as analysed by two American scholars, R. A. Lewis and R. H. Rowland. Their figures, some of which are reproduced in Table 6, show that between 1926 and 1939, the period of most rapid urbanization in the USSR, the outstanding areas for population growth were the Far East, Kazakhstan, East Siberia, the Volga–Vyatsk region and the Donetsk–Dnepr region. The average annual increases here were between 10.5 and 12.5 per cent. Between 1939 and 1959 Kazakhstan, West Siberia, the Urals, East Siberia, Moldavia and Central Asia led the way, the rate now being from about 3.5 to 4.5 per cent. The period 1959–66, however, saw a very marked change. (These years are taken because they provide the census figures, and not because the changes necessarily started then.) Several of the 'old' centres of most rapid growth – East and West Siberia, the Far East and the Urals – fell well below the national average, while Moldavia, Central Asia, Kazakhstan, White Russia and the Central Black Earth region were in the lead. At the same time the percentage of town dwellers grew most quickly in the Donetsk–Dnepr, Central Black Earth, Volga–Vyatsk, North-west and White Russian regions. The development of new urban centres and enlargement of old ones has traditionally been a most painful social process in the Soviet Union, largely because of the low priority given to housing and public amenities.

In this introductory chapter we have tried only to outline some of the main problems of the growth and distribution of the Soviet population. The exercise is, however, very pertinent to our study of Soviet society, in that many of these problems have a big impact on the country's social structure and social institutions.

30. The exception is the drift of young people from village to town, which is dealt with in chapter 7.

2

The Official Theory of Classes and
Social Development

THE Soviet Union is a country whose government stipulates a
fairly rigid doctrine of State and society which both influences
official policies, and is used to justify them. It is only natural that
an officially approved interpretation of class structure and social
development should be part and parcel of this scheme.

There is, furthermore, a long historical precedent for an
official sociology. Russian rulers for the better part of a millen-
nium promoted a system of legally fixed classes or *soslovia*, whose
existence was enshrined in an approved philosophy of Tsardom.
This practice has been common to many lands, but the Russian
form was more rigorous than many. The *soslovia* were arranged
in a hierarchical manner, with those most vital to the functioning
of the State at the top: their significance and development are in
themselves an entire branch of Russian history.[1]

There is much to be said for beginning our survey of Soviet
social structure with an account of Soviet official concepts, their
origin and development. Although they are inadequate for most
purposes, successive Soviet leaders have tried to shape Soviet
society in accordance with them, and much of the statistical
information available to us is from this mould. When we have
looked at this problem we can go on in other chapters to analyse
Soviet society from a finer standpoint, using methods and indices
generally applied by sociologists outside the communist world.

The Soviet authorities have always claimed that their theories
of social structure are based on Marxist thought. Marx himself
was not so much interested in social hierarchies or stratification
as in the existence and interplay of a few very cohesive classes.
He recognized that individuals would have different tastes,

1. *The History of classes (soslovia) in Russia*, written by V. O. Klyuchevski
in 1886, comes to mind in this respect.

abilities and needs, and would never in this sense be equal. But he did not really pursue the social implications of this. Modern industrialized society, he held, was for economic reasons polarizing into two opposing classes of poor workers and rich capitalists or landlords, while the intermediate groups were being gradually absorbed by one or the other. The gap between rich and poor could only broaden, and a revolutionary situation had to develop. For the purposes of his theory these developments transcended all 'intra-class' distinctions. Marx considered that the central determinant of 'class' was relationship to the means of production; on this depended such secondary class characteristics as the standard of living and class consciousness.[2] At the same time he may not have been completely satisfied with this interpretation himself, for, as we know, he died without leaving a final definition of what he meant by 'class'.

Lenin adopted Marx's basic idea of the polarization of society under capitalism, and his definition of class in these conditions was basically economic and deterministic in the Marxist sense. He followed Marx in including a very strong psychological element, and the internal cohesiveness of a given class was no less essential to his analysis.[3]

2. These problems have been treated by many able scholars including S. Ossowski, *Class Structure in the Social Consciousness*, London, 1963, p. 69 ff.

3. 'Classes', he wrote in June 1919, 'are large groups of people which differ from each other by the place they occupy in a historically definite system of social production, by their relation (in most cases fixed and formulated in laws) to the means of production, by their role in the social organization of labour, and, consequently, by the dimensions and method of acquiring the share of social wealth that they obtain. Classes are groups of people one of which may appropriate the labour of another owing to the different places they occupy in a definite system of social economy.' (V. I. Lenin, *A Great Beginning*, from the *Essentials of Lenin*, Vol. II, London, 1947, p. 492.) This formulation has its weaknesses. The first element in it – the place occupied in the 'historically definite [i.e. determined] system of social production' – is at best crude historicism. The classes' 'role in the social organization of labour' apparently covers the more legalistic aspects of employment which under capitalism were supposed to be controlled by the bourgeoisie anyway. Lenin talks of the 'dimensions and method of acquiring the share of social wealth', but omits any specific reference to the important problem of income. The touchstone of 'ability to appropriate the labour of another class' is, of course, useless as a tool for analysis in the short run. All of his indices are primarily occupational. They do not explicitly include such important

Yet his primary concern was Russia, and from his point of view Marx's theories left two major questions unanswered. Firstly there was the problem of bringing about a socialist revolution in a land where the supposedly revolutionary force – the urban proletariat – was but a small minority (see Table 7). Marx had always had a very low opinion of the revolutionary potential of the peasantry, which formed the vast majority of the Russian population. Secondly there was Marx's failure to say anything of substance about the administration of society after the Revolution. So even when Lenin had managed, by a combination of good luck and singlemindedness of purpose, to snatch political power, he still had to supply most of the solutions for the immense problems of government and social development in Russia.

He set out his main ideas in documents like the April 1917 *Theses*, and *The State and the Revolution*, written some four months later, though many of them can without difficulty be traced to earlier works, and some were modified later for severely practical reasons. The concepts were elaborated in a rather popular form in Nikolai Bukharin and Evgenii Preobrazhenski's *ABC of Communism*, published in 1921. The underlying and essentially Marxist premise of these works was that a communist government could not only foretell the general course of social development on its territory, but was somehow morally obliged to take strong measures, in the name of the proletariat, to encourage it. This, in the case of Russia, implied the destruction of the 'capitalist' class, the creation of a massive proletariat and the re-education, or proletization, of the peasantry. The numbers of people who were to be 'reclassed' were, of course, enormous, as may be seen from the table. Lenin held that the former specialists and State officials, the 'bourgeois intelligentsia', could be controlled and used in the interests of the socialist society during the first stage of its development. Eventually they would be replaced by a socialist intelligentsia drawn from the workers and peasants themselves. The application of this prin-

---

yardsticks as education or prestige. The definition as a whole was tailored to fit Lenin's concept of capitalist societies, and not Soviet reality. Despite all its inadequacies, Soviet sociologists are still obliged to claim that it is valid.

ciple in the Red Army during the Civil War was a major element in the Bolshevik success.

TABLE 7. *The Class Composition of the Soviet Union*

Class	1913	1924	1928	1937	1939	1959	1968
Percentage breakdown							
Employees	3.0	4.7	5.6	45.7	17.7	20.1	22.9
Workers	14.0	10.1	12.0		32.5	48.2	54.8
Collectivized peasants & craftsmen in cooperatives	—	1.3	2.9	48.8	47.2	31.4	22.27
Individual peasants & free craftsmen	66.7	75.4	74.9	5.5	2.6	0.3	0.03
Bourgeoisie, landowners, traders & kulaks	16.3	8.5	4.6	—	—	—	—
Numerical breakdown (millions)							
Total population	159.2	137.7	150.0	163.4	170.6	208.8	236.7
Employees	4.8	5.2	8.4		30.2	42.0	54.1
Workers	22.3	15.2	18.0		55.4	100.6	129.8
Collectivized peasants & craftsmen in cooperatives	—	1.8	4.4	79.7	80.5	65.6	52.7
Individual peasants & free craftsmen	106.2	103.8	112.3	9.0	4.4	0.6	0.1
Bourgeoisie, landowners, traders & kulaks	25.9	11.7	6.9	—	—	—	—

Sources:

Percentage breakdown: *Narodnoe Khozyaistvo SSSR v 1961*, p. 27, *Nar. Khoz. SSSR v 1968*, p. 35, *Nar. Khoz. SSSR v 1969*, p. 30, *SSSR i zarubezhnye strany, stat. sbornik*, Moscow, 1970, p. 24.

Numerical breakdown: Total population 1913, 1939 (census of 17 January within existing boundaries), 1959 from *Narodnoe khozyaistvo SSSR v 1961*, pp. 7 and 8; 1924, 1928, 1937, estimates and hypothetical figures from F. Lorimer, op. cit., pp. 30, 135; 1968, from *Narodnoe khozyaistvo SSSR v 1968*, p. 7. Other totals calculated.

Lenin added to Marx's rather scanty notion of the dictatorship of the proletariat the concept of a union of the proletariat and the poor peasantry, in which the former would be the dominating force. This was in effect his answer to the problem of how to fit the Russian peasantry into a Marxist scheme, and it formed the basis for later Soviet theories of 'friendly' classes. The union would continue until all the 'capitalist elements' remaining in Soviet society had been removed, or, in Bukharin's more moderate formulation, absorbed into the family of the toiling masses. By this time society would be largely homogeneous anyway. Relations between classes were meanwhile to be manipulated by all legal, political and economic means at the disposal of the leadership.

These concepts, which were highly dictatorial in character, determined most Bolshevik policies after 1917. There was, in fact, hardly a sphere of Soviet life which was not affected by them. They led to the excesses of War Communism and the Civil War; they left an indelible imprint on Soviet economic and legal theory. The Constitutions of 1918 and 1924 stipulated that franchise in the urban areas, which were predominantly working-class, was to be five times more favourable than in the rural ones, while former 'exploiters' were excluded from the vote (for what it was worth) altogether. Admission to the Party (a much more important matter) was easiest for persons of proletarian or poor peasant extraction, less so for other peasants and small craftsmen, and most difficult for 'employees', which still meant the old bourgeoisie. Although the introduction of the New Economic Policy in March 1921 signified the acceptance of a more flexible approach in the economic sphere – including a reduction of the pressures on petty capitalists, private traders and *kulaks*, together with a slackening of the misconceived drive for social equality – Lenin's theoretical framework was still *de rigueur*. Only his time-scale for social development lengthened as the post-revolutionary years added to his experience of statesmanship.

LENIN AND BUKHARIN ON SOCIAL DIVERSITY

The Soviet leader's doctrinaire acceptance of a Marxist two-class scheme in the sphere of political theory did not, of course, prevent him from viewing the social diversity which surrounded him with a severely practical eye. Lenin's understanding of intra-class divisions is a topic which still awaits the enthusiastic attention of a young Ph.D. student. Even so, the most cursory examination of the eighteen hundred or so references to 'class' in the fourth edition of his work provides ample illustration of his realism.[4]

He viewed the bourgeoisie, which occupied one place in the 'historically determined system of social production', as a very heterogeneous group, comprising capitalists, landowners, state functionaries, churchmen, etc., who were all motivated by rather different political and economic aims. He saw considerable variety in the working class, which he tended to dissect by trade or occupation. The wage and rationing policies to which he subscribed during the period of War Communism and after differentiated between workers on the basis of their importance to the economy. He was, again, acutely aware of variations in the workers' level of political allegiance to Bolshevism – which is what he really meant when he talked about class consciousness. Workers who supported his party, or faction, were the most 'advanced'; those who did not were merely 'egoistic individuals' who had temporarily fallen under bourgeois influence and should be thrown out of the proletarian family. Any mass desertion of the workers from his cause (to return, for example, to the villages) he called 'declassification'.[5]

By such means as these Lenin admitted social diversity in the proletariat, while maintaining the principle of its social unity for political purposes pure and unsullied, at least to his own satisfaction. The working class, as a class, was suspect only in those capitalist lands which had moved into the phase of colonialism, for then there might be a split between an élite group of workers who benefited from the exploitation of the colonies, and the rest, who continued to suffer harsh exploitation at home.

Lenin's solution of the peasant problem after the revolution was based precisely on the presumption that there were profound social cleavages in this class. Indeed, he thought of it as falling into three distinct parts. First there were the so-called rich peasants, or 'kulaks', whom he sometimes termed the 'rural bourgeoisie' and who were destined to tread the path of all capitalist exploiters. At the other extreme were those whom he

4. The fifth edition has at the time of writing not been provided with its own thematic reference volume.

5. Vol. XXXII, p. 176, and Vol. XXI, p. 479.

called the 'exploited peasants, the poor people and their friends', the 'rural proletariat'.[6] Between them came the middle peasantry. After the Revolution, he claimed, the poor peasantry and some of the middle peasants would join the workers in the union we have just mentioned. The other middle peasants would side with the kulaks – and be treated as such.

It is relevant to recall that Lenin, in good Tsarist tradition, went to extraordinary lengths to amass information about Soviet economic and social development. Indeed, by the mid twenties the Bolsheviks must have been amongst the best informed of all national leaders in this respect. The Central Statistical Administration (Ts. S. U.) was established as early as July 1918, and the first Soviet census of workers and employees in industry was attempted in the same year. The first census of the population was organized as early as 1920. In the ensuing years many narrower surveys were promoted: between 1919 and 1922, for example, 12,000 workers' and employees' budgets were collected and analysed, and after 1923 this became an annual exercise. In 1922 over 9,000 peasants' budgets were similarly processed. Workers' and peasants' nutritional needs and their use of time were other principal objects of study. Some of these investigations were conducted for Gosplan under the guidance of the economist S. G. Strumilin. Much of the data collected may have been of questionable quality: but it must have been ample for an objective appraisal of the Leninist concepts. Unfortunately, the Soviet leaders were not interested in faulting their own theories. Sociology, as an independent academic discipline, was virtually banned in 1922, so that 'unmarxist' interpretations were out of the question.

Nikolai Bukharin was generally regarded as the outstanding Party theoretician after Lenin died. He was always doctrinaire, but exhibited a deeper interest in social structure. Perhaps the pragmatic studies of the mid twenties owe something to his presence in the leadership; by that time his outlook was a little more flexible.

The fullest expression of his views was contained in his book *Historical Materialism, a System of Sociology*, published in Moscow in 1921. Bukharin recognized, apart from the exploiters and

6. Vols. XXVI, p. 331, XXVII, p. 191, XXIX, p. 124.

the exploited, four *types* of class, some associated with capitalism, others to be found in the post-capitalist stage of development. The first were the 'intermediate' classes which (like the technical intelligentsia in capitalist society) were not really in either of the principal camps. Next came the 'transitional' classes, which Bukharin defined as 'groups which have come from a preceding form of society, and which are decomposing in the present state of society, thereby giving birth to various classes with opposing roles in production'. He took the peasantry as an example, for this class would, he held, break down into bourgeois and proletarian elements. Thirdly, there was a type of mixed class composed of people who had two or more occupations which carried different class status. Bukharin gave as an example here a railway worker who hired someone to tend his garden. Lastly there were the 'declassed' elements – the lumpenproletariat, beggars and 'bohemians'.

'Reality', wrote Bukharin, 'is a motley picture with all its social-economic types and relations ... it would be naive to suppose that every class is a thoroughly unified whole, all parts being of equal importance, with Tom, Dick and Harry all on the same level.' And again '. . . the difference in being is also reflected in consciousness. The Proletariat is unequal in its consciousness, as it is unequal in its position. It is *more or less* a unit as compared with the other classes, but not with regard to its own various parts.' It was 'divided into a number of links of varying strength'. In fact, he wrote, and quite logically, 'It is the heterogeneity of class which makes a party (i.e. the Communist Party) indispensable.'[7]

This must be one of the most elastic interpretations of the Soviet social fabric ever to have come from the leadership. Though dogmatic in its origins, it allowed scope for serious investigation. The concept of society as 'a motley picture' could eventually have opened the door to very pragmatic sociological analyses which were potentially destructive of Lenin's (or for that matter, Marx's) notion of class homogeneity. Bukharin himself was evidently not fully aware of this danger, and the triumph of Stalinism effectively removed it.

7. N. Boukharine, *La Théorie du Matérialisme Historique*, Paris, 1927. Quotations from pages 306–8, 330–32.

STALIN'S FORMULATION

Stalin's contributions to class theory were, by comparison with Lenin's or Bukharin's, modest in the extreme. He was concerned primarily with transforming the USSR into a mighty, industrialized power under his own personal leadership, and social theory interested him only in so far as it could be made to justify or further these aims. He proclaimed himself a convinced Marxist–Leninist: but there is no doubt that he interpreted all the basic concepts of these doctrines in the manner most suited to his own needs.

His first major actions after he had defeated his opponents in the top leadership were to accelerate industrial growth by means of the Five-Year Plans, extend his control over the agricultural sector through collectivization, and suppress the remaining 'capitalist elements' in town and country. Private industry and trade were all but abolished, that is with the exception of the peasant market. New political pressures were brought to bear on the 'bourgeois' specialists who had, until then, quietly served the régime, and many were dismissed or arrested. The training plans for a new technical élite were greatly extended. The Church was weakened. Only individual craftsmen were allowed to continue working as of old, provided that they did not indulge in the capitalist pursuit of hiring labour. In the countryside the *kulaks*, together with masses of peasants whose opposition to the régime had been too vociferous, were dispossessed and transported to places like Central Asia or Siberia. The overwhelming majority of peasants were obliged to unite within the strict bonds of the collective farm system, and by 1939 only a few remained outside it. At the same time younger peasants were drafted into the towns to man the new factories, and the working class grew rapidly, as shown in Table 7. This was social engineering in an extreme form.

Stalin justified the increase of pressure on former capitalist elements (a term which he interpreted in the widest possible sense) by his famous thesis of the sharpening of the class struggle. The remaining capitalist elements would, he held, intensify their resistance as the Soviet Union moved towards communism. This was totally un-Marxist and in direct opposition to Bukharin's later formulations, but it fitted the dictator's theory of capitalist encirclement and his attacks on Bukharin's softer line in economic affairs.

These changes meant that by the late thirties all but a very small percentage of the population could, with some slender justification, be termed 'working class' or 'peasantry', the capitalist-bourgeois elements having been totally extracted. It is, of course, impossible to believe that either of these classes was in any important respect less varied and internally differentiated than before: Stalin's glib formula merely meant that this variety should no longer be taken into account, at least in discussions of theory.

He set out what became the standard formulation in his speech to the Eighth Congress of Soviets in November 1936 on the project of the new constitution. Both the working class and the peasantry, he claimed, had undergone profound transformation. The working class was no longer exploited, and it owned, in the aggregate, the means of production. Indeed, it could not be called a 'proletariat' any longer. The peasantry, too, was a new peasantry, since it too was free from exploitation and, as a result of collectivization, cooperatively owned the means of production. Stalin considered that collective ownership, though superior to private ownership, was inferior to social or state ownership (a point of view with which Marx would probably have disagreed). This implied that the peasantry should be regarded as an inferior class, which would mature only when it passed through the collectivized stage and become a genuine rural working class. This inferiority, a dim reflection of Marx's impatience with men of the soil, was ensured by several provisions of collective farm law. Stalin further stipulated that in the absence of 'exploitation' relations between these classes could not be anything but amicable and friendly.

Stalin's theory might have ignored the possibility of social differentiation or friction within the classes, but, as we shall see below, his practical policies promoted many obvious inter- and intra-class distinctions. That he had a hierarchical scheme in mind is very evident from his famous description of the professional Party cadres as soldiers who held different ranks in an army. It is not improbable that social differentiation in Stalin's

Russia reached a degree unknown in any industrialized state of the day. We cannot go into this fascinating problem here, but there is evidence to show that whereas the leading group in Stalin's hierarchy enjoyed an incredible degree of economic and political power, the least privileged sections of the community – the poorest peasants and numerous political prisoners – were deprived enough to warrant the description of serfs or slaves by outside observers.[8] Stalin's social policies left an imprint on the configuration of Soviet society which is visible today.

The third social group in Stalin's scheme was the intelligentsia. His definition of this was, to say the least, peculiar. He chose to call it a *prosloika*, which can best be translated as 'through-' or 'cross-stratum'.[9] It was not a class because (as other theorists were to claim, though unconvincingly) it had no independent relationship to the means of production. Thus it could not play a separate part in the political life of the country. As a 'cross-stratum' it was not really distinct from the two classes, which supplied eighty or ninety per cent of its members – the remainder came from the old bourgeois intelligentsia. Nevertheless, it enjoyed 'equal rights' in Soviet society, it was 'in harness' with the workers and peasants, and was constructing a classless society with them. A socialist intelligentsia was unique to the Soviet Union. Stalin gave no hint that this group was anything less than homogeneous either.

There is little doubt that these rather incongruous attributes were only a camouflage: the new intelligentsia was in reality Stalin's upper class. As so many of his policies showed, he was anxious to increase its size and power to an optimal point, for it formed the base from which he ruled the country. The combination of a 'cross-stratum' and two 'classes' was most peculiar. It was useful only in that it underscored two basic types of social distinction which are still important water-sheds in Soviet society, the first being occupation, which clearly separates worker and peasant, and the second education, by which the intelligentsia is distinguished from other social groups.

How would relations between these friendly groups develop?

8. A viewpoint expressed in S. V. Utechin, *Russian Political Thought*, London, 1964, p. 236.
9. The ordinary Russian word for stratum, or layer, is *sloi*.

Stalin appeared to follow Lenin in accepting the concept of a period of convergence, culminating in a classless society. Changes in the working class, the peasantry and the intelligentsia meant, he said

... firstly, that the dividing lines between the working class and the peasantry, just as between these classes and the intelligentsia, are being effaced, and the old class exclusiveness is disappearing. This means that the distance between these social groups is being reduced all the time.

Secondly, that the economic contradictions between these groups are falling away, and being effaced.

And finally, that the political contradictions between them are also falling away and being effaced.[10]

The Constitution of 1936, which was supposed to mark the completion of the building of socialism in the country, served as a vehicle for Stalin's class formula. It is ironical that Bukharin should have been involved in drafting it. It extended the franchise to all citizens, regardless of class, in recognition of the fact that exploitation was no more. All adult members of Soviet society had the same rights and duties. In like manner the Party statutes approved at the Eighteenth Party Congress, in March 1939, abolished distinctions between admission procedures for persons from different social groups – though this change was as much a consequence of the ending of mass political purges as it was a reflection of the new class formulations.

Stalin's last pronouncements on the subject of social development were contained in *The Economic Problems of Socialism*, a short work published in October 1952. Here we find, in the main, a re-statement of his class convergence theory, though with some embellishment. The peasantry would become more like the working class as collective ownership of the means of production was transformed into state ownership. Village would come to resemble town, primarily in the amenities it provided for the inhabitants. A reduction in the gap between mental and

10. *Voprosy Leninisma*, Moscow, 1953, p. 551. The contradictions which Stalin had in mind were based on different relationships to the means of production, but in conditions of socialism they were not 'antagonistic' in character.

physical labour would take place as more people received advanced training, thus ensuring a fusion of both classes with the intelligentsia.

Stalin now, however, rebuked those comrades who thought that *all* the class differences, as he defined them, would disappear altogether, even under communism. This, he said, was not possible, owing to the profound differences in conditions of production; only the *basic* divergences would go. This was doubtless his way of hinting that the social distinctions which he had so actively encouraged contained a real element of durability.

The advent of Stalinism dealt a heavy blow to the study of social phenomena, albeit in the rather rigid forms which it had assumed in the twenties.[11] Sociology, even in its most orthodox interpretation, lost its right to be considered as a separate discipline. After Bukharin's disgrace one Abram Deborin held brief sway as the most authoritative theoretician. Deborin maintained that historical materialism was, in itself, a 'sufficient framework for the explanation of social phenomena'.[12] Though the Deborinists were in turn swept away for 'inadequate attention to the tasks of Marxism–Leninism', Stalin never allowed sociology to regain its status as an independent branch of the social sciences.

He sponsored far-reaching changes in data collection. The general trend seems to have been towards maintaining the coverage of the twenties, but with more specialization and a concentration of the collecting processes in the Central Statistical

11. This interesting topic still awaits proper investigation by historians. Soviet statisticians and sociologists have, in recent years, devoted a number of interesting (if not totally satisfactory) chapters to problems of what we would call the history of sociological research in the twenties and thirties. Some of those which deserve attention are to be found in the following works: A. I. Ezhov, *Organizatsia statistiki v SSSR*, Moscow, 1968, *Istoria sovetskoi gosudarstvennoi statistiki*, Moscow, 1969 (family budgets, income); I. Ya. Matyukha, *Statistika byudzhetov naselenia*, Moscow, 1967 (rural sociology); Yu. V. Arutyunyan, *Opyt sotsiologicheskovo izuchenia sela*, Moscow, 1968 (time studies); V. G. Kryazhev, *Vnerbochee vremya; sfera obsluzhivania*, Moscow, 1966. A few of the details we mention here were taken from *Statisticheski slovar*, Moscow, 1966, and M. I. Florinsky, *Encyclopedia of the Soviet Union*, New York, 1963.

12. Paolo Ammassari, 'Ideologia e Sociologia nell'Unione Sovietica', in *Rassegna Italiana di Sociologia*, Jan.–March 1964, p. 69.

Administration (which was even merged with Gosplan for a few months in 1930). Some People's Commissariats did additionally develop their own systems. There was a sharp reduction in the amount of statistical material actually published. The compilation of annual statistical handbooks for the USSR was discontinued in 1936, though many other sources of a similar kind had petered out in the late twenties. Particularly disappointing was the closure of the labour journal *Statistika truda* in 1929. A number of institutes dealing with sociological topics, including the extremely important Institute of Demography, the Institute of Experimental Statistics and Statistical Methodology, and the Institute of Economic Growth (Institut konyunktury) were shut down. Studies of other 'negative' social phenomena, like suicide, came to a halt after 1929. Strumilin's time-use studies, which had produced some very revealing results earlier, were stopped in 1936.[13] We have already commented on the suppression of the 1937 and 1939 census returns. The unfavourable attitude which the Party leadership adopted towards social research meant that even a strongly Marxist interpretation of many social phenomena was greatly impeded. By the end of the thirties there were too many unpleasant problems, which, from Stalin's point of view, were better left unexplored.

KHRUSHCHEV'S INNOVATIONS AND THE NEW CRITICISM

After Khrushchev's denunciation of Stalin at the Twentieth Party Congress in January 1956 it was not unreasonable to hope that the late dictator's class formulation might be changed. Its crude simplicity was, after all, a monument to the dictator and a barrier to sensitive scholarship. Khrushchev went so far as to declare that Stalin's theory of sharpening class conflict was erroneous, and at one point expressed a reservation on his attempted discardment of the term 'proletariat'. The two-class-one-stratum scheme was, however, retained. A Central Committee decree of 30 June stated that the development of Soviet society had been restricted, but not fundamentally changed, by

13. G. S. Petrosyan, *Vnerabochee vremya trudyashchikhsya v SSSR*, Moscow, 1965, p. 5.

the 'cult of the personality'. The old formula found a place in the Third Party Programme which was approved in October 1961, and was reiterated in the article on classes in the *Philosophical Dictionary* which went to press in September 1963. The cautious Brezhnev leadership duly inserted it in the 1967 *Theses on the Fiftieth Anniversary of Soviet Power*.

This does not mean that the official understanding of the formula has not been modified. Khrushchev was not much of a theorist, and close associates like Suslov or Ilichev were too conservative to suggest much. But the Soviet leader did try, in his inimitable fashion, to pour some new parsnip wine into the old bottles.

Perhaps his most significant idea was that the Soviet Union would develop into a 'state of the whole people'. The entry of the Soviet Union into the period of the 'extensive construction of communism' (which was his concept too) would, he held, be accompanied by the long-awaited erasing of the distinctions between towns and country on the one hand, and mental and physical labour on the other. The fusion of nationalities would be completed. Worker, peasant and *intelligent* would be as one. But the working class would somehow maintain its identity, and remain the leading force in society.

Communism was described in the Party programme in economic rather than social terms; it would involve a degree of development and provide a standard of living superior to that enjoyed by the most advanced capitalist countries. Communist society would definitely be classless. However, the old Marxist formula – 'from each according to his ability, to each according to his needs' – which was repeated in the text of the programme reintroduced the old ambiguity about how 'equal' people can be if their abilities are different. Khrushchev declared that the condition of full communism would be achieved in the brief term of twenty years. The Soviet Union would catch up with the USA in the per capita output of certain foodstuffs and overtake it in five. Though the Soviet leader's thoughts on social development retained their respectability after his dismissal, his timescale was quietly dropped.[14]

14. Brezhnev hardly mentioned the programme in his detailed report to the Twenty-third Party Congress in March 1966.

A new factor in this concept of social advance was the more immediate emphasis on homogeneity. It was backed on a practical plane by Khrushchev's efforts to narrow differences both between the three social groups and inside them, and extend (at least superficially) the powers of voluntary and social, as against state, organizations.

Yet the most exciting development of the post-Stalin period is not the leadership's attempt to imbue new life into an arid Stalinist paradigm, but the way in which it has been criticized. This has been possible only as a result of the virtual rebirth of Soviet sociology, which was a direct result of Khruschev's more liberal policies. This event may for convenience be linked with the establishment of the Soviet Sociological Association in the summer of 1958: by 1967 this body embraced no less than 79 organizations and 580 individual scholars.[15]

The new sociology was sanctioned by the Party because the leaders hoped it would help them elucidate and solve social problems which they could not handle very well otherwise. But the reappearance of sociology as an independent discipline inevitably meant that questions, and quite searching ones, would be asked about social structure, for that is, after all, the essence of the study. One must conclude that the authorities realized this at a fairly early stage, and decided they could tolerate and control research and publication. This explains the odd situation in which the old formula is reproduced in all propaganda documents, but virtually replaced by more realistic analyses in scholarly writings.

In fact there is hardly a prominent sociologist who has not departed from it in one way or another. The All-Union Congress on social structure which was organized in Minsk in January 1966 provided many vivid illustrations of this fact. At this meeting (to take but two examples) V. S. Semenov, a leading and in many respects rather orthodox specialist on social structure, stated that the present scheme 'could no longer satisfy Soviet scholars', while Ya. V. Arutyunyan, a prominent rural sociologist, declared 'everybody recognizes that the (official) concept of

15. *Pravda*, 23 November 1967. Professor G. P. Frantsev put the number of persons professionally engaged in sociological research a t 2,000 in *Partynaya zhizn*, No. 24, 1967.

class structure is not adequate to cover the concept of social structure, for the latter is broader and more intricate'.[16]

The main trend of criticism may be summarized fairly easily. Scholars tend to start with an orthodox formulation and move on to emphasize indices of class which, though recognizably within the Lenin definition, were thought of by him as rather secondary or deductive. Thus the old concept of the relationship to the means of production has been stretched to include categories like the degree to which a job is skilled or mechanized, and the income which it provides. Indeed, Soviet sociologists are obviously fascinated by the social effects of income differentials, though they have to treat the problem very cautiously in print. Occupational differences are, it is suggested, at the root of very significant cultural ones.

The next stage is to claim that these secondary indices can, in certain cases, become more important than relationship to the means of production, and overshadow the basic worker/peasant and intelligentsia/non-intelligentsia distinctions. Some sociologists have even gone so far as to claim that intra-class differences will outlive the inter-class ones, and will survive even when Soviet society becomes truly communist. This can only suggest the conclusion that communist society itself will be unstable as a result of their presence. It is noteworthy that this tendency towards objective analysis has entailed the recognition of major social problems – such as unorganized migration from village to town, inequality of educational opportunity and social mobility, etc. – which were taboo before.

No single author provides a consistent exposition of this line of argument, but it can be easily illustrated from the work of several. Let us begin with V. S. Semenov, who has adopted a liberal-orthodox position. In an article which appeared in

16. The reports at the congress were published, evidently in an amended form, in two volumes (*Problemy izmenenia sotsialnoi struktury sovetskogo obshchestva*, and *Klassy, sotsialnye sloi gruppy v USSR*, both edited by Ts. A. Stepanyan, V. S. Semenov and others, Moscow, 1968). Mr K. E. Wädekin has published a brief analysis of other conference documents which came into his hands (*Osteuropa*, Heft 1, p. 23, 1968). These were evidently circulated in advance of the conference, which was held in January 1966, and not January 1965 as Mr Wädekin states. Much criticism of a similar nature has been expressed in Soviet learned journals.

September 1965, he claimed that there were four types of social division in Soviet society.[17] The first ran between worker and peasant, the second between mental and physical labour, as of yore. The third was the distinction between people's way of life in town and country. This was by no means original, but it was not explicit in the old formula. Semenov's fourth distinction was, however, already outside the Stalinist framework, for it covered differences between groups within a given class. He was careful to emphasize that these intra-class differences (whose ideological pedigree, as he probably realized, owed as much to Bukharin as to Lenin) were of a secondary and subordinate nature, but the mere recognition of their existence was a step forward.

These ideas were regurgitated in the party journal *Kommunist* in the spring of 1968 by the well-known economist G. Glezerman. Now, however, they were used as a means for emphasizing the importance of income differentials in the social structure, and stressing that problems like social and educational inequalities, social mobility and migration from the village should all be studied in depth.[18]

Many sociologists concerned with problems of labour come very close to asserting that the 'content' or 'character' of labour is the central factor in social stratification. The classification of society into workers and peasants is in itself a division by occupation, but the sociologists in question have in mind a much more searching analysis within each of these classes. Thus L. N. Kogan stated at the Minsk symposium that other indices like education, income, living conditions and way of life all ultimately depended on 'the character of labour'.

M. N. Rutkevich, writing in April 1966, took another logical step by stating that when large numbers of people, for example the workers, have the same relationship to the means of production, then the secondary distinctions between them become dominant; and what is more, these distinctions will remain even after the classes have fused together.[19] Yu. V. Arutyunyan provided the obvious conclusion to this line of argument when he claimed, on the basis of his study of rural society, that these

17. *Voprosy Filosofii*, No. 9, 1965, p. 142.
18. *Kommunist*, No. 13, p. 28.
19. *Filosofskie Nauki*, No. 4, 1966, p. 23.

secondary indices can already make intra-class differences more important than inter-class ones. This was in effect a way of reversing the order of Semenov's indices and saying that the worker–peasant split is *not* the most important dichotomy in Soviet society.

Many other daring, though uncoordinated, suggestions for change have been made from time to time, and a few of them deserve mention here. One sociologist, O. N. Alterovich, stated that new classes of 'agricultural workers' (i.e. state farm workers) or 'non-urban workers' should be added to the worker–peasant scheme, because they in many respects occupied an intermediate position between the urban working class and the peasantry. G. Glezerman suggested that under socialism the classes could have differing interests, i.e., that they would not be totally amicable even then. S. L. Senyavski held that there were no 'pure' classes as officially defined. Members of a single family could be formally separated by class distinctions if one worked in a collective farm and another in a factory, even though they had been brought up and lived together. Another scholar, R. G. Vartanov, actually proposed that the term 'class' be rejected altogether in favour of 'stratum', because Soviet classes are 'non-political'.[20] The most charitable interpretation of this particular view is that the workers and peasantry do not have incompatible political views: one cannot believe Vartanov was saying they were devoid of political power. But the implication is that Soviet classes are not classes as Marx envisaged them, and this is not an officially approved point of view. Many of these arguments, incidentally, have centred around the position of the intelligentsia, but this is a subject we shall treat in chapter 5.

The official reaction to this theorizing has been unequivocal. At the Minsk symposium Z. A. Stephanyan rejected criticism of the official formula and denied that any new classes or strata could be discerned in the Soviet Union. He came out against attempts to merge the intelligentsia with the workers or peasants which some of the interpretations implied. He also rejected the thesis that intra-class differences could override all others, for this, he said, would deny the working class its leading role. His statement made it clear that the Soviet leadership's fondness for

20. *Problemy*, op. cit., p. 119.

the old scheme did not spring merely from respect for a Stalin tradition. The concept of a distinct and undivided working class is essential to the ideology of the Communist Party, which has always claimed to represent it. If important divisions were admitted to exist among the workers, or the leading role of their class put in doubt, the ideological premises of the Party would be shaken. The Party leadership evidently fears that any important modification of Soviet social theory would have precisely this result. Moreover, any reappraisals might be retrospective, with disastrous effects on Soviet historiography.

The retention of the old formula has not stopped questioning; but it seems that Soviet sociologists will have to work within the officially approved framework for a long time to come. If this is so, there is room for cautious optimism. The existence of an official sociology has not stifled useful sociological investigation in other lands of the Soviet bloc. This may be a pointer for Russia.

3
Worker and Peasant –
Some Institutional Distinctions

THE official formula, for all its bareness, is useful in that it emphasizes principal watersheds in Soviet society, including the distinction between the average worker and the average peasant. The 'intelligentsia', or more broadly, 'employees', are much less distinctive concepts. They merge with the classes, especially the 'working class', and for purposes of generalization may even be considered part of them. Most Soviet social statistics are in fact presented for two categories only, 'workers and employees', and 'peasantry'.[1]

The worker–peasant distinction is, of course, primarily an occupational and locational one. In the Soviet context it is also one of different relationships to the means of production, since the workers use state-owned, and the peasants cooperatively-owned, machinery. These distinctions are reinforced by a number of others, especially in matters of legal status, standard of living, educational achievement, cultural tastes, and time-use. Here we shall address ourselves to the first three of these five facets, leaving culture and time-use for discussion in Chapter 6. A chronological treatment of even these divergences would clearly take us deep into the social history of the USSR, so we shall base our analysis on the situation as it stood in the mid or late sixties.

The Bolsheviks abolished all existing titles and ranks, from Tsar down, on 24 November 1917. Stalin's 1936 Constitution appeared to ensure complete equality for all Soviet citizens, but it was backed by a substantial body of law which in many important respects relegated the peasant to the status of second-class citizen. A goodly number of these measures are, in one form or another, still in force today, and provide some justification for

1. Soviet sociologists have on occasions appealed for more flexibility; see note by V. N. Shubkin, *Voprosy Filosofii*, No. 8, 1964, p. 24.

thinking of the workers and peasants as 'estates', in the old European sense of the word, rather than as classes.

The most significant legal distinctions between them are at present enshrined in such documents as the Collective Farm Model Charter of November 1969 for peasants and the Principles of Labour Legislation of the USSR and Union Republics of July 1970 for workers. These form the basis for collective farm and labour law. In addition a host of internal passport and residence provisions, some published and some not, are relevant. All this legislation regulates the standing of workers and peasants in such important matters as residence and employment rights, working conditions, social insurance, property rights and form of income. We will take each of these topics in turn, concerning ourselves with legal postulations rather than administrative practice; but considerable departures from legal norms will be mentioned when necessary.[2]

RESIDENCE AND EMPLOYMENT

Residence in all kinds of urban settlements (and in a few rural areas which are near large towns, in 'closed' zones or near frontiers) is regulated by the so-called passport régime. This requires that citizens acquire an internal passport on reaching the age of sixteen and renew it periodically afterwards. The great majority of collectivized peasants, it will be noted, are not eligible for a passport. It might seem at first sight that they would be pleased to be without this tedious document, but this is by no means so, mainly because its absence impedes movement to a town.

The existing system was founded in December 1932, ostensibly to 'improve the enumeration of the population of towns, workers' settlements and building sites, and free them from persons not engaged in productive labour . . . kulaks, criminals and other anti-social elements'. In fact, the authorities used the

2. Other branches of Soviet civil and criminal law do not generally distinguish between Soviet citizens who are members of collective farms and those who are not. A few elements of local custom law are, however, apparently observed among peasants even now, especially in family relations. These practices are permitted by the authorities when they do not overtly contradict civil law. (E. L. Johnson, *An Introduction to the Soviet Legal System*, London, 1969.)

passport régime as a means of reducing undesirable labour mobility at a time of rapid industrialization. The only publicized changes which have been made since then include some simplification and amendments to allow for Soviet territorial gains during the war.[3]

The passport, which has to have an approved residence stamp, is issued by the local militia. If the holder wishes to change his place of residence permanently he must get the formal permission of the militia in his chosen area before he moves in. This is only a formality in small towns and the less desirable spots where there is little pressure on public amenities, but may present a major difficulty in places like Moscow, Leningrad and republican capitals, which have more to offer their inhabitants. It is no secret that outsiders are all but excluded from permanent residence in Moscow, for example, and some people find that registration there can be procured only by bribery. This system may seem strange to a Britisher or an American, but internal passports, albeit with much less restrictive provisions, are obligatory in several West European countries.

The overwhelming majority of collective farm members who live outside areas where there is a passport régime face special problems when moving. If they wish to go anywhere for more than a month they must obtain a pass from the local village Soviet. This document legalizes their absence, and enables them to apply for a temporary residence permit or, if they go to a town, a passport with a residence stamp. The chairmen of village Soviets are traditionally reluctant to issue these passes, or *spravki* as they are called, and getting one is recognized as a major hurdle in village life. Overcoming it may absorb the energies of the rustic mind for a long period.

A change of residence, in town or country, often means a change of job. Since the adoption of the law of 25 April 1956 workers and employees who are not on special contracts may leave their jobs after giving two weeks' notice to their employers.

3. Details on the Soviet internal passport system are to be found in the *Bolshaya sovetskaya entsiklopedia*, Vol. 44, Moscow, 1939, p. 322, Vol. XXXII, Moscow, 1955, p. 200; *O soblyudenii obshchestvennogo poryadka i pravil blagoustroistva v Moskve*, Moscow, 1958, p. 406; *Slovar pravovykh znanii*, Moscow, 1965, p. 309.

This may, in certain cases, entail a reduction in their social insurance benefits and affect old age pension rights, but the present provisions are not too oppressive.[4]

At the same time it is only fair to note that the situation has been much less favourable in the past. Although the 1922 Labour Code explicitly granted workers the right to terminate their employment at will, this right was attenuated with the introduction of the Work Book (a sort of labour passport) in December 1938, and then suppressed altogether by the law of 26 June 1940.[5] This was the end of free labour relations in the Soviet Union until 1956. The imminence of war may have provided some justification for introducing this harsh measure, but it could have been repealed much sooner.

The legal bonds between the peasant and the collective farm are much tighter. Most young people from 'workers' families take any job they want, or can find, when they leave school. Collective farm children are in a different position. Under the terms of the 1969 Statutes those who reach the age of sixteen, and wish to do so, may apply to the board of the farm for membership. There is, however, a very interesting point at issue here, since a youngster who decides not to apply has no automatic right to leave the village. A pass may be legally refused. Thus there seems to be a real element of compulsion on him to join the farm. The question of whether young peasants try to evade collective farm membership, or whether farm administrations are anxious to have them, is an intricate one, and obviously depends on a large number of factors, personal and economic. There is overwhelming evidence, however, that young peasants in most areas try to get away if they can. They evidently object to having a job virtually thrust upon them.

Withdrawal from a collective farm is hardly less complicated than moving out of the village altogether. In most cases the peasant has to have the permission of the *kolkhoz* board and general assembly of members – which may keep him waiting up to three months. The most common outlets are transfer to work

4. The regulations are in fact rather complicated. See for example, *Trudovoe pravo, entsiklopedicheski slovar*, Moscow, 1969, entries under 'social insurance', etc., and *Sovetskoe trudovoe pravo*, Moscow, 1966, pp. 307, 318.

5. Solomon Schwarz, *Labor in the Soviet Union*, London, 1953, Chapter 3.

in industry through an official state hiring organization, participation in an organized migration scheme to a newly developed region, transfer to a state farm, or call-up for obligatory military service. If a peasant commits a serious misdemeanour he may be expelled. Family ties also provide sufficient grounds for leaving, and it is not unknown for young girls to marry passport holders with this in mind.[6]

A peasant's departure from the farm is in any case likely to have an adverse effect on the wellbeing of his family, since a smaller household means, amongst other things, a smaller private plot; loss of even part of this valuable asset can be in itself a severe sanction. A further disadvantage of peasant status is that the household, rather than the individual, is taken as a unit for other purposes, including taxation. The statutes contain, however, a provision for a final settlement between the departing peasant and the farm, and desertion is not in itself a criminal offence.

Not all of the persons living and working on a collective farm are members. Farm administrations have the specific right to hire outsiders for work which is beyond the capabilities of their members. This means that most agricultural specialists, and a few others, such as teachers and cultural workers, are brought in from the towns on short-term contracts. Though part of the collective farm community, they are not subject to these irksome restrictions. Nevertheless, it has been government policy to encourage them to take membership. By 1957 rather more than half of the agricultural specialists in farms were members, having either joined, or risen, from the ranks of the unskilled.[7]

It is worth digressing for a moment to observe that the legal ties of residence and occupation have in practice been far from effective in keeping peasants on the collective farm. No numerical analysis of the use – or abuse – of the escape clauses is available to us. But the fact that more peasants have left than the authorities intended is evident from the big discrepancies between the planned and actual growth of the non-peasant labour

6. A brief discussion of some of these provisions may be found in V. K. Grigoriev (ed.), *Kolkhoznoe pravo*, Moscow, 1962, p. 114.

7. I. F. Pankratov, *Osnovyne prava i obyazannosti rukovodyashchikh kadrov kolkhoza*, Moscow, 1957, p. 73.

force (Table 8). The plan figures, which can only be rough approximations, allow for both natural increase and the influx from the collective farm sector. But if we presume the planners' forecast of the first variable to be fairly reliable, then it seems that since the war something like a million able-bodied peasants a year have been leaving the farms in excess of government expectations.[8] Of course, the plans, or for that matter local regulations, may have been revised during the five-year periods to allow for migration which could not be stopped.

TABLE 8. *Planned and Actual Growth of the Non-Peasant Labour Force, 1946–65, millions*

Years	Planned Growth	Actual Growth	Surplus
1946–50	6.25	10.2	4.0
1951–5	6.0	10.0	4.0
1956–8	plan abandoned	4.2	—
1959–65	8.0	19.0	11.0

Sources:
Narodnoe khozyaistvo SSSR v 1965, p. 557; *Direktivy KPSS, Sovetskogo pravitelstva po khozyaistvennym voprosam*, Vol. 3, Moscow, 1958, p. 686; N. S. Khrushchev, *Stroitelstvo kommunizma v SSSR*, Moscow, 1962, p. 427; *XXI S'ezd KPSS (stenograficheski otchet)*, Vol. II, p. 525; Solomon Schwartz, *Labor in the Soviet Union*, London, 1953, p. 29.

WORKING CONDITIONS AND SOCIAL INSURANCE

The regulations covering the activities of Soviet workers and employees while on the job in the late sixties were approved by the State Committee for Labour and Wages on 12 January 1957.[9] They stipulate that people must work honestly and conscientiously: observe factory regulations: be punctual: devote all their time to the work in hand: carry out the production tasks allotted to them: fulfil norms, respect state property, observe

8. This would have been included in the total losses of peasant population which may, in some years, have been over two and a half million. (See Chapter 7, below.)

9. *Sbornik zakonodatelnykh aktov o trude*, Moscow, 1965, p. 544.

safety regulations and keep work-places clean. Violation of these rules is punished severely by Western standards. Punishments range from a rebuke or reprimand to transfer to a lower, worse-paid, position for three months. The more serious misdemeanour of truancy (defined as one day's absence from work without good reason, or arrival at work in a drunken state) may in addition be punished by a temporary reduction in pension rights, or dismissal.

Once again, we must remember, however, that these rules replaced a considerably harsher régime. The regulations in force from January 1941 to 1957 stipulated that workers were not allowed to walk about or converse with one another during working hours, and they were bound to *over*fulfil their norms systematically. These requirements were supplemented by laws and decrees which came close to turning normal factory employment into a form of forced labour. The law of 26 June 1940, for instance, which prohibited unauthorized quitting, made both lateness and truancy (then much more stringently defined) into criminal offences punishable by up to six months' corrective labour at the worker's place of employment, and authorized a wage cut of up to twenty-five per cent. Though these oppressive provisions were being ignored fairly widely by the early fifties, they were formally swept away only by the law of 25 April 1956.[10]

Legal pressure on the peasant to work hard and efficiently is much more immediate, and is built into the collective farm statutes. The farm managements have to face a problem which is unknown in the factory or state enterprise, for whereas the worker or employee may normally be expected to get on with the work in hand, the peasant has every incentive to spend as much time as possible working not on collective farm land but on his private plot, from which he may gain a third or more of his sustenance.

The post-Stalin leadership has been reluctant to abandon the old hostility to the private sector, a hostility both ideological and economic in character. Khrushchev adopted a more tolerant

10. The autumn of 1969 and spring of 1970 were characterized by calls from responsible officials to tighten labour discipline and centralize hiring in an effort to restrict turnover and improve productivity. This rather threatening development is, at the time of writing, limited to reports of individual cases, and has not been backed up by changes in the law.

policy towards private husbandry in 1953, but other important measures which he promoted in this sphere could not really be thus described. On 10 March 1956, for example, he promulgated a law on the Model Charter which specifically empowered the collective farm authorities to reduce the size of the plot if any member of the household was not working in the public sector. This important provision was retained in the 1969 version of the Charter. After 1958 he began another squeeze in the form of a levy on the produce of the plot, though this was relaxed after his dismissal. Unpalatable though the existence of the private plot is, its importance to the economy has prevented the authorities from stifling it altogether. Hence the uncertainty of the official approach.

Throughout most of the history of the collective farm, the existence of the private plot has made minimal norms for participation in work in the public sector a sheer necessity – that is, if collectivized agriculture were to work at all. The first annual minimum of labour days was established by law in 1939. After March 1956 it was fixed individually by the farm administration, but this move can best be interpreted as an attempt to improve the system rather than dismantle it. A similar provision has been retained in the new Model Charter.

The worker, as we have seen, lays himself open to sanctions from the management if he breaks the regulations of his enterprise. An erring peasant is, if anything, in a more vulnerable position. This is partly because the farm administration controls so many aspects of his private and working life, and partly because the economics of collective farming push him to great, sometimes illegal, reliance on the private plot. If the peasant does not spend enough time at work in the public sector the farm administration is empowered to raise the agricultural tax on his household by fifty per cent, or reduce the size of his private plot. If he refuses to do his full stint consistently he may be excluded from the farm altogether, which again may mean a reduction in the plot, from which all the other members of his household will suffer. Of course we have no means of knowing how often these legal sanctions are applied. In so far as many peasants stay on the land only because of their private plot, such repressive provisions may defeat their own object.

Labour protection is another sphere in which the peasant is at a disadvantage – though agricultural labour is by its very nature considerably more difficult to protect than work in office or factory. Soviet workers may normally not begin to toil until they reach the age of sixteen (fifteen-year-olds may take employment only with the specific approval of the enterprise trade union organization), and there are many restrictions on the types of work anyone under eighteen can do. Workers have a guaranteed six- or seven-hour working day and the equivalent of at least twelve working days' holiday per annum. In so far as their average working day over the year must not exceed seven hours, workers in state farms (as opposed to peasants) are also covered by these provisions. All workers are eligible for many social insurance benefits, including sick pay and an old-age pension which may be calculated from their best period of earnings but in no instance fall below thirty roubles a month. Retirement normally begins at sixty for men and fifty-five for women, though certain categories of workers may be pensioned off younger. Full pension rights are enjoyed by those who have a twenty-five or twenty-year work-stage behind them, i.e. the great majority of people in normal employment. It is true that these provisions have at times been ignored or suppressed, that they have tended to be devalued by inflation, and that there has not been any un-employment benefit for able-bodied persons since October 1930.[11] Nevertheless, they are not bad by international standards.

The peasant, on the other hand, may start work as soon as he can walk, and indeed peasant children, as in many countries, are expected to help their parents from an early age. Membership of the collective farm brings full adult responsibilities from the age of sixteen. No maximum working hours have ever been fixed for collective farmers, but there is no doubt that they are expected to work much longer than workers in non-agricultural institutions: an agricultural handbook published in 1953 suggested a nine-hour day during the winter, extending to twelve or fourteen hours at other times.[12] The 1969 Charter stipulated that the

11. An apparent resurgence of unemployment led to calls in the autumn of 1969 for a reinstitution of this benefit, disguised as redundancy or retraining benefits.

12. *Kniga kolkhoznika*, Moscow, 1953, p. 262.

kolkhoz itself should regulate these questions, and no statutory limits were mentioned.

The peasant has no guaranteed holiday. A commentary published in December 1962 stated that the nature and length of rest periods 'were to be fixed by the collective farms themselves, depending on the state of their economies, conditions of work and opportunities available'. Only those peasants 'who had taken an active part in communal labour and who had fulfilled the fixed minimum of labour days (or work norms)' were eligible for them anyway.[13] In practice, of course, a holiday is an economic impossibility for the majority of peasants, quite apart from the fact that they are busiest in the summer. The new version of the Charter makes only a fleeting reference to annual paid leave, but contains specific provisions for the release of pregnant women and mothers with young babies.

Up until the summer of 1964 the peasant lagged far behind the worker in matters of social insurance. The collective farms were expected to run their own sickness benefit schemes and care for their own aged; and as the public sector of agriculture was generally in a parlous state, funds were not usually available for these purposes. At the same time, by paying direct and indirect taxes, the peasant was contributing to the State budget from which most of the benefits enjoyed by the workers were ultimately drawn.[14]

Khrushchev took a big step towards righting this double injustice when in July of that year he introduced old-age pensions, sickness and maternity benefits for members of collective farms, to be financed from a central state fund. These provisions were formally incorporated into the Charter. It is true that they have remained much less generous than in other sectors – the minimum rate for a peasant's old-age pension, for example, is only twelve roubles a month, and eligibility begins five years later for both men and women. Collective farmers, it is true, retain the right to the use of their private plot while receiving a pension.

13. *Spravochnik po selskokhozyaistvennomu zakonodatelstvu dlya predsedatelya kolkhoza*, Moscow, 1962, p. 47.

14. The two outstanding examples of such taxes were the old system of obligatory deliveries of produce to the state at low prices, and the indirect taxes levied on all goods sold in State shops in rural areas.

Membership of the collective farm still in practice precludes a man from the marginal benefits of trade union membership; but an important and invidious legal distinction between the 'estates' has been removed.

SOURCES OF INCOME

Another major legal distinction between worker and peasant is the way in which they are paid. Persons employed in state enterprises and institutions receive a wage or salary subject to fixed state minima, on either a time-rate or a piece-work basis. In addition they can earn bonuses for overtime or over-fulfilment of norms. In normal circumstances the basic wage is assured.

The peasant is supposed to derive his main income from the output of the public sector of the collective farm. But by the time Stalin died he was in a very unenviable position. His income was payable in kind or money, and was residual, that is, received only after the farm had made all its obligatory deliveries to state bodies. The peasant also had the right to the produce of his private plot, which he could consume or sell. This manner of payment might have been satisfactory in a prosperous country with highly developed farms and a benevolent government. The low productivity of Soviet collectivized agriculture, however, combined with low prices for obligatory deliveries, and the continuous official pressure on the private plot, meant that the peasant's income was both unreliable and insufficient for his needs.

Payment for work done in the public sector was, until the late fifties, calculated on the basis of the so-called labour day, or *trudoden*. A day's work could equal more than one *trudoden* if it was exceptionally laborious or required extra skills. In the course of the year each peasant notched up a number of these units, according to the amount and type of work that he did. Payment for them was determined only in the autumn, when the collective farm had met all other obligations. In the meantime the peasant had to manage on the previous year's takings and the produce from his private plot. Many collective farmers had to find temporary jobs in local industry to make ends meet.

The first important relaxation of these blatantly unfair pressures came in September 1953, when Khrushchev raised the state prices for deliveries of agricultural produce and stipulated a more tolerant attitude towards private livestock holding. In March 1956 he introduced guaranteed monthly advances to the peasants of up to twenty-five per cent of the collective farm money income from all sources, or fifty per cent of the money income from the actual sale of agricultural produce. Subsequently a regular wage fund was set up, so that payments to collective farm members ceased to be merely residual. State demands on collective farms were generally much reduced during his tenure of office. This alone could not bring about any miraculous change in poor villages, but at least it meant that the need for kinder policies had been recognized.

A few other significant changes have been made since Khrushchev went. Since 1966 the labour-day has been largely replaced by a piece-work tariff system, in some ways similar to that operative in state farms. By the beginning of 1969 over 92 per cent of all collective farms had apparently gone over to it. In addition, 95 per cent of them, it was claimed, gave guaranteed monthly advances (though these, of course, varied with output, unlike the guaranteed minimum wage in other sectors of the economy).[15] Payment in kind also became much less common.

In the early fifties only 34 per cent of peasant income from the public sector was in money, but the figure had apparently risen to over 80 per cent by 1963.[16] The peasant is still heavily dependent on his private plot: as we shall see in a moment, by the late sixties it was, in one way or another, still providing about a third of his consumption needs.

As far as legal distinctions are concerned, we may on the basis of this survey draw some fairly safe conclusions. The post-Stalin period has witnessed a steady closing of the legal gap between the peasantry and the working class, yet the status of the former is still markedly inferior. The conservative character of the 1969 Model Charter makes it appear unlikely that the discrimination against the peasant will disappear completely in the near future. The old legal barriers between the two estates cannot be re-

15. *Ekonomika selskogo khozyaistva*, No. 1, 1969, p. 7.

16. D. A. Morozov, *Trudoden i torgovlya v kolkhoze*, Moscow, 1968, pp. 138–9. The 1969 charter still specifically authorized payments in kind.

moved while the collective farm remains. Discrimination of this kind is, however, probably less important to the peasant, in practical terms, than deficiencies in his standard of living and cultural amenities, a subject to which we shall now turn.

STANDARDS OF LIVING

There are many ways of measuring a person's standard of living. The indices we shall use for our own summary assessment of the gap between worker and peasant are income (as far as it can be assessed, in roubles), the different patterns of food consumption, and the levels of trade in urban and rural areas. A few other data relating mainly to time-use and cultural pursuits we shall leave for discussion in Chapter 6. These are not the only figures available for purposes of comparison, but they are the handiest for giving an idea of the existing gap.

The differential between worker and peasant income is a mystery of long standing, though a few Soviet scholars have of late made brave attempts to unravel it. There is no doubt that total peasant income was, in the last years of Stalin's rule, much lower than that of workers; the problem is whether there is still a lag, and if so, how great it is.

A set of figures produced by the Soviet economist I. F. Suslov showing the relative sizes of incomes of persons employed in industry, state farms, and collective farms (state farm workers being regarded as a sort of intermediate category) is given in Table 9. He claimed that by 1965 the peasant was earning, *from the public sector* of the collective farm, only little more than half as much as the worker, though the gulf between them had narrowed appreciably during the preceding seven years.[17]

This brings us to the associated problem of assessing the income from the peasant plot. The plot, incidentally, is not a purely peasant institution, in so far as all workers have the right to one, and many workers in or near rural areas take advantage of this. But compared to peasant holdings, the workers' private

17. Figures provided by the 1967 handbook of labour statistics, *Trud v SSSR*, p. 134, also show the same trend, mainly due to a rapid improvement in the well-being of the peasantry. But the categorization is vague, and it is hardly possible to compare these data with Suslov's.

TABLE 9. *Changes in the Level of Wages of Collective Farmers
and Workers in State Enterprises* (%)

Average annual wage of persons employed in	1958	1960	1963	1964	1965	(Plan) 1970
(a) Industry	100	105	115	116	123	148
(b) State farms	100	103	124	131	139	165
(c) Collective farms	100	90	123	146	169	233
Wages in collective farms as a % of wages in industry *	40	34	43	50	55	64
Wages in the collective farm as a % of wages in state farms *	70	61	67	75	82	96

*Exclusive of income from the peasant private plot. See the comment on
workers' plots in footnote 18.
Source:
I. F. Suslov, *Ekonomicheskie problemy razvitiya kolkhozov*, Moscow, 1967,
p. 172.

sector is quite small.[18] One Soviet observer has stated that in the
late sixties the peasant's plot provided, on average, over a third
of his entire income. M. I. Sidorova gave the following proportions for peasant income sources in her book on the subject in
1969: Total income: 100. Earnings from the public sector: 37.8;
value of garden plot produce: 34.3; value of state and collective
farm pension, medical services and schooling: 19.5; income from
state enterprises and cooperatives: 7.2; other income: 1.4.
Naturally the mix would vary considerably from one family to
another.[19]

18. In 1962, according to N. S. Latugin, of the 33 million plots in existence
7 million belonged to state farm workers and 10 million to other workers and
employees. Of all persons living in families with plots, about 40 per cent were
workers. This gives, however, a false impression of the workers' holdings,
since the maximum size of a worker's plot was 0.15 hectares as compared to
half a hectare for the peasants which means a 'maximum area' ratio of 2.5
million hectares as against 8 million for the peasants. Much of this was probably in the hands of state farm workers; but if the income from workers' plots
is averaged out over the much larger working class it sinks to almost negligible proportions. See N. S. Latugin, *Problemy sblizheniya urovniya zhizni
rabochikh i kolkhoznikov*, Moscow, 1965, p. 5, and *Kratki yuridicheski slovar-
spravochnik dlya naseleniya*, Moscow, 1962, p. 376.

19. M. I. Sidorova, *Obshchestvennye fondy potrebleniai dokhody kolkhoznikov*,
Moscow, 1969, p. 143. See also K. E. Wädekin, *Privatproduzenten in der*

Some economists have expressed the opinion that total peasant income as a result must almost have reached worker level.[20] The problem is, of course, fearfully complicated. Besides the difficulty of determining the volume of output of peasant plots, there is that of pricing it: at the same time the enormous regional and temporal variations all but invalidate generalization. It seems evident, however, that given this double burden the peasant has to work harder than the worker for every rouble he earns.

Different levels of income are usually accompanied by different consumption patterns. But workers and peasants both have characteristic sets of tastes and preferences which would hardly be effaced by a mere equalization of incomes. Figures for worker, employee and peasant budgets which were published in the Soviet journal *Ekonomicheskie nauki* in 1963 illustrated some of the existing divergencies (Table 10).[21] Despite their many weaknesses these data are worthy of our attention.[22]

The peasant, it appears, consumed an extremely large proportion of his income in the form of food. Indeed, it seems that but for the private plot nearly all of his income could go on this. He

---

sowjetischen Landwirtschaft, Köln, 1967, Chapter 2, for estimates of the weight of private plot production up to 1965.

20. At the Westfield Conference held in London in April 1968, there was a discussion of an excellent paper by Mr K. E. Wädekin on labour in Soviet agriculture. F. Seton (Nuffield College, Oxford) suggested that agricultural incomes might be 20-40 per cent lower than industrial ones at that time. Specialists in Soviet economics who were present, however, thought that the gap between peasant and worker incomes had probably been all but closed. The well-known Soviet sociologist T. I. Zaslavskaya suggested that peasant income in the RSFSR in 1962 was 62 per cent of that of workers', and 73 per cent of that of state farm workers'. (See her article on labour movements in R. V. Ryvkina (ed.), *Sotsiologicheskie issledovaniya*, Novosibirsk, 1967, p. 157.) She did not make it clear whether this included the income from the private plot: presumably it did.

21. These figures are adduced by D. A. Morozov, *Trudoden, dengi i torgovlia na sele*, Moscow, 1965, p. 211.

22. Particularly columns 1 and 2. Column 3, which covers the 'industrial employee' category, is from a methodological point of view less satisfactory. The coverage of this term is not explained, but it probably embraces all categories of mental labour, that is both highly trained specialists with a high standard of living and low-grade service personnel, who are more akin to workers. For discussion of this practice (which causes continual headaches) see pp. 141-9.

TABLE 10. *Expenditure Structure of Families of Collective Farmers, Workers and Employees in Industry, Per Capita Per Annum, as % of All Expenditures*

Itemization	Collective farmer	Industrial worker	Industrial employee
Expenditure, or value of consumption of all products, including:	100	100	100
Food	58.1	43.0	44.2
Clothing, linen, footwear	15.1	16.1	19.6
Cultural and household goods, furniture	4.4	5.9	6.5
Building materials, repairs, construction	6.2	1.0	1.0
Visits to cinema, theatre, other cultural and educational needs, payment of personal services (cures, laundry, baths, hairdressers, transport, communications, etc.)	2.8	4.3	4.4
Payment for communal services (water, gas, electricity, heating)	—	1.4	1.7
Other	13.4	28.3	22.6

Source:
Ekonomicheskie nauki, No. 5, 1963, p. 44.

devoted less than a fifth of it to clothing and cultural goods, and nothing to communal services. He spent, however, much more on building materials, repairs and construction, the reason being that peasants are usually expected to house themselves. It is unfortunate that such a large proportion of each budget is not itemized.

The table yields other interesting insights if we bear in mind that at the time when it was compiled the industrial workers (who are the best-paid of all workers) were earning considerably more than the peasants. Thus if we were boldly to increase the percentages in the 'industrial workers' column by, say, 40 per cent and think of the resulting figures as some 'real value' equivalent, we would discover that in real terms the peasant was spending rather less than the worker on food, or, to put it in another way, was eating a quantity of food which was worth less. The lag in peasant consumption of all other commodities and services (with the exception of building materials) would become much more apparent. His expenditure on furniture and cultural and household goods would have been about half that of the worker, reflecting more primitive domestic arrangements. The fact that the peasant's expenditure on communal services was nil did not, obviously, mean that he managed without all of them. He merely had to find other, and presumably far less convenient, sources of supply: his central heating was cut with a saw in the forest and his water lugged in a pail by one of the women in his household.

The figures for industrial employees are less meaningful, for the reasons we suggested in the last footnote. It is clear, however, that people in the category had, on the whole, a more opulent consumption pattern than the workers or peasants. They spent a larger proportion of their income on clothes and the secondary comforts of life.

Some interesting figures on the consumption of different *kinds* of food were published in the Soviet statistical handbook for 1967, and these are reproduced in Table 11. They presumably cover food from all sources (including the peasant's private plot). It will be noted that the consumption levels for the two social categories are about equal only in milk and eggs. In 1967 peasants were eating 24–40 per cent less meat, fish and, surpris-

TABLE 11. *Consumption of Basic Foodstuffs in the Families of Workers, Employees and Collective Farmers (Per Capita Per Annum, in Kilograms)*

| | Workers and employees | | | Collective farmers | | |
	1960	1966	1967	1960	1966	1967
Meat and bacon fat (including poultry and natural by-products)	44	46	49	30	35	37
Milk and milk products (calculated in the form of milk)	245	265	279	228	246	260
Eggs (number)	117	131	137	122	133	141
Fish and fish products	12.0	14.5	14.8	5.4	7.9	8.2
Sugar	32.4	37.6	38.5	18.2	28.3	31.2
Oil	5.9	6.5	6.8	4.1	5.4	5.8
Potatoes	132	129	125	168	154	148
Vegetables and melons	74	79	85	59	56	65
Grain products (bread calculated in the form of flour, grain, beans, macaroni products)	153	145	143	188	176	172

Source:
Narodnoe khozyaistvo SSSR v 1967, Moscow, 1968, p. 697.

ingly, vegetables, than the workers and employees. They consumed significantly more low-quality foods, like flour and potatoes. At the same time the table seems to indicate that the diet of the peasants was improving more quickly than that of the other group.

The backwardness of the village, which bears more heavily on the peasant than anyone else, is also clear from figures available for trade turnover in urban and rural areas, Table 12. In 1967

TABLE 12. *Turnover of Retail Goods in the State and Cooperative Networks (for Urban and Rural Settlements, Roubles Per Head of the Population in 1967)*

	Towns and urban settlements			Rural areas		
	including			*including*		
	All goods	*Comestibles*	*Other goods*	*All goods*	*Comestibles*	*Other goods*
USSR	734	421	313	270	150	120
RSFSR	740	442	298	322	194	128
Estonia	1,018	543	475	337	196	141
Azerbaidzhan	546	296	250	109	59	50
Lithuania	973	495	478	172	95	77
Kazakhstan	597	336	261	329	179	150

Source:
Narodnoe khozyaistvo SSSR v 1967, Moscow, 1968, p. 718, adapted. Estonia and Azerbaidzhan had the highest and lowest republican turnovers respectively. Lithuania and Kazakhstan had the largest and smallest differentials.

the per capita figure for the USSR as a whole was nearly three times as high in the towns as in the country. The discrepancy varied from 1.8 for Kazakhstan to 5.7 for Lithuania. The numbers of shops and booths were about equal in each sector, but given the scattered nature of rural settlement, this meant that the village network was far from adequate. In any case the shops and establishments were much smaller. Of the 211,000 catering establishments registered at that time only 62,000 were in the villages.[23] In 1965 there were 417,900 persons employed in enterprises offering 'non-industrial' services in the towns, and

23. *Narodnoe khozyaistvo SSSR v 1967*, p. 741.

only 62,400 in similar jobs in the country. The volume of work done was valued at 626.7 million roubles in the first case, and 75.8 million roubles, or about a ninth of that figure, in the second.[24] Obviously, many rural inhabitants went to the towns to shop. But the known inadequacy of transport facilities, and the distances involved, must have made this in itself a considerable burden.

Before leaving the problem of living standards we should perhaps recall a point which has been made often, but which bears repeating. This is that aggregated figures, especially when they cover millions of individuals, can conceal a great deal. Thus although the peasants as a group may have fared worse than the workers and employees, a more sensitive statistical treatment could show that the top layer of peasants (containing, most obviously, those with good private plots near large towns) were better off than the poorest workers and employees, or conversely, that the economic gap between the poorest peasants on one hand and the richest workers and employees on the other was much greater than that illustrated here. This would certainly be so if the state farm workers were categorized with the peasants, as some Soviet sociologists suggest they should be. Variations of income within the working class and peasantry are dealt with in Chapters 4 and 6.

In general, however, it seems that despite a narrowing of income differentials, the living standards (in the broadest sense) of the peasantry were by the late sixties still markedly below those of the workers and employees.

EDUCATIONAL LEVELS

The most comprehensive data available on educational achievement at the time of writing are from the returns of the 1959 All-Union Census, some of which are shown in Table 13. The figures are now a little out-dated in that the distinctions they reveal have softened somewhat. Data in the 1968 statistical handbook for all kinds of education above seven-year school level show that the peasants are slowly creeping up.[25] But the eradication of their

24. *Narodnoe khozyaistvo SSSR v 1965*, p. 599.
25. *Narodnoe khozyaistvo SSSR v 1968*, p. 34.

TABLE 13. *Educational Levels of the Labour Force by Social Group, circa 1959 (both sexes, per 1,000 persons)*

Rural and urban population	Higher, incomplete higher and middle special	General (10-year school)	Incomplete general (7-year school)	Primary (4-year school) and over	Less than 4 years of schooling
All social groups	109	64	260	331	236
Workers	20	59	307	418	196
Employees	490	145	258	92	15
Collective farmers	9	23	194	355	419

Source:
All-Union Census, 1959, p. 111. Figures for incomplete primary education are calculated as a residue, as they were not given in the returns.

educational backwardness is a long-term project, not least because young people whose educational achievements are greatest tend to desert the village as soon as they can.

Table 13 also illustrates the expected predominance of the employees. The differences between the social groups were very marked in the sphere of higher education; whereas the peasants could boast but 9 individuals per thousand with any education beyond the general school, the workers had 20 and the employees had 490. The workers greatly out-distanced the peasants in the incidence of full general schooling. Figures from the census also showed that whereas 66 persons per thousand of the urban labour force had ten years of schooling or more, only 20 per thousand of the rural peasantry reached this level.

The officially approved concept of Soviet society as being a society divided into two classes can be supported by several persuasive arguments. The peasantry is still separated from the working class and employees not only by obvious occupational and locational characteristics, but also in its legal status, standard of living and educational achievement. The political distinctions, which we shall deal with later, are not inconsiderable either. The proclaimed policy of the Soviet leadership is to close this gap, and it seems that in general some progress, albeit cautious, is being registered.

4

Soviet Workers, Rich and Poor

IT has long been a commonplace among Western sociologists to regard a person's income as an important – sometimes the most important – factor in determining his place in society. This is a sufficient reason for beginning our survey of the structure of the Soviet working class from that angle.[1] The other highly important indices of occupation, education and prestige we shall consider in Chapter 5.

Income, of course, is a tricky concept to use. In 'capitalist' states it may include a person's 'earnings', and sums which he does not have to work for. These may be from private sources, or be unearned benefits like pensions or state subsidies. Income is not synonymous with 'wealth', which may more properly be regarded as accumulated income of various kinds. A man's wealth in the form of personal property – say a flat or a car – may exercise a much bigger influence on his life than the amount of money he has to live on. But all things considered, per capita income, earned and unearned, is a reasonable measure of general wellbeing. This is as true for Russia as for any other land, the main difference being that apart from state subsidies there is little legal unearned income to be taken into account. (Illegal income is an important factor, but imponderable.)

The major problem that confronts us when we try to apply these concepts to the Soviet working class is the all-too-familiar one of a shortage of data. A few published studies of the distribution of wages and the distribution of families by per capita income do, however, permit some tentative conclusions. We shall

1. We are using 'working class' as a shorthand term for all Soviet citizens who are not members of collective farms, that is, in the sense it is used in Chapters 2 and 3. It includes 'employees', the intelligentsia, and low-grade service personnel, unless otherwise stated. The only excuse for this rather unsatisfactory practice is that it enables us to avoid tedious verbosity at many points in the argument. Specific references to other groups will be made where necessary.

begin by summarizing these materials. Then we can pass on to some Soviet investigations of how differences in income are linked with distinct styles of life.

INCOME DISTRIBUTION AND GOVERNMENT POLICIES

A good deal has been published since the mid sixties on *average* wage levels in different branches of industry, and increases in these averages, real or apparent, are now always made public. But *distribution* is still something of a state secret. This is irritating in view of the fact that the government has always retained the right to plan wage and bonus rates and fix enterprise wage funds. Since as far back as the twenties it has also encouraged extensive surveys of family budgets; by 1967, for example, 51,000 of them, covering some 200,000 souls, were being followed regularly.[2] This material must provide the comrades in the Central Statistical Administration with a mass of data for analysis. Published sources, however, are mostly limited to accounts of laws modifying wage tariffs (which are a good step removed from what people actually earn), discussions of methodology, and descriptions of shifts in distribution which are difficult to interpret and suspiciously stereotyped in exposition.[3]

In these circumstances the few figures and graphic representations to appear in print are of particular interest. Those on which we have chosen to base our conclusions here are shown in Figures 5 and 6. In a cohesive, 'equitable' society one would expect the wage curve to be symmetrical, with the arithmetical mean of all wages in the middle. This mean would not be pulled to the left, down the wage scale, by a preponderance of people earning little, and the base of the curve would be narrow, reflecting a narrow range of income. This state of affairs is illustrated

2. *Vestnik Statistiki*, No. 4, 1967, p. 62, and A. I. Ezhov, *Statistika i metodologia pokazatelei sovetskoi statistiki*, Moscow, 1965, p. 316. For a brief account of the history of family budget surveys in the USSR see also article by M. Kaser in *Soviet Studies*, July 1955.

3. A careful documentation of the announced changes in differentials between wage rates is to be found in M. Yanowitch, 'The Soviet Income Revolution', *Slavic Review*, December 1963. There is a brief bibliography of Soviet works on this problem in the *Soviet Studies Information Supplement*, April 1970 number.

in Figure 5. It is one which hardly ever exists, since in most societies a majority of people earn relatively little – thereby shifting the peak of the curve to the left – while a few earn a lot, stretching the bottom right hand side of the curve out along the wage axis.

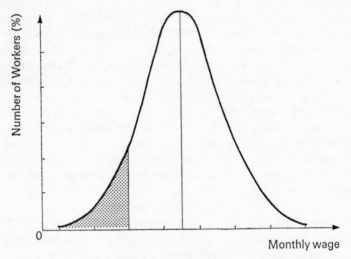

FIGURE 5. *Model Distribution of Workers by Wage**

*This was evidently intended as an illustration of a fairly equitable distribution of wages. The vertical line in the dead centre of the curve represents the modal wage (i.e., that earned by the largest number of people) and also the median wage (i.e., that which divides all earners into two groups of equal size).

The shaded area was intended to represent that section of the workers who would be affected by a rise in minimal wage rates.

Source:

A. G. Aganbegyan, V. F. Maier, *Zarabotnaya plata v SSSR*, Moscow, 1959, p. 229.

The curves showing actual wage distributions for 1946 and 1966 in Figure 6 are both irregular, and seem to illustrate the effects of well known government policies.

Stalin launched his campaign against 'harmful egalitarianism' in 1931, and big differentials in earnings were characteristic of the Soviet working class until Khrushchev began his far-reaching reform of wage structures in 1956. Stalin's policies evidently produced the very pointed and lop-sided curve which Loznevaya proposed for 1946. The most common wage was low, half of the workers and employees earned comparatively little, and the great majority of people earned less than the average wage, which meant that the happy minority earned a great deal.

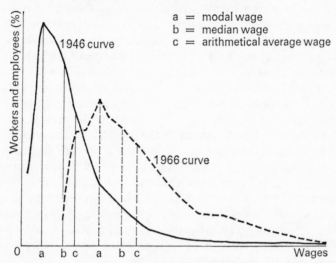

FIGURE 6. *Distribution of Workers and Employees in the National Economy of the USSR by Earnings, 1946 and 1966*

Source:

M. Loznevaya, 'Matematicheskie metody v planirovanii zarabotnoi platy', *Sotsialisticheski Trud*, No. 10, 1968, p. 127.

Khrushchev's policies were directed towards making Soviet society more egalitarian, for the masses if not for the party and government élite. He introduced many measures designed to ease existing inequalities.

Firstly, he sponsored several increases in wages, both for low-paid workers and across the board. In September 1956 a minimum wage was established at 270–350 old roubles (the equivalent of 27–35 'new' ones), depending on the branch of the economy and the urban/rural location of the enterprise. As a consequence the worst-paid workers were said to have had rises of up to 33 per cent. Between 1959 and 1962 the minimum was again raised, this time to 40 or 45 roubles; a further rise took place on 1 January 1968, when the minimum was fixed at 60 roubles a month.[4]

In addition, workers in the trading network (who were badly paid) and teaching professions have had their own increases. In May 1960 the lower-paid categories of workers and employees were released from the payment of income tax, though it should be borne in mind that this in most cases would not have amounted to more than 5 per cent of their earnings, as the top rate for well-paid bachelors was only just under 13 per cent.[5] Khrushchev's plans to abolish income tax altogether were quietly abandoned, presumably because the economy would not stand the strain.

The increases in minimum rates were accompanied by a thorough, and long overdue simplification of the intricate state-approved wage tariff system. By the early fifties the system was chaotic. Apart from extreme, unwarranted differentials between given wage scales and within them, there were anomalous rates which permitted people doing the same job in different factories to earn widely different wages. In many cases the basic wage formed only a small percentage of total earnings – the difference being made up by swollen bonus payments. Khrushchev's aim was to remove these distortions and reduce the differentials between workers of varying skills.

Between 1956 and 1965 the most extreme differentials within scales were reduced from 1:4.1 to 1:2.6 and the proportion of the bonus in wage payments fell sharply. Differentials between whole branches of industry were also noticeably narrowed. Industrial workers got an average rise of 9 per cent but workers on state farms and in the service industries, who were traditionally amongst the worst off, found themselves 20 per cent richer.[6] From early 1955 there were multiple improvements in pension schemes and other forms of social insurance, again mainly to the benefit of the underprivileged.

There was also a far-reaching simplification of the system of

4. Volkov, A. P., and others, *Trud i zarabotnaya plata v SSSR*, Moscow, 1968, p. 424; S. P. Figurnov, *Stroitelstvo kommunizma i rost blagosostoyania naroda*, Moscow, 1962, p. 144. The currency reform which introduced one new rouble to ten old ones was introduced on 1 January 1961.

5. *Spravochnik po nalogam - sboram s naselenia*, Moscow, 1968, p. 17.

6. A. P. Volkov, op. cit., pp. 301–2.

salaries for managers and technical personnel.[7] The object was again to bring rates under better control and reduce the opportunities for easy acquisition of supplementary benefits. The number of salary schemes in industry, for example, went down from 700 to 35, while the bonus rate for plan fulfilment was reduced from 30 or 40 per cent to 15 per cent of the standard rate. The new regulations stipulated that bonuses for overfulfilling plans should not exceed 40 to 60 per cent of the basic salary.[8] This meant a downward pressure on the upper layer of salaries.

The overall result seems to have been a marked change in the distribution of earnings. Loznevaya's curve for 1966 is, in fact, much more 'egalitarian' than her curve for 1946. The fall in the proportion of people getting very low wages caused the peak of the 1966 curve to drop down the vertical axis, and move to the right, that is up the wage scale. At the same time the larger proportion of people getting salaries somewhat above average raised the right-hand slope. We may recall in passing that this tendency was not confined to the working class. The period saw a marked improvement in the wellbeing of the peasantry, and possibly some narrowing of differentials inside the collective farm. This meant that all sectors of society were affected by the movement.

Changes in the distribution of earnings must have meant some realignment of per capita income. There are sound reasons for believing that in industrialized societies this tends to be more equitably distributed than are earnings throughout the labour force. Such is, after all, the main object of state subsidies, transfer payments to the poor, ill and old, free education and the imposition of income taxes on the more opulent.

7. The Soviet statistical category is ITR, 'engineers and technical workers'.

8. Volkov, op. cit., pp. 343–4. M. Yanowitch, in the article cited above, was concerned with the administrative means by which the 'spread' of earnings was narrowed in the fifties and early sixties. He emphasized the importance of the damping effect of increasing weight of the basic wage as against bonus in people's pay. The administrative changes, though of fundamental importance, are not directly related to the distribution of take-home pay, which interests us. An account of the changes in labour legislation and wage minima in the post-Stalin period is to be found in M. Dewar's article, 'Labour and Wage Reforms in the USSR', in *The Soviet Economy*, ed. H. G. Shaffer, London, 1963.

Soviet economists usually stress this point, and S. P. Figurnov claims to have illustrated it in his curves for wage and income distribution at the end of the fifties (Figure 7). His income curve is indeed more 'equitable' than his wages curve, showing more people near the average income line. Figurnov stated that if an 'overall differential' in earnings for workers and employees throughout the economy were taken as 1, then the differential between incomes would only be 0.88. A study of 888 family budgets in Sverdlovsk in 1966–7 showed that the State provided, through subsidies, etc., 46.4 per cent of the income of the poorest families, and only 11.5 per cent of that of the richest.[9]

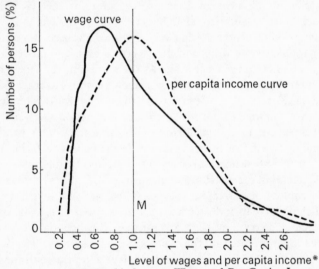

FIGURE 7.   *Relationship between Wage and Per Capita Income Distribution*

*Expressed as a proportion or multiple of the median, M.

Source:

S. P. Figurnov, op. cit., p. 158. This is not his own calculation: he gives sources for it.

The drive towards egalitarianism in earnings was very pronounced in these years. If it did not produce an even more equal distribution of income, it is because it must have been opposed by some very powerful forces.

9. S. P. Figurnov, op. cit., p. 158; D. Stadukhin and M. Khaverson, *Ekonomicheskie nauki*, No. 12, 1967, p. 22.

The first originated from government policy itself. The post-Stalin leadership never envisaged anything approaching a return to 'harmful egalitarianism' which Stalin had attacked so bitterly. The 1961 Party Programme stipulated, it is true, a 'continuous narrowing' of wage and income differentials, but was not explicit about the end result.[10] The current tasks of communist construction still require that labour be rewarded according to its quantity and quality. Thus B. M. Sukharevski, an expert on wage structure, claimed in 1968 that existing differentials would actually increase, so as to reflect, when necessary, the greater physical exertion demanded by some jobs and offset the unattractive nature of others. He mentioned specifically the need to raise the wages of certain middle-grade groups because the increase in the minimum rates of January 1968 had brought the lowest-paid group too close to them. Here Sukharevski was in fact repeating a directive of the 1965–70 Five-Year Plan. The long-term reduction of differentials, he claimed, not very logically, would come about by further rises in minimal rates, a rapprochement between the lower-paid, middle- and higher-paid workers, and the movement of workers out of old-fashioned, unattractive (and presumably ill-paid) jobs which would be replaced by more advanced ones.[11]

It would, again, be naïve to imagine that all Soviet people actually favour more egalitarianism. Those who benefited most from the old differentials – the upper layers of the bureaucracy, managers, specialists, and the most favoured workers – would of course tend to frown on change and look for ways of increasing their income to compensate for it.

The generous rises in minimum wages were coupled with the reform of the wage structure, which meant lesser increases for many of the more intermediate categories. Piece-work, bonuses and incentive payment schemes have always allowed a good deal of quiet creep, regardless of all government controls. The very secrecy which continues to shroud the top wage bracket strongly suggests excessive earnings, while there do not seem to be any published laws specifically limiting the salaries of the highest-paid personnel. If such reductions had been an important

10. *Party Programme*, part II, section II.
11. A. P. Volkov, op. cit., p. 296.

element in Khrushchev's policies we would no doubt have heard more about it. On the contrary, muted criticism of excessive income differentials has occasionally appeared in the works of individual Soviet researchers.[12]

Finally, there is the important question of price movements. Increases in the cost of commonly used consumer goods bear more heavily on the poor. The Soviet government possesses a unique prerogative in this area, in so far as it retains the right to set prices for the overwhelming majority of goods and services available. Its record, however, has not been altogether happy. Although the policy has been to hold prices for consumer goods more or less steady, price rises were authorized in 1958, 1962, and 1966. The increases of June 1962 were a particularly serious setback for the egalitarian trend, for as a result of them a number of staple foods, including meat, milk and butter, cost up to a third more. Purchases of food, as we shall see, take up a larger proportion of the poorer family budget.

There was, incidentally, evidence that the so-called economic reform, launched in 1965, also initially tended to be inegalitarian, in so far as managers and specialists gained greater financial benefits. This disparity seems, however, to have been smoothed over subsequently.[13]

12. For example, M. S. Kukushkin, discussing the national wage policy in 1965, complained about unjustifiable gaps between the wages of many production workers on the one hand, and some administrative workers on the other. 'It is difficult to explain', he wrote, 'why the wage of one worker should be twenty or thirty times greater than that of another.' He was evidently thinking of disparities between the lowest-paid workers and the top management. In a very large enterprise headed by a successful management this kind of differential might in fact be just possible. *Narodny dokhod*, Leningrad, 1965, p. 156.

13. For hints of these difficulties see *Sotsialisticheski Trud*, No. 2, 1967, p. 28, and *Planovoe Khozyaistvo*, No. 4, 1967, p. 8. Opposition of all kinds may be the explanation for the surprising stability recently revealed in differentials between the average monthly earnings of three of the statistical groupings used in Soviet industry – workers, I T R and low-grade service personnel. The figures for 1955–66, as published in *Trud v SSSR* were, in percentage terms,

	Service personnel	Workers	ITR
1955	100	112.6	186.4
1966	100	118.3	170.2

POVERTY IN THE WORKING CLASS

Published income data are most revealing, however, when they are seen in the light of recent statements by Soviet scholars regarding what the minimum per capita income for a non-peasant family should be.[14] This upsurge of interest was no doubt prompted by the emphasis which the Party Programme laid on consumption needs. By the mid sixties some convincing studies had been done, and a line of sufficiency stipulated. We may presume that it had tacit official approval.

Writing in 1962, when the government was in the process of introducing a 40–45-rouble minimum wage, S. P. Figurnov suggested vaguely that this line was somewhere near 35 roubles, though he may have been referring to an earlier period when the minimum wage was at that level or below.[15] However, in a book published in 1967 the economists G. S. Sarkisyan and N. P. Kuznetsova, came out for a recognized minimum of 51.4 roubles per head. They claimed that this was the sum necessary to ensure a modest standard of living for a typical urban family of husband, wife and two children in a simply furnished flat.[16] The basic figures they use were calculated by the Labour Research Institute in 1965 and these are reproduced in Table 14. In an essay which went to the press early in January 1968, D. N. Karpukhin and N. P. Kuznetsova, suggested almost the same figure, which included allowances for state subsidies and transfer payments.[17] Their argument is worth quoting in detail, because it leads to some interesting conclusions.

The gap between service personnel and ITR closed only by about six per cent. Relatively, the workers benefited most of all. Of course, the differentials within each group on which these averages are based did narrow. Rises in the minimal wage rates would have affected workers as well as service personnel.

14. The family has been taken as the unit for analysis in the USSR for the obvious reason that per capita income is a function of the earnings of adults, spread over their children and dependants and supplemented by various state subsidies. This is a common statistical practice.

15. op. cit., p. 105.

16. G. S. Sarkisyan and N. P. Kuznetsova, *Potrebnosti i dokhod semi*, Moscow, 1967, p. 66.

17. A. P. Volkov, op. cit., p. 413.

A normative consumption budget for minimal material provision at the present time (1966–70) was worked out for a standard, typical worker's family of four people (the father is in a mechanized job, the mother works in easy production conditions, a 13–14-year-old son and a 7–8-year-old daughter are at school). Approximate calculations show that a monthly income of a little over 200 roubles is needed to satisfy their minimal requirements . . . A per capita monthly income of fifty roubles can serve at the present time and for the next few years as a criterion for planning the minimal level of income for the families of workers and employees . . . At the present time the proportion of wages in the total income of an industrial worker's family with a per capita income of fifty roubles a month is on the average 75 to 80 per cent. [The remainder comes from the State – M.M.] If we apply this ratio to a budget for covering minimal material needs then the minimum wage in a family with two working members must be about 150 roubles, or 75 roubles for each worker. There is, however, a definite ratio between the wage of the first working member and that of the second. Thus in the group of families which have a per capita income of 50 roubles a month, the wage of the second working member makes up about 40 per cent of the total wage. It follows from this that in a budget for covering minimal material needs the wage of the second working member must stand at 60 roubles and that of the first at about 90 roubles a month.[18]

The wage-sex differentials are interesting but since we have so little data on women's wages we shall base our conclusions on a common 75-rouble wage or 50-rouble income. This figure is, to judge from the items listed in Table 14, not so much the sum needed to avoid *want*, as that required to provide a sort of minimum of wellbeing acceptable to Soviet planners.

It covers a diet of the cheaper foods, though even these, it will be noted, take up a surprisingly large proportion of the budget. The average for families in advanced industrialized societies would probably be near a quarter. Twenty per cent of the Soviet minimum budget goes on a wardrobe of low-grade but adequate clothes, and a sufficient amount of plain furniture. A small fridge and a television set are included in the durable consumer goods, but no carpets, electrical appliances or car. Rent is only a small consideration in this budget, but then most Soviet families live in rather cramped accommodation which sometimes

18. A. P. Volkov, op. cit., pp. 423–4.

TABLE 14. *Volume and Structure of Expenditure for the Minimum Material Provision of a Family*

Expenditures	Monthly sums, roubles and kopecks	Percentage of total expenditure
Food	115.00	55.9
Clothing, etc.	43.00	20.9
Furniture, crockery	5.50	2.6
Cultural, sports, household goods	4.50	2.2
Haberdashery, toiletries, medicine	2.70	1.3
Tobacco, matches, wine, spirits	5.50	2.7
Subtotal: consumer goods	176.20	85.7
Housing and communal services	11.00	5.4
Holidays, cures	2.80	1.4
Cultural and educational needs	3.60	1.7
Hairdressing, steam baths, laundry	4.70	2.3
Transport and communications	4.80	2.3
Other expenditures, including subscriptions to clubs	2.50	1.2
Subtotal: services	29.40	14.3
Total expenditure on the family	205.60	100.0
Total expenditure on one member	51.40	—

Source:
G. S. Sarkisyan and N. P. Kuznetsova, *Potrebnosti i dokhod semi*, Moscow, 1967, p. 66.

amounts to no more than one room. Education is basically free and transport subsidized – in this respect anyone on a minimal budget would have no undue worry. (Though medical services are free, incidentally, medicines outside hospitals must be bought at substantial prices.) However it seems unlikely that an annual holiday would be possible on the proposed allotment unless it were at subsidized rates, while the allowance for incidental expenses, such as alcoholic beverages and entertainment, is very small and practically excludes family visits to the cinema or theatre.

The fifty roubles, then, would have covered an existence of Soviet-style pinched comfort in the mid sixties providing – and this is important – that all the necessary consumer durables had been obtained. The budget appears to allow in effect for depreciation costs but not initial capital purchases. Thus major acquisitions by a young couple setting up house would be possible only with help from outside or at the cost of a sharp fall in their standard of living. Soviet households are not, on the whole, well provided with capital goods. By 1968 there were 27 million TV sets, 25 million washing machines, 13.7 million refrigerators and 5.9 million vacuum cleaners, for perhaps sixty or seventy million hearths.[19] We do not, incidentally, know how many of these appliances were working.

All the indications are that a large proportion of the Soviet working class was, in the late sixties, still a long way from achieving this suggested minimum, either in earnings or income. The average wage rate for workers and employees was in itself suspiciously low, if viewed from this angle. In 1967, for example, it was put at 104.7 roubles a month. A rough calculation shows that if we exclude pensioners, forget about army conscripts and students, etc., this meant a per capita sum of only 54 roubles for the working class as a whole, though this was exclusive of transfer payments.

Some idea of the actual size of the underprivileged group may be gained from a number of sources. The Soviet economist E. I. Kapustin has provided sufficient data on minimal wage rates to enable us to estimate that in 1967 over 20 per cent of all persons employed in the highly paid building industry, and more than 60 per cent of those in the textile and food industries (where wages were low) were earning less than 75 roubles a month.[20] According to another source, in 1965–6 about 30 per cent of all

19. *Narodnoe khozyaistvo SSSR v 1968*, Moscow, 1969, p. 596. The number of independent households does not appear to be available, but the order of magnitude for 1968 given here is suggested by the 1959 census. At that time there were 50.3 million families of two members or more, 12 million persons with families but living alone, and 9.3 million without any relatives at all. Some of these may have lived in hostels, others shared. If the number of people living alone is deducted from the 208.8 million population at that time, and the figure divided by the number of families with two members or more, we are left with an average family of 3.75.

20. A. P. Volkov, op. cit., pp. 326–7. The numbers of workers involved and their wage rates were taken from *Trud v SSSR*, Moscow, 1967, pp. 152, 145.

workers and employees in Belorussia were in the 'very lowest paid category'.[21]

At the same time the few studies of the distribution of Soviet

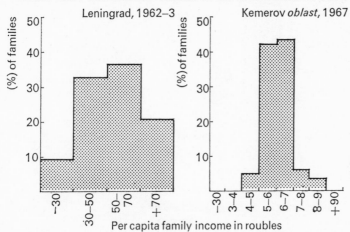

FIGURES 8–9.   *Per Capita Income Distribution in the USSR, Selected Surveys*

Sources for Figures 8–11 and details of samples *

Figure 8 Source: L. S. Blyakhman, A. G. Zdravomyslov and O. I. Shkaratan, 'Problemy Upravlenia dvizheniem rabochei sily', in *Trud i lichnost*, Leningrad, 1965, p. 140.

The data in this figure were provided as family background information to a study of labour mobility. The sample included 10,720 workers of 25 Leningrad enterprises of various types. The survey was conducted in 1962 and the first three months of 1963. The authors seem to have gone to some lengths to choose a representative sample, but warn that it is not necessarily so.

Figure 9 Source: E. G. Antosenkov and L. A. Shishkina, article in *Izvestia Sibirskogo Otdelenia Akademii Nauk*, Vypusk 3, 1968, p. 32.

21. E. A. Lotukhina, *Realny dokhod i zhiznenny uroven trudyashchikhsya*, ed. M. Z. Bora, Minsk, 1966, p. 68. D. N. Karpukhina and N. P. Kuznetsova in A. P. Volkov, op. cit., stated that the proportion of families having both working members on the absolute minimum salary scales was less than 1 per cent of all families in the country, and that the income structure of these families was anyway different, as the state subsidy here 'rose to 34 or 40 per cent'. They wished to imply by this that there are very few families at the absolute bottom of the income scale. Their statement does not mean very much for it only requires one working member to earn a rouble more than the statutory minimum in order to place his family outside this category altogether.

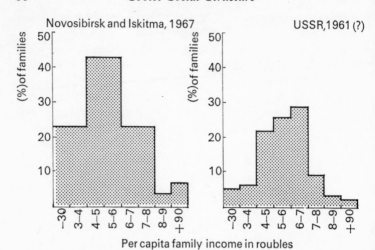

Per capita family income in roubles

FIGURES 10–11.   *Per Capita Income Distribution in the USSR, Selected Surveys*

Figure 10 Source: A. Yu. Shapirov, article in *Izvestia Sibirskogo Otdelenia Akademii Nauk, Seria Obshchestvennikh Nauk,* Vypusk 1, 1968, p. 33. Novosibirsk and Iskitma were taken as examples of large and small towns. The statistical work behind these figures was not explained.

Figure 11 Source: S. P. Figurnov, *Stroitelstvo kommunizma i rost blagosostoyania naroda,* Moscow, 1962, p. 156.
The data are described merely as 'selected'.

*These examples have been chosen because they were reasonably clear, involved fairly large samples – and were known to the author. An interesting study of standards of living in Sverdlovsk (which had much in common with those given here) was published by D. Stadukhin and M. Khaverson in *Nauchnye Doklady Vysshei Shkoly, Ekonomicheskie Nauki,* No. 12, 1967, p. 28.

families by per capita income which have been published in recent years strongly suggest the same sort of conclusion. We have chosen four of the most revealing for comment here.

Figure 8 shows how the families of nearly 11,000 workers from various branches of industry in Leningrad were distributed over four main income groups in 1962–3. The authors were careful to point out that the results need not have been representative of Leningrad, and that the sample differed in some important characteristics from the Soviet working class as a whole. The workers in this survey, for example, were younger, and their level of education was distinctly higher. The large proportion of people getting less than 30 roubles a month may have included a disproportionately large number of juniors and apprentices. But these problems apart, it is clear that a large proportion of families were in the lowest capital income-group. Perhaps the authors wished to discourage generalization from this basis.

Figure 9 shows the results of a survey of family income conducted amongst some 4,000 workers in the coal mines of Kemerovo *oblast* in 1967. The level of income was much higher and the per capita distribution more equitable, in that most families were in the middle of the scale. This may be accounted for partly by changes in the wage structure which took place in the sixties, and partly by the fact that wages in the coal industry tend to be better than in industry as a whole anyway.

A much less favourable picture is revealed in Figure 10. This shows how the families of workers in such poorly paid branches as trade, catering, and public amenities in the Siberian towns of Novosibirsk and Iskitima were faring at about the same time. The distribution here is rather comparable with that shown by the Leningrad survey in Figure 8. It is worth noting that these branches employ a high percentage of women, so possibly only few husbands and wives would work in them together. The family incomes on which Figure 10 is based, then, probably allow for the employment of one partner in a better-paid job. But by the same token family incomes of workers in laborious, male-dominated industries like mining probably include a low figure for wives engaged in less lucrative employment, so the figures may be more comparable than appears at first sight.

Figure 11 is the most intriguing, and possibly the most revealing of our examples. Taken from S. P. Figurnov's book, which went to press in July 1962, it apparently represents the genuine distribution of all families of workers and employees by per capita income throughout the country.[22] Two presumptions have had to be made, however. The first is that the figures really cover all workers and employees, since the author nowhere states this explicitly. The second is that the income groups are indeed as we have shown. No income figures were given, so it

22. *Stroitelstvo kommunizma i rost blagosostoyania naroda*, as noted above, Moscow, 1962, p. 157.

has been necessary to fit a hypothetical set into the eight slots. This is not quite so outrageous as might seem at first, because we can just about guess the values of the two extreme columns from current Soviet practice, and then all we have to do is divide the difference between them by six. In fact the distribution of income so obtained is credible and lies somewhere between the extremes we have found in the local studies. The per capita income of about three quarters of the families was between 40 and 80 roubles, while minorities of 11 per cent and 14 per cent had incomes of under 40 roubles and over 80 roubles per capita respectively.

In three of these four studies a very considerable proportion of the sample of families is under the 50-rouble per capita income line. The figures were 42.7, 4.8, (probably) 40, and 32.8 per cent respectively. Of these the last may well be representative of Soviet non-peasant society in the early sixties. Of course these studies are of different years, and we do not know enough about them to judge their comparability. Nevertheless, all things considered, they seem to support the conclusion that by the mid sixties a third or more of the Soviet working class could be thought of as 'poor' by accepted Soviet standards.

It is tempting to pause at this point and ask who the poor were. From the standpoint of the sociologist this means correlating their income – or lack of it – with things like occupation, educational levels, and style of living. The last of these will be dealt with below, and we shall have something to say about occupation and educational attainments in Chapter 5. Here it will be convenient merely to comment on the branches of the economy in which they worked and their most typical occupations. Table 15 has been compiled for this purpose. The least developed and worst-paid sectors were the housing and communal services, the health services, trade, catering and the state farms. In the 'industrial' sector, which we have shown as one item, wages varied from averages of 195.3 roubles in coalmining to 76.1 roubles in the sewing industry. On the whole forestry, textiles and the food industry had the lowest average rates of pay.[23] In addition people working for local authorities tend to earn considerably less than those doing similar jobs for

23. *Trud v SSSR*, Moscow, 1968, pp. 140–44.

TABLE 15. *Average Monthly Wages in the Soviet Economy,*
*1967 (Non-*kolkhoz *Sector, in Roubles)*

Sector of the economy	Average wage
Science and supporting enterprises	122.0
Construction (building and repair personnel)	118.1
Transport (all types)	115.0
State and economic apparatus, administration offices of cooperative and public organizations	112.5
Industry (production personnel)	111.7
Education (schools, colleges, and cultural institutions)	96.5
Credit and insurance institutions	93.0
State farms and subordinate agricultural enterprises	84.1
Trade, catering, supplies	82.5
Health services	82.4
Housing and communal services	78.6
The economy as a whole	103.0

Source:
Trud v SSSR, Moscow, 1968, p. 139. Figures cover workers and employees
and are arranged by order of magnitude.

the central ministries. At times work in rural areas has been
paid at lower rates than in the towns.

The poorer workers in the Soviet Union, as elsewhere, have
tended to have unskilled or semi-skilled occupations. A short list

TABLE 16. *Selected Occupations with Low Wages*
(Monthly, in Roubles, about the mid sixties)

Occupation	Average Wage	Occupation	Average Wage
Office worker	45–60	Shoemaker	46–55
Cashier	50	Seamstress	46–50
Labourer	50–60	Laundress	46–55
Storeman	50–60	Nurse	45
Lift operator	46	Shop assistant (junior)	55
Weighing scale operator	50–65	Cleaner	46–55

Sources:
S. Kh. Guryanov, L. A. Kostin, *Trud i Zarabotnaya plata na predpriyatii,*
Moscow, 1967, pp. 192 ff.
D. V. Pravdin, and others, *Zarabotnaya plata rabotnikov neproizvodst-*
vennoi sfery, Moscow, 1967, pp. 65, 135.

of low-paid jobs culled from a few wage handbooks may be found in Table 16. It will be noted that there are several numerically important white-collar and light manual occupations amongst them. In 1966 the average wage for the industrial 'employee' was about 17 per cent lower than that for the industrial 'worker'.

The Soviet Union is by no means unique in having very large numbers of people living below accepted subsistence levels. An American survey of March 1966, for example, showed that some 15.4 per cent of the population were classed as 'poor persons', i.e. members of families with an income of less than 3,000 dollars per annum. It is tempting to think of the American poor as having much in common with their opposite numbers in the Soviet Union: but given the differences in the way of life, it is hardly possible to make a meaningful comparison. The overwhelming majority of poor people in America were town-dwellers, though the *incidence* of poverty was higher in the country. The poverty rate among coloured Americans considered separately was above the national average: in 1966 some 41.4 per cent of them were classed as 'poor'.[24]

THE INCOME OF THE PRIVILEGED

There is not a great deal we can say about that part of the Soviet working class where per capita income was above 50 roubles a month. Most worker and low-grade employee families were probably in the 50–70-rouble range. Here, presumably, at least one working partner would have had a skilled or highly skilled job in one of the better-paid branches of industry.

There does not seem to be any consensus of opinion amongst Soviet sociologists about dividing lines inside the middle or upper working class (if we may use these terms), but, as the data on life-styles will show, they have a tendency to consider people with an income of from 40 or 50 to 70 or 75 roubles as being in one category, and persons with more as being in another. L. S. Blyakhman, for example, observes this distinction in some of his work, and describes the first group as 'provided for' (we would

24. *Statistical Abstract of the U.S.*, Washington, 1968, pp. 324–9; also the *Social Security Bulletin*, January 1965, p. 11. The non-white population totalled 9.6 million at that time.

perhaps say 'comfortably off') and the second as 'highly provided for'.[25] We do not really know enough about this sector of Soviet society to say whether this is a good dividing point. Sociologists who use a 100-rouble guide-line are probably moved more by a sense of numerical symmetry than anything else.

The problem of the people in the uppermost income brackets is no less intractable. We have so far in this chapter used the term 'working class' to designate all social groups apart from the peasantry. At the same time it is apparent that the richest people in Soviet society are best thought of as being part of the intelligentsia, which is in so many respects distinctive. No comprehensive study of their income has been published, though figures for the All-Union average earnings of engineers and technical personnel (ITR), who make up a large part of the intelligentsia, are, as we have noted, available. Thus in 1966 persons in this category in industry had an average salary of 150 roubles, while the 'workers' earned 104.4 roubles and 'employees' 88.2 roubles.[26]

Really senior personnel are considerably better off. Table 17 contains some data relating to senior administrators in the late fifties. The basic range for directors (or managers) was then the equivalent of 190 to 400 new roubles a month. The average rate for engineers and technical personnel in industry in 1960 was, interestingly enough, something under 133 roubles.[27] We can be quite sure, however, that few directors would have been satisfied with their basic rate, as Soviet labour law allowed them access to many different kinds of production bonuses. Thus under the terms of rules introduced in July 1959 directors could increase their salaries by 10–15 per cent if they fulfilled their production plan, and then by 1.5 per cent more for each per cent of over-fulfilment. Some were eligible for supplements because they worked in the higher wage zones: some could hope to receive a 'personal salary' of up to 350 new roubles a month for doing particularly responsible work, exclusive of bonuses.[28] Few

25. In A. G. Zdravomyslov and V. A. Yadov, *Trud i razvitie lichnosti*, Leningrad, 1965, p. 140.

26. *Trud v SSSR*, p. 139.   27. ibid., p. 139.

28. *Sbornik zakonodatelnykh atkov o trude*, Moscow, 1965, pp. 279, 317–323, 325 ff.

TABLE 17: *Salaries of Selected Senior Industrial Personnel (Figures Converted to New Roubles)*

No.	Occupation	Monthly salaries according to category of factory			
		I Cat.	II Cat.	III Cat.	IV Cat.
1	2	3	4	5	6
1	Director	350–400	310–360	250–300	200–250
2	Chief Engineer	320–370	280–330	200–270	190–220
3	Assistant Director, Second Engineer, Chief Mechanic, Chief of Department (production, technical & technical control)	250–300	200–250	150–210	150–180
4	Chief of Department (designing, planning, labour organization, supplies & sales)	190–220	160–190	140–160	110–130
5	Chief of Safety Department, Senior Despatcher	160–190	140–170	120–140	110–130
	Chief of Sector or Bureau Despatcher	130–150	120–140	110–130	100–120
7	Senior Engineer, Senior Designer, Senior Economist	110–135	110–135	100–120	100–120
8	Engineer, Designer, Economist	100–120	100–120	90–110	90–110
9	Technician	75–90	75–90	70–85	70–85

Source: L. Kostin, *Wages in the USSR*, Moscow, 1960, p. 60.

directors would be enterprising enough to hit every jackpot: but there is no doubt that by the end of the sixties salaries of 500–700 roubles a month were not uncommon amongst them.

Snippets of information on the salaries of some of the topmost earners have been collected by a few Western observers, but no one, as far as we are aware, has attempted to systematize them.[29] It may well be that there is a sort of 'lower élite' of a few

29. Some examples to hand are: A. Inkeles and R. Baier, *The Soviet Citizen*, New York, 1968, p. 113. These figures relate to the year 1940. N. Dewitt, *Education and Professional Employment in the USSR*, Washington, 1961, p. 542; John Gunther, *Inside Russia Today*, London, 1962 edition, p. 68; Arvid Broderson, *Soviet Labor*, New York, 1966, p. 176; E. C. Brown, *Soviet Trade Unions and Labor Relations*, Cambridge (Mass.), 1966, p. 298; J. A. Newth, *Soviet Studies*, Vol. 12, 1960–61, p. 196.

million souls, comprising specialists, technical personnel, factory managers, senior government officials, research workers and artists, etc., whose per capita family income is in the one-hundred to two-hundred-rouble range.[30] This may be capped by an upper élite composed of the few thousand most prominent families in the state, whose earnings may be very much greater. That the top salaries can be extremely high is beyond doubt. John Gunther mentioned the figure of 1,500 new roubles a month for the President of the Academy of Sciences, 1,200 for the rector of an important university, 600 for a senior government official and 400 for an army colonel. It is recognized among the Soviet public that individuals can earn much more if they occupy one of a few thousand top ministerial or Party posts, or are famous for their endeavours in the arts or sciences. Royalties are high and prizes generous. Moreover, it is reliably reported that many people in this category can hope for very significant supplements to their income from at least two semi-confidential sources. Regular sums may be offered to leading technical and administrative personnel 'for technical progress', and one-time payments may be made 'for a rest-cure', without a medical certificate or verification of treatment being needed. Some categories of personnel also have access to special shops and an excellent, closed trade network, at least part of which functions under the aegis of the Central Committee itself. This is doubtlessly a very important sociological phenomenon, but one which is scarcely open to investigation.

LIFE-STYLES AND SPENDING PATTERNS

Money is important in so far as it can be used to improve one's way of life. This simple truth is, of course, as relevant inside the Soviet Union as it is in the West. Soviet society, like all industrialized societies, shows great variety in the spending patterns

30. N. Ryabkina and N. Rimashevksya, writing in *Sotsialisticheski Trud*, No. 7, 1966, claimed that some 1.5 per cent of all 'workers and employees', or just over one million persons, earned more than 200 roubles. The West German scholar K. E. Wädekin hypothesized an upper class (or stratum, as he calls it) of about 5.8 million, or 11.8 per cent of the population in 1959, 'Zur Sozialschichtung der Sowjetgesellschaft', *Osteuropa*, Heft 5, 1965.

of different income-groups, and these are reflected in the Soviet budget studies of recent years. Yet when thinking about this, we must remember that the way a person spends his money depends not only on the amount he has. He will be influenced by many other factors, such as his age, sex, family position, occupation, education and cultural background, not to mention the availability of goods and services. The element of chance cannot be excluded. Thus although it may be true to say that certain spending habits are associated with a certain level of income, the relationship is by no means simple.

TABLE 18. *Income and Consumption (as a Percentage of Income and as Calculated in Roubles by the Writer)*

The average annual income per capita of the family: materials of a survey conducted in Moscow workers' families

	As a percentage of income						Calculated in Roubles					
Per capita Income monthly	Food	Clothes	Furniture Cultural Goods	Housing & Communal Amenities	Non-Material Expenses	Other Expenses & Savings	Food	Clothes	Furniture Cultural Goods	Housing & Communal Amenities	Non-Material Expenses	Other Expenses & Savings
44	55.5	12.4	4.1	3.4	7.4	17.2	24.4	5.5	1.8	1.5	3.2	7.6
82	45.9	15.4	7.4	2.4	9.1	19.8	37.6	12.6	6.1	2.0	7.5	16.2
113	40.2	15.9	6.6	2.2	8.2	26.9	45.4	18	7.5	2.5	10	10

Source:
V. F. Maier and P. N. Krylov (eds.), *Planirovanie Narodnogo Potreblenia v SSSR*, Moscow, 1964, p. 93.

Table 18 shows how three separate groups of Moscow families spent their income in the early sixties. They are all described as 'workers'' families but we must not take this appellation too seriously. The first group (with a monthly income of 44 roubles) was probably representative of many poorer workers' households: the others may be better thought of as belonging to the middle and upper working class, and intelligentsia. The original breakdown was given in percentages of total expenditure, but in the second table we have converted it into roubles for a reason which will be apparent in a moment. The survey was conducted in the early sixties and embraced an undisclosed number of families, though we would probably be justified in accepting the consumption patterns it shows as generally valid for many other big towns.

According to these figures, the Moscow rich had a very different way of life from the Moscow poor. The latter spent over half of their income on food – which is what the compilers of the minimum budget suggested. The richer ones devoted 40 per cent of their income to it. But in terms of roubles, this obviously meant a totally different diet, as one obviously eats far better for forty-five roubles than for twenty-four. Differences in expenditures on clothing, and particularly furnishings, were no less significant. The poorer families set aside about 5.5 roubles per head every month for the former and 1.8 roubles for the latter: the figures for the opulent families were 18 and 7.5 roubles respectively.

Expenditure on housing and communal amenities, though small, also varied significantly: the richer families spent nearly twice as much as the poorer on them. Though Soviet housing remains in statistical darkness, this difference may be significant. Rents vary according to the income of the tenant, the quality of the accommodation and the number of square metres it contains. Thus although we have no means of knowing exactly what elements these figures covered, it is by no means improbable that the richer families were in fact paying for more and better living space. To digress for a moment, data published on the accommodation occupied by 8,500 women in Gorki showed that over a fifth of them were living in unsatisfactory conditions (Table 19). The figures available for four urban areas which are reproduced in Table 20 show that the majority of people were very cramped indeed, but that there was, at the same time, a group of 9 to 14 per cent who were distinctly favoured. These families may have been at the top of the income scale, and thus have had the heavier rent bills as implied in Table 18.

The item we have translated in Table 18 as 'non-material expenses' (*netovarnye raskhody*) was not explained, but it probably included payments for cultural amenities and transport. The richest families spent more than three times as much as the poorest on them. The sums listed under 'other expenses and savings' varied by a factor of four between poor and rich: it is a

TABLE 19. *Distribution of 8,500 Women in Gorki by Type of Housing*★

Type of housing	%
Baraki (temporary one-storeyed wooden huts with rooms for several families)	13.6
Hostels	4.0
Shared rooms	5.0
Private flats	5.5
Other accommodation (mainly state-owned or cooperative flats)	71.9

★Osipov states: ' 10% of the families studied lived in cramped quarters and had less than 9 sq. metres of living space.' [i.e. per family – M. M.]

Source:

G. V. Osipov and others, *Rabochi klass i tekhnicheski progress*, Moscow, 1965, p. 246.

TABLE 20. *Distribution of Families by Amount of Living space, 1958*

N.I.I.T.★ studies	Families	Amount of living space (metres²) per head		
		up to 7	7–9	+9
Moscow	100	77.2	11.4	11.4
Leningrad	100	85.7	—	14.3
Tbilisi	100	82.0	9.0	9.0
Pavlovo-Posad	100	81.1	7.5	11.4
N.I.I.T.-Ts. S. U.★ mass study	100	71.5	14.4	14.1

★ Study conducted by the Labour Research Institute and Central Statistical Administration (USSR).

Source:

V. G. Kryazhev, *Vnerabochee vremya i sfera obsluzhivania*, Moscow, 1966, p. 72.

pity that no details of them were provided. We may note in passing that in general configuration the budget of the 44-rouble families is not at all unlike the minimum budget suggested by G. S. Sarkisyan and N. P. Kuznetsova. In most cases families with a monthly income of 82 roubles per head lay between the other two groups, though their expenditure pattern was closer to that of the upper one.

In 1967 V. F. Maier, one of the scholars involved in this work, published some data from another study, based, it seems, on the same three income-groups, though in this case he merely termed them 'insufficiently provided for', 'of average income' and 'well provided for'.[31] These data indicated that all families were spending about five per cent more of their income on comestibles than before, though the relationships between the groups stayed about the same. Curious were his figures for 'paid services', not shown separately in the earlier study. Poor families spent 7 per cent of their income – some three roubles a month – on these, while families in the top group spent 12 per cent of theirs, that is 13.6 roubles. V. F. Maier again did not say what he meant by this term, but it may well have covered another widely reported, but uninvestigated, phenomenon – the employment of domestics to help with house and children, especially on a part-time basis.

LIFE-STYLES AND TIME-USAGE

Expenditure on goods and services is not the only way of judging how an individual lives. The amount of time which he devotes to a given range of activities is also very revealing, for in practice the poor tend to have one pattern of time-usage, and the rich another. We must, of course, remember that, as with money expenditure, a mass of extraneous factors will have an influence on how a person spends his time; these will vary from one activity to another in a most intricate manner. Nevertheless, all things considered, a basic relationship between income and time-usage may be discerned and usefully explored.

As we noted in Chapter 2, time studies were in vogue in Russia in the twenties. The present wave of interest began with the resuscitation of sociology in the late fifties, and by 1966 major

31. V. F. Maier, *Vestnik Moskovskogo Universiteta*, No. 2, 1967, p. 31.

surveys were being carried out by literally dozens of groups of sociologists.

Soviet time-use studies have, however, a number of defects which from our point of view detract from their value, and since we shall have recourse to such studies several times in this book, it would be just as well to summarize their most common short-comings here. The first springs from the fact that Soviet re-searchers usually seem more concerned with finding means to improve economic efficiency or ascertaining the impact of given government measures than with exploring the social significance of differences in the patterns of time-usage. This means that many important activities which are irrelevant to these aims are not explicitly dealt with, at least in the published results. Many topics are obviously forbidden. No work bearing on such inter-esting social groups as high-standing officials, the unemployed, or criminals (to mention but three) have, to this writer's know-ledge, ever been published. The influence of factors like housing standards, the availability of consumer goods or car-ownership on the use of time has so far been excluded. Many of the prob-lems which are of most interest to us are thus dealt with only in passing, and this means that we often have to try to extract from studies something which the researchers were not really concerned with. Finally, many studies are restricted in scope and in their published form produce results which are contradictory and defy generalization. If we feel justified in using them, it is because despite all these drawbacks they throw a great deal of light on Soviet social structure.

The categorization of time-uses has been a subject of debate in the USSR since 1958, and a number of schemes have been proposed.[32] A fairly detailed one covering non-working time-uses by Professor G. A. Prudenski is considered to be fairly authoritative. It is set out in Table 21. The main distinction is between working and non-working time; the latter is divided into four sub-sections – time associated with work, time spent on domestic and other tasks, time spent satisfying 'physiological' needs, like eating, sleeping and washing, and 'free' time spent

32. A brief account of these developments may be found in G. S. Petrosyan, *Vnerabochee vremya trudyashchikhsya v SSSR*, Moscow, 1965, p. 5 ff.

on leisure pursuits. The time-use data we shall use below fits, with few exceptions, into these categories.

TABLE 21. *Time Expenditure*

A	*Working time*
B	*Non-working time*

    (*a*)   Time associated with working activities, dressing, travel, etc.

    (*b*)   Time devoted to material and everyday (domestic) needs:
         Shopping
         Cooking
         Laundry
         Other household work
         Child care
         Personal toilet
         Work in garden plot
         Other needs

    (*c*)   Time devoted to physiological needs:
         Eating
         Sleeping

    (*d*)   Time devoted to leisure (free time):
         With children
         Study
         Social-political work
         Creative/Artistic work
         Sport
         Holiday & Amusements
         Other leisure activities

Source:
Scheme of G. A. Prudenski, in V. I. Bolgov, *Rabochee vremya i uroven zhizni trudyashchikhsya, Novosibirsk,* 1964, p. 13 (slightly simplified).

Figures from a study of workers in Krasnoyarsk in 1963 are reproduced in Table 22. Unfortunately little was revealed about the nature of the sample, but it seems that all workers, regardless of income, spent approximately the same amount of their time working and travelling to or from work. Neither did the time they spent eating and sleeping etc., seem to correlate with

TABLE 22. *Workers' Time Budgets (as a Percentage of All Time-Uses, by Income-group, Krasnoyarsk Krai Survey, 1963)*

Family per capita income (roubles)	Working time	Non-working time linked with work	Time spent on domestic duties	Time spent on satisfying physiological needs	Free time	Total
up to 50	24.5	7.3	9.5	37.0	21.7	100
51–75	25.0	7.7	10.1	36.6	20.6	100
over 75	24.5	7.5	5.1	37.1	25.8	100

Source:
V. A. Artemov and others, *Statistika byudzhetov vremeni trudyashchikhsya*, Moscow, 1966, p. 91. Data from this investigation (conducted in 1959 and 1963) have been used by a number of sociologists whose findings are adduced in this study.

income. The evidence of another survey, however, suggests that richer folk worked longer. The results of a 1959 Novosibirsk study of 230 families (Table 23) indicated that persons in the 75-rouble bracket and above worked up to an hour and a quarter a day more than those at the lower end of the scale. The explanation for this apparent contradiction may lie in extra overtime,

TABLE 23. *Working Hours by Income-group (in Hours and Minutes, Novosibirsk Survey, 1959)*

Family per capita income (roubles)	Working time	Time spent on material and everyday needs
up to 20	4.37	8.01
20–35	6.08	5.55
36–50	6.40	5.39
51–75	6.54	5.29
76–100	7.24	4.52
over 100	7.07	4.41

Source:
V. I. Bolgov, *Vnerabochee vremya i uroven zhizni trudyashchikhsya*, Novosibirsk, 1964, p. 65, per capita of over-16s in families. Novosibirsk study, embracing 230 families, in 1959.

or in the sampling itself. The working day of 4.37 hours which is given for people earning under twenty roubles reflected, presumably, part-time employment, or the special conditions for juveniles.

The most striking variation was in the time spent on domestic chores; this was far smaller in the upper income group. Surveys conducted in Erevan (1963), in Novosibirsk and Krasnoyarsk (1959) also showed that more opulent people had fewer household duties than their poorer neighbours (Tables 23, 24 and 25). This may be another indication that richer families had domestic help, though it is not the only possible explanation: more demanding work or a propensity for restaurant meals could be other causes.

TABLE 24. *Use of Non-working Time by Income-group,*
(as % of All Time-uses, Erevan Survey, 1963)

		Total non-working time (100%)			
Family per capita income (roubles)	*Time associated with work (A)*	*Time spent on domestic chores (B)*	*Time spent on physio-logical needs (C)*	*Sub-total A, B, C*	*Time spent on leisure pursuits*
up to 30	9.1	24.9	45.9	79.9	20.1
31–50	10.0	22.8	45.6	78.4	21.6
51–75	8.8	16.2	48.9	73.9	26.1
76–100	6.2	12.9	51.4	70.5	29.5
over 100	8.7	10.9	51.0	70.6	29.4

Source:

G. S. Petrosyan, *Vnerabochee vremya trudyashchikhsya v SSSR*, Moscow, 1965, p. 111. Study of 3,363 workers, employees and ITR in Erevan, over 3 days – working day, Saturday and Sunday, 1963–4.

In Table 25 V. I. Bolgov distinguishes between time-use patterns of 'workers' on the one hand and engineers and technical personnel in the same income groups on the other. Apart from the fact that it is difficult to imagine workers' families having a per capita income of 100 roubles or more, the data are rather puzzling. The distinctions between income groups were much more marked for ITR than for workers. Only in the top-most group did the latter spend much more time on domestic chores than workers. At another point in his book Bolgov shows, on the basis of the Novosibirsk survey, that whereas only 26.5 per cent of the workers and employees in the 20–35-rouble income-group bought cooked lunches, 64 per cent of those with over a hundred roubles did so. The poorer people evidently tended to take their own food to work with them, or not to eat until they got home.

TABLE 25. *Time Spent on Material and Domestic Chores among Workers and ITR* by Income-group (in Hours per Week, Krasnoyarsk Krai Survey, 1959)*

Family per capita income (roubles)	Workers	ITR
up to 20	23.8	—
21–30	26.6	28.1
31–50	25.8	26.5
51–100	23.1	22.4
over 100	20.5	14.3

*Engineers and Technical Personnel.

Source:

V. I. Bolgov, op. cit., p. 31. Based on 1,000 time budgets.

Differences between the patterns of the sexes in this sphere quite override differences between income groups. Soviet men and women are by no means equal when it comes to cooking, cleaning, and minding the children. Some of the more striking discrepancies are illustrated in Table 26, which is based on data from a survey carried out before 1961 in Kostroma. It is obvious that despite the improvements claimed since the twenties (Table 27) the Soviet married woman with children still carried the major part of the domestic burden. Her duties in this respect took at least twice as long as her husband's. If she had to do a full-time job as well she spent an hour a day less sleeping and eating, and had a full two hours less leisure time. She could console herself only with the thought that as a woman she could expect to live some seven years longer than her spouse.

TABLE 26. *Workers' Time Budgets by Sex (Married Couples with Children; Hours and Minutes per Working Day, Kostroma Survey, pre–1961)*

Non-working time	Family with children	
	Man	Woman
Time linked with production work	1.44	1.43
Domestic chores and toilet	2.40	5.17
Sleeping and eating	8.18	7.18
Subtotal	12.02	13.78
Leisure time	3.54	1.55
Other time expenditures	0.20	0.38
Total, all non-working time	15.76	15.71

Source:
G. S. Petrosyan, op. cit., p. 103. Abstracted from a table devoted to differences between the sexes in families of different sizes. The totals in the Soviet text are both overstated by 0.8 but this discrepancy is not explained.

If, however, we analyse the domestic burden of women in different income-groups, we still come upon very palpable social distinctions. A recent Moscow study indicated that poorer women spent twice as much time on household duties as richer ones: in fact, only the time spent on cooking seemed to be fairly constant (Table 28). The poorest women spent just about three times as long as the richest looking after the children, cleaning,

TABLE 27. *Changes in the Expenditure of Time on Material Needs and Domestic Duties by Sex, 1923–59 (Hours and Minutes per Working Day)*

Sex	1923–4	1959	
		Novosibirsk	Moscow
Women	10.00	7.14	5.16
Men	2.46	2.30	2.03

Source:
V. I. Bolgov, op. cit., p. 47.

and shopping. Washing clothes seemed to be almost the prerogative of the poor. Of course, the smaller amount of time spent looking after children may have been related to the fact that the richer women in the sample had fewer of them, but no explanation of this kind was given.

TABLE 28. *Women's Use of Time by Income-group* (*Working Day, in Hours and Minutes, Certain Moscow Factories*)

Family per capita income (roubles)	Time spent on					
	Cooking	Care of children	Cleaning	Laundry	Shopping	Total
up to 30	1.50	0.35	0.35	0.40	1.20	5.0
31–50	1.25	0.25	0.25	0.35	0.55	3.45
51–75	1.20	0.10	0.20	0.20	0.30	2.40
76 or over	1.20	0.10	0.10	0.05	0.30	2.15

Source:
V. G. Kryazhev, *Vnerabochee vremya i sfera obsluzhivania*, Moscow, 1966, p. 109. The totals are overstated by 1.2 to 0.4. This discrepancy may be explained by lack of an 'others' column.

Time devoted to the garden plot is perhaps one of the clearest indices of social stratification in the Soviet Union. Although plots are characteristic of the peasant household, a significant number of the workers' families have the use of some land for private food production.[33] The 1959 Krasnoyarsk study showed that whereas the poorest people spent up to 44 per cent of all time devoted to domestic needs on tending their plots, the richer families spent less than 3 per cent of it, which could mean either that only a tiny proportion of them bothered to keep plots at all, or that they had outsiders to work them (Table 29). The distinctions which Bolgov made between workers and ITR personnel in the same income groups were again not very meaningful.

Lastly we come to free time or leisure. Prudensky understands this as time devoted to a whole range of social and political activities (not all of them voluntary), including part-time study. The

33. Chapter 3, p. 65, footnote 18.

TABLE 29. *Time Spent on Garden Plot by Income-group (in Hours, and as % of Time Spent on Material Needs and Domestic Duties, Krasnoyarsk Krai Survey)*

Family per capita income (roubles)	Workers		ITR	
	Hours	% as above	Hours	% as above
up to 20	2.6	43.8	—	—
20.1 to 30	9.4	35.4	11.9	43.0
30.1–50	6.2	24.0	5.5	20.8
*50.1–100	2.9	12.5	2.5	11.2
over 100	0.6	2.9	0.5	3.5

*Possibly 60–100. There appears to be a misprint in the Soviet text.
Source:
V. I. Bolgov, op. cit., p. 33.

Erevan survey showed that the amount of leisure time available to the individual increases sharply towards the top of the income scale (Table 24). That a greater proportion of free time is associated with a higher income was also shown by the 1963 Krasnoyarsk survey (Table 22). This study yielded further information on the distribution of free time by sex. It seems that while, in that area, the richest men had three times as much free time as the poorest, the gap between rich and poor women was less than 70 per cent (Table 30). Bolgov's figures did not, apparently, reveal any striking difference in the amount of

TABLE 30. *Monthly Fund of Free (Leisure) Time Available to Workers, by Income-group and Sex (in Hours and Minutes, Krasnoyarsk Krai Survey, 1963)*

Family per capita income (roubles)	Free time	
	Men	Women
up to 20	89,45	75,39
21–35	128,03	53,74
36–50	130,46	65,32
51–75	131,03	91,19
76–100	166,36	110,60
101 or over	266,44	131,05

Source:
V. A. Artemov and others, op. cit., p. 119.

leisure time available to workers and ITR in the same income group (Table 31).

TABLE 31. *Weekly Fund of Free (Leisure) Time Available to Workers and ITR by Income-group (Hours per Week, Krasnoyarsk Krai Survey, 1959).*

Family per capita income (roubles)	Workers	ITR
20.1–30	17.5	15.3
30.1–50	20.7	21.1
50.1–100	24.8	24.7
over 100	30.0	31.1

Source:
V. I. Bolgov, op. cit., p. 29.

The different income-groups, however, put their free time to very different uses. Richer people spent up to *nine times* as much of their free time in the pursuit of learning as members from the poorer families (Table 32). 'Self-improvement' (presumably reading and attending lectures) and study taken together absorbed over 14 hours a week at one extreme and under 5 hours at the other. In Table 33 we reproduce some figures on actual reading habits. The differences shown here are not quite so spectacular. Even so it appears that whereas only 13.5 per cent of the poorer workers in the sample borrowed from a public library in 1959, 39.3 per cent of the richer ones did so. The other

TABLE 32. *Use of Free (Leisure) Time by Income-group (Hours per Week, Krasnoyarsk Krai Survey)*

Family per capita income (roubles)	No. of budgets examined	Time spent on		
		Study	Self-education	Total
up to 20	41	0.8	4.1	4.9
21–30	104	0.9	3.7	4.6
31–50	234	2.3	4.7	7.0
51–100	304	3.7	6.1	9.8
over 100	174	7.3	6.8	14.1

Source:
V. G. Baikova and others, *Svobodnoe vremya i vsestoronnee razvitie lichnosti*, Moscow, 1965, p. 88.

results are not easily interpreted. It is noteworthy that the middle group apparently read more books and newspapers than the upper one, perhaps indicating a greater yearning for knowledge – and social advancement.

TABLE 33. *Reading Habits by Income-group, over One Year, 1959*

Family per capita income (roubles)	No. of books average per family	% of group subscribing to newspapers	% of group borrowing books
up to 40	31	66.6	13.5
40.1–70	60	80.7	32.8
over 70	46	75.0	39.3

Source:
F. Yu. Aleshina, article in *Industry and Labour in the USSR*, ed. G. V. Osipov, London, 1968.

It would obviously be too much to ask that sociological data derived from different sources should always give a clear-cut picture, or serve as a basis for far-reaching conclusions. Indeed it is evident from the few items we have dealt with here that they often raise almost as many questions as they answer. Petrosyan's Erevan study, for example, shows considerable differences in the amount of time which workers spent preparing for, or travelling to and from work, and this does not seem to have been a function of income at all. He himself does not provide any explanation. Bolgov shows that people from the higher income-groups spent twice as much time as their poor neighbours in the 'sphere of the public services'. This may be merely a reflection of the fact that they ate out or shopped more often; but he does not explain exactly what he had in view, and outside observers are left with another minor puzzle. All the studies we have used are restricted in area and scope, and many important details of the samples are missing.

Nevertheless, they do present an impressionistic picture of the gradation by income in the Soviet working class, and allow us to measure some of the social fissures engendered. We can only hope that with time the more obvious gaps in our knowledge will be filled from new sources.

5
Soviet Workers – Jobs and Education

In the last chapter we were concerned with the distribution of income in the Soviet working class and variations in modes of life associated with it. We shall now turn to the problem of occupational and educational hierarchies.

Apart from its intrinsic interest, this exercise will serve as an introduction to two cogent problems which have been investigated by Soviet sociologists in some depth, namely, how positively or negatively people view their own productive activities, and how education affects their tastes and habits. These questions assume particular importance in the context of Soviet social and political development. Soviet citizens who are really dissatisfied have fewer opportunities of voicing dissatisfaction, or bringing about change, than people in most Western societies, and there is no question of emigration for those who are desperate. On the other hand the state authorities claim that the steady improvement in educational levels is a major Soviet achievement which will eventually transform the outlook of Soviet man into something entirely admirable.

Evaluating and stratifying jobs is no easy task, as managers, trade unionists and labour economists have long since discovered. The problem is that most occupations are composed of a number of elements which are not easily measured, and are related in an intricate, and possibly unstable, manner. Thus different jobs require different kinds of mental or physical skill, and even attitudes of mind. They may be more or less mechanized, and demand a greater or lesser degree of physical exertion. Some will be more monotonous, demand less initiative, or have fewer separate operations in them than others. The two (albeit inadequate) elements on which most Soviet practical analyses are based are the degree of physical or mental skill required, and the extent to which the work is mechanized. These are the bases for findings we shall present here.

Unfortunately Soviet sociologists and statisticians have provided far fewer insights into the occupation structure than one would wish, even within this narrow framework. They are, after all, in rather an equivocal position. The Soviet government exercises an unprecedented prerogative in influencing the occupational structure of the labour force, while the wage rates, which it also fixes, themselves represent a kind of official value judgement on jobs. Labour surveys are conducted frequently, and detailed statistical material must be available in the offices of the Central Statistical Administration. The conditions for research, analysis – and publication – would seem to be basically propitious. But on the other hand the contradictions between the manner in which the occupational structure of the Soviet working class is supposed to develop, and its actual configuration, present some knotty ideological and practical problems which hardly lend themselves to frank treatment.

The theory of development is briefly as follows. Jobs are supposed to increase in number, thus providing the conditions for full employment: the quantity of *skilled*, mechanized jobs will, however, grow relatively much faster. There will be more skilled occupations of known types, and new *kinds* of skilled work will be created. The number and proportion of unskilled, dirty jobs will fall. This trend is seen to result from a healthy population growth, good economic progress, mechanization, and finally automation. Automation will not mean unemployment because workers will be switched to other jobs, retrained or given shorter hours in an organized fashion.

The prospects for the people who will fill these jobs are bright. Their levels of skill will increase: workers will eventually become indistinguishable from specialists: a greater proportion of them will move into highly skilled and mechanized (or automized) jobs and into the new kinds of jobs available. Fewer of them will be engaged in crude physical labour, and the physical element will be reduced in all kinds of work.

All this would be very nice if it did not carry a number of unwelcome implications. The first is that workers will get more and more specialized in their trades as mechanization progresses; but greater specialization unfortunately does not readily fit the Marxist principle of an increasingly homogeneous society. The contradiction cannot be easily resolved. Marx, after all, envisaged a state of affairs in which there would be a high degree of interchangeability between men and jobs. This was for him one aspect of social equality. Thus although Soviet analysts can welcome any proof of improvement in the occupation structure, they must at the same time insist that what they call 'narrow profiles' or specializations are disappearing, at least for most of the labour force.

Automation raises other questions. This is only in a very rudimentary stage in the USSR so far, but it seems that in general automized equipment can be run by people with *less* skill. Soviet observers maintain that automation in capitalist lands leads to the 'dequalification' of the labour force. Automation is a desideratum of the Soviet ideologues, but so is a greater fund of specialized skills in the working class. In the event they try to conform with the Marxist prognosis by talking about a narrowing of the gap between workers and the intelligentsia through smaller wage differentials and a rise in the general educational level of the workers. Nevertheless, these are points of potential conflict between ideology and reality.[1]

Finally there is a practical difficulty, which for official purposes is best left unexplored; it is that the Soviet economy still contains an uncomfortably high proportion of persons in unskilled and unmechanized jobs.

THE DISTRIBUTION OF SKILLS AND MECHANIZATION

Let us take the problem of skill in the Soviet working class first. We shall for the moment restrict ourselves to workers in industry and construction, for which figures are most readily available. In 1968 there were about 24 million persons classified as 'workers' in industry and 5 million in construction, out of a total of about 56 million in the economy as a whole. Any generalizations

---

1. A very unsuccessful attempt to grapple with their problems was made by A. P. Osipov in a now standard article, 'Tekhnicheski progress i izmenenie professionalnoi struktury rabochego klassa' in *Sotsiologia v SSSR*, Vol. 2, Moscow, 1966, p. 10.

we make on this basis will therefore cover a large part of the labour force.[2]

All trades in the Soviet Union are broken down into grades, or *razryady*. The *razryad* may best be regarded as a sort of composite measure of difficulty: a recent Soviet encyclopedia states that it covers the 'complexity, exactness, degree of responsibility, conditions of labour, and other factors involved' in the work.[3] There are four sets or scales of *razryady* in industry and three in construction, each scale being composed of between six and ten *razryady*, with the hardest jobs coming at the top of the scale, i.e. in the sixth, etc., *razryady*. The scales are designed to fit trades which are more or less difficult to master. In 1965 only 10 per cent of the workers in industry were outside them altogether.[4]

In like manner the workers' technical and working abilities are graded on scales of *kvalifikatsii* which in fact correspond to the *razryady*. The worker is supposed to apply to the management when he thinks he is competent enough to be moved onto a higher *razryad*. Totally unskilled work is classified at the bottom of the *razryad* scales, and should be done by people with a low qualification rating.

What can we say about the distribution of skill among Soviet workers? Figure 12 has been constructed to show the percentage of workers in each *razryad* at the time of the August 1965 labour census. In fact the distribution seemed to be reasonably 'regular'. Nearly half of the workers were at that time in grades three and four, which was in the middle, or just above the middle, of the most important scales. The relatively large number of people in grade one would, of course, be partly explained by the fact that newcomers to the labour market and people who were incapable of sticking at any job for long, would tend to congregate there. But it also reflected the large proportion of unskilled jobs in the economy. The top of the hierarchy would be occupied by older

2. Figures from *Trud v SSSR*, Moscow, 1968. 'Workers' at that time made up about two thirds of the non-peasant labour force. The remainder consisted of two important categories of personnel which we shall treat separately below: a, medium and highly skilled specialists, or persons who did specialist work without the formal training needed for it, and b) low-grade employees like clerks, cleaners and watchmen, etc.

3. *Trudovoe pravo, Entsiklopedicheski Slovar'*, Moscow, 1969, p. 403.

4. *Trud v SSSR*, Moscow, 1968, pp. 150–52.

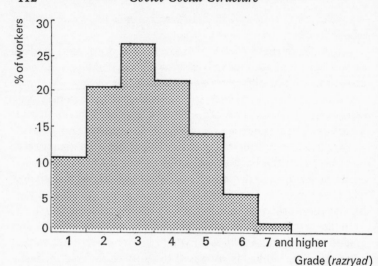

FIGURE 12.   *Distribution of Soviet Workers in Industry and Construction, by Skill*

Source:

Trud v SSSR, Moscow, 1968, pp. 81, 121, 150, 152 (calculated).

workers or the more able people from the middle age-groups. We must not, of course, forget that this breakdown is rather artificial: the assessment of a worker's skill must bear a significant subjective element, and also depend on factors like the conditions of work, the actual availability of a more skilled job, and even personal relations with the management. There may be a tendency for managers to bunch their workers in the middle grades.

TABLE 34. *Breakdown of Soviet Workers* (rabochie) *by level of Skill* (%)

Level of skill	1925	1927	1950	1959	1962
Highly skilled and skilled	18.5	40.5	49.6	51.7	61.0
Semi-skilled	41.3	34.1	47.9	46.4	24.0
Unskilled	40.2	25.4	2.5	1.9	15.0

Sources:

F. V. Konstantinov and others, *Stroitelstvo kommunizma i razvitie obshchest-vennykh otnoshenii*, Moscow, 1966, p. 69 (chapter written by V. S. Semenov); E. L. Manevich, op. cit., p. 19.

A very rudimentary and unsatisfactory classification of Soviet workers by skill which crops up from time to time in Soviet sources is shown in Table 34.[5] No definition of the degrees of skill used, or the apparent jump in the number of highly skilled workers in 1927, is offered. The figures for unskilled workers in 1950 and 1959 are obviously absurd, as indeed one Soviet economist has pointed out.[6] To judge from our own Figure 12, the classification 'highly skilled and skilled' must have begun as low as the third *razryad*, while workers in the first *razryad* made up the 'unskilled', and those in the second the 'semi-skilled' groups. The analysis (if we may grace it with that term) does, however, have some interest in that it purports to show a long-term rise in the proportion of highly skilled workers at the expense of semi-skilled and unskilled workers. There may, furthermore, have been a marked acceleration in the fifties. The pattern of Soviet industrialization and training policies would suggest this.

In the USSR, as in other lands, there is a marked degree of correlation between skill and income; in other words, the most skilled layers of the working class tend to be the richest, and vice versa. A principal object of the *razryad* system is, after all, to relate remuneration to skill. The differentials between the lowest and highest *razryady* since the reform of 1964–5 have been 1:1.8 and 1:2.6, depending on the scale.[7]

As will be evident from the discussion in Chapter 4, wage depends not only on *razryad*. Take-home pay is affected by such things as bonuses, overtime payments and regional supplements, not to mention losses through breakdowns, failure of raw material supplies, or illness. All of these may make a highly skilled man in one set of circumstances worse off than an unskilled labourer in others. This is illustrated in data provided by L. S. Blyakhman from a study of labour mobility among 10,720 workers of selected trades in Leningrad in 1962–3 (Figure 13). From these we see that although more skill usually meant better

5. See, for example, I. A. Stepanyan, V. S. Semenov, and others, *Problemy izmenenia sotsialnoi struktury sovetskogo obshchestva*, Moscow, 1968, p. 214; A. A. Zvorykin, *Nauka, proizvodstvo, trud*, Moscow, 1965, p. 102; E. L. Manevich, *Problemy obshchestvennogo truda v SSSR*, Moscow, 1966, p. 19.

6. V. E. Komarov, *Stroitelstvo kommunizma i professionalnaya struktura rabotnikov proizvodstva*, Moscow, 1965, p. 65.

7. A. P. Volkov, op. cit., p. 302.

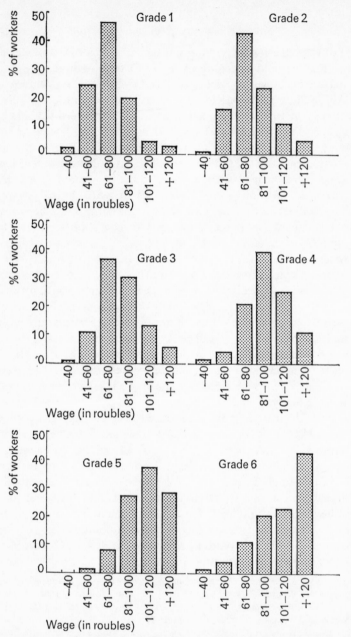

FIGURE 13. *Percentage of Workers in Different Wage Groups, by grade of skill*

pay, there were big discrepancies. The average wage in the most skilled grade, for example, worked out at just over a hundred roubles: yet there were some people earning more than this in all the lower grades.

TABLE 35. *Breakdown of Soviet Workers by Level of Mechanization of Labour* (%)

Type of occupation	1948	1954	1959	1962
Workers in mechanized jobs and workers engaged in repair and servicing of equipment	44.3	47.9	50.0	56.0
Including: Workers in mechanized jobs, motor mechanics, crane drivers, operatives, etc.	25.1	29.5	31.5	39.4
Workers servicing machines and mechanisms (setting, repairing, etc.)	7.3	7.5	7.9	9.4
Manual labourers	55.7	52.1	50.0	44.0

Source:
A. I. Notkin, *Struktura narodnogo khozyaistva SSSR*, Moscow, 1967, pp. 210–11. Chapter by V. E. Komarov and V. M. Moskovich. An analysis of figures for 1965 in V. V. Krevnevich, *Vliyanie nauchno-tekhnicheskogo progressa na izmenenie struktury rabochego klassa*, Moscow, 1971, indicates that further progress towards mechanization was extremely slow. Automation was insignificant.

An idea of the advance of mechanization in the USSR may be gained from the data in Table 35.[8] The figures as they stand

8. This apparently differs somewhat from the scheme adopted by the USSR Central Statistical Administration for the labour censuses of 1959, 1962 and 1965, which included the following categories: (*a*) automized jobs, (*b*) controlling machines and mechanisms, (*c*) repairing machines and mechanisms, (*d*) physical work loading and servicing machines, (*e*) physical work without machines or mechanisms, sometimes with simple instruments. It has been criticized by many Soviet observers for being 'economic' rather than 'sociological', and for not being particularly clear or consistent, which is why so many improvements have been suggested. Comment on its strengths and

Source for Figure 13:
L. S. Blyakhman, A. G. Zdravomyslov, O. I. Shkaratan, 'Problemy upravlenia dvizheniem rabochei sily', in *Trud i razvitie lichnosti*, ed. A. G. Zdravomyslov and V. A. Yadov, Leningrad, 1965, p. 180.

reveal that, judging by British or American standards, by 1962 there was still a very low level of mechanization in the USSR.[9] Despite steady progress, 44 per cent of all Soviet workers were still engaged in manual jobs without machines. We know from other sources that in 1959 9 per cent more were engaged in physical work, loading and servicing machines. The manual labour would, of course, have been both skilled and unskilled, but we may safely presume that the latter predominated heavily, since modern industry offers few openings for unmechanized craftsmanship. This is another way of saying that people doing unmechanized jobs must also have tended to be the least skilled; this particular relationship, however, still awaits proper investigation at the time of writing. A recent survey of seventy Uzbek factories seemed to show a close degree of correlation between the level of mechanization in them and the average level of skill and education of their workers (Table 36).

We would expect to find that workers in the least mechanized jobs, like the workers with the lowest skill ratings, are the poorest – the principal exceptions being labourers whose work requires exceptional physical effort, or the few craftsmen with considerable manual dexterity. No systematic study of this problem has appeared either, but a mass of indirect evidence supports the

---

weaknesses (with proposed changes) may be found in the following: the article by V. Ya. Suslov in R. P. Davykin, *Rabochi klass SSSR na sovremennom etape*, Leningrad, 1968; the article by Z. I. Fainburg and G. P. Veinberg, *Vliyanie tekhnicheskogo progressa na kharakter truda*, Moscow, 1964, p. 38 ff., V. E. Komarov, *Stroitelstvo kommunizma i professionalnaya struktura rabotnikov proizvodstva*, Moscow, 1965, p. 58 ff. As far as we are aware no really detailed systematization of data on occupations from any of the censuses has been published.

9. The proportion of 'unskilled manual workers' in the British labour force, as revealed by the 1961 census, was about 8.3 per cent, while the 'labourers, except farm and mine' group in the US labour force in 1960 made up only about 5.3 per cent. Both of these figures were probably understatements: the American figure in particular could probably be doubled by the addition of unskilled farm and mine workers, etc., and some of the 2 million persons who did not specify their work. Even so, the pool of unskilled manual labour evidently made up a far smaller proportion of the labour force in these two countries. (UK census returns for 1961, published by H.M. Stationery Office, 1966, socio-economic group tables, pp. 2–3, and *Statistical Abstract of the USA*, Washington, 1967, p. 232.)

TABLE 36. *Correlation Between Mechanization, Education and Skill Levels of Workers*

Level of mechanization of production processes (not defined)	Average razryad	Average educational level (no. of years in school)
Up to 20%	1.3	3.9
21–30%	1.41	4.2
31–40%	1.78	4.4
41–50%	3.1	5.8
60–70%	3.7	6.4
70%	4.1	7.2

Source:
T. Abdushukurov, M. Abdulaev.
Zakonomernosti kulturno-teknicheskogo progressa trudyashchikhsya v sovremenny period stroitelstva kommunizma, Tashkent, 1966, p. 40.
The table was compiled on the basis of an analysis of the materials of the Department of Industry of the Institute of Economics, Academy of Sciences, Uzbek Republic.

contention. Nearly all of the lowest-paid jobs listed in Table 16 were quite unmechanized. The people with the lowest incomes, as we have observed, tend to work in the least favoured branches of the economy, like light industry, textiles, catering, public services, and these have been traditionally neglected investment-wise. A study of physical fatigue conducted in Novosibirsk in the mid sixties showed that people in the lowest income brackets tended to get tired at work more often than the higher wage

TABLE 37. *Relationship Between Fatigue and Per Capita Income (workers who normally get very tired as a percentage of all workers in the given income-group)*

	Per capita family income-groups (without state subsidies) in roubles per month			
	Up to 30	30–49	50–89	90–129
% of workers	57.1	30.1	27.6	24.7

Source:
G. N. Charkasov, *Sotsialno-ekonomicheskie problemy intensivnosti truda v SSSR*, Moscow, 1966, p. 121.
From a survey of 1,900 workers of the basic trades of the machine building enterprises in Novosibirsk.

earners (Table 37). This sort of evidence points to the conclusion that unskilled labourers in the less mechanized jobs make up the poorer sections of the working class, while workers in the more highly mechanized ones are better off.

TABLE 38. *Changes in Occupation Structure of Soviet Industry* (*Number of Workers, in Thousands, Except First Line*)

Occupation	1948 (1 May)	1959 (1 Aug.)	1962 (1 Aug.)	1965 (2 Aug.)	1948–65 proportional change
All workers (millions)	10*	17.8	20.1	22.2	2.2
Highly skilled–mechanized occupations:					
Fitters	710	1527	2021	2366	3.3
Machine tool operators	505	1011	1221	1336	2.6
Mechanics	290	890	1070 .	1242	4.2
Electricians	206	343	464	641	3.1
Welders	66	193	283	360	5.4
Drivers†	182	253	276	336	1.8
Unskilled-mechanized occupations:					
Labourers	659	790	787	914	1.4
Loaders	371	571	587	648	1.7
Warehousemen	87	199	239	284	3.3
Blacksmiths	72	52	49	43	0.6

*Estimate.
†Probably best regarded as coming between the two groups.
Source:
Trud v SSSR, Moscow, 1968, pp. 81, 177–9. Selected data and years.

The data we have adduced so far supports the claim that both skill and mechanization levels have shown a general tendency to rise. We have mentioned only global figures, though examples taken from individual enterprises are abundant. But the trends are not wholly favourable, as a closer look at some of the occupation data included in the 1968 statistical handbook on labour reveals. We have chosen for comparison six of the most skilled and four of the least skilled occupations (Table 38). This selection is probably sufficient for purposes of illustration.[10]

The most important categories of skilled workers doing mechanized jobs in industry did indeed increase in size faster than the industrial labour force as a whole between the labour census years of 1948 and 1965. But labourers and loaders, the two most sizeable unskilled categories, increased by 40 and 70 per cent respectively, while the number of warehousemen trebled. (This last development is slightly intriguing: it was probably due to an increase in stocks and a greater locational dispersion of them.) The number of drivers, a fairly key category in the economy, rose by much less than the average rate. The only listed category of manual labour which actually shrank, incidentally, was the tiny one of skilled blacksmiths who worked by hand. The implication is clear. Improvement in the occupation structure will be slower than the authorities hoped, and large numbers of unskilled workers in low-grade jobs will be characteristic of the Soviet economy for a long time to come.

OCCUPATIONAL PRESTIGE

Occupations can also be ranged by how desirable people think they are. Work in the Soviet Union naturally varies in its attractiveness: the fact that an academician and a charwoman might be both struggling for communism will not blind them to the vast prestige difference between their jobs. Proclaimed adherence to the state ideology, as far as we can judge, does not seem to affect the individual's attitudes to this problem in any measurable degree.

Not surprisingly, Soviet sociologists have been a little hesitant to explore invidious differences of this kind, but since the mid sixties a few interesting studies have appeared. One which was conducted by a group of sociologists in Novosibirsk about 1965 was designed to elucidate how 231 men and 109 women of various manual trades in a building project evaluated 45 trades and professions ranging from the most demanding to the least

10. Our aim in choosing these data was to illustrate the overall trends in a simple manner. Soviet observers who have touched on this problem produce far more impressive results by limiting themselves to the best developed branches of industry, rather specific jobs, or individual enterprises, see A. P. Osipov, op. cit., B. I. Eremeev, Chapter III, section 3, in Ts. A. Stepanyan and others, *Klassy, sostsialnye sloi i gruppy v SSSR*, Moscow, 1968, etc.

skilled.[11] The study suffered from a number of shortcomings: for example, the overwhelming majority of occupations in the questionnaire were definitely 'blue-collar': only seven were in the 'employee' bracket; of these three (accountant, economist, and nursing sister) were really service personnel, and only four (doctor, agronomist, research worker, and teacher) properly belonged to the intelligentsia. The sample of participants was small, and the range of jobs in which they were employed narrow.

Some interesting details were nevertheless revealed. The men and women were asked to allot to each of the jobs in the list from one to ten points, according to their estimate of its desirability, or *privlekatelnost*. The opinions of the participants were re-assuringly complex, with some significant differences of evaluation between the sexes. The men gave radio technician, engine driver, welder, research worker and steel producer (in that order) seven points or more: the reader may care to pause for a moment to consider these somewhat astonishing preferences. The women's choices, on the other hand, were closer to what we would expect. They put research worker, doctor, teacher, (house) painter, economist and tailor first. The pattern of choice of the least desirable jobs was practically common to both sexes and fairly obvious: nobody liked work that demanded heavy physical labour. These were the jobs which gained three points or less:

Men	Women
1. Labourers	1. Labourers
2. Loaders	2. Loaders
3. Navvies	3. Navvies
4. Tackle-handlers	4. Tackle-handlers
5. Forestry workers	5. Forestry workers
6. Communication workers	6. Blacksmiths, press-operators
	7. Stock rearers
	8. Field workers
	9. Motor roller operators
	10. Bulldozer operators
	11. Tractor drivers
	12. Instrument-makers
	13. Repair mechanics

11. Article by V. A. Kalmyk, F. M. Borodkin and I. N. Spesivtseva in *Sotsiologicheskie issledovania*, ed. R. V. Ryvkina, Novosibirsk, 1967, p. 289.

The women, in general, were more precise about their preferences than the men, and placed more jobs right at the bottom of their lists.

A number of sociologists have studied the attitudes of young people to their jobs, or to the work they would like to do when they leave school. These choices are in themselves an index of occupation prestige, though again judged from the angle of a specific section of society. The best study to hand at the time of writing was done by V. V. Vodzinskaya on the basis of a questionnaire sent to 624 young people about to graduate from five general schools in Leningrad in 1964.[12] The main weakness of the sample was, as she readily admitted, its narrowness: all the children were of urban background, and probably from relatively opulent families. Nevertheless her findings correlated very closely with the assessment of experts and (she claimed) much more extended surveys of school leavers conducted elsewhere. V. V. Vodzinskaya attempted to determine which of four components of a job – its social prestige, the possibilities it offers for personal fulfilment, its 'creativeness', and pay – were most important in determining young people's attitudes to it. The conclusion that she came to is that social prestige was the main element in their choice. In the course of her argument she provided curves showing the standing of eighty occupations in accordance with these indices, and picked out the following twenty as the most and least desirable occupations (in descending order of preference):

Most Popular
1. Research worker in physics
2. Engineer or radio technician
3. Research worker in medicine
4. Engineer-geologist
5. Research worker in mathematics
6. Research chemist
7. Radio technician
8. Pilot

12. Article by V. V. Vodzinskaya in G. V. Osipov and J. Szczepański, eds., *Sotsialnye problemy truda i proizvodstva*, Moscow and Warsaw, 1969, p. 39. We cannot, of course, hope to do full justice to Vodzinskaya's work in a few lines.

  9. Chemical engineer
10. Research worker in biology
11. Doctor
12. Specialist in literature and the arts
      . . . . . [13]
55. Turner
      . . . . . [13]
62. Milling machine operator
      . . . . . [13]

Least Popular
75. Shop assistant
76. Clerk, accounts clerk, comptometer operator
77. Painter, mason, plasterer
78. Agricultural worker
79. Compositor
80. Worker in public amenities.

The discrepancy between this line-up and the preferences of the male building workers in Novosibirsk illustrates, of course how precarious generalizations about the social prestige of jobs can be.

Investigations of this type, though interesting, do not provide more than a general impression of occupation status in the USSR – of course, they are not intended to. Important considerations like the attractiveness of political influence which obviously goes with many of the top jobs, or public deprecation of the most menial ones, are not explored. The best Western studies published to date do not do much to fill this gap, but they have indicated that at least in the years preceding the Second World War the Soviet prestige hierarchy for urban jobs resembled the American one.[14] It seems that the abundance of unskilled, unmechanized jobs in the Soviet Union does not in itself raise people's opinion of this kind of labour.

13. Omissions as in Vodzinskaya's published version.
14. A. Inkeles and R. Bauer, *The Soviet Citizen*, Harvard, 1959, p. 76 ff., and A. Inkeles, *Social Change in Soviet Russia*, Harvard, 1968, Chapters 9 and 10. The information given there is based on a 1950–51 survey of some 2,700 war-time émigrés from the USSR.

OCCUPATION AND ATTITUDES TOWARDS LABOUR

Let us now turn to some of the sociological investigations which Soviet scholars have made on the basis of occupational groups. The most interesting and revealing of these studies have been concerned with finding out how satisfied workers of various occupation groups are with their jobs. An outstanding analysis of this problem, based on a survey of 2,665 young workers under 30, was conducted by a group of sociologists under the guidance of V. A. Yadov and A. G. Zdravomyslov in Leningrad in 1963. We must, however, preface our account of this work with a few methodological details.[15]

Firstly, the scheme of occupations which Yadov and Zdravomyslov use is a little more sophisticated than that given in Table 35, as it is an attempt to categorize jobs not only by the degree to which they are mechanized, and the level of skill they require, but also by the degree to which they are rhythmic and monotonous.[16] The resulting framework has six categories, which are explained in the notes to Figure 14.

Secondly, the Yadov–Zdravomyslov analysis of workers' attitudes towards their jobs is inevitably rather intricate, since it is an attempt to distinguish and evaluate all the main social and personal factors. The final analysis rests, however, on four composite elements. The first of these contains what they call the three 'objective' indices, that is, the degree of responsibility and conscientiousness shown by the worker, his 'labour initiative', or concern for the efficiency of the productive process, and his level of discipline, all of which are expressed in output, and plan fulfilment. The second element is satisfaction with the actual operations performed, and the third, satisfaction with the trade or 'profession'. The fourth element is the 'comprehension of the

---

15. A. G. Zdravomyslov, V. P. Rozhin, V. A. Yadov, *Chelovek i ego rabota*, Moscow, 1967. Other studies have appeared on this theme, but some are sloppy, at least in their published form, and inspire less confidence. See, for example, G. V. Osipov and others, *Rabochii klass i tekhnicheski progress*, Moscow, 1965; K. K. Platonov, *Lichnost i trud*, Moscow, 1965. We shall refer to the Leningrad study discussed here and later as the Yadov–Zdravomyslov study, since V. A. Yadov and A. G. Zdravomyslov evidently organized it. This is not to belittle the important contributions made by other scholars.

16. Zdravomyslov, op. cit., p. 32.

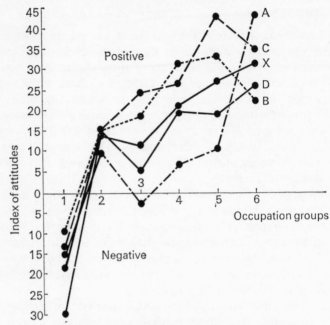

A: attitude towards labour by 'objective indices'
B: index of satisfaction with work
C: index of satisfaction with trade
D: index of comprehension of social significance of work
X: composite index, the arithmetical mean

FIGURE 14.   *The Relationship of Occupation Group and Attitude towards Labour*

Source and Notes:

A. G. Zdravomyslov, V. P. Rozhin and V. A. Yadov, *Chevolek i ego rabota*, Moscow, 1967, p. 227.

Zdravomyslov's six labour categories are as follows:

1. Unskilled physical labour.
2. Labour on a conveyor belt, demanding medium trade training. Exacting rhythm.
3. Mechanized labour, demanding medium trade training. Exacting rhythm.
4. Control of automatic equipment, medium trade training, no repair abilities.
5. Skilled physical labour, demanding high level of trade training (fitters).
6. Control of automatic equipment and repair of same, demanding high level of trade training.

social significance' of the work. All of these are measured on a positive–negative scale.

Some results from this part of the study are shown in diagrammatic form in Figure 14. It is evident that people doing unskilled and unmechanized physical labour (a category which is, we must remember, very extensive in society as a whole) have very negative ratings on all four counts, and the people doing the most skilled and mechanized work generally have very positive ones. This in itself is an interesting observation. But the actual relationships between the indices are rather complex, especially in the upper occupation groups. Thus although people in group six have the best objective indices – they are more conscientious, disciplined, etc. – they are not particularly satisfied with the day-to-day tasks that they have to fulfil. The authors attempt to explain this by the relative monotony of the work, but add that the phenomenon requires investigation. People doing 'mechanized labour demanding medium grade training, with an exacting rhythm' (which must be an important and growing category if industry is to develop), also have negative objective indices.

These apparently innocent findings may have disconcerting implications for the development of Soviet society. Yadov and Zdravomyslov's sample has better indices than the Soviet non-peasant labour force as a whole; the sample is more educated, younger, better provided with cultural and other amenities, and more socially homogeneous. It may be that the reactions of the Soviet working class in the aggregate are worse. We may surmise that people in the upper parts of it are much more satisfied with their lot than those at the bottom. 'Class solidarity' cannot be very meaningful in this particular respect. The passage of more workers to more skilled and mechanized jobs may indeed cause a rise in the general level of satisfaction, but important sources of discontent will remain, especially if workers become more demanding. And that still leaves the problem of people who are left with the nasty jobs. Some 16 per cent of all the workers in the Leningrad sample were dissatisfied, or very dissatisfied, with their work, and over 12 per cent disliked their trades.[17] Another study of the attitudes of 600 workers in Gorki and Moscow

17. Zdravomyslov, ibid., pp. 386, 387.

revealed that 15.2 per cent were dissatisfied with their work there.[18] Soviet writers naturally claim that dissatisfaction in capitalist lands is much more widespread, but this is a very debatable point. Alex Inkeles's study suggested that Americans, in this respect at least, were happier.[19]

Yadov and Zdravomyslov also go into the question of what prompted the people in different occupation groups to choose the jobs they were in. (Vodzinskaya was concerned with young people's evaluations, as distinct from their intentions or the availability of work.) The conclusions are set out for men and women separately in Figures 15a and 15b. Sex differences, it appears, were again very important. Men in all the occupations of the sample rated the wage factor fairly low. Women tended to think of financial return much more, particularly if their work was in one of the lower groups, or, interestingly, required a certain amount of training and manual dexterity, as in group five. Men in unskilled jobs placed force of circumstance highest amongst the reasons for their choice, but this became steadily less important in more skilled and mechanized jobs. It was a much less significant factor for women. Interest in the job was generally higher among men than among women; and whereas it became progressively more important through the six groups for men, it remained at a fairly constant level for the other sex. Perhaps all this meant that women were rather more reluctant to work at all in cases where they had the added burden of domestic duties.

A number of sociologists have attempted to correlate occupation group with such things as participation in efficiency drives at work, and cultural tastes, but the results which have come to our notice have been disappointing. Some of the data provided by the Leningrad economists N. B. Lebedev and O. I. Shkaratan on worker participation in a 'rationalization and invention' campaign in the machine-building industry of Leningrad in 1965 are reproduced in Table 39. These campaigns have been organized from time to time to encourage workers to make their own suggestions for improvement of the work process, and their re-

18. See article by A. A. Zvorykin in *Sotsiologia i ideologia*, ed. L. A. Volovik, Moscow, 1969, p. 79.

19. A. Inkeles, *The Soviet Citizen*, p. 104.

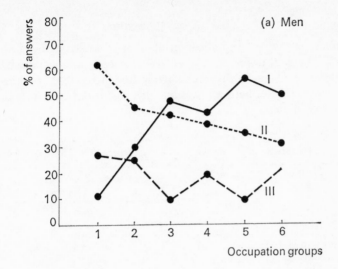

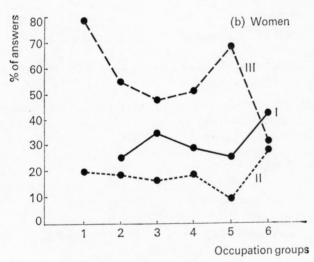

I: trade seemed interesting
II: circumstances precluded any other choice
III: pay was attractive

FIGURE 15. *Motivation for Job Choice amongst Young Workers:*
*Six 'controlled' Occupation Groups**

*Occupation groups are identical with those in Figure 14.
Source:
A. G. Zdravomyslov and others, *Chelovek i ego rabota*, Moscow, 1967, p. 159

actions provide some indication of their enthusiasm for their jobs. There is, unfortunately for our purposes, also a financial element involved, in that fees ranging from 10 to 5,000 roubles may be paid; but here we presume that this is not dominant in people's interest.

TABLE 39. *Relationship of the Character of Labour to Participation in the Rationalization and Invention Movement* (%)

| | Participants as a % of all workers in group | | |
Occupation groups	Constantly	Not constantly	Never
Scientific technical	7.5	32.8	59.7
Skilled (mainly manual) labour	16.3	46.0	37.7
Semi-skilled (mainly manual) labour	4.4	21.2	74.4
Low-grade mental labour	4.7	15.4	79.9
Unskilled physical labour	0.9	9.1	90.0

Source:
N. B. Lebedev and O. I. Shkaratan, *Ocherki istorii sotsialisticheskogo sorevnovania*, Leningrad, 1966, p. 241.

Naturally, the opportunity for invention and rationalization varies from one job to another; men handling highly mechanized or automized processes have less scope for this than those engaged in work which is only partly mechanized, or requires manual skills, so a difference in rationalizing activities need not be a consequence of attitude alone. Shkaratan and Lebedev's study showed that the onus of the campaign was borne by skilled workers who operated fairly simple, standard machine tools. The participation rates of unskilled labourers was negligible, while the other categories did little better.

Data supplied in a book edited by G. V. Osipov on the cultural demands of workers in the Gorki *oblast* from an occupational standpoint suggested that the workers in the more intricate jobs had more developed cultural interests, but this is not surprising if we presume that they were more skilled and (to anticipate a few pages) better educated.[20] At the same time there were apparent anomalies: workers with automized jobs, whom one

20. *Industry and Labour in the USSR*, London, 1967, p. 107.

would not expect to be the most backward, had rather un-developed cultural tastes, like the unskilled labourers. An investigation of 840 workers in the First Moscow Ballbearing Factory in 1963 by S. T. Guryanov provided more insights.[21] It showed, for instance, that involvement in dressmaking and sewing classes varied from 2 per cent of the most skilled group of workers to 48 per cent among the least skilled; this was, no doubt, a reflection not only of cultural interests, but also of economic necessity and the sex composition of the samples. As far as part-time study was concerned, Guryanov showed that semi-skilled and unskilled workers were amongst the least interested. The study suffered, however, from inadequate presentation of the data, and some of the figures were somewhat suspect. Guryanov claimed, for example, that in six months even the least avid readers in his sample read more than nine books each. Soviet newspapers may well make their readers yearn for more digestible fare, but this level nevertheless seems suspiciously high. Perhaps pamphlets are included, but then the statement does not mean much.

GENERAL EDUCATION AND THE WORKING CLASS

Educational attainment is another major starting point for sociological analysis in the USSR. We shall have a good deal to say about the nature of Soviet education and the relationship of the Soviet school to different groups of society in Chapter 9. Here we will restrict ourselves to comment on such problems as educational levels in the working class, the correlation of education with income and occupation, and the extent to which educational attainment has been seen to influence people's attitudes and way of life.

The Soviet government has, over the years, made enormous strides in building up the country's school system, and it is not our intention to belittle this achievement. At the same time official figures show that a considerable proportion of the workers still have a meagre educational background. According to the 1968 statistical handbook, 50 per cent of the workers in all branches of the economy had less than seven years of general schooling behind them as late as January 1967. A survey of the

21. S. T. Guryanov, *Sotsializm v SSSR*, Moscow, 1965.

educational levels of workers in the automized enterprises of the Gorky *oblast* in 1961 showed that even there 48 per cent of them had not reached the seventh class.[22] A fairly far-reaching improvement over the next one or two decades may, it is true, be expected as more and more young people are encouraged to stay on at school. Nearly half the relevant age-groups were taking their school-leaving certificates, or *attestaty zrelosti*, in the late sixties. Nevertheless, the Soviet working class still lags behind the United States in this respect: by 1965 87.4 per cent of all American sixteen- and seventeen-year-olds were still enrolled in school.[23]

The Soviet authorities have long since declared that a lack of financial means is no bar to learning in the Soviet Union. This implies that all members of the working class, regardless of income or occupation, enjoy equal educational opportunities. No correlative studies have ever been published on this delicate topic, but a great deal of indirect evidence suggests that the average educational level rises from the lower to the higher income groups in society. A higher education, as we shall find in a later chapter, is achieved much more frequently by children of the intelligentsia, who are mostly in the upper income brackets, and there are doubtless gradations in achievement between children from the lower income-groups as well.

An interesting investigation of the extent to which people from the different income-groups indulge in *part-time* study was conducted on the basis of the above-mentioned sample of 10,720 Leningrad workers (Table 40). The figures show that despite significant differences between the sexes (men being much more ready students than women) the proportion of part-time students doubles between the 20–30- and 70–100-rouble income groups. There are anomalies at the extreme ends of the income range for which there are no obvious answers. The relatively high proportion of women students in the under-twenty-rouble income-group is one of these. The large number of

22. *Narodnoe Khozyaistvo SSSR v 1968*, p. 34; no separate figure is given for the low-grade 'employees' who are not specialists; G. V. Osipov, *Rabochi klass i tekhnicheski progress*, Moscow, 1965, p. 152. The Soviet definition of automation is probably suspect.

23. *U.S. Digest of Educational Statistics*, Washington, 1966, p. 4.

part-time students in the 20–30-rouble income group may merely mean that many people who wish to study but cannot do so on a full-time basis take part-time or temporary jobs which pay little. The fall-off in the numbers of part-time students from the richest families is in itself not unexpected, because these families can presumably afford to support their children while they study at full-time institutions.

TABLE 40. *Income and Participation in Part-time Study*

| | % of persons studying | | | |
| | On all courses | | At vuz level | |
Family per capita income (roubles)	Men	Women	Men	Women
Up to 20	—	8.4	—	—
21–30	12.7	4.7	2.2	0.3
31–40	11.8	5.6	1.9	0.7
41–50	10.5	7.2	2.0	1.3
51–60	15.4	8.1	2.8	1.9
61–70	16.3	8.0	3.2	1.3
71–100	23.8	9.8	4.3	2.2
+100	18.5	10.2	4.1	—
Average	16.2	6.9	3.0	1.4

Source:
L. S. Blyakhman, A. G. Zdravomyslov, O. I. Shkaratan, 'Problemy upravlenia dvizheniem rabochei sily', in *Trud i lichnost*, Leningrad, 1965, p. 184.

It might be expected that the best-educated workers in the Soviet Union would also be the most skilled. Academician Strumilin, the doyen of Soviet economists, and, incidentally, a pioneer in this field, claims to have proved by investigations conducted in the twenties that people with better general educational background acquire new skills more quickly, and his findings have been used as an argument for increasing financial allocations for education. References to his work are still frequent and its validity has apparently been upheld by concrete investigations. Thus a study of workers at the Vladimir Ilich factory in Moscow in the early sixties purported to show that whereas workers with five to six years of general schooling took, on average, five years to move up one *razryad*, those who completed seven classes needed only just over three: a ten-year general education shortened the time to a year and a half.[24]

The Yadov–Zdravomyslov study has, however, cast considerable doubt on this proposition. As the authors pointed out, the important thing is not so much whether people with more education *can* learn quicker (and thus rise faster in the skill hierarchy) as whether they are allowed to, or have the opportunity to. In fact, these scholars said, the evidence by the mid sixties was contradictory. Probably the masses of new workers with higher educational levels could not be promoted.

TABLE 41. *Educational Levels in the Most Common Manual Trades*

Manual trade	Number of workers with 7 classes or more (per thousand)	Number employed (millions)
Turners	667	0.928
Electricians	633	1.290
Tailors	568	0.840
Storekeepers, weighing scale operators	562	0.904
Fitters	529	3.039
Metal workers	495	0.782
Drivers	427	3.174
Carpenters	386	0.778
Labourers	333	2.462
Loaders and porters	271	1.703
Nurses, nursemaids	270	0.894
Joiners	238	2.091
Cleaners	147	1.733
Lorry drivers	147	0.784
Watchmen	87	2.030

Source:
1959 All-Union census, pp. 161, 177.

At the same time there is no doubt that better-educated workers tended to predominate in the more highly mechanized and skilled jobs, at least at the time of the 1959 census. We are not in a position to measure this accurately, but substantive evidence that it was so is shown in Table 41. Here the fifteen most common manual trades, employing from just under 800,000

24. Article by V. M. Zhamin in *Ekonomicheskaya Gazeta*, 28 April 1965.

to over 3 million persons each, and comprising in all about 23 million persons (just over half of the non-agricultural manual labour force) have been listed according to the proportion of practicants with more than seven years of general schooling. From this selection we see that whereas only 8.7 per cent of the country's two million watchmen had been in school for longer than seven years, the corresponding figure for the highly skilled turners (lathe-operators) was 66.7 per cent. The most educated workers, incidentally, were a relatively small group of some 70,000 compositors and allied workers: according to the census 87.8 per cent of them had seven years of general education or more. They were followed by watchmakers and jewellers, with about 70 per cent. A study of 2,888 Leningrad workers and employees conducted by O. I. Shkaratan in 1965 gives the same sort of evidence.[25] Whereas skilled and semi-skilled workers in his sample had 8.3, 8.2 and 9.1 years of general education behind them, the unskilled manual labourers had only 6.5 (Table 42). Shkaratan's figures, incidentally, illustrate the principle that the more skilled workers have, by definition, had more *special* training for their jobs. His highest grade of worker spent three times as long as the unskilled manuals on courses of this kind. Table 42 yields some other interesting information, particularly on differences of a political nature, to which we shall return in Chapter 8 below.

EDUCATION AND ATTITUDES TOWARDS LABOUR

The impact of general education on the Soviet worker's way of life and outlook is considered by the Soviet authorities to be of immense importance, for the educational system is thought to play a major part in shaping the new Soviet man. The problem has many ramifications. Soviet scholars have looked into the economic, socio-political and moral feedback from education, and usually come to positive conclusions.

Here we cannot hope to do more than review a few of their findings. We have just mentioned the problem of how far education helps Soviet workers improve their abilities and master new

25. Unfortunately the only version of this study we have seen was in a very inadequate article printed in *Voprosy Filosofii*, No. 1, 1967.

TABLE 42. Analysis of a Labour Force Sample by Eight Indices

Type of profession or trade	Length of general training (years)	Grade of skill	Wage (roubles per month)	Length of specialist training	CPSU or Komsomol member	Social activities*	Age	Length of time in industry (years)	Total no. of persons
Managers, directors	13.6	—	172.9	41.5	CPSU 54.4 Koms. 6.4 neither 39.2	84.2	41.8	17	92
High-grade mental labour – draughtsmen	14.0	—	127.0	51.9	CPSU 19.8 Koms. 20.4 neither 59.8	70.4	35.7	13.5	135
Medium-grade mental labour – technicians, accountants	12.5	—	109.8	40.3	CPSU 19.6 Koms. 23.2 neither 57.2	82.4	36.8	14	287
High-grade physical & mental labour – skilled machine operators etc.	8.8	4.8	129.0	13.3	CPSU 23.4 Koms. 14.2 neither 62.4	79.2	35.3	15.5	67

					CPSU / Koms. / neither				
Skilled manual labour – fitters, welders	8.3	3.9	120.0	11.4	CPSU 16.2 / Koms. 21.2 / neither 62.6	60.7	39.1	13.5	1002
Semi-skilled manual labour	8.2	3.2	107.5	7.1	CPSU 12.2 / Koms. 27.3 / neither 60.5	54.3	35.7	11.4	837
Semi-skilled mental labour – service personnel, ordinary office staff	9.1	—	83.6	8.5	CPSU 7.8 / Koms. 19.3 / neither 72.9	54.5	32.3	14.1	353
Unskilled manual labour	6.5	3.0	97.5	4.08	CPSU 3.7 / Koms. 10.1 / neither 86.2	35.1	39.2	14.5	115

* Percentage of persons who participated (in each group). Terms undefined.

Source:

O. I. Shkaratan, *Voprosy filosofii*, No. 1, 1967, p. 37.

skills. We shall now take two other aspects of education which are of manageable dimensions. The first is how it affects the worker's attitude to his job, and the second is the manner in which it influences his use of time.

The first problem was examined in some detail by the Leningrad scholar A. A. Kissel on the basis of data which was also used in the Yadov–Zdravomyslov analysis.[26]

Kissel's work as published suffered from certain imperfections, principally his failure to disengage education properly from factors like age, sex, and social background, which may have been just as important. Nevertheless, he does come up with some apparently interesting results. He showed that people with more general education did indeed have a more altruistic and conscientious attitude towards labour, which was doubtless rather reassuring for the state ideologues (Table 43). Nearly thirty per cent of the least educated thought that their pay packet was 'the main thing', while only just under sixteen per cent of them held the 'social significance of labour' to be of primary importance. Of the workers with ten or eleven years of general education behind them only 7 per cent put money first, and 25 per cent apparently took the extreme altruistic view. Among people with middle special or higher education the result was even better (though these people should be thought of as being in the intelligentsia). This rather rosy picture was unfortunately spoilt by the fact that at least sixty per cent of the people in every group still had their wage packet very much in mind.

Kissel showed, in another set of figures, that the better-educated workers were involved in 'social activities' more often than the others. The weakness of his argument here, however, is that this might be more easily explicable by age differences: after all, workers with a full general education would certainly be amongst the youngest.[27]

The Yadov–Zdravomyslov study revealed what was described

26. A. A. Kissel, 'Uroven obrazovania rabochego i otnoshenie k trudu', in *Trud i lichnost*. Yadov and Zdravomyslov also cover this material in *Chelovek i ego rabota*, p. 267, but from a broader perspective. Here we shall draw on both.

27. The meaning of the term 'social activities' and associated problems are dealt with in Chapter 8.

TABLE 43. *Workers' Understanding of the Social Significance of Labour by Educational Level*

Education	1		2		3		4		Total No.
	No.	%	No.	%	No.	%	No.	%	
Up to 4 classes	28	29.7	31	32.9	20	21.5	15	15.9	94
5–6 classes	109	26.2	138	33.2	101	24.3	68	16.3	416
7–9 classes	220	14.6	471	31.4	442	29.5	367	24.5	1500
10–11 classes	39	7.0	149	26.6	232	41.4	140	25.0	560
Middle special & incomplete higher	3	3.2	30	31.6	35	36.8	27	28.4	95
Averages	399	15.0	819	30.7	830	31.1	617	23.2	2665

Columns

% of workers who believe that:

1. Any work is good if it pays well.
2. The wage is the main thing but the significance of work is also important.
3. The significance of work is the main thing but the wage is also important.
4. Work is good when it allows you to be of use (to society) and when it makes you feel needed.

The percentages add horizontally.

Source:

A. A. Kissel, op. cit., p. 123.

as a 'rather serious social problem' in the correlation of satisfaction and occupation. Kissel's analysis indicated that in the lower occupation groups the more educated people tended to be less satisfied with their jobs than those with less education.[28] Yadov and Zdravomyslov showed that this held good for the 'objective' indices of attitude to work as well; in other words, more education

28. Kissel, op. cit., p. 122; Yadov and Zdravomyslov, op. cit., p. 279. The writers give the average number of classes of general schooling attained by workers who were satisfied and dissatisfied, and who worked efficiently or inefficiently in each occupation group. One cannot help feeling that this particular phenomenon could have been illustrated much more vividly.

did not make them perform better. This implied that, given the existing occupation structure, more general education was not really called for, since it only made the people who were stuck in low-grade jobs more dissatisfied. The solutions which Yadov and Zdravomyslov proposed were that workers should be progressively moved into more demanding work in a planned and orderly manner; that everybody should have a broader and more comprehensive training; that employment and placement services should be improved; and that there should be a more liberal attitude on the part of the authorities towards floating labour. Any cut-back on general education would, they thought, be socially unjustifiable. The measures against 'loafers' which were introduced by the Brezhnev leadership in the autumn of 1969 and spring of 1970 ran directly counter to such enlightened attitudes.

From the point of view of workers' attitudes to their jobs, then, the spread of general education seems to be a mixed blessing.

Education may have many subtle effects on a person's way of life outside his place of work. V. D. Patrushev is well known in the USSR for his studies of time-use, and a book he wrote recently together with a number of other sociologists attempts an analysis of this relationship.[29] The data used was from the surveys conducted in Krasnoyarsk Krai in 1959 and 1963. The breakdown of time-uses shown in Table 44 was compiled from results collected in 1959, apparently on the basis of a sample of 1,000 time budgets.[30]

The Table illustrates firstly important differences between the sexes. We have already seen that women at all levels of income devote very much more time than men to domestic activities. They also have less leisure. Patrushev's figures suggest that the more educated women have roughly the same sort of pattern as the *richer* women, at least in so far as they, too, spend less time on

29. V. D. Patrushev, *Vremya kak ekonomicheskaya kategoria*, Moscow, 1966.

30. Some details on the first Krasnoyarsk survey are to be found in V. I. Bolgov, *Vnerabochee vremya i uroven zhizni trudyashichikhsya*, Novosibirsk, 1964, p. 7. Patrushev is not specific about the sample. The object was to determine how the shortening of working hours affected the way people used their non-working time, though this particular aspect is not directly relevant to our study of the class structure.

domesticities and more looking after their children. The male side of the table does not lend itself to easy interpretation, except to show the obvious fall-off of involvement in work on private plots amongst the more educated.

TABLE 44. *Time Spent on Domestic Labour and Free Time amongst Workers by Educational Level (in Hours, over Six Working Days)*

	Educational level						
	Men				Women		
Time devoted to:	Under 4 classes	5–9 classes	Middle special & incomplete higher	Higher	Under 4 classes	5–9 classes	Middle special & incomplete higher
Domestic labour including:	14.8	13.2	11.1	10.9	32.4	26.7	23.6
Shopping	1.8	2.1	2.6	1.5	4.7	4.0	3.7
Cooking	1.4	1.6	1.7	1.2	10.2	8.2	6.5
Cleaning	2.4	1.7	1.2	3.3	4.2	3.7	3.3
Care of clothing	0.6	0.5	0.8	0.6	4.4	3.9	3.4
Care of children	2.8	2.9	1.9	2.7	4.0	3.4	4.2
Knitting, sewing, repairs	1.2	1.0	0.4	1.6	2.3	2.5	1.4
Work in garden plot	4.6	3.4	2.5	—	2.6	1.0	1.1
Free time including:	17.1	20.1	24.0	23.4	8.7	14.5	18.7
Study	1.2	4.0	6.4	6.8	0.5	3.0	7.1
Self-education	4.4	5.7	6.3	5.8	1.3	3.0	3.8
Social work	0.3	0.1	0.3	0.7	0.2	0.2	0.7
Amusement	8.2	7.5	8.3	5.1	4.7	6.1	5.8
P.T. and Sport	0.6	0.8	0.8	3.3		0.1	0.3
Amateur hobbies	0.2	0.2	0.2	—	0.1	0.1	0.2
Rest	1.0	0.9	0.7	0.3	0.7	1.1	0.3
Other	1.2	0.9	1.0	1.4	1.2	0.9	0.5

Source:
V. D. Patrushev, op. cit., p. 112.

Both men and women with a better educational background seem to study more – education being in this sense self-productive. They read more, and indulge in 'social activities' more often. People in the top educational bracket are shown to be far keener on sport. A study of leisure habits in Erevan revealed similar traits, and a very limited questionnaire conducted in one

of the workshops of the Urals Machine-building Factory provided yet more supporting evidence.[31] It would be pleasant if we
could generalize on these figures, and this seems, at first sight,
entirely possible. It would not, however, be fair to ignore facts
which do not fit this pattern. One study conducted in Leningrad
flatly contradicted some of these findings, and showed that
interest in part-time study and sport tended to *fall* amongst the
better-educated workers, while reading habits varied tremen-
dously and did not tie in at all well with schooling. All that can
be said is that on the present balance of evidence this is best
regarded as an unexplained discrepancy.

Conclusions are not easily arrived at when so much is unknown
and so much has to be inferred. But a few general observations
are perhaps in order. If we expected to find big differences of
income, material wellbeing, skill, education, cultural interest,
and outlook in the Soviet 'working class' we have not been
disappointed; some of these differences we have even been able
to measure. If we presumed that there would be a strong element
of polarization in the distribution of social assets – as in most
industrialized societies – then our survey has provided ample
illustration of the fact. The Soviet working class is clearly strati-
fied into various layers; a higher or lower level of income tends
to go with more or less skill, education, material wellbeing, etc.
There are sets of attitudes and patterns of time-use which
correspond with these gradations to an interesting degree.

So marked a degree of differentiation has, of course, rather far-
reaching implications. It does not merely disprove the simplistic

31. Some of these patterns are discussed in G. S. Petrosyan, *Vnerabochee
vremya trudyashchikhsya v SSSR*, Moscow, 1965, p. 112 ff. (with references
to a Sverdlovsk study), while the Urals Machine-building Factory survey is
dealt with in M. T. Yovchuk, and others, *Pod'em kulturno-tekhnicheskogo
urovnya sovetskogo rabochego klassa*, Moscow, 1961, p. 264. This study was
conducted in 1960. A slightly different version of the free-time section of the
Patrushev table is to be found in V. I. Bolgov, op. cit., Novosibirsk, 1964,
p. 116. Bolgov here refers to a sample of 1,200 time budgets. An analysis of
the minor discrepancies between these findings would be long and rather
tedious, so we have decided to spare ourselves and the reader. For a source in
English see F. G. Durham, *Use of Free Time by Young People in Soviet Society*,
Centre for International Studies, Massachusetts Institute of Technology,
mimeograph, January 1966.

theories of social development which are still part and parcel of
the official ideology. Indeed, disproof is hardly needed. It
implies the existence of a set of stresses and strains in Soviet
society to which, perhaps, insufficient attention has been paid in
the past. Soviet ideologists admit that 'non-antagonistic' contradictions are possible in a socialist society. In practical terms the
distinction between 'antagonistic' and 'non-antagonistic' does
not seem to mean very much, though we would not wish to
imply that we think a 'revolutionary situation' is at hand.

The most and least privileged groups in Soviet urban society
play very different roles in the life of their country. Perhaps inevitably, people at the top of the social hierarchy are the most
socially active, in the sense that they have more responsible jobs,
spend more, live better, have more advanced cultural tastes.
Apart even from their relationship to political power (which we
shall touch on in Chapter 8) they seem to embody the virtues of
a 'progressive' working class, as envisaged in the state ideology.
The least privileged workers are much more passive and apathetic, more concerned with earning their daily bread, and more
negative in their outlook. Indeed, it would probably not be unfair to think of the top layer of the working class as a latter-day
Soviet version of Lenin's 'pro-capitalist' workers, that is, those
who benefited most from the existing order, and were most
anxious to sustain it.

THE INTELLIGENTSIA – SIZE AND DEFINITION

No survey of Soviet social structure would be complete without
special reference to the intelligentsia. We have, it is true, referred
to this group frequently in our analysis of income differentials
and the occupation structure, but we have not attempted to
define it. This is a good point to look into this question, since
membership of the intelligentsia is mainly a matter of educational achievement.

The intelligentsia occupies a very special place in Soviet
society. *Intelligenty* usually hold key positions in the state
administration, and membership of the intelligentsia confers
considerable social prestige. Its existence is essential to the
system of social mobility. The intelligentsia is not by any means

confined to the towns: but as the rural contingent is very small and would probably regard itself as part of a single Soviet intelligentsia anyway, we shall make our generalizations about the whole group here. Some of the traits specific to the rural intelligentsia will emerge in Chapter 6.

The problem of definition is also a problem of size. Lenin described the intelligentsia in May 1904 as a group including 'not only littérateurs, but all educated people, representatives of the free professions in general, representatives of mental labour (brain workers, as the English say) as distinct from representatives of physical labour'. This definition seems to lay main emphasis on educational achievement and a superior position in the occupational hierarchy: but like so many others it has been subject to very elastic interpretation in the Soviet Union. The interpretations in vogue by the late sixties were of two basic types. The first, proposed by predominantly orthodox-minded scholars or party officials, attempted to make the term very wide and voluminous. This was partly in response to the official theory of social development which requires the intelligentsia to expand and merge with the working class or peasantry, as one factor in the abolition of the old distinction between mental and physical labour. The other argument for a broad definition is that a large intelligentsia may be regarded as a tribute to party policies.

This rather absurd approach may be traced back several decades, at least to Molotov's speech on the third Five-Year Plan in 1939.[32] It entails including in the intelligentsia all workers of 'predominantly mental labour', that is, all employees (or *sluzhashchie*, as they are called in Russian) from highly skilled specialists down to the humble clerks, cleaners and watchmen. It still crops up in statistical handbooks, and was specifically mentioned in the 1959 census returns. A. K. Kurylev and I. Ya. Kopylov, two sociologists who should have known better, mentioned it in a booklet on social relations.[33] By 1968 there were some 28.8 million persons, or about 35 per cent of the total labour force, doing 'predominantly mental' work in the USSR.

---

32. A point made by B. Meissner in *Sowjet-gesellschaft im Wandel*, W. Kohlhammer Verlag, 1966, p. 97.

33. *Formirovanie kommunisticheskikh obshchestvennykh otnoshenii*, Moscow, 1965.

Since employees have families, albeit small ones, this would also mean that up to a third of the entire population would have to be included in the social group.

Happily, most Soviet sociologists now adopt narrower and more realistic definitions. V. S. Semenov, perhaps the most prominent analyst of social structure in the Soviet Union at present, takes this line. In an essay published in 1966 he defined the intelligentsia as persons of 'mental, *intellectual* labour',[34] thus drawing a distinction between *intelligenty* proper and 'mental' workers who performed the less demanding service functions. The 1959 census returns, on which he based his analysis, listed 20.4 million persons as engaged in predominantly mental labour. Semenov held that only 12.7 million of these should be included in the intelligentsia proper, the rest being merely low-grade service personnel. The corresponding figures for 1968 would have been about 19 and 9.5 million.

Semenov went on to subdivide the intelligentsia of 1959, as he defined it, into three distinct groups. The first of these was particularly interesting. It contained some 2.4 million 'responsible persons in state and economic administration and social organizations' who were listed as follows:

Managers (*rukovoditeli*) of state administrative organs and public organizations and their subsidiary departments	392,131
Managers of enterprises and their subsidiary departments	955,224
Financial control workers and accountants	963,229
Juridical personnel	78,711
Total	2,389,295

This rather innocent-seeming body is, in fact, the uppermost tip of the Soviet labour force; here we have the people who, in their working hours, really control the Soviet Union. Semenov's

34. See F. V. Konstantinov (ed.), *Stroitelstvo kommunizma i razvitie obshchestvennykh otnoshenii*, Moscow, chapter 4, p. 166. The italics above are ours.

grouping is about as near as Soviet sociologists have come to defining publicly an élite in their society.

The second group comprised the technological and economic personnel (engineers and technicians who were not senior enough to be included in the first group), agricultural specialists, planners, and economists. They numbered just under five million. The last group of some 5.3 million persons contained the 'scientific and cultural' intelligentsia: these were research workers, medical personnel, teachers, artists and writers, in other words, the creative sector of society.[35]

M. N. Rutkevich, who is one of the most respected Soviet sociologists, and is perhaps less rigid in his views than Semenov, has preferred to use a more rigorous definition still. He regards the intelligentsia as a 'social group or stratum composed of persons who are professionally engaged in highly qualified mental labour which requires middle special or higher education'.[36] This is a more explicit definition than Semenov's and emphasizes the professional aspect. It does, however, leave a loophole in that persons who occupy intelligentsia-type positions without formal training may be included. This is important because perhaps a third of all professional posts are still occupied by such people.[37] M. N. Rutkevich had claimed in an earlier article that the 1959 census figures for mental workers contained an intelligentsia of roughly 10 million, a group of 8 million 'employees', and another of 2 million workers who shouldn't

35. We have taken Semenov's scheme since it represents a fairly conservative, though defensible point of view. Semenov himself claimed that Marx's three-part breakdown of the intelligentsia lay at the base of it (though Marx was thinking in terms of a capitalist society). He quoted the Marxist definitions as follows: (*a*) persons of intellectual labour who participate directly in the productive process, (*b*) persons creating, by their mental labour, goods which may be sold (like books and pictures), (*c*) persons whose creation is inseparable from the act of creating, e.g. doctors, teachers, orators. The statistical handbook for 1958 contained a categorization of the Soviet intelligentsia (numbered at 15.4 million) which, though cruder, is not dissimilar from Semenov's. (*Narodnoe khozyaistvo SSSR v 1958*, p. 672.)

36. Article in *Nauchnye doklady vysshei shkoly, Filosofskie nauki*, No. 4, 1968, p. 22.

37. *Trud v SSSR*, p. 297. The Soviet term is *praktiki*. The figure varied, for example, from 22 per cent for directors to 43 per cent for technicians in industry.

have been listed in that category at all.[38] The 1968 equivalent of Rutkevich's intelligentsia would therefore have been in the region of 17 million.

A perusal of the Soviet sociological literature of the last few years reveals other suggestions along these lines. Other authors, departing from the same premises as Semenov and Rutkevich, have modified the mixture of social groups in the intelligentsia to suit their own tastes, and ended up with somewhat larger or smaller numbers.[39] Fortunately, there is no pressing need for us to take all viewpoints into account here. We may conclude our summary with mention of a view which appears to have the seal of Party approval for practical, if not for propaganda, purposes.

The *Theses* which were issued by the Party to mark the fiftieth anniversary of the October Revolution contained no definition of the intelligentsia as such, but they did strongly imply that it consisted of persons with higher or middle special education who were employed in the economy. In 1959 these numbered 8.7 million, and in 1968 14.9 million, or about 13 per cent of the total labour force.

Most Western observers, of course, would regard all these propositions with a certain scepticism; in most Western countries a degree from an institution of higher education or its equivalent is taken as the only badge of intellectual maturity. And many university teachers are very sceptical about *that*. But if we adopt this yardstick for the USSR, then we would conclude that there were just over six million *intelligenty* employed in the Soviet economy in the autumn of 1968. In addition about 400,000 persons had degrees, but were not employed: most of these were presumably housewives and pensioners.[40] We can, of course, only guess at the size of the VUZ-trained intelligentsia as a social group, since we know little about dependants, and we cannot adequately treat the problem of families where one working

38. G. V. Osipov (ed.), *Sotsiologia v SSSR*, Moscow, Vol. 1, p. 393.

39. I. E. Vorozheikin, for example, reduced the 1959 figure by 2 million souls when he excluded all lower grade managers and financial and legal staff: see I. E. Vorozheikin, and others, *Sovetskaya intelligentsia*, Moscow, 1968, p. 330. E. L. Manevich, on the contrary, included certain categories of office workers and employees, and arrived at a total of $17\frac{1}{2}$ million, see E. L. Manevich, *Problemy obshchestvennogo truda v SSSR*, Moscow, 1966, p. 20.

40. *Narodnoe khozyaistvo SSSR v 1968*, pp. 34, 559.

member is an *intelligent* and others not. But it would probably be reasonable to think of the Soviet degree-holding intelligentsia with their families as numbering 15–20 million, or six to eight per cent of the population. Though considerably less than the Soviet authorities claim, and a long way behind American attainment, this is still a very creditable dimension.[41]

How far does the way of life of the Soviet intelligentsia differ from that of other groups in Soviet society? No explicit studies of this question seem to have been published, but a great deal of sociological data on other themes casts light on it, for the simple reason that the intelligentsia may often be identified with certain élite groups, through occupation and income. We have already noted that members of the intelligentsia have the best jobs and probably enjoy a better standard of living than any other social group. They often seem to work longer hours, but have fewer household duties and more leisure time at their disposal. They are more interested in studying and serious cultural pursuits.

They are, of course, also different in ways which find expression only in the unregistered comments of the people, or in literature; they are regarded as having a different standard of manners, and a more elevated way of life. Members of the intelligentsia possibly get drunk less often, and enjoy a feeling of community which sometimes evokes the hostility of outsiders. Perhaps the day will come when these factors, too, will come into the realm of sociological research.

The debate on how best to define the Soviet intelligentsia has, not surprisingly, been linked with the criticisms of the official concept of classes which we dealt with in Chapter 2. Recently many Soviet sociologists have attempted to redefine the relationship between the intelligentsia and the workers and peasants in a manner which is hardly compatible with the official class

41. Comparisons of this kind are difficult, but there is no doubt about American supremacy. In the USA in March 1959 7.9 per cent of the population aged twenty-five and over had completed four years of college, and this figure rose to 9.4 per cent four years later (*U.S. Digest of Educational Statistics*, Washington, 1966, p. 9). The figure for completed higher education among the same age groups in the USSR at the time of the 1959 Census was 3.2 per cent (*All-Union Census*, 1959, p. 74). By 1968 this figure was probably still less than 6 per cent. The comparability of standards is another problem, but they were probably not too disparate.

scheme. M. N. Rutkevich has discussed what he considered to be the main 'aberrations' in a number of articles, and we could do worse than conclude our own brief survey with his exposition of them.[42]

Rutkevich begins by demolishing three views of the intelligentsia which he thinks are totally unacceptable. The first of these equates the intelligentsia with all persons involved in 'predominantly mental labour', in the spirit of the old Molotov formula. The second narrows the term to cover only creative workers, that is, artists, research workers and scientists. This proposal was made by the Yugoslav sociologist Janičevic at a conference on social structure held in Prague in June 1963. It would have meant including in the Soviet intelligentsia only the third group in Semenov's scheme, or part of that group. Rutkevich thus avoided both extremes of size. The third suggestion which he rejects out of hand is that the intelligentsia should be taken to include just people of courteous bearing: this probably arose through a linguistic coincidence, insofar as the Russian adjective *intelligentny* may mean 'intelligent', 'of the intelligentsia', or, by popular association, 'well-mannered'.

He then turns to a detailed criticism of two groups of sociologists who attempt by different means to incorporate the intelligentsia partially or completely into the working class and the peasantry, thus denying it any separate existence. The Polish economist Z. Bauman expounded this view at the Prague conference and it was evidently accepted by a number of Soviet sociologists. Thus Rutkevich takes the Leningrader T. S. Batalina to task because she held that all non-peasant mental workers should be regarded as part of the working class. It could, of course, be argued that this view was in line with Lenin's definition of class, since all non-peasants in the USSR have the same relationship to the means of production. Rutkevich held that it was wrong to consider relationship to the means of production to be the only index of class. In like manner he reproached A. P. Kirsanov and Yu. V. Arutyunyan for merging the country-based intelligentsia with the peasantry (though this was hardly a fair assessment of

42. Articles in *Filosofskie Nauki*, No. 4, 1966, *Sotsiologia v SSSR*, Moscow, 1966, p. 393, and Ts. A. Stepanyan, V. S. Semenov, *Klassy, sotsialnye sloi i gruppy v SSSR*, Moscow, 1968, p. 136.

their published views). Such solutions were also undesirable in that they implied the splitting of the intelligentsia into urban and rural components.

The second group of sociologists whose view Rutkevich found unacceptable contained people like K. P. Buslov and O. I. Shkaratan. They had suggested that only administrators, teachers, doctors, artists, etc. should be included in the intelligentsia: all technical personnel (Semenov's second group) should go into the working class. A valid distinction could indeed be made, Rutkevich argued, between productive and 'service' functions, but it was not as important as the occupational and educational characteristics which distinguished the intelligentsia as he defined it from the rest of society. Rutkevich was thus concerned, in all his arguments, to preserve the concept of the intelligentsia as a cohesive entity – which is probably justified by the facts of social life.

EMPLOYEES AND SERVICE WORKERS

The 'employees' in the sense of low-grade non-manual workers have received singularly little attention from Soviet sociologists. V. S. Semenov, in his analysis of the 1959 census returns, considered them to consist of the following groups:

Office workers and accounts clerks	3,439,636
Transport employees (conductors, guards)	334,752
Persons employed in communications	476,360
Persons employed in trade and catering	1,882,162
Persons employed in communal amenities, public services	2,283,104
Total	8,416,014

but this scheme is not accepted by everyone. A. M. Shunkov, who wrote a small book about employees in the mid sixties, took the term to mean junior office workers, or persons who did some kind of paper-work or accounting, regardless of the actual conditions of labour.[43] He indicated, moreover, that there were

43. A. M. Shunkov, *Organizatsia truda sluzhashchikh*, Moscow, 1965, p. 10.

considerable anomalies and variations in day-to-day usage. Legal consultants and statisticians who would normally be highly trained are often considered as 'employees' rather than 'specialists': in institutions and organizations where there are no highly trained technical personnel even the senior administrators put themselves in the 'employee' category for statistical purposes.

There is no doubt that the employees usually come towards the bottom of the income hierarchy, as we have noted. Shunkov gave a list of typical salary rates which showed that all except the senior employees were earning well below 75 roubles a month at the time.[44] We would expect a good proportion of them to be in the urban poor, and have the same style of life.[45]

As to the future of employees in a communist society, M. N. Rutkevich suggested that as low-grade toilers they would gradually disappear.[46] Some of them would be transubstantiated into workers handling automatic equipment, some of them would move into various other jobs, and yet others would become fully-fledged specialists. 'This progressive development', wrote Rutkevich, 'is intimately bound up with the use, for administrative purposes, of ever more complicated technology, from dictaphones and copying apparatus to cybernetic machines.' The use of these contraptions in the West has not, however, had this effect: and in view of the Soviet tendency to develop bureaucracies, Rutkevich's forecast seems to be a very long-term one indeed.

44. ibid., p. 96.
45. Shunkov gives some details of a 1964 time-use study conducted amongst them, but the sample was too small to make the results very convincing; ibid., p. 54 ff.
46. *Nauchnye doklady vysshei shkoly, Filosofskie nauki*, 1966, No. 4, p. 27.

6

Collective Farm Society

SOCIAL stratification in the Soviet village has traditionally been a subject of debate in the Soviet Union. The Bolshevik leaders were interested in the problem in the first decades of their rule both because the peasantry made up the overwhelming mass of the population, and because they regarded the 'correct' development of social relations in the village as essential for the success of their rule. We have already mentioned that studies of peasant income differentials were vigorously promoted in the twenties. Although, to quote one authority, 'in the end no valid and authoritative study of this intractable problem was ever produced', the Party Leaders' interpretations of the results obtained had a profound influence on the disputes among them and the course of Party policy.[1]

It is tempting to return to these debates, and sift the findings on which they were based. But that is a task for historians. Of more direct interest to us are the facts which have been revealed in recent years by the 1959 All-Union Census, the statistical handbooks and a few Soviet scholars who have been allowed to conduct investigations in approved localities and publish some of the results.

The problem of analysis now, however, assumes a rather different form. The direction of research, and the information provided, bears not so much on the social stratification of the peasantry, understood in the sense of the unskilled men of the soil, as on the collective farm as a community. The distinction is, of course, important. Although the collective farm is dominated in terms of numbers by the peasant, it contains several other important social groups, some of whom may not even be members. A few studies also cover non-collective farm rural society, which has its own structures and characteristics. We shall, however, in this chapter, take the peasant and the collective farm

1. M. Lewin, *Russian Peasants and Soviet Power*, London, 1968, p. 49.

community as our main point of reference, and bring in other groups only for purposes of comparison.

The Soviet collective farm community has been shrinking for many years: between 1953 and 1968 the peasant population in fact fell by about 23 million souls. Peasants are already a minority in rural areas. According to the 1968 estimates, the rural population of the USSR amounted to 105.7 million persons, while the peasants, as a social group, numbered 53.7 million. A few million of these, however, dwelt in urban areas (the figure in 1959 was 3.2 million), sometimes as a result of 'freak' administrative divisions, sometimes, no doubt, because market garden *kolkhozy* were enclosed in urban boundaries.

The decline in numbers, as we shall see in the next chapter, is explained mainly by the outflow of people from collective farms into state farms and urban or rural industry. Large numbers of peasants have found themselves transformed into state farm workers in their own villages as a result of economic reorganization.

The reduction in the size of the peasantry has been accompanied by an enlargement of the collective farm as an administrative unit. Between 1953 and 1968 the total number of farms, including a few which specialized in fishing and handicraft work, fell from 93,300 to 36,200, partly through amalgamation, partly through conversion into state farms. This means that the average number of peasant households per farm rose from 220 to 420, and a farm usually absorbed several settlements. In 1966, for example, just a half of collective farms in the USSR contained between two and five of them (Table 45).

The social structure of the collective farm, as it stands at present, has many unique features. The Soviet authorities have been constrained, in the interest of economic efficiency, to introduce into a mechanically inept peasant community groups of persons equipped with various kinds of high or middle grade technical skills. Many of these persons are not of rural origin at all. This means that collective farm society (like the collective farm itself) is really a product of administrative convenience. The government has had to take account of this in the occupation and income structures which it has encouraged: obviously, there could be no question of 'egalitarianism' on the level of the mass of unskilled peasants. Most Soviet sociologists recognize this and use the main occupation groups as a basis for their analysis. Education and social status in the collective farm seem to correlate closely with the other two indices. We, too, shall take occupation as our starting point.

TABLE 45. *Distribution of Collective Farms in the USSR by Number of Settlements (as % of total)*

	No. of settlements per farm				
Year*	1	2-5	6-10	11-15	15+
1961	16.7	46.1	20.4	7.4	9.4
1965	14.8	47.9	21.2	7.7	8.4
1966	15.4	49.5	20.3	7.2	7.6

*1 January. The definition of 'settlement', however, varied somewhat from one region to another.
Sources:
Narodnoe khozyaistvo SSSR, 1962, p. 340; *1964*, p. 398; *1965*, p. 412.

THE OCCUPATIONAL STRUCTURE OF THE FARM

The information available to us on the labour force of the collective farm is patchy, and there are many activities which go virtually uncharted. The main occupation groups are, however, recognized statistical entities, and we know a fair amount about them.

They are four in number. First there are the administrative personnel and specialists, next the so-called 'mechanizers', (or agricultural machinery operators), thirdly the poultry and livestock farmers or handlers, and fourthly the ordinary field workers. The last are essentially the rump of the old Russian peasantry; in statistical returns they are sometimes designated as 'field workers without any recognized speciality' and treated as a residue. The figures for these groups, as shown in the 1959 census and later sources, are reproduced in Table 46.

It would, of course, be wrong to imagine that the economic wellbeing of the collective farm community depends only on these four groups. Frequent reference is made in official and unofficial sources to a number of others without which Soviet agriculture would not be able to function at all. These include the builders (important because collective farms have to do most of their own construction work), minor administrative and service personnel, and a variety of rustic handymen. Two important groups of able-bodied peasants are conversely not involved in agriculture at all: some have jobs in local towns or state enterprises, so as to make a better contribution to the family budget, whilst others work in non-agricultural subsidiary enterprises

TABLE 46. *Distribution of Persons Engaged in Predominantly Physical Labour in Collective Farms, Circa 1959*

Type of occupation	Number	%
Brigadiers of all kinds, and like occupations	595,392	2.1
Mechanizers (excluding ordinary drivers)	1,600,996	5.5
Livestock handlers, milkmaids, shepherds, swineherds, poultry farmers, etc.	4,356,667	15.2
Other minor agricultural occupations, vine tenders, specialized gardeners, irrigation workers, etc.	183,502	0.6
Occupations without designation of speciality (i.e. unskilled field workers)	21,991,868	76.6
Total	28,728,425	100

Source:
1959 All-Union Census, p. 159, simplified. The order of occupations has, however, been retained. The statistical handbook *Narodnoe khozyaistvo SSSR v 1968* provides extra items of information for 1968 as follows: total labour force, average for year, public sector only, 18.1 million; senior administrators, specialists, brigadiers, etc. (1 April 1969) 531,849; mechanizers: 1,992,000 (pp. 446 ff.).

within the collective farm, producing (to quote a recent example) paper clips instead of potatoes. Finally we have to remember that all members of peasant families are drawn into farm work at harvest time: that the collective farm can in time of need call on the services of up to 12 million superannuated pensioners, and that up to the late sixties perhaps four or five million able-bodied peasants were engaged exclusively in tending private plots.[2]

These extra magnitudes are alarming, but we shall proceed on

2. Figures from *Narodnoe khozyaistvo SSSR v 1968*, pp. 446, 604.

the reasonable assumption that they do not invalidate the basic four-tier occupation structure shown in Table 46. We are probably justified in regarding the social groups which correspond with the main occupations as the main pillars of collective farm society, and the relationships between them as being the stuff of any sociological analysis thereof. At least, this must be so until sources of information improve.[3]

The 'top people' in the collective farm are the chairman, vice-chairman (or chairmen), accountant, and highly skilled specialists – veterinary surgeons, botanists and agricultural engineers. They are often, as we shall see in Chapter 10, of non-peasant, or even urban origin. Soviet statisticians usually include in this group brigade leaders and the managers of cattle and poultry farms, though these are mostly without extended training and may have been merely promoted from among the more able peasants. In April 1969 the whole group numbered 531,849, or about three per cent of the average annual labour force working in the *kolkhoz* public sector. Of these 326,000 or 1.9 per cent were specialists with higher or middle special education.

The authorities have long been desperately anxious to increase the numbers of specialists. Khrushchev devoted particular attention to it in his first major post-Stalin speech on agriculture in September 1953. The presence of specialists on the farm is indeed vital if Soviet agricultural performance is to be improved. But, as we shall see in other chapters, there is considerable difficulty in getting them to stay. Despite the authorities' pro-

3. It is important to bear in mind that much of the data relating to the collective farm labour force is very provisional or approximate in character, partly because of the seasonal nature of agriculture, and partly as a result of the organization of work. To take but two examples: the number of persons participating in work in the public sector in 1959, when weather conditions were reasonably normal, varied from 18.0 million in January to 30.7 million in July. Only a small proportion of the harvesting labour force came from outside (*Selskoe khozyaistvo SSSR*, Moscow, 1960, p. 460). The 1959 census listed 24.2 million persons as employed in agriculture without special skills, but added in a footnote 'apart from members of their families engaged in work on the private plots, who numbered 9.8 million'. (By 1968, as we have noted, there was probably a marked fall in this figure, but this may not be enough to explain the discrepancy.) Faced with fluctuations such as these, we can only crave the reader's extreme indulgence. When possible we have used published annual averages.

claimed intentions, the specialist core is increasing much more slowly than anticipated.

The so-called service personnel – clerks, store-keepers, char-women, watchmen, chauffeurs, postmen, etc. – are sometimes grouped with the administrative and technical categories. Most of these occupations are undemanding and require very little training. An exception may be jobs connected with 'cultural activities', which are occasionally included in this group. It is difficult to know how many of them there are; one source said they made up 2.5 per cent of the *kolkhoz* labour force in 1962.[4] In 1969 administrative and service personnel of all kinds were said to comprise 7 per cent of the total collective farm labour force, which would bring the figure for service personnel alone up to about 4 per cent, or 800,000.[5]

Despite the outflow of specialists, the administrative staff as a whole has tended to grow. Complaints about this have been frequent for many years, and many instances of such staff making up 10 or 12 per cent of the labour force have been quoted.[6] Given the unpopularity of work in agriculture this is quite understandable. An office or service job would appeal to many (especially young) people, who did not want to be mere peasants, but could not easily leave the farm. The authorities have tried to control this evil, albeit not very successfully, by stipulating that only a small percentage of the farm income should be set aside for these salaries.

The next major group in our scheme is composed of the mechanizers, that is tractor drivers, mechanics, combine harvest operators, and ordinary drivers. The last are sometimes omitted from this group by outside observers, as driving requires con-siderably less skill than the handling of agricultural machinery. In 1969 there were just under 2 million mechanizers, including 1,429,000 tractor drivers and combine harvest operators, and 563,000 drivers. Altogether they must have made up about 11 per cent of the *kolkhoz* labour force.[7]

4. E. S. Karnaukhov and M. I. Kozlov, *Puti povyshenia proizvoditelnosti truda v selskom khozyaistve*, Moscow, 1964, p. 76.

5. V. Danilov, *Ekonomicheskie Nauki*, No. 3, 1969.

6. I. I. Dmitrashko, *Vnutrikolkhozyne ekonomicheskie otnoshenia*, Moscow, 1966, p. 167.

7. *Narodnoe khozyaistvo SSSR v 1968*, p. 454.

If the specialists are the mental élite of the Soviet collective farm, the mechanizers are the skilled élite of the manual labour groups. They were transferred to the *kolkhozy* only in March 1958, when the Machine and Tractor Stations, which formerly controlled agricultural implements, were reduced to the status of repair centres. The mechanizers' work, wrote T. I. Zaslavskaya, a specialist on social problems in the village,

has characteristics which basically distinguish it from other types of *kolkhoz* labour. Firstly, it presupposes significantly more skill. Tractor drivers' training in agricultural mechanization schools lasts one or two years. This training permits mechanizers to transfer to industrial employment comparatively easily . . . There are, however, drawbacks: work on a tractor demands a lot of physical strength. The fierce vibration often causes professional ailments . . . During the basic agricultural campaigns mechanizers work from dawn to dusk, and spend the night in covered lorries at the work-brigade post. Long periods away from home and family make their work burdensome.[8]

In these few sentences Zaslavskaya has mentioned the great dilemma which faces most mechanizers, and which is thwarting the Soviet authorities in their efforts to promote the growth of this group inside the collective farm. On the one hand young male peasants are attracted by the prospect of learning a skill and doing more responsible work which is better paid. But once they have become mechanizers they find that they can earn more for less effort outside the collective farm and outside the agricultural sector altogether. This is part of the general problem of the drift from the land, and it explains why the group has been static in size for nearly a decade.

Next in level of skill come the builders. We have in view here builders who are actually members of the collective farms, and not workers employed on construction sites in rural areas. Collective farm builders were not listed separately in the 1959 census, and no recent figure seems to be available for them; but in 1962 they numbered just under half a million and made up 1.6 per cent of the collective farm labour force.[9]

The number of peasants who are engaged in non-agricultural

8. T. I. Zaslavskaya, *Raspredelenie po trudu v kolkhozakh*, Moscow, 1966, p. 207.
9. E. S. Karnaukhov, op. cit., p. 76.

pursuits within the farm has never, to our knowledge, been specifically divulged. Some of the statistical handbooks do, however, draw a distinction between members of the collective farm who are 'employed in agricultural work in the public sector', and those who are merely 'employed in the public sector'. The gap between the two in 1967 was 1.7 million, or 12 per cent of the average annual labour force; this then, may have included, apart from some administrative and service personnel, the builders, and all 'non-agricultural' peasants. As to the peasants employed outside the farm, two Soviet economists, V. Ya. Churakov and L. I. Suvorova, evidently using unpublished figures from the *kolkhoz* annual returns, stated in 1965 that 8 per cent of the able-bodied collective farm labour force were employed in state enterprises or were studying at full-time institutions.[10]

Cattle rearing, dairying, and poultry farming, etc., are usually regarded as women's work in the village. In 1959 just over 4 million persons, or 14 per cent of the *kolkhoz* labour force, were engaged in it. This work, wrote Zaslavskaya,

is mostly more skilled and complicated than the average job in the field. It is organized in strict accordance with a daily timetable, demands veterinary knowledge and skills, a facility for handling beasts, equipment, machinery. Physically, in most branches of stock rearing, it is harder than field work. A long working day is characteristic of it, and it often has to be done far from the peasant's place of residence, or any cultural or communal amenities. Output is paid at piece-rates . . . It is not seasonal in character.[11]

In the course of her discussion of labour mobility Zaslavskaya indicated that whereas the field worker had only 656 roubles' worth of equipment at his disposal, the livestock breeder had 2,860 roubles' worth. This reflected a higher degree of mechanization and the fact that animals have to be provided with buildings. Much of the work in this sector is therefore under cover.

The simple unskilled peasants who work in the fields make up the remaining two thirds of the collective farm labour force. It is they who bear the main brunt of feeding Soviet society. Their work is laborious, boring and usually ill paid.

10. *Ispolzovanie trudovykh resursov v kolkhozakh i sovkhozakh*, Moscow, 1967, p. 23.
11. op. cit., p. 197.

They are undoubtedly the least understood social group in the collective farm. In the twenties the peasantry was commonly divided into four main categories – the *batraki*, who were in principle landless and hired themselves out; the poor peasantry, who generally had land but no animals; the middle peasantry who had both; and the kulaks who were rich enough to hire labour. The divisions, naturally, were not always clear and there were lively arguments about them. Since the social surveys available at the time of writing do not reveal much about distinctions within the group of unskilled field-workers as such we cannot imitate that practice. We shall attempt to do no more in this chapter than indicate the extent of the fluctuations in well-being between the richest and the poorest of them, and illustrate some of their common social characteristics.

The occupations in the collective farm, like those in other sectors of the economy, vary considerably in prestige and attractiveness. This is perhaps a good point to comment on this factor. The most useful analysis which has come to our notice was done by T. I. Zaslavskaya on the basis of a survey of some 1,600 young people in two collective and two state farms of the Novosibirsk *oblast* in 1966. They were asked certain questions about their own jobs, and their answers were tabulated on a five-point

TABLE 47. *Assessments of Collective Farm Occupations*

	Specialists	Drivers	Brigadiers	Tractor drivers	Milk-maids	Peasants
Overall assessment of labour	4.25	4.0	3.6	3.58	3.51	2.9
Interest in content of labour	4.00	3.85	3.8	3.37	3.16	2.67
Estimated prestige of labour	3.5	3.39	3.6	3.45	3.38	2.9

Source:
T. I. Zaslavskaya, *Trudovye resursy sela*, p. 230. 1600 young people, aged 16–30 years, of 2 state farms and 2 collective farms in Novosibirsk *oblast*. (Assessments are measured on a 5-point scale.)

scale. In Table 47 we have singled out those indices which seem to be most revealing, namely their overall assessment of their work, the extent to which it interested them, and their own evaluation of its prestige.

Results for three indices are remarkably close, and accord with the distribution of skills. Specialists are at the top of the scale, and unskilled peasants at the bottom. The only occupation people seemed uncertain about was that of an ordinary driver, which earned a low prestige rating but a high general assessment. This may have been because the shortage of transport in the Soviet village can give anyone who has access to a vehicle welcome opportunities for travel to towns and earning money on the side.

THE INCOME HIERARCHY IN THE COLLECTIVE FARM

Although no comprehensive wage or income figures for the collective farm seem to have been assembled, there is no doubt that there is usually a set of differentials which matches the occupational structure outlined above. The effect of income from the private plot is difficult to judge, but it probably tends to help the poorest relatively more. We shall take the basic income from the public sector of each group in turn, beginning at the top: then we shall comment briefly on the probable effects of the private sector.

The best-paid man in the *kolkhoz* is usually the chairman. His salary under existing arrangements depends in the first instance on where the local soviet has placed him on the republican salary scale (the current RSFSR version of which was approved by the Council of Ministers in 1966). This decision depends in turn on the size and output of his farm: there is a ceiling of 300 roubles a month for large enterprises, and a floor of 80 roubles a month for small ones. There is, however, a system of bonuses which may increase his basic rate by up to 50 per cent.

We have no means of knowing what the average bonus stands at, or, indeed, how the country's 36,000 or so chairmen are distributed on the republican scales. The probability is that most of them are in the middle. Thus in 1962, of the 619 chairmen in the Bashkir Autonomous Republic, over 400 earned between

146 and 181 roubles a month: the scale at that time probably extended from the equivalent of 100 to 250 new roubles.[12] Writers on this subject frequently complain that chairmen have a sinful tendency to inflate their own incomes, and there have even been cases of them thinking up their own bonuses. K. A. Shaibekov, for example, writing in 1963, quoted instances where chairmen's earnings had risen to fifteen or nineteen times those of the unskilled workers on their farms.[13]

Vice-chairmen are entitled to up to 90 per cent of the chairman's earnings, and other responsible administrators and specialists get from 60 to 90 per cent, in descending order of skill. These rates are recommended in all-union legislation.[14] In addition, all persons in this category may earn bonuses and get supplements of up to 15 per cent for long service. Eighty per cent of their salaries is paid monthly, and the remainder on the fulfilment of output plans. The formal income of the management of collective farms is not, incidentally, much below that of similar categories in the state farms.

The material benefits of responsibility do not, however, end with formal earnings. The chairman and his closest associates have considerable influence in the enterprise, and direct access to all the produce of the public sector in addition to that of their private plots. All this can be of great benefit to them, especially if they are not too scrupulous. In addition they have first call on amenities like transport, a telephone, and electric light, which may be scarce and can make a vast difference to one's standard of living in the countryside.

The service personnel are apparently amongst the lowest-paid people in the farm. In 1966, for example, the basic earnings varied from about 70 roubles a month for workers in cultural and educational institutions down to 40 roubles a month for watchmen and cleaners.[15] Sometimes much lower rates are

12. I. D. Laptiev, *Nakoplenie i potreblenie v kolkhozakh*, Moscow, 1967, p. 224.

13. K. A. Shaibekov, *Pravovye formy oplaty truda v kolkhozakh*, Moscow, 1963, p. 225. Other insights into this problem may be found in P. P. Pyatnitsky and others, *Denezhnaya oplata truda v kolkhozakh*, Moscow, 1960, p. 121.

14. Laptiev, op. cit., p. 228; K. A. Shaibekov, op. cit., p. 234.

15. M. M. Baranov, *Novye progressivnye formy oplaty truda v kolkhozakh*, Moscow, 1967.

recorded.[16] Yet it is not improbable that many of the more menial jobs were filled by old frail people who either lived with their families or could get extra sustenance from their private plots.

Unlike the administrative and service personnel, the main manual groups are all on piece-rates and, as we indicated in Chapter 2, draw an income in money and kind from several sources. Payment in kind is extremely difficult to measure and price, so that Soviet statisticians, always shy when it comes to

TABLES 48 and 49. *Distribution of Income from the Public Sector of Collective Farms by Occupation Group*

TABLE 48. *Amur* Oblast, 1965

Occupation	1 Average annual No. of persons	2 Man-days worked per annum	3 Average monthly income (roubles)
Brigadiers	286	307	134.00
Farm managers	151	324	126.90
Tractor drivers	4,062	254	87.78
Ordinary drivers	873	277	102.81
Milkmaids	1,444	320	100.17
Herdsmen	904	334	104.44
Calf-minders	773	322	91.15
Swineherds	615	326	97.20
Fieldworkers	7,698	176	39.06
Totals and averages	22,098*	250	81.27

These tables were originally compiled to show the relationship between the number of labour-days worked in the public sector and income.

*The sum of the figures in this column is 16,806. No explanation is provided for the discrepancy.

Source: M. F. Kovaleva, *Stimuly povyshenia effektivnosti selskokhozyaist-vennogo proizvodstva*, Moscow, 1968, p. 256.

16. V. A. Morozov (op. cit., p. 120) quotes one instance of a charwoman and watchman earning between ten and a half and eighteen roubles a month, a derisory sum even in a *kolkhoz*. Prompted, perhaps, by intelligent neighbours, they complained to the local Soviet that their earnings fell below those of the minimum statutory requirements for 'employees'. Technically, as collective farm members, they were not covered by those provisions, but Morozov does not tell us what decision was reached.

TABLE 49. *Stavropoloski Krai, 1961**

Occupation	1 No. of persons who worked in course of year	2 Man-days worked per annum	3 Average monthly income (roubles)
Tractor drivers & combine harvest drivers	2,887	222	68.0
Herdsmen (local)	2,491	312	81.9
Swineherds	708	302	77.9
Shepherds	1,254	298	68.5
Milkmaids	1,966	291	68.3
Calf-minders	529	287	64.2
Poultry farmers	853	276	57.0
Non-agric. workers and builders	3,235	247	56.5
Fieldworkers and persons engaged in auxiliary labour	33,871	121	21.5
Total	47,794	—	—

*25 collective farms only.
Source:
I. F. Suslov, op. cit., p. 174.

questions of personal income, have another reason for reticence.
The occasional pieces of information to find their way into print are thus of particular interest. In Tables 48 and 49 we reproduce two sets of figures compiled at *oblast* level, and relating, with the exception of one item, to incomes in the manual groups. We see from Table 48 that in the Amur *oblast* in 1965 brigadiers and farm managers received 127–134 roubles for work in the public sector, while the field workers at the bottom of the scale took home only 40 roubles. The livestock handlers earned between 91 and 104 roubles. The position of the mechanizer group was ambiguous, since the less skilled drivers earned more than the tractor drivers; this must have been due to a combination of local circumstances unknown to us. Earnings depended, of course, not only on tariff differentials, but also on the number of days worked. The unskilled peasants who had lower rates and

worse jobs had much less incentive to toil in the public sector: thus, while the livestock handlers notched up 320 to 334 days, the field workers averaged only 176. It seems probable that the mass of them had to choose between trying to get higher earnings through hard work with livestock, or relying on a minimum input of man-days in field work in the public sector, plus more attention to their own private plots.

We will leave the reader to draw his own conclusions on the not dissimilar income pattern in twenty-five collective farms of the Stavropol Krai in 1961. In this case a figure for non-agricultural workers and builders has been included. They come below the livestock handlers, but are much above the field workers and persons engaged in auxiliary labour. The differential between the top and bottom earnings of the manuals is nearly a factor of four: in the Amur *oblast* four years later it was just over two and a half. These examples are, of course, only offered as individual illustrations, but in fact they seem to be reasonably compatible with the income differentials published for mechanizers, livestock handlers and field workers in the RSFSR in 1964 (Table 50). In the poorer farms the average mechanizer earned 3.46 times as much as the field worker: in the richer farms the differential went down to 1:1.5, but the average for the whole of the republic was 1:2.14. The livestock handlers' incomes were between the two, but in all cases closer to the unskilled peasants.

TABLE 50. *Income Distribution. Ratios for Mechanizers, Livestock Handlers and Field Workers, RSFSR 1964**

Type of farm Occupation	Poorest (man-day payment −1.5 r.)	Middle range (man-day payment 2–3 r.)	Richest (man-day payment + 3 r.)	All farms
Fieldwork	100	100	100	100
Livestock handlers	157	108	—	127
Mechanizers	346	176	150	214

*Presumably without income from private plots.
Source:
Voprosy Ekonomiki, No. 3, 1966, p. 67.

The differentials between the top and bottom of the occupation hierarchy are probably somewhat dampened by the existence of the private sector. The private plot is, after all, one of the main reasons why unskilled peasants work so little in the public sector, and earn so little from it. As we noted in Chapter 3, the plot was by the mid sixties probably providing a third or more of the income of the average peasant. No proper analysis of the involvement of different social groups in this sector has, to our knowledge, been published by Soviet scholars, but two facts are obvious.

Firstly, the more privileged people in the farm do not have access to more land – except, perhaps, by abuse of their influence. The size of the plot has, by law, nothing whatever to do with the occupations of its users, provided they are employed in the public sector of the farm; the determining factor is the number of farm members in the given household who participate in the work of the public sector – allowance being made for pensioners, etc.

Secondly, there is the purely mathematical factor. If all plots of a standard size produce roughly the same amount, then the output of the plot of a poorer family will represent a much larger proportion of that family's income than would be the case in a richer household. Indeed, the evidence is precisely that poorer people put more time and effort into their plots, so they may get rather more out of them. We would suggest therefore that the levelling tendency is real, but hardly enough to alter seriously the overall alignment of incomes we have described. Our general conclusion must be that the income differentials in any given collective farm are very great indeed: and that since the farm is a fairly small unit this inequality must be very apparent to all members.

THE PROBLEM OF REGIONAL VARIATIONS

The data at our disposal have enabled us to construct a model of income distribution in the collective farm which allows a chairman to receive many times as much as a simple fieldworker.

The income of each of the occupation groups involved is, however, characterized by extreme regional variations, and we

TABLE 51. *Variations in Peasant Income by Union Republic*

Union republics listed in order of total individual peasant income, 1966 (% of average for USSR)		Union republics by peasant income from public sector only, 1966 (% of average for USSR
Estonia	191	217
Latvia	155	108
Lithuania	132	95
Kazakhstan	116	194
RSFSR	102	120
Georgia	100	21
Turkmenia	95	126
Ukraine	94	96
White Russia	94	66
Moldavia	86	74
Uzbekistan	79	76
Kirgizia	78	116
Armenia	76	32
Azerbaidzhan	68	36
Tadzhikistan	61	89

Source:
M. I. Sidorova, op. cit., pp. 161, 168.

cannot allow these to pass without mention.[17] Apart from geographical location, the proximity of a town or road (which will allow a farm, or the individual peasant, to dispose of produce in a *kolkhoz* market) may easily have a considerable effect on income. Indeed, some Soviet scholars consider that these variations

17. Peasant income, being closely related to weather conditions, government policy, etc., obviously shows considerable annual fluctuations. In addition, there are long-term trends, not always upwards. These ups and downs have been the subject of many studies. In general agricultural output improved steadily between 1953 and 1959, but in the decade which followed the increases in output barely kept pace with the rise in the population. Recorded improvements in the peasants' standard of living have owed not a little to increased payments for state purchases of farm produce, state subsidies, etc. We have reluctantly omitted a chronological treatment of changes in the income of the various occupation groups, since the scarcity of data would make it very speculative.

contribute substantially to the peasant's underprivileged status vis-à-vis the workers, whose wage rates are much more standardized. Even figures for such large areas as republics, which average hundreds of thousands, if not millions, of incomes, show great swings. The figures in Table 51, taken from M. I. Sidorova's book, are meant to illustrate this. In 1966 the total per capita income of the Estonian peasant household was more than three times that of the Tadzhik peasant household, and nearly twice the average for the whole country. The same source shows that if we leave out income from the private plot, the extreme range between republics – in this case Estonia and Georgia – went up to a factor of ten! The Georgian peasant's total income was near the national average, but his earnings from the public sector were only 21 per cent of it. If any proof were required, incidentally, that Georgia has retained the closest Soviet equivalent of uncollectivized agriculture, it is here. Armenia and Azerbaidzhan were not far behind. T. I. Zaslavskaya noted in a discussion of peasant income that in 1962 there was not a single union republic, nor, in the RSFSR, economic region, in which payment for a day's work varied by less than a factor of 4.5. In eleven unspecified economic regions and republics it was more than fifteen!

The extensive introduction of money payments in the collective farm in lieu of payment in kind has involved the use of piecework tariffs not unlike those operative in industry, with the more skilled members of the collective at the top. But it is doubtful whether this has reduced regional fluctuations significantly: in 1960 the ratio of the top and bottom grades in the Pskov *oblast* was 1:1.4, while in the Krasnodar Krai it was 1:5.0

Figures on differentials between the three occupation groups shown in Table 50 indicate that regional fluctuations must be greatest amongst unskilled peasants and least amongst mechanizers. The permitted fluctuations in rates of pay for administrative staff are, of course, specifically designed to meet the requirements of farms in different regions. The income differentials between occupations in any given farm must be affected by the general level of prosperity, but we have no data to hand on these intricate relationships.

Some Soviet observers state that the general improvement in peasant wellbeing over recent years has been accompanied by a tendency for regional and occupational differentials to get smaller. Thus T. I. Zaslavskaya claims a 'significant' narrowing of the between regions over the period 1954–62. A writer in the journal *Ekonomika selskovo khozyaistva* wrote that between 1965 and 1967 the salaries of *kolkhoz* chairmen rose on average by 8 per cent, but milkmaids, tractor drivers and field workers earned 14, 20 and 28 per cent more respectively.[18] State old-age pensions for the peasantry, introduced in the summer of 1964, helped the poorest section of collective farm society, and the improvements in the financial relationship between the State and the collective farms may also have encouraged this tendency.

At the same time it is hardly to be doubted that the majority of peasants in the lower layers of the occupation hierarchy are still very poor, both in absolute terms and in relation to everyone else in the Soviet village. Although no 'peasant poor' or contemporary *bednyak* element has been delineated, Soviet sociologists have shown themselves to be very much aware of the problem. T. I. Zaslavskaya, for example, has produced figures to show, albeit in a roundabout way, that in all the economic regions of the USSR in 1962 there was a big lag between actual peasant earnings per labour day and the rates enjoyed by the average state farm worker (which Zaslavskaya took as the 'social norm' for the given region), Table 52. The peasant income, measured thus, was between 8 and 52 per cent lower. The average for the country, she held, was 40 per cent. The table also provides another illustration of the great regional fluctuations in the payment of the working day.

There is not a great deal that can be said about educational achievement among occupation groups in the collective farm, apart from indicating the most common levels for each one.

About half of the administrative or managerial group have the advantage of higher and middle education; by April 1968 some 75 per cent of all collective farm chairmen had proper professional training, but the proportion fell rapidly in less responsible jobs. The mechanizers, who may be thought of as forming the next layer, must by definition have had the benefit of some

18. No. 1, 1969, p. 8.

TABLE 52. *Necessary* and Actual Differences in the Payment of a Working Day for Collective Farmers, by Economic Region, Early Sixties*

Economic Regions	Pay of a collective farmer's working day as a % of average for USSR		Actual level of payment for a working day as a % of the 'social norm' for the region
	Actual	Necessary	
Volga-Vyatsk	72	101	48
Central	81	102	52
North-West	81	101	53
South-West	77	91	57
Western Siberia	112	132	57
Urals	96	110	58
Central Black Earth	96	110	58
Eastern Siberia	118	129	61
Far East	158	156	68
Transcaucasia	91	87	70
South	99	94	71
Volga	132	123	72
Kazakhstan	116	108	72
Central Asia	123	92	90
Northern Caucasus	140	102	92

*'Necessary' is a translation of Zaslavskaya's term: it should be understood as what certain economists think desirable.
Source:
T. I. Zaslavskaya, *Raspredelenie po trudu v kolkhozakh*, Moscow, 1966, p. 80.

low-grade technical training. This need not, however, have been in a school – many were taught on the job. The lowest level of educational achievement is not surprisingly to be found among the mass of livestock handlers and fieldworkers: this explains the extremely low rates of schooling recorded for all *kolkhozniki* in the 1959 census. But here age is important; the younger people tend to be much better educated than their elders.

The general level of education on the farm is kept down by the steady outflow of young people. Figures available for the educational achievements of the rural 'workers' and 'employees' show that in 1959 they easily outdistanced the peasants, though they themselves lagged well behind the townsfolk (Table 53).

TABLE 53. *Educational Levels of the Rural Labour Force, circa 1959 (Persons of Both Sexes Who Have Employment, by Social Group, per 1,000 Persons)**

	Higher, incomplete higher and middle special	General (10-year school)	Incomplete general (7-year school)	Primary (4-year school) and over	Less than 4 years of schooling
All rural groups	59	36	221	352	332
Workers	12	35	264	435	254
Employees	487	127	265	104	17
Collective farmers	9	23	194	355	419

* See source note for Table 13.
All-Union Census 1959, p. 115.

LIFE-STYLES IN THE SOVIET VILLAGE

Differences in occupation, income and education are associated, in village as in town, with different styles of life. We shall now turn to a few of the more interesting analyses of this problem to come from the pens of Soviet scholars. But first a word on the nature and sequence of our presentation. Being from different sources these studies do not quite fit together, and we can do no more than present some of the more important points from them.

We shall begin with an analysis of the housing conditions, private plot use and livestock holdings of the main social groups in a Ukrainian village, as published by the Soviet rural sociologist Yu. V. Arutyunyan. Then we shall go on to a number of interesting time-use studies which appeared in a book by V. Ya. Churakov and L. I. Suvorova in 1967. A few cultural indices are included here. Finally we shall review another Arutyunyan study, this being an attempt to compare the cultural tastes and habits of social groups in three widely scattered rural areas. Arutyunyan also applied the time-use index for this purpose.

In 1963 Arutyunyan conducted a detailed study of the living conditions of a random sample of 2,364 inhabitants of the

Ukrainian village Terpenie and the state farm Akerman which was located in two adjoining settlements.[19] Here we shall limit ourselves, for the sake of brevity, to the results from Terpenie where the bulk of his sample lived.

TABLE 54. *Quality of Accommodation in the Village of Terpenie, 1963 (Percentage Distributions)*

Sector	Socio-occu-pation group	Roofs		Walls		Floor	
		Straw or reed	Tile or iron sheeting	Brick, reed or plaster	Clay	Earthen	Wooden
Enterprises	A	—	100	71.4	28.6	—	100
	B						
	C	3	97	11	89	8	92
	D	10	90	14	86	25	75
State institutions	A	3	75	43	57	3	97
	B	—	100	22	78	10	90
	C	4	96	13	87	7	93
	D	7	93	20	80	29	71
Collective farms	A	—	100	75	25	—	100
	B	—	100	20	80	—	100
	C	6	94	37	63	13	87
	D	12	88	16	84	30	70

Socio-occupation group
A = Mental skilled   C = Physical skilled
B = Mental unskilled   D = Physical unskilled
Source:
Yu. V. Arutyunyan, *Opyt sotsiologicheskogo izuchenia sela*, Moscow, 1968, p. 96 (selected indices).

Terpenie, as Arutyunyan freely admitted, was an unusually fortunate village, being well-built and 'progressive'. It was also the subject of sociological investigation in the thirties, and this permitted a few chronological comparisons, usually of a flattering

19. *Opyt sostsiologicheskoyo izuchenia sela*, Moscow, 1968; *Voprosy Filosofii* No. 5, 1966, and No. 9, 1968. The total population of Terpenie in 1963 was 5,158 persons.

nature. Arutyunyan's sample covered people working not only in the collective and state farms there, but also in industry and state institutions. In his treatment of this data, however, Arutyunyan has presumably put the state farm workers in the industrial enterprise sector, since they were few in number. He used four occupation groups for his analysis – mental and physical, each being subdivided into skilled and unskilled. In the agricultural sector this corresponded roughly to specialists, service personnel, mechanizers and unskilled peasants, taken to include livestock handlers. He was able on this basis to illustrate some interesting social distinctions, both between the economic sectors and the groups inside them.

Some of his more revealing data on housing are reproduced in Table 54. From these we see that a much larger proportion of the people in the upper occupation groups of each sector had stone-walled accommodation, while most of the others managed with clay dwellings. Hardly any of the specialists' dwellings had earthen floors, but 25–30 per cent of the accommodation occupied by unskilled manuals did. (An earthen floor in the Ukraine betokens not so much dire poverty as cultural backwardness.) At least eighty per cent of all families in each sector had a separate house, the only exception being the service personnel in state institutions. The number of rooms did not conform to any easily recognizable pattern, so we have not reproduced these indices in the table. Good roofing was fairly general, even among the unskilled peasantry.

Some of Arutyunyan's data on the distribution of certain household commodities are of interest. There appears to be a very real gradation in the possession of divans, bookcases and sideboards – three pieces of furniture one associated with a higher, or more Westernized, standard of living (Table 55). In most cases these objects were encountered at least twice as often in the households of specialists as in those of unskilled workers or peasants. Photographs, on the other hand, were more common in poorer households. Ikons present a special problem: though classified as 'decorations' they were, no doubt, often kept for their religious significance. Their incidence in the families of the unskilled workers in each sector was many times higher than in the families of specialists; half of the unskilled peasant and worker households, and nearly a third of the unskilled workers in state institutions, had them.

Land and animal holdings are key factors in the village. As far as garden plots and sown land are concerned, we find that about 80–100 per cent of the families in all social groups – with the

TABLE 55. *Household Effects and Decoration in the Village of Terpenie, 1963*

		Effects			Decorations	
Sector	Socio-occupation group	Divan	Book-Shelf	Side-board	Photo-graphs	Ikons
Enterprises	A					
	B	71.4	71.4	14.3	42.9	14.3
	C	68	48	17	83	24
	D	24	53	5	90	53
State institutions	A	60	73	27	43	3
	B	47	44	30	75	25
	C	63	47	23	60	20
	D	32	40	4	80	29
Collective farms	A	75	75	—	75	—
	B	80	60	40	80	—
	C	67	50	21	23	50
	D	54	38	12	54	48

Source:
Yu. V. Arutyunyan, op. cit., p. 97 (selected indices).

exception of service personnel of the state institutions – were provided for (Table 56). Arutyunyan indicated in a footnote that this exception may have been due to the fact that most people in this category were youngsters who had not established themselves in life. Some of them might have been living with their families, or were unwilling to get tied down, but this was a problem, he said, which awaited further research.

The holdings of livestock by all social groups outside the collective farm were limited. However, there were dramatic variations between social groups inside it. Three quarters of the specialists had a cow; but fewer of the service personnel, the mechanizers, unskilled peasants, were so blessed. Fifty per cent of the first group had pigs, but only 21 per cent of the last. It seems, then, that privately owned livestock was a real status symbol in this particular instance.

We have given Arutyunyan's Terpenie findings in a little detail, because he appears to have produced a competent if restricted sociological survey of the village. His data on the neighbouring state farm settlements of Zarechnoe and Lugovoe showed, on the whole, a similar pattern.[20]

TABLE 56. *Private Plot Holdings in the Village of Terpenie, 1964 (Percentages)*

Sector	Socio-occupation group	Land		Animals	
		Sown land*	Garden plot*	Cow	Pig
Enterprises	A				
	B	100	85.9	—	—
	C	80	90	7	17
	D	100	100	24	5
State institutions	A	80	87	7	10
	B	56	59	9	6
	C	87	93	10	20
	D	86	86	11	14
Collective farm	A	100	100	75	50
	B	80	80	20	40
	C	79	94	33	21
	D	79	79	31	21

*The writer does not explain the distinction.
Source:
Yu. V. Arutyunyan, op. cit., p. 95 (selected indices).

Arutyunyan was as interested in the relationships between similar social groups in different economic sectors as the distinctions between different groups in the same sector. He tried to illustrate not only the vertical range of wellbeing between peasant and specialist inside the collective farm, but also the horizontal relationship between, for example, rural worker and peasant. A major conclusion of his study is that the less skilled people at the bottom of each sector are closer to one another than they are to the specialists at the top of their own. This might

20. op. cit., p. 100.

seem to us a fairly innocuous and not unexpected finding. In the Soviet context, however, it could easily be taken as a criticism of the official view that the main divisions in Soviet society are 'vertical' rather than 'horizontal'. The latter implies rifts between the haves and have-nots.

Arutyunyan evidently believed that his findings were of some general validity, and we can hardly do other than give him the benefit of the doubt. But this does not mean that we should accept what he said quite uncritically. If he managed to illustrate, in rather concrete terms, that there is a significant lowering of material and cultural standards as one goes down the occupation scale in all sectors of Soviet rural society, this does not exclude the possibility of local exceptions, which may, indeed, be numerous. Regional variety seems to be a strong characteristic of the Soviet village. Even in Lugovoe and Zarechnoe all social groups, skilled and unskilled, seemed to keep pigs to an equal degree, while holdings of cows increased, rather than decreased, towards the bottom of the scale. Here the skilled manual workers (mechanizers) were on the whole the best provided for.[21]

So much for material differences. Let us now turn to the social distinctions in the way people use their time. We may begin with some of the basic differences between peasant, state farm and industrial worker, as illustrated in a recent study (Table 57). This covered four *oblasts* of Central Russia, so it was probably representative for much of the Soviet population.[22] In considering the findings we must not, however, forget the methodological

21. Details given by T. I. Zaslavskaya and V. N. Ladenkov on the housing occupied by specialists and mechanizers in collective and state farms in the Novosibirsk *oblast* show yet another pattern, the main distinctions here running between the types of farm. In the *kolkhozy* specialists had at least one square metre per head more living space than mechanizers; the differential between these occupational groups in state farms was rather more marked. A much larger proportion of both specialists and mechanizers had their own private houses in the collective farms. For other details see T. I. Zaslavskaya and V. N. Ladenkov, 'Sotsialno-ekonomicheskie uslovia sozdania postoyanikh kadrov *v* selskom khozyaistve Sibiri', *Izvestia Sibirskovo otdelenia A.N. SSSR, seria obshchestvennykh nauk*, No. 11, 1967, p. 39.

22. V. Ya. Churakov and L. I. Suvorova, *Ispolzovanie trudovikh resursov v kolkhozakh i sovkhozakh*, Moscow, 1967, p. 90. Each of these categories presumably included specialists, but they would have been too few significantly to affect the inter-group relationships.

difficulties involved. The first lies in the enormous seasonal variations in the farming community's daily timetable; there are times when its members work from dawn to dusk, and others when they have comparatively little to do. Secondly, while workers and employees have days off and clearly delineated working hours, it is by no means easy to distinguish between work-days and rest-days on the farm and there is hardly any rest at all in the sowing and harvesting periods. The figures given here relate only to working days in July. The third difficulty is not new to us. Sex differences, as we have seen, can have an overriding influence on time usage; this is as true for the peasant as for the urban household.

Fortunately the data in Table 57 allow us to take this factor

TABLE 57. *Time Budget of Collective Farmers, State Farm Workers and Industrial Workers (July 1963, working day, in %)**

Time expenditure	Collective farmers		State farm workers		Industrial workers	
	Men	Women	Men	Women	Men	Women
1. Total working time in collective farm, state enterprise or institution	37.0	27.0	29.5	18.9	28.7	28.3
2. Non-working time linked with work	4.6	4.0	4.0	2.5	6.8	5.8
3. Household duties including garden plot	10.3	26.3	11.0	33.3	8.5	19.3
4. Satisfaction of physical needs (eating, sleeping, toilet)	36.6	34.5	38.7	36.0	38.3	36.3
5. Free time	9.4	5.2	14.7	7.8	16.8	9.5
6. Other time expenditures	2.1	3.0	2.1	1.5	0.9	0.8

*Slightly simplified for clarity.
Source:
V. Ya. Churakov and L. I. Suvorova, op. cit., p. 90. On the basis of TsSU (RSFSR) studies in the Ivanovo, Sverdlovsk, Gorki and Rostov *oblasts.*

into account. Sex distinctions are again seen to be at least as important as social ones. Women in collective and state farms carried a 12 to 30 per cent heavier work-load than men, in terms of hours. They spent much less time than their menfolk in formal employment (both in the collective farms and state sectors), but far more in their own household or on the garden plot. As far as the workers were concerned, men and women evidently had an almost equal working day, but again the woman spent an extra 10 per cent of her time in household duties. On working days women in each sector had only just over half as much free time as men.

There were, nevertheless, clear differences in time use patterns between the three sectors, quite independently of those connected with sex. Whereas the male peasant spent 11 hours daily working in the collectivized sector, at home, or in his garden plot, the state farm worker toiled for $9\frac{1}{2}$ hours, and the industrial worker for just over nine, though the last did spend a little more time than the others, preparing for, and travelling to, work.[23] The figures for women were just under thirteen hours, $12\frac{1}{2}$ hours and just under $11\frac{1}{2}$ hours respectively. This led to big social differences in the amount of free time available, from the 1 hour and 48 minutes enjoyed by the average peasant to the 3 hours and 18 minutes which the workers in industry had.[24]

A good analysis of how peasants, state farm workers and industrial workers spent the free time which remained at their disposal in the month of June is to be found in another study adduced by the same authors (Table 58).[25] This is in effect a cultural index.

The differences between the sexes were again, in many instances, greater than between the sectors. But having said this we must admit that social distinctions were once more very evident. Thus, industrial and state farm workers devoted up to six or seven times as much of their non-working time as the peasants to bringing up their children, studying, and improving their work skills. Of course, June is a busy month on the land, and in

23. That is 47.3, 40.5 and 37.2 per cent respectively, the sum of items 1 and 3.
24. Average for men and women taken together.
25. ibid., p. 92.

peasant families these activities were probably the first to suffer on this account. Many of the children, for example, may have been out in the fields themselves.

TABLE 58. *Free Time Expenditures of Collective Farmers, State Farm Workers and Industrial Workers, June 1963*

Time expenditure	Collective farmers		State farm workers		Industrial workers	
	Men	Women	Men	Women	Men	Women
Total free time including:	100.0	100.0	100.0	100.0	100.0	100.0
1. Education of children	0.7	1.2	3.3	7.1	4.5	4.4
2. Study and improvement of skills	1.5	—	2.4	8.0	9.5	8.0
3. Social work	8.2	8.2	9.5	17.0	5.4	8.8
4. Creative work	—	—	0.9	—	1.2	—
5. PT and sport	3.7	—	5.7	—	5.0	1.4
6. Rest and recreation (leisure)	85.9	90.6	78.2	67.9	74.4	77.4

Source:
V. Ya. Churakov and L. I. Suvorova, op. cit., p. 92.

An analysis of 'rest and recreation', or leisure activities proper, is to be found in Table 59. The relationships are complicated, and we shall leave the reader to make his own perusal. We may, however, make the following comments. People in each sector devoted approximately the same proportion of their time to reading newspapers (though women were at an obvious disadvantage), and the state farm workers and industrial workers seemed to absorb far more 'literature' than the peasants. Women industrial workers outdid their menfolk in this respect. Industrial workers watched television and listened to the radio much more than the peasants and state farm workers, who appeared to see more films, etc. As far as amateur musical activities were concerned, the male industrial workers in the sample left everyone else far behind, possibly because of their known proclivity for brass bands. The peasants spent considerably more time receiving guests or visiting relatives and friends, and were fonder of 'unoccupied leisure', i.e. doing nothing.

TABLE 59. *Leisure Time Expenditures of Collective Farmers, State Farm Workers and Industrial Workers, June 1963*

Time expenditure	Collective farmers		State farm workes		Industrial workers	
	Men	Women	Men	Women	Men	Women
Total leisure time including:	100.0	100.0	100.0	100.0	100.0	100.0
1. Reading newspapers	10.4	2.7	10.9	4.0	11.7	4.7
2. Reading literature	5.1	2.7	15.9	4.0	13.3	15.1
3. Listening to radio, watching TV	9.6	5.2	12.8	7.8	25.0	19.8
4. Visits to cinemas, theatres, museums exhibitions*	10.4	7.8	11.5	18.4	4.4	6.6
5. Visits to dance halls, parks*	6.1	6.6	6.5	6.6	7.7	5.6
6. Singing, dancing, playing musical instruments	0.8	—	2.4	1.3	6.7	2.7
7. Receiving guests, visiting friends and relations	19.0	24.7	10.9	21.1	8.3	15.1
8. Unoccupied	38.8	50.3	29.2	36.8	22.9	30.5

* Including travelling time.
Source:
V. Ya. Churakov and L. I. Suvorova, op. cit., p. 92 (section on free time).

Inside the collective farm itself we find a rather interesting array of distinctions by occupation group (Table 60). We shall again restrict ourselves to commenting on a few of the more important items, beginning with working hours. Of all occupation groups, the male livestock handlers worked the longest day in the public sector. It amounted on average to 42.5 per cent of their time, or nearly eleven hours. At the other extreme were the

TABLE 60. Time Budget of Collective Farmers by Occupation Group, June 1963, (Expenditures Expressed as % of 24 Hours)

Time expenditure	Administrative and managerial staff, specialists		Service personnel and others		Mechanizers		Cattle rearers		Fieldworkers	
	Men	Women	Men	Women	Men	Women	Men	Women	Men	Women
1. Working time in the collective farm*	39.1	35.1	33.5	29.9	38.5	14.9	42.5	34.2	33.2	22.5
2. Free time linked with work in the collective farm	5.4	5.1	3.9	3.0	4.4	2.8	4.7	4.9	4.6	3.7
3. Working time of persons employed in state enterprises and institutions†	—	—	—	0.3	—	16.7	—	—	0.1	—
4. Free time linked with work in state enterprises and institutions	—	—	—	—	—	2.8	0.1	0.1	0.1	—
5. Time spent on handicrafts	—	0.1	0.5	0.8	0.2	—	0.1	—	1.2	0.3
6. Household duties (except work on garden plot etc.)	2.4	12.8	3.9	12.4	2.5	12.4	1.9	10.8	3.2	14.1
7 Work on garden plot (or similar)	4.0	9.9	9.2	11.1	5.4	6.2	6.7	10.0	8.3	15.3
8. Satisfaction of physical needs (eating, sleeping and toilet)	34.2	32.2	36.9	35.4	37.1	38.3	34.9	33.5	37.9	34.9
9. Free (i.e. unoccupied) time	11.0	4.8	9.6	5.4	10.3	5.2	7.9	4.4	9.3	6.9
10. Other time expenditures	3.9	—	2.5	1.7	1.6	0.7	1.2	2.1	2.1	2.3

* Public sector only.
† Presumably concerning collective farm members, mostly women, who are employed outside the farm.

Source:
V. Ya. Churakov and L. I. Suvorova, op. cit., p. 94.

service personnel and unskilled peasants, who devoted only 33.5 per cent of their time, or eight hours to such work. But a relatively low proportion of time spent in the public sector was, not surprisingly, balanced by a heavier investment in the garden plot. The poorer people spent more time on it than the richer ones, while women in all the groups were more involved than men, this trend being particularly marked amongst the field workers. The amount of time spent on domestic chores (other than the private plot) was remarkably even throughout – though the women always bore most of the burden. The groups that had the heaviest working day – the administrative personnel, specialists and stock rearers – not unexpectedly spent the least time eating and sleeping. Nevertheless people in the top occupations had more leisure time at their disposal than those in the less skilled ones, partly because they spent less time on private plots. If the administrative and specialist group had plots and livestock holdings (as in Terpenie) then we must infer that they hired others to do the work for them. The investment of time in the private plot seemed to be unexpectedly small; we have, after all,

TABLE 61. *Time Expenditures of Collective Farmers Who Work Only on Their Private Plots (24-Hour Time Budget, Working Day, as %)*

Time expenditure	Men	Women
Working time in the collective farm and state enterprises	—	0.3
Free time linked with work in the collective farm	—	0.1
Time spent on handicrafts	14.4	1.0
Household duties including:	23.9	45.1
Time spent on garden plot	18.5	20.4
Satisfaction of physical needs (eating, sleeping, toilet)	43.1	38.7
Free time including:	16.8	10.4
Receiving guests	2.2	2.4
Unoccupied leisure	9.4	5.8
Other time expenditures	1.8	4.4

Source:
V. Ya. Churakov and L. I. Suvorova, op. cit., p. 96.

concluded that the peasant was gaining a third or so of his liveli-
hood from it at that time. The answer to this puzzle probably lies
in Table 61, which gives time budgets for peasants who worked
only on their private plots. They were presumably not included
in the other figures: many Soviet observers have noted that they
are mainly old people and women. The men 'privateers' involved
apparently had a relatively easier life – they certainly spent more
time eating and sleeping, and had considerably more free time –
a large proportion of which they spent in 'unoccupied leisure'.
But their womenfolk worked harder than anyone.

Finally, we come to Arutyunyan's analysis of cultural differences between occupation groups in villages of the Lukhovitski
raion in Moscow *oblast*, and the Tartar and Chuvash Autonomous Republics, as reflected in the possession (rather than use) of
certain cultural goods.[26]

Since we do not have space to consider all the divergences
here (and that would be rather a tiresome exercise anyway), we
shall take only what appear to be the most interesting. Before we
do so it behoves us to recall a point we made earlier – that
people's cultural tastes and habits are a product of many factors,
not least their educational background, and that the link with
occupation may be quite indirect. Although Arutyunyan uses
occupation groups as a basis for his analysis, he is himself very
much aware of this fact.

The possession of personal libraries, television sets and newspaper subscriptions by persons employed in collective farm,
state farm and industry in Lukhovitski *raion* is shown in Table
62. We have omitted figures for ordinary radios, as most people

26. This passage was written before the cultural indices of Arutyunyan's
Terpenie (Lugovoe, Zarechnoe) study became available. We decided not to
revise what was set down, or replace it by the new Terpenie data, partly
because the latter seemed to accord very largely with that provided by the
samples discussed here, and partly because there is something to be said, in a
survey study such as ours, of bringing in a variety of investigations. In *Opyt
sotsiologicheskogo izuchenia sela* Arutyunyan used up to fourteen indices of
cultural level, including possession of various kinds of literature, timepieces,
bicycles, motor-cycles, sewing machines, radios and musical instruments. He
showed that in general the specialists in each of the three sectors were two or
three times more likely to have most of them than people in the least skilled
occupation groups. The other groups fell between these extremes. (*Opyt*, pp.
98, 102.)

TABLE 62. *Possession of Reading Matter and Television Sets (Lukhovitski* Raion, *Moscow* Oblast)*

Cultural indices in the family	Collective farms				State farms				Enterprises and institutions			
	A	B	C	D	A	B	C	D	A	B	C	D
Have library	50	20	38	20	58	17	31	24	61	26	23	10
Subscribe to 2 or more newspapers	79	45	53	39	77	50	62	14	84	76	59	29
Have a television set	79	45	38	25	81	70	88	46	73	65	68	41

*Groups: as in Table 54.

Figures for the possession of radios are universally high, 62–95 per cent, and have been omitted. Absence of a radio set does not mean much as it may have been counterbalanced by rediffusion.

Source:

Yu. V. Arutyunyan, article in *Voprosy Filosofii*, No. 9, 1968, p. 125.

had a set. All things considered, the level of cultural interest measured in this way seems to have been rather lower in the collective farm than outside it. Although the distribution of libraries was fairly even, many more of the rural industrial workers took two or more newspapers, while both state farm and industrial workers were much more frequent possessors of television sets. Of course, the purchase of a TV depends not only on a desire to see the programmes, and the ability to pay, but also on the availability of the apparatus so this was not in itself a good index of cultural avidity. The state farm workers here were evidently better off than those covered by the Churakov–Suvarova study mentioned above. But if the figures given for items 6 and 8 in Table 59 would lead one to believe that collective farm communities lagged behind the workers in their cultural tastes and habits, this study seems to provide some confirmation.

There was also a clearly marked gradation between occupation groups inside each sector. The usual pattern was for between half and four fifths of the specialists to have the said objects. They were followed, at some distance, by the skilled manual workers. The service personnel and the unskilled manual labourers tended to be the worst off, and with one or two exceptions were less than half as well provided for as the specialists. Arutyunyan found approximately the same distribution in the Tartar and Chuvash areas, though sometimes the positions of unskilled mental workers and skilled manuals were reversed.

TABLE 63. *Use of Free Time* (% *of Persons Questioned*)

Question: What do you do most often in your free time?	Social (occupation) group*					Average for the sample
	A	B	C	D_1	D_2	
Tataria						
Answers:						
Domestic duties, child care	47	69	69	72	79	68
Watch television	43	44	20	21	33	29
Read	42	25	9	10	4	13
Go to cinema, dancing	30	34	28	23	27	23
Just rest, most often sleep	7	13	3	13	20	12
Study, improve my working skills	23	13	2	4	3	7
Chuvashia						
Answers:						
Domestic duties, child care	50	51	59	75	82	67
Watch television	36	33	23	21	17	16
Read	35	13	15	12	10	11
Go to cinema, dancing	31	24	25	13	4	16
Just rest, most often sleep	9	18	18	8	10	7
Study, improve my working skills	10	4	7	3	2	5

*Groups A, B, C, as in Table 54. D_1 = livestock handlers, D_2 = unskilled labourers.
Source:
Yu. V. Arutyunyan, op. cit., p. 127.

The results of Arutyunyan's survey of the use of free time by occupation groups in two villages in the Tartar and Chuvash regions are shown in Table 63. It appears that people who had the more responsible jobs again spent much less time doing household chores and looking after the children – Arutyunyan takes the two items together. Radio and television entertainment seem to have been more the prerogative of the privileged, but this trend was much less clear in the Tartar village than in the Chuvash one. Reading was vastly more popular amongst administrative personnel, specialists, and service personnel, than in the manual groups. Part-time education and self-improvement seem to have followed the same pattern, though the mechanizers in Chuvashia were, it seems, much fonder of these pursuits than their brethren in Tataria. Whereas the cinema and dances seem to have been attended by all social groups in the Tartar *oblast*, it evidently had superior social overtones in Chuvashia. Quite clearly, inactive rest was more common at the bottom of the Tartar social hierarchy; the picture in the Chuvash region was more complex, but at least may serve as another reminder of the difficulties of generalization. Arutyunyan's survey of cultural habits by sex in the Lukhovitski *raion* seems to show that people at the top of the socio-occupational scale were more active than those at the bottom, and that the social gradation was much more marked amongst women than amongst men (Table 64).

TABLE 64. *Preferred Cultural Pursuits in Villages of the Lukhovitski* raion, *by Sex*

| | | Percentage breakdown | | | | | | | |
| | | Men | | | | Women | | | |
Socio-occupation group	No. of persons in group	Radio	News-papers	TV	Literature	Radio	News-papers	TV	Literature
A Intelligentsia	71	71	93	64	88	81	86	45	96
B Employees	66	81	88	37	78	80	84	67	83
C Mechanizers and other skilled workers	68	81	85	60	78	—	—	—	—
D Unskilled workers	196	82	82	57	67	65	50	39	47

Source:
Yu. V. Arutyunyan, op. cit., p. 129.

Arutyunyan also gave some interesting data on the ideals of different occupation groups in this area (Table 65). His results indicated that people in the less skilled groups seemed to be rather less concerned with interesting work or family happiness, and more anxious to achieve a measure of material wellbeing.

TABLE 65. *Life Ideals of the Inhabitants of the Lukhovitski* raion

Question: What does 'a good life' mean to you?	A		B		C		D	
	Men	Women	Men	Women	Men	Women	Men	Women
No. of persons questioned	59	50	29	83	240	—	122	232
Answers:*								
1. Have good interesting work	71	78	76	69	63	—	53	47
2. Have a happy family life	63	72	76	62	58	—	51	54
3. Live in sufficiency, in comfort	43	50	55	43	65	—	67	62

*Expressed as a percentage of each group.
Source:
Yu. V. Arutyunyan, op. cit., p. 131.

Finally, some variations in the degree of satisfaction with living conditions and cultural amenities in the Tartar and Chuvash villages by occupation group are shown in Table 66. This table, though our last, is, in fact, quite an important one, for it reveals that the intelligentsia and highly skilled mechanizers were more demanding and less satisfied with what they had. This naturally raises very far-reaching questions about how successful the government can be in persuading better-educated people to stay in the village. The more cultivated people are, the more reason they have for complaint. Several Soviet observers have commented on the grave implications of this phenomenon.

If we stand back from these numerous observations, the considerable material and cultural variety of Soviet village society becomes very apparent. Yet it is a variety in which a great deal of order is apparent. The lines of differentiation which run between social groups and between sectors are unmistakeable. As far as the collective farm community is concerned, the specialists and responsible administrative personnel lead a markedly different way of life from everyone else; it is possible to measure some of the ways in which they are materially and culturally more

TABLE 66. *Proportion of Persons Satisfied With the Work of Mass Cultural Institutions and General Amenities in the Village*

						Percentages	
		No. of persons questioned		Satisfied with the work of mass cultural organs		Satisfied with the general amenities in the village	
Socio-occupation group		Tartar ASSR	Chuvash ASSR	Tartar ASSR	Chuvash ASSR	Tartar ASSR	Chuvash ASSR
A	Intelligentsia	60	71	38	29	25	29
B	Employees	32	67	41	31	16	22
C	Mechanizers	71	65	52	42	35	36
D_1	Cattle rearers and others	133	58	64	53	48	50
D_2	Unskilled labourers	105	66	52	51	37	40
	Totals and averages	401	327	55	46	40	38

Source:
Yu. V. Arutyunyan, op. cit., p. 124.

advanced. The same may be said, though to a lesser extent, of the mechanizers. The rearguard of village society is formed by the mass of the peasantry, which lags well behind everyone else in nearly every index we have examined.

7

The Drift from the Land

THE history of Soviet society has been characterized by a massive shift of the population from agriculture to industry, and from village to town. The USSR is by no means unique in this respect, for all industrializing societies go through the same process. Soviet internal migration, however, prompted for long periods by administrative order and big differentials between urban and rural standards of living, has taken place on an unprecedented scale and at great speed. The social consequences have been far-reaching.

We shall begin our own brief survey of this interesting phenomenon with some data on the extent of migration and the main directions it has taken. For the purposes of analysis we shall follow the usual practice of Soviet sociologists, and think of the village as composed only of collective farm, state farm, and rural industrial sectors. (Sometimes, it is true, they also distinguish between large and small towns.) This simple scheme is represented in Figure 16. We must remember that apart from the movement in both directions between all sectors, each sector has its own natural growth potential. We shall then outline the main rural-urban migratory trends in the Khrushchev and post-Khrushchev periods in so far as the inadequate population and labour force figures permit. Next we shall comment on some observed regional variations in the pattern and illustrate the main population flows *inside* the urban and rural sectors.

This, however, is in a sense only a preliminary exercise. Our main concern will be to present some of the more competent studies of the social implications of migration to be published by Soviet sociologists in recent years. The problems that are dealt with in this work are the nature and causes of migration (particularly from village to town), the kinds of people who are most frequently involved, and the facility with which they adapt to urban life.

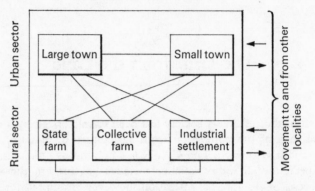

Migration may take place in each direction along the lines shown

FIGURE 16. *Urban Rural Migration: Schematic Representation*

THE MAIN CURRENTS

Figures for population of rural areas between 1954 and 1968 are given in Table 67. We shall begin with the period 1954–64, as this coincided with Khrushchev's distinctive agricultural policies.

The total rural population, as may be seen, varied remarkably little in size, and apart from an increase in the years 1955 and 1956 (perhaps primarily as a result of the Virgin Land campaigns) remained at a level of about 107–8 million. This did not mean, of course, that no one left the land. The natural increase of this vast segment of the Soviet population, even allowing for a moderate birth-rate, must have been in the region of a million and a half a year, and this was covered by people leaving. In addition we must allow for some returnees. It would probably be reasonable to think of the overall outflow as being in the order of two million a year.[1] We may well ask what sector of the village they came from.

This is not difficult to answer, at least in general terms. The same period saw spectacular changes within collective farm, state farm and rural industrial populations, though they were changes of different kinds. The collective farm population fell by at least 20 million. If we again allow for natural increase and

1. The urban population rose by 35 million over the same period; this figure would cover natural increase, the influx from the land, and the administrative reorganization of villages into towns or workers' settlements.

some immigration, we may surmise that the average annual loss of population to the collective farm community as a whole was at least two and a half million, though the rate of fall slowed down considerably in the last years of the period.

TABLE 67. *Rural Population Changes 1954–68*

	Population (millions)					
				Annual absolute change		
	Collective farm (peasant)	Other rural*	Total rural	Collective farm	Other rural	Total rural
1954	—	—	107.4	—	—	+0.7
1955	c. 76.6	31.5	108.1	+ 0.1	+ 1.5	+1.6
1956	c. 76.7	33.0	109.7	—	—	+0.3
1957	—	—	110.0⎫	−11.2⎫	+10.3	−0.7
1958	—	—	109.3⎭	⎭		−0.5
1959	65.5	43.3	108.8⎫	− 5.0⎫	+4.1	−0.3
1960	—	—	108.5⎭	⎭		−0.6
1961	60.5	47.4	107.9	− 2.7	+ 2.8	+0.1
1962	57.8	50.2	108.0	− 0.7	+ 0.8	+0.1
1963	57.1	51.0	108.1	− 1.0	+ 0.8	−0.2
1964	56.1	51.8	107.9	+ 0.3	− 0.6	−0.3
1965	56.4	51.2	107.6	− 1.8	+ 1.3	−0.5
1966	54.6	52.5	107.1	− 1.6	+ 0.9	−0.7
1967	53.0	53.4	106.4	+ 0.7	− 1.4	−0.7
1968	53.7	52.0	105.7†	—	—	—

*N.B. This column in fact understates the rural, non-collective farm population, due to the few million peasants who were resident in urban areas. The collective farm rural population is therefore somewhat smaller. The figure for 'urban peasants' at the time of the 1959 census was 3.2 million. This circumstance does not, as far as we can tell, appreciably affect the chronological relationships.

† The figure for 1969 was 104.7 million.

Sources:

K. E. Wädekin, 'Landwirtschaftliche Bevölkerung und Arbeitskräfte der Sowjetunion in Zahlen', *Osteuropa Wirtschaft*, No. 1, 1967, p. 40; *Narodnoe Khozyaistvo SSSR*, corresponding years.

Population figures are not published for the state farm and rural industrial sectors separately, and we can only infer what happened in them from the changes in the size of their labour force. The number of persons employed in the state farms rose from 2.6 million in 1954 to 8.1 million in 1964, that is, it increased by a factor of three. True, most of this expansion came from the reorganization of collective farms rather than from mechanical movement: between 1955 and 1967 some 4.6 million of their workers, or three quarters of the registered growth in the labour force, were former peasants who had been recategorized. In view of our comments in Chapter 3 the reorganization must have had important implications for them.

The number of persons employed in the rural industrial sector can be estimated only by indirect means, and only for three of the years in the period which interests us. It seems, however, that the figure rose modestly by about a million and a half (from 8.5 million to 10 million) between 1950 and 1966.[2]

Only part of the increase in the size of the non-collective farm sectors can be explained by natural growth. Moreover, we know that the Soviet government's efforts to persuade townspeople, especially school-leavers, to work in them were generally unsuccessful. The only mass exodus to the village which has been announced resulted from the Virgin Land campaigns, but these involved hardly more than a million people altogether. It seems safe to infer, then, that the collective farm was the main source of supply for labour in state farms and rural industry. As we shall see in a moment, all three sectors provided migrants for the towns.

The changes of government policy which followed Khrushchev's removal in the autumn of 1964 evidently affected these trends, and this is to some extent reflected in our data. The total rural population had begun to decrease in 1963, but by 1969 the annual crude fall reached a million a year. The unfavourable

2. Figures for the state farm labour force come from *Trud v SSSR*, pp. 24 and 126. The figures for the non-agricultural rural labour force (ibid., pp. 22, 38) were arrived at by subtracting the state farm labour force from the total labour force 'in rural areas', though this is only given as a percentage of the total 'worker and employee' labour force for the whole country. This charge would have meant an increase of perhaps 4–5 million in the *population* of the rural industrial sector. K. E. Wädekin, using other sources, has suggested that it rose by as much as 10 million between 1955 and 1965, and that the final figure for 1965 was 37–38 million. (See his article 'Landwirtschaftliche Bevölkerung und Arbeitskräfte der Sowjetunion in Zahlen', *Osteuropa Wirtschaft*, No. 1, 1967.)

demographic position in the countryside and more administrative boundary changes may have been partly responsible for this, but an increase in migration to the towns was probably the main factor. If we again make an allowance for the relevant factors, we may presume that this movement was by then running at something over 2 million a year.

As far as the collective farm population was concerned, we see that while the general fall continued, small increases were registered in 1965 and again in 1968, the implication being that at these points the exodus was counterbalanced by immigration and natural increase. The same sort of thing had happened, but more obviously, after the death of Stalin. We can suggest reasons for the increase in 1965. Khrushchev's pension schemes, introduced in the summer of 1964, were followed, after his departure, by a relaxation of government pressure on the private plot, and a less restrictive policy towards the collective farm. In 1966 and 1967, however, the outflow must again have been well over two million. The slight reverse in this trend registered for 1968 is, at the time of writing, not easily explicable. The general malaise in rural society would incline one to believe that it was only temporary.

The labour force of the state farms grew until 1966 when, by a new method of reckoning then used, it numbered 9.3 million. After that it virtually stopped. We may presume that the state farm population moved accordingly. This was largely a consequence of the new leadership's rejection of Khrushchev's policy of rapidly turning collective farms into state farms.

It is not easy, on the material at present to hand, to say much about the population of the rural industrial sector in these years. We have noted that it was formerly subject to moderate expansion. It seems unlikely that it has recently absorbed more than a small proportion of the population of other sectors, at least on a permanent basis. The general conclusion on all these movements must be that the post-Khrushchev policies towards the peasant did not substantially affect the continued migration from the collective farm or benefit the other rural sectors. If more peasants indeed went into them (rather than straight into the towns) the labour turnover in them merely increased, so that they lost more people to the urban centres.

The fact that the flight from the land is a major, long-standing phenomenon in the USSR does not, of course, mean that all regions are equally affected. An analysis of the outflow from rural areas for the years 1959–63 by the Soviet demographer V. I. Perevedentsev showed that in the Volgo–Vyatka, North Western and Central regions it was nearly twice the average for the whole country, whereas in Moldavia, Central Asia and the North Caucasus it was only 32–53 per cent of the national average.[3] In general, as V. I. Perevedentsev noted, a lower outflow from the villages was characteristic of the non-Russian republics. This was, no doubt, due partly to ethnic and cultural factors, and partly to the higher incidence of state farms in them. He pointed out that only in one area – Kazakhstan – did the numbers moving into the villages exceed those who left.[4]

A number of regional studies highlight another aspect of the problem. This is the considerable migration *within* the urban or rural sectors of the USSR, i.e. from town to town or village to village. Thus V. I. Perevedentsev, in a study of population movements in four *oblasts* and one *krai* of Western Siberia, showed that of all new migrants to the towns between 1956 and 1960, some 46 per cent came from other towns, and only 54 per cent from rural areas (Table 68). The proportion of rural migrants among new arrivals in the towns varied considerably from one *oblast* to another: those *oblasts* with a higher proportion of rural inhabitants in the total population, or larger urban concentrations, tended to have more former villagers amongst the newcomers. Perevedentsev pointed out, incidentally, that there was a tendency for people who left the villages to go to towns near their old homes – which tends to confirm the proposition that most migration takes place within *oblasts* or fairly small administrative units.

Not everyone who leaves a particular village ends up in a town. A most interesting study by the Novosibirsk sociologists T. I.

3. Chapter in D. I. Valentei and others (eds.), *Narodonaselenie i ekonomika*, Moscow, 1967, p. 106.

4. The rural population of four other economic regions actually increased (North Caucasus, Transcaucasia, Central Asia and Moldavia), but the crude increase was probably less than natural increase, indicating an overall loss by migration anyway.

Zaslavskaya and L. D. Antosenkova showed that of all the people who were known to have arrived in the villages of the Novosibirsk *oblast* between 1961 and 1966, 47 per cent were from other villages: of those that left, 33 per cent moved to other villages. These figures, which were said to come from official sources, are shown in Table 69. The writers indicated, in addition, that men tended to be rather more mobile than women; just under 138,000 men, as opposed to 117,000 women, migrated. The subordinate trends were not significantly different, except that a larger proportion of the women who left the villages moved to towns. The writers were careful to add the following proviso: '. . . judging by the change in the overall size of the rural population and the extent of its natural growth, the actual size of the resultant population movement is at least twice that which is accounted for here.'[5]

TABLE 68. *Urban–Rural Origins of Persons Moving into Towns in Western Siberia (1965–60, % of All Arrivals)*

Region	Arrived from other towns	Arrived from the country
Omsk *oblast*	22	78
Tomsk *oblast*	31	69
Novosibirsk *oblast*	41	59
Kemerovo *oblast*	67	33
Altai *krai*	27	73
West Siberia (average)	46	54

Source:
V. I. Perevedentsev, *Migratsia naselenia*, Novosibirsk, 1966, p. 102.

Movement from town to village is, of course, taking place all over the USSR, the point being that it is much weaker than the drift in the opposite direction. This was clearly the case in the Novosibirsk *oblast* in 1961–6, where just over half of the people arriving in the villages came from the towns. Perevedentsev has

5. Figures on six rural soviets of the Sverdlovsk *oblast* for 1961–3 show that of some 947 migrants just over 13 per cent went to other villages of the same *oblast*; see F. N. Rekunov, in Ts. S. Stepanov and V. S. Semenov (eds.), *Klassy* etc., Moscow, 1968, p. 122.

TABLE 69. *Migration into and out of Rural Districts (Villages)
of the Novosibirsk Oblast (by Origin and Destination of Migrants)
1961–6*

Direction of flow	Total
Arrived in rural districts	254,736
from towns	123,325
from villages	119,021
unknown	12,390
Left rural districts	307,036
for towns	199,451
for villages	100,137
unknown	7,448
Resultant population movement	− 52,300
(out of/into village)	
with towns	− 76,126
with village	+ 18,884
unknown	+ 4,942

Source:
T. I. Zaslavskaya and L. D. Antosenkova, in *Sotsialnye problemy trudovykh resursov sela,* T. I. Zaslavskaya (ed.), Novosibirsk, 1968, p. 23.

TABLE 70. *Urban and Rural Population Movements in the West
Siberia Economic Region (Number of Persons Leaving Towns for
Villages per 100 Arrivals from Villages)*

Region	1956	1957	1958	1959	1960	1956–60*
Omsk *oblast*	57	67	63	52	49	57
Tomsk *oblast*	86	58	70	44	47	60
Novosibirsk *oblast*	79	88	60	56	57	67
Kemerovo *oblast*	72	78	64	57	69	68
Altai *krai*	75	77	70	60	63	68
West Siberia (average)	78	76	66	56	60	67

*Annual average.
Source:
V. I. Perevedentsev, op. cit., p. 103.

provided some interesting figures on the position in Western Siberia in 1956–60 (Table 70). These show that there the towns lost to the villages between 44 and 88 persons for every hundred gained, the proportion varying by *oblast* and year. In 1960, for example, for every 100 persons who came to the towns of Tomsk *oblast* from the villages, only 47 persons went back, whereas in the Kemerovo *oblast* the loss was 69. Understandably, each location has its own delicate balance of factors which influences the pattern of migration. This is not to deny the importance of individual choice, or fortuity.

SOME LOCAL PROBLEMS – STATE FARM AND COLLECTIVE FARM

T. I. Zaslavskaya and I. D. Antosenkova also provided some data on migration in and out of two collective and two state farms in the Novosibirsk *oblast*. These establishments were not, they claimed, typical, and perhaps for this reason gave no details of their size; but they are useful as examples of channels of flow. Anyway, the writers would hardly have investigated them in depth if they had been completely unrepresentative or totally unsuitable for generalization. Table 71 is reconstructed from a written analysis of immigration given in the article (this accounts for the slight discrepancies in the figures).

TABLE 71. *Origins by Residence of Migrants to 2 Collective and 2 State Farms (Novosibirsk Oblast, 1961–6)*

Arriving in the collective farms		
from villages	33	66
from small towns	12	25
from large towns	4	9
Totals	49	100
Arriving in state farms		
from villages	280	50
from small towns	192	33
from large towns	116	20
Totals	580	100

Source:
T. I. Zaslavskaya, op. cit., p. 38.

The figures show that while over the six years the *kolkhozy* attracted 49 persons, the state farms got 580. This must reflect, at least in part, their relatively greater desirability to outsiders. Moreover, the state and collective farms evidently draw people from other sectors in quite different proportions. The only people from large towns to go into the collective farms, according to the writers, were specialists who were directed there – and there were only four of them in the years under review. Twelve people came from small towns, and 33, or two thirds, from other rural areas. The state farms, on the other hand, drew 116 souls, a fifth of the total, from large towns, and nearly two hundred, or a third, from small ones. The influx from other rural areas was, by *kolkhoz* standards, enormous, amounting to about 290 persons.

Migration out of the state farms differed in character from that out of the collective farms. The state farms lost 46.5 persons per thousand inhabitants as an excess of departures over arrivals, whilst the collective farms lost 19.9 per thousand. The conclusion which Zaslavskaya draws from this is that the turnover in the state farms was much higher. Of every 100 persons who left them, over fifty went to the large towns, and thirty to small towns; thus only a meagre 20 per cent remained in rural areas. Migrants from the collective farm, however, had a different set of preferences: a third went to large towns, a third to small towns, and a third stayed in the country. In other words, although towns, large and small, attracted the lion's share of people moving out of both types of farm, the large towns appealed significantly more to state farm workers. The majority of intra-rural migrants, said the writers, made for the state farms. As a result, they observed,

the state farms serve as a sort of transit point, and the former collective farm member who has adapted himself to one may either move on to another state farm (usually near a town), to a small town, or directly to Novosibirsk itself. This circumstance simplifies the process of forming state farm cadres: there are many who wish to work in them. But it also promotes an unusually high fluidity of cadres, which cannot but affect production, the level of labour organization, and morale. There are state farms in Novosibirsk *oblast* where 40–50 per cent of the workers change every year.[6]

6. T. I Zaslavskaya and I. D. Antosenkova, op. cit., p. 39.

It seems, indeed, that these enterprises often compete for migrants to replenish their labour forces. In a recent article R. Ivanova criticized 'unhealthy' competition for people between state farms in Siberia.[7] The general drift, it appears, is from state farms with poorer living conditions to those with better ones, and thence into state enterprises for servicing agricultural machinery, which offer mechanizers the advantage of 'a work-day with labour norms and better rates of pay'. The annual turnover in the state farms of the Novosibirsk *oblast* in the nine years 1959–67 was, presumably for this reason, 19 per cent of the labour force. In the state farms of the Far East it was even higher.

Once they get into the towns the migrants' occupation pattern again seems to evolve in a fairly standard manner. No study of this has come to our notice, but V. S. Nemchenko has put forward the following hypothesis:

Young people up to twenty years of age go from agriculture mainly into construction and industry. This is to be explained . . . by the low standing of farm work in the eyes of young people, including those from the village, this being linked with the deterioration in the conditions of labour and living conditions there. People who are a little older in turn leave construction and go into industry, also as a consequence of the poorer working conditions which new arrivals straight from the village have to put up with. Young people from the towns, or village youth who have become acclimatized to urban life, will not tolerate them. Some of the workers aged thirty or over leave work in construction and industry as well, and move into the sphere of non-material production. They take mainly service jobs – which again evidently reflects the comparative laboriousness of work in the first two sectors.[8]

7. *Voprosy Ekonomiki*, No. 4, 1969, p. 135.

8. From *Voprosy teorii narodonaselenia pri sotsialisme*, ed. D. I. Valentei and others, Moscow, 1967, p. 138. See also V. I. Perevedentsev, *Migratsia naselenia*, Novosibirsk, 1966, for comment on movements in Krasnoyarsk and Novosibirsk, in 1960. Migrants to the towns in this case went mostly into construction; hardly any entered the better-paid branches of machine-building (p. 124).

THE MIGRANTS – MOTIVATION AND AGE-GROUPS

The principal cause of migration from the village, is, of course, the opportunity for betterment, in the widest possible sense, in the town. A study of how people rate the attractions of urban life was done by T. I. Zaslavskaya and some of her colleagues in 1966.[9] Their sample consisted of 291 questionnaire replies from families in the Novosibirsk *oblast* whose members had migrated. The coverage of this study was admittedly small, but we reproduce the analysis it produced in the belief that this was basically sound (Table 72). Over twenty per cent of the migrants were prompted to move by material necessity, while fifteen per cent just wanted to live in a town. It is noteworthy that a third moved for the purpose of getting more education or specialized training. Women, incidentally, seemed to be influenced by material considerations rather more than men. The study contained an analysis of these motives by the ages and educational achievement of the migrants, and purported to show how the pattern of motivation changed over time.

TABLE 72. *Distribution of Village Migrants to Towns by Motivation for Migration, All Age-Groups* (%)

Motive for migrating	Both Sexes	Men	Women
Material necessity	20.6	16.7	23.6
Desire to study	18.9	22.2	16.3
Desire to acquire a skill	13.4	11.9	14.5
Desire to live in a town	15.5	17.5	13.9
Family circumstances	10.7	8.7	12.1
Bad relations with the management	2.4	4.8	0.6
State of health	1.7	2.4	1.2
Other motives	11.0	9.5	12.2
No reply	5.8	6.3	5.6

Source:
T. I. Zaslavskaya, op. cit., p. 29.

Note: The distribution (which totals 100% in each case) was presumably made on the basis of each migrant's principal stated motive. Several sets of results used in this study are of this type; see Tables 73, 74, 89. Obviously this method is in some cases less than satisfactory.

9. T. I. Zaslavskaya, V. N. Ladenkov, V. D. Mirkin, L. D. Antosenkova *Sotsialnye problemy trudovykh resursov sela*, Novosibirsk, 1968.

Amongst the younger people the desire for more education and training was relatively more important – 55 per cent of the under-twenties named this as their motive, whereas only 11 per cent of those over twenty-six did so. On the other hand, family considerations and the desire to live in a town were much more prominent among the latter.

Of the worst-educated migrants (those with four classes or less of general schooling), nearly 30 per cent were prompted to move by material considerations, and another 20 per cent wished to enjoy the urban way of life: none of them were interested in more education, and many did not even complete the questionnaire (Table 73). The motivation of people with 7–8 years of schooling was close to the average for the whole sample – 15 per cent were moved by a desire for more education and 18 per cent sought some low-grade training. Of the people with a full general education, however, nearly half migrated in order to continue their studies.

TABLE 73. *Motivation for Migration and Level of Education of Migrants* (%)

	Education at time of migration (classes)			
Motive for migrating	*4 or less*	*5–6*	*7–8*	*9–11*
Material necessity	29.2	22.6	23.1	10.0
Desire to study	—	—	15.4	47.1
Desire to acquire a skill	4.2	11.3	18.1	8.7
Desire to live in a town	20.8	22.6	14.7	10.0
Family circumstances	8.3	13.1	18.8	6.2
Bad relations with the management	8.3	3.6	2.1	—
State of health	4.2	1.8	1.4	1.4
Other motives	8.3	18.8	7.7	11.4
No reply	16.7	6.2	7.7	1.4

Source:
T. I. Zaslavskaya, op. cit., p. 31. See note to Table 72.

The changes in the pattern of motivation over time merit consideration, in that they may reflect a shift in the attitude of village folk towards the town. The figures available are shown in Table 74. It appears that after 1953 material necessity greatly diminished as a factor in out-migration from the village, while the desire to live in the towns, and presumably enjoy urban amenities, grew. Many more people moved for family reasons – the authors claimed because more village parents wanted to give their children a better education. The desire for education and training among adults apparently remained almost constant.

TABLE 74. *Changes in the motivation for Migration to Towns 1953–66* (%)

Motive for migrating	1953–7	1958–63	1964–6
Material necessity	32.0	15.9	12.2
Desire to study	20.6	17.2	18.4
Desire to acquire a skill	11.3	15.2	12.2
Desire to live in a town	12.4	16.6	18.4
Family circumstances	6.2	10.3	20.4
Bad relations with the management	—	3.4	4.1
State of health and other reasons	17.5	21.4	14.2

Source:
T. I. Zaslavskaya, op. cit., p. 33. See note to Table 72.

This small survey is not without interest, but we should not forget that it may have important methodological weaknesses. It is not excluded (as the authors themselves suggest) that a whole layer of motives connected with the very nature of work and life in the village has been left uncovered.

A more extended examination of this motivation takes us into the realm of mathematics, which can find no place in so limited a framework as ours. Nevertheless, some of the conclusions of a vast survey of 10,000 people conducted in 200 settlements throughout the R S F S R in 1967 are reasonably digestible.[10] This survey took the form of an attempt to elucidate the relative weights of the circumstances which, in the opinion of migrants, prompted them to move.

The authors distinguished twenty factors, which they grouped separately by theme and in order of general importance. The two methods give rather different patterns, since factors which come together in any thematic group – economic, for example – may vary greatly in importance.

10. Presented by T. I. Zaslavskaya and V. N. Ladenkov in an article in *Izvestia Sibirskogo otdelenia Akademii nauk SSSR Obschchestvennye nauki*, No. 11, Vypusk 3, 1967.

The contents of each of the four *thematic* groups seem, at first sight, rather unconnected, but a little reflection will show that they do, in fact, fit together.

The first of these contains motives linked with the *standard of living*. Here we find the average wage, number of cinemas, the development of retail trade, and the number of teachers and medical workers in attendance. The availability of state-owned housing and nurseries for young children, together with home electricity consumption, are also included.

The second group, at first sight rather desperate, is basically *demographic*: here we find the cohesiveness of the population structure and its growth (which affects the presence of young individuals and young families), the proportion of persons of local nationality, the incidence of persons with middle and higher education, and the density of the railway network.

The third set of factors reflects *industrial development* and

TABLE 75. *Factors Influencing Migration from the Soviet Village*

Primary factors: (66% responsible)	1. Average wage in the state farms of *oblast* 2. Cinema attendance 3. Per capita retail trade turnover 4. No. of teachers } per '000 population 5. No. of medical personnel } per '000 population 6. Rate of natural increase of population
Secondary factors: (44% responsible)	1. Household use of electricity 2. Proportion of women among *Sovkhoz* workers 3. Proportion of young people aged 16–29 in rural population 4. Percentage of houses without electricity 5. Density of railways 6. Amount of state-owned living space (on state farms)
Tertiary factors: (26% responsible)	1. Average no. of working days per state farm worker 2. Average income from garden plot 3. Average size of the settlement 4. Density of the local population 5. Proportion of non-Russians (in autonomous republics) 6. Percentage of rural population in the locality (i.e. urbanization) 7. Amount of electricity consumed in homes 8. Percentage of children in nurseries

Source:
T. I. Zaslavskaya and V. H. Ladenkov, op. cit., p. 41.

level of technical progress. These include the proportion of employed women, the proportion of agricultural population in the area, the percentage of houses with electricity, and the average employment rate of the year. The last set of (two) factors may be thought of as _geographic_, namely, the density of the population and the average size of the rural settlements.

When regrouped by _order of importance_ all of the factors form the pattern shown in Table 75. The major ones were weighted as 66 per cent, the secondary ones 44 per cent and the lesser ones 26 per cent responsible for migration. The overlap of the figures is presumably explained by the fact that each set was calculated independently of the others, but the authors provided little detail on their methodology.

All the evidence at our disposal points to the fact that the great majority of people leaving the village are young and able-bodied. Two Soviet scholars, L. Denisova and T. Fadeeva, showed that over 60 per cent of the people who moved into towns throughout the Soviet Union in 1964 were aged between sixteen and twenty-nine, and of these 56 per cent were men and 44 per cent women.[11] A study of migration from the rural areas of the Novosbirsk _oblast_ over the five years 1959–63 showed that by 1964 a large proportion of the young people had gone (Table 76). The outflow peaks corresponded with the beginning of schooling, the completion of seven and ten classes, and the onset of the pension age.[12]

These age-groups are not only the most able-bodied, but also the best educated and trained of the farming community. That mechanizers make up a considerable proportion of them is evident from the Central Statistical Administration returns. The figures in Table 77 which cover the five years 1964–8, show that over 600,000 disappeared annually, a loss almost equal to the rate at which they had been trained. This means that the average trainee spent no more than three years in agriculture. Between 1968 and 1969 there was even a small absolute fall of some 5,000 mechanizers in the collective farms.[13] All this is regarded as

11. _Vestnik statistiki_, No. 7.1965.

12. V. I. Perevedentsev, op. cit., 1966, p. 112.

13. _Narodnoe Khozyaistvo SSSR v 1968_, p. 454. The number of mechanizers in Soviet agriculture as a whole apparently rose by a very modest 26,000.

TABLE 76. *Age of Migrants from the Village (Novosibirsk* oblast, *1959–63)*

Age-groups	Outflow by 1964 (as % of given age group in 1959)	Given age groups as % of outflow
15	18.5	3.1
16	20.1	2.9
17	35.4	4.9
18	39.8	3.0
19	46.9	2.7
20–24	32.2	15.6
25–29	18.9	11.8
30–39	12.1	14.6
40–49	9.9	6.6
50–54	6.6	2.5
55–59	3.8	1.2
60+	11.9	10.3
Average	12.3	—

Source: V. I. Perevedentsev, op. cit., p. 112. Under-fifteens omitted. They comprised 20.8% of the outflow as given in the third column.

extremely ominous by the authorities, for the mechanizers are destined to replace the unskilled peasant and ultimately change the very nature of Soviet agricultural production. They are important, too, in that their improved educational background is supposed to raise cultural levels in the village. In this respect they are second only to the specialists, who are far fewer in number.

This long-standing and widespread desertion inevitably has a deleterious effect on the life of the Soviet village. We have already had occasion to mention the imbalance of the sex ratio in the countryside. The outflow of young people has also led to the age structure in the village being much worse than in the towns.

Evidence on the ages of people going back to the village, incidentally, is contradictory. Zaslavskaya's data on Novosibirskaya *oblast* suggests they are older than the out-migrants, but figures for Kazakhstan in 1963–4 do not indicate any substantial difference (N. Zabelin and S. Sundetov, *Ispolzovanie trudovykh resursov v voprosakh balansa truda,* Alma-Ata, 1966).

TABLE 77. *Training of Mechanizers for Agriculture and Number of Mechanizers Employed (Thousands)**

Mechanizers	1964	1965	1966	1967	1968
Numbers trained	921	772	714	764	657
Annual increase in numbers employed (state and collective farms)†	106	144	105	94	38
Annual increase in numbers employed as % of those trained	11.5	18.7	14.7	12.3	5.8

*All types (tractor-drivers, combine harvest operators and assistants, drivers, for both state and collective farms) included.

†Figures for 1 April of each year. 1,135,000 mechanizers were trained in 1963.

Source:
Narodnoe Khozyaistvo SSSR v 1968, pp. 454, 565, and *1965*, pp. 443, 585.

This is easily visible from the figures provided by the 1959 census for the population in rural and urban areas.[14] The effects on the labour force have been, as may be seen from Table 78, very far-reaching. There are fewer able-bodied toilers in the lower age-groups, and far more juveniles and elderly people. Thus whereas in industry only one person per thousand was

TABLE 78. *Age Distribution of Employed Population (Selected Branches of the Economy, per Thousand Persons)*

Branch of the economy	up to 16	16–19	20–29	30–39	40–49	50–54	55–59	60 and over
All the economy	5	94	322	252	174	70	41	42
Industry	1	101	395	260	153	52	24	14
State farms	10	124	319	227	171	69	42	38
Collective farms	12	107	260	207	181	87	62	84

Source:
All-Union Census 1959, pp. 51, 117.

14. *All-Union Census*, 1959, p. 51.

under sixteen years of age, and 14 per thousand over sixty, the corresponding figures for state farms were 10 and 38, and those for the collective farm 12 and 84.[15] It is doubtful whether there has been any improvement in the position in more recent years.

SETTLING DOWN IN TOWN

No figures seem to be available for the activities of the drifters who did not manage to find a niche in the town and returned to the village forever. But how quickly do those who stay in the towns get used to their new way of life? In their 1966 investigation of migrants from 291 families T. I. Zaslavskaya and her colleagues endeavoured to measure the process of settling down by four indices – acquisition of more education and specialized training, better (i.e. more skilled) work, higher pay, and more living space. Let us trace their main conclusions.[16]

Just under two thirds of the erstwhile rustics did not, it appears, bother to raise their general education level at all, or as the case may be, get any middle special or higher education to

TABLE 79. *Distribution of Rural Migrants by Length of Extra Schooling in Town*

Years of extra schooling in town	No. of persons	% of sample
1–2 years	38	13.1
3–4 years	50	17.4
5–6 years	10	3.4
7–8 years	4	1.4
Subtotal	102	35.3
Did not study	187	64.7

Source:
T. I. Zaslavskaya, op. cit., p. 65.

15. A point commented upon by V. Ya. Churakova and L. I. Suvorova, op. cit. p. 25.
16. The investigation encompassed material on migration for the preceding five years. Some details are given in the source; see source note, Table 69.

follow it (Table 79). Half of the remainder obtained an extra four years of schooling. Of course, the migrant's performance tended to depend on the education he had before. The least and most educated groups showed the best results in this respect: the first because they needed education to get anywhere at all, the second, presumably, because they came to the town precisely in order to continue their studies. Although the proportions of people studying were the same for both sexes, men tended to do a year more than women. Other figures show that no less than 59 per cent of all migrants obtained low-grade training for specific jobs, but it is noteworthy that no less than a third of them had already received some such training in the village.

TABLE 80. *Change in the Type of Work Done by Migrants*

Original occupation in village	Total*	Occupation in town, 1966, %			
		Unskilled labourers	Skilled workers	Foremen Mechanics, etc.	Mental workers
Unskilled labourers or collective farmers	62	26.3	49.1	5.3	19.3
Mechanizers and drivers	35	20.0	68.5	2.9	8.6
Skilled workers in general trades†	40	7.7	74.4	12.8	5.1
Mental workers	18	16.6	27.8	27.8	27.8

*Includes only persons who worked before migrating.

†Trades like fitter, mechanic, which are not specific to one branch of industry or one enterprise.

Source:
T. I. Zaslavskaya, op. cit., p. 72.

As far as finding skilled work was concerned, the study revealed a rather mixed picture (Table 80). Three quarters of the formerly unskilled went into something more demanding; but none of the other groups fared so well. Twenty per cent of the mechanizers and drivers ended up doing less skilled work. Of the 'qualified workers' – those with a more widely applicable skill –

three quarters found themselves in roughly the same skill category. The mental workers (a mixed category) were spread out all over the spectrum. As the writers implied, skill-wise the village lost more than society gained from the movement examined in this particular sample.

TABLE 81. *Distribution of Migrants by Supplementary Education and Wage Increases in Town*

| Extra wage (roubles) | % of those who | | Average (%) |
	continued their education	did not continue their education	
up to 30	25.0	26.9	26.2
31–50	22.2	20.9	21.4
51–70	11.1	25.4	20.4
71–90	19.4	11.9	14.6
91–110	13.9	7.5	9.7
111 or over	8.4	7.4	7.7

Source:
T. I. Zaslavskaya, op. cit., p. 74.

The overwhelming majority of migrants greatly increased their earnings. This was the result of three factors: higher wage rates, extra training, and the general rise in wages over time. Extra education, it will be noted (Table 81), did not bring a clear benefit to everyone: this doubtlessly depended on its nature and other circumstances. The most impressive increases in earnings, according to the writers, took place within three years of moving, and were thus a consequence of the existing wage differentials rather than of the migrants having obtained more education or skills. The fact that people could expect such a jump was undoubtedly a major factor in prompting them to leave the village. But it may be presumed that their expenditure patterns assumed an urban character and some of their expenses rose.

Acquisition of accommodation seemed to follow a path of gradual improvement (Table 82). During the first three years nearly half of the migrants either lived in a dormitory or shared a room, perhaps with several others. Just over a third got permanent accommodation and the rest lodged with relatives. But as the years went by, the proportion of people with their own room,

TABLE 82. *Living Conditions of Migrants and Length of Residence in Town*

Length of residence in town (years)	Distribution of migrants by type of housing, as % of the sample						
				Have own accommodation	including		
	Live in a hostel	Hire a bed	Live with relatives		a room	a flat	a house
1–3	26.2	21.2	17.5	35.1	10.1	12.5	12.5
4–6	15.8	14.5	14.5	55.2	13.2	32.8	9.2
7–10	7.5	3.8	7.5	81.3	24.6	32.2	24.5
11–15	7.1	7.1	—	85.8	2.4	73.8	9.6
16 or over	—	—	3.8	96.2	7.6	69.0	19.6
Average	14.3	11.8	10.7	63.3	12.2	36.8	14.3

Source:
T. I. Zaslavskaya, op. cit., p. 76.

flat, or even house slowly increased, until by the eleventh year of urban residence nearly 86 per cent were in this category.

The authors of this study, in reviewing the process of adaptation, claimed that it is an effective method of social advancement for former villagers, and they expressed no surprise that of the 291 persons questioned only three intended to return, in time, to the village. In fact it seems that it took the average person about four years to settle down, though accommodation was a problem for much longer.

The economic and social implications of the government's long-standing neglect of the peasant, and the flight from the land which it has provoked, are extremely grave. This fact is recognized by observers both within the Soviet Union and abroad. Nearly all agricultural areas now suffer from a shortage of labour, especially young and skilled labour, in periods of intense activity. The present well-established migratory trends can only exacerbate this, to the obvious detriment of output. Moreover, since the point is now being reached when there is a shortage of skilled labour to man agricultural machinery, there is a real danger that further investment in agriculture, though desperately needed, will bring ever smaller marginal returns. The plans to transform Soviet rural society into a happy reflection of an ideal urban society, well-educated, socially homogeneous and contented, are far from being implemented.

Analyses of migration show that the drift from the land is a very intricate phenomenon: the reasons for it are many, and the removal of a few marginal grievances are hardly likely to make villagers want to stay at home. Zaslavskaya and her colleagues reject as useless the old Stalinist administrative restrictions on movement. They recognize that some of the main social problems, like the demographic imbalance which leads to a shortage of young people as marriage-mates and friends, themselves encourage further out-migration. Neither can the problem be reduced to one of mere investment. A whole set of social conditions has to be changed.

The task, indeed, is now so vast that it is difficult to see how it can be fulfilled. Changes in the payment and status of the collectivized peasant introduced during Khrushchev's tenure of office, and the slightly more benevolent policies introduced since 1968 have on occasions slowed down the outflow from the village, but as far as we can see, not halted it. The new collective farm statutes approved in November 1969 were on the whole conservative, and held out no hope of a radical improvement in the legal position of the peasantry – which would have at least been a step in the right direction.

What is the government to do? Clearly, its long-term aim must be to reduce the agricultural labour force to the smallish, efficient force characteristic of advanced industrialized lands. Most of the peasants have to be transformed into workers anyway. On the positive side it must be recognized that the outflow of technically skilled peasants, i.e. mechanizers, is a method, albeit a relatively inefficient one, of providing new labour for industry. In the short term, however, there is a need to slow down the drift of young people from the village drastically. Are we therefore to expect further massive increases in social benefits for the peasantry? Greater freedom to work the private plot, uneconomic and politically undesirable though this type of farming may be? A tightening up of administrative measures for keeping the peasant on the farm – despite their proven inadequacy in the past? Or more massive imports of agricultural produce from abroad? It is noteworthy that in some parts of the country collective farms officials have been offering young people extra bonuses to stay on the land, which means that they get more for doing the same work as the older generation. But this can hardly be a satisfactory solution. The Soviet authorities will succeed in closing the rift between town and country, and providing the Soviet people with a good and varied diet, only if they can solve these daunting problems.

Part II

POLITICS, EDUCATION AND
EMPLOYMENT

8

The Party and Society

THE Communist Party of the Soviet Union has long been the object of intensive study. It has attracted the avid attention of historians, political scientists and journalists both inside the Soviet Union and abroad for nearly as long as the Bolsheviks have been in power. Despite a shortage of really reliable information, many works have been devoted to its historical development, formal structure and leading figures. The manner by which it controls the State (for it is an organized apparatus of rule as much as a political party) and its relations with other organizations have been carefully explored. Our task here is not to repeat or summarize facts already treated competently by others. Rather shall we endeavour to throw light on a few problems concerning relationships between the Party and society which have been revealed more recently in Soviet published materials not widely available to readers in the West.

We have just used the term 'apparatus of rule' to describe the Party. It is, of course, important to remember that the Communist Party has two very distinct types of membership. The core of the organization consists of a bureaucratic group of anything up to three hundred thousand full-time officials – *apparatchiki* – whose working life is devoted entirely to running Party, and ultimately state, affairs.[1] These are the people who manage the hierarchy of territorial Party committees (with their subordinate departments) up and down the country. The seats in

1. In Western sources estimates for the early and mid-sixties range from 100,000 up to about 240,000; see references in Rigby, op. cit., p. 348, footnote, and article by G. Fischer in *Soviet Studies*, Vol. XVI, No. 3, January 1965. It is interesting that N. E. Ovchinnikov, a Party official writing about 1964, suggested that the number of paid (i.e. full-time) Party officials was something below 150,000 for the whole country. These were assisted by over 300,000 volunteers who in theory at least were unpaid for their efforts. See G. E. Glezerman and V. G. Afanasiev, *Opyt i metodika konkretnykh sotsiologicheskikh issledovanii*, Moscow, 1965, p. 212.

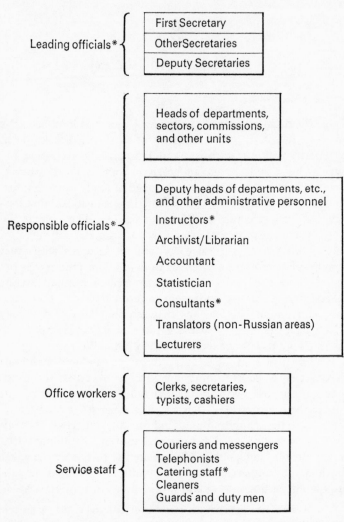

FIGURE 17. *Hypothetical Occupation Structure of a Party Committee at Raion Level (Full-time Personnel)*

Sources:
Details culled from *Spisok abonentov leningradskoi telefonnoi seti*, Leningrad, 1965, pp. 99–100, and *Spravochnik partiinogo rabotnika*, Moscow, 1957, pp. 406–7.

any Party committee or bureau are in theory elective, but in practice the most responsible ones are filled by full-time officials whose nomination is suggested, or at least approved, by a higher organ.

The full-time apparatus of any given committee, from republic down to the local district, or *raion*, is, of course, itself an organizational entity, with the familiar socio-occupational gradations. The main groups in it are probably the leading officials (all ostensibly elected), responsible officials (some elected), their supporting office staff, and service personnel, rather as illustrated in Figure 17. In addition there may be part-time workers (who, it appears, usually aspire to permanent posts), and a large number of voluntary helpers – Party members who may or may not hold elective posts. Many of these get time off from their full-time jobs in order to indulge in Party activities. The number of Party workers of all kinds may vary from a few dozen in a *raion* committee up to several hundred at the *oblast* level. The peak of the apparatal pyramid, which comprises about four thousand territorial organizations in all, is the Party's Central Committee, located in vast administrative offices in Moscow. This body alone may contain several thousand persons.

Very little is known about the Party apparatus; indeed the variations in the estimates of its size are themselves indicative of our ignorance. If this is one of the most closely guarded secrets of Soviet society, the reason is not far to seek. The existence of a powerful and centralized organizational machine staffed by permanent officials largely negates the principles of democratic

---

* Notes on Figure 17
The distinction between *leading* workers and *responsible* workers is ours.
Instructors are Party officials who can be entrusted with various duties either on the premises or elsewhere. They may act as senior receptionists, or may be sent out to check on the fulfilment of Party directives in non-Party organizations. *Consultants* may be specialists (lawyers, economists, etc.) whose knowledge is needed for administrative decisions. *Catering staff* have been included because some Party organizations have their own eating facilities. A good buffet can be a major attraction for this kind of work.

Party organizations frequently employ part-time workers to supplement the full-time staff. They also rely on the services of 'activists' who have their full-time jobs outside the Party but usually hold elective positions in the committee.

control in the Party, and indeed rule by the Soviets. It provides proof, if any were needed, of the concentration of power in the hands of the small group of men who lead the Party.

Only a few very restricted categories of professional Party workers are open to anything approaching sociological analysis. Scanty figures covering things like educational background, age and career patterns are available for members of Party organs at the All-Union or republican levels; something is known about the background of a few heads of Central Committee departments and the first secretaries of the hundred or so *oblast* and *krai* committees in the provinces. We know virtually nothing about the rest. The Party is not, of course, unique in this respect: other administrative hierarchies, such as the soviets, ministries, and social organizations are also closed to investigation. Few governments welcome investigation of their bureaucracies, but the Soviet authorities take secrecy to a rare extreme. At the same time the Party propagandists like to claim that a large proportion of members partake in the running of Party affairs. In 1967, for example, some 2.7 million communists (i.e. Party members) were said to occupy 'elective' positions; this figure included the leading, and some responsible, personnel in the territorial Party organs illustrated, but the great majority of positions were at the lowest and least significant level, that is in the third of a million or so primary organizations of factories, farms, shops and offices.

The mass, or ordinary, membership of the Party is more open to generalization than the bureaucratic core, though not to proper analysis. Between 1953 and 1968 the number of people in the Party grew from just under 7 million to just over 13 million, which works out at a little under 9 per cent of everyone over the joining age of eighteen.[2] The post-Stalin leadership has shown an interest in proving that the Party membership is representative of society at large, and this doubtless explains why publication of data on its social composition was resumed in 1965; the practice had ceased in the early thirties when Stalin was preparing for the purges.[3]

2. We have based this estimate on the figures from *New Directions in the Soviet Economy*, cited in footnote to Figure 4, p. 19.

3. 'KPSS v tsifrakh', in *Partiinaya zhizn*, No. 10, 1965, and No. 15, 1967;

It is possible, on this basis, to explore a few of the quantitative relationships between the mass membership and various groups in Soviet society – an exercise closely relevant to our study of the social structure of the USSR. In this context we shall also suggest some reasons why people join the Party at all.

THE PARTY MEMBERSHIP AND SOCIAL GROUPS

The leadership of the Communist Party takes a very close interest in the social composition of the mass membership, and, by extension, the Party coverage or 'saturation' of different groups in Soviet society.[4] One of the most important elements in the Central Committee apparatus, the 'Party Organs' Department, as it is now called, was created specifically to manipulate 'cadres', and this, according to all the evidence, includes controlling intakes by 'social position'. It is probable that the Party Organs Department, which is usually headed by a man who enjoys the confidence of the leading faction in the Politbureau, issues all the necessary directives in circular letter form to subordinate Party organizations. Control has to be discreet, since the Party rules, like the Constitution, do not distinguish between Soviet citizens by their social provenance. Instructions eventually reach the town and district committees which are in direct contact with the primary organizations that admit all new members. This is the point at which the policy of the leadership on questions of intakes is implemented. All new candidatures are then checked and approved at the local town or *raion* Party office. Admission policies over the years have varied, and may not always have been fully effective; but there has not been any known departure from the principle of strict central control, at least since the early twenties. Discrepancies between the Central Committee policies and intakes in the matter of the social position of the candidates

see also 'Ob itogakh priema v partiyu i izmeneniakh v sostave KPSS za 1967', in *Spravochnik partiinogo rabotnika*, 1968, p. 539.

4. Indeed, the second factor may be more important. We use the term 'saturation' in the sense in which Mr H. Rigby understood it in his excellent study *Communist Party Membership in the USSR, 1917–1967*, Princeton, 1968. Readers who are interested in the deeper chronology of these trends could not do better than consult those pages.

have been due, most likely, to people mis-stating their social status so as to improve their chances of admission.[5] Only a small proportion of the members leave the Party before they die, so membership, except in time of repression or purge, is normally regarded as terminable by death. The generally accepted way to leave is to omit to pay the nominal membership fees. Demonstrative departure, or exclusion, can lead to the loss of one's job, unemployment, and other misfortunes.

The standard categorization of social groups in the Party since the twenties has been the worker-peasant-employee one with which we are familiar.[6] Fortunately, the recent reports on Party membership have also contained information on some other sub-groups, and this allows us to make a rather more sensitive analysis. But let us take the triadic scheme as our starting point. The social composition of the Party (thus understood) is compared with a corresponding breakdown of Soviet society in Table 83.[7] It is at once evident that in the late sixties the 'employees'

TABLE 83. *Representation of Social Groups in the Party, circa 1967*

Social group	As % of society	As % of Party
Employees*	23.9	45.9
Workers	53.5	38.1
Peasants	22.6	16.0

*The official estimate for all workers of predominantly mental labour at the beginning of 1969 has been inserted here.
Sources:
Social groups: *Narodnoe khozyaistvo SSSR v 1967*, p. 35; *1969*, p. 30.
Party membership: *Kommunist*, No. 15, 1967, p. 95.

5. An instance of how these requirements were imposed (or avoided) locally in the mid thirties may be found in the Smolensk documents; see M. Fainsod, *Smolensk under Soviet Rule*, London, 1958, p. 78. A favourite loophole was to quote 'social origins', i.e. one's former 'social position' or that of one's parents, rather than one's existing social position if the other was more satisfactory.
6. Rigby, op. cit., p. 159, etc.
7. We proceed on the assumption that the Party definitions exactly fit those used in the statistical handbooks.

(which here means all persons of predominantly mental labour) had the highest representation in the Party, both in absolute numbers and proportionately to the size of their social group. The workers and peasants, conversely, provided fewer Party members than purely proportional considerations would demand. Furthermore, the weight of employees may here be understated. In the last years of Stalin's rule the proportion of 'workers' in the Party declined relative to 'employees', and the efforts to push up worker and peasant representation which were made after his death may have introduced a plebeian bias into many candidates' interpretation of their social position.

The weight of the 'employee' element conceals, in fact, the dominance of the intelligentsia. Managers and specialists, who in 1967 made up, at a generous estimate, 14 per cent of the total *labour force*, occupied a third of the places in the Party. At the other extreme the unskilled peasants, who comprised perhaps 20 per cent of the labour force, took up only 7 or 8 per cent of these places.

These disproportions are matched by wide variations in the percentages of members of given socio-occupational groups who were in the Party, in other words, the extent to which those groups were saturated. Some of the figures gleaned on this most interesting topic are shown in Table 84. Let us begin with some comments on the groups which make up the intelligentsia.[8]

The 1967 official report suggested that about 4.2 million people, or perhaps one out of every four of administrative personnel, managers and specialists were full or candidate members of the Party.[9] It is, in fact, probably safe to assume that a much

8. Some of these figures have been taken directly from official sources, others arrived at by rough calculation, particularly of data from the 1967 report on Party membership. Except where specific sources are given they should be regarded *only* as indications of an order of magnitude.

9. The groupings for specialists which were included were: (1) Managers of organizations, establishments, enterprises, construction sites, state farms, and their structural subdivisions; (2) Engineers and technical workers, agricultural specialists; (3) Workers (*rabotniki*) in science, education, health, literature and the arts; (4) Workers (*rabotniki*) in trade, catering, supply and sales enterprises. Two (presumably non-specialist) groups included in the 1965 report but not in that of 1967 were 'workers [*rabotniki*] in control, accounting and office services', and 'other employees'. It will be noted that this comes very close to a definition of the intelligentsia.

TABLE 84. *Party 'Saturation' of Selected Social and Occupational Groups*

Source ref.	Groups	Saturation rate %	Year
	Administrative, industrial and service personnel		
1	Managerial staff and specialists	25	1967
2	Engineers	33	1968
3	Workers	9	1967
4	Service personne	13	1967
	Intelligentsia (non-production)		
5	Candidates & doctors of science	+50	1968
6	Teachers	25	1968
7	Doctors	20	1968
	Persons employed in government an social organizations		
8	Deputies to Supreme Soviet USSR	75	1966
9	Deputies to Supreme Soviets Union & Autonomous Republics	67	1966
10	Deputies to Local Soviets	45	1969
11	Trade union officials, Chairmen of Committees	48	1967
12	TU officials, members of Committees	28	1967
13	Secretaries of Komsomol organizations	20	1968
	Collective farm personnel		
14	Chairmen	94	1959
15	Agronomists & other specialists	50	1968
16	Mechanizers	23	1965
17	Cattle rearers	24	1965
18	Peasants	5	1965

Sources:

Items 1, 3, 4: Estimate, *KPSS v tsifrakh*, 1967, and data alluded to in Chapter 5.

Items 2, 5, 6, 7, 15: *Kommunist*, No. 16, 1969, p. 17.

Items, 8, 9, 10: *Pravda*, 26 March 1967 and 22 March 1969, sources quoted in E. M. Jacobs, *Soviet Studies*, University of Glasgow, July 1970, p. 68.

Items 11, 12: *Spravochnaya kniga o profsoyuzakh*, Moscow, 1968, p. 7.

Item 13: *Kommunist*, No. 14, 1968, p. 47.

Item 14: *Selskoe khozyaistvo SSSR*, Moscow, 1960, p. 474. The exact figure given is 93.5 per cent.

Items 16, 17: *Pravda*, 6 June 1965, quoted in V. S. Aleksandrov and A. G. Lashin, *Sotsialno-politicheskoe i kulturnoe razvitie sotsialisticheskogo obshchestva*, Moscow, 1969.

Item 18: Estimate, as residue, from source quoted for items 16, 17.

higher proportion of the country's *senior* administrative personnel were in it. The same report revealed that nearly 940,000
Party members were working in 'organs of state and economic
management, in the apparatus of the Party and social organizations'. No identical formulation appears in any of the available
collections of statistics, but the 1967 handbook on Soviet labour
did list a category of 'workers in the apparatus of state and
economic management and in the managerial organs of cooperative and social organizations', which numbered 1,640,000.[10] If
these formulations are roughly comparable, then well over half of
this narrower administrative group must have been in the Party.
The report, moreover, gave a figure of 460,000 for communists
who were 'managers [*rukovoditeli*] of organizations, institutions,
enterprises, building sites, state farms and their structural subdivisions'; this may have covered the more senior amongst them,
and indicated an even higher saturation rate. Some regional data
for the years 1950–61 analysed by H. Rigby suggest that nearly
all of the industrial managers who were prominent enough to be
deputies to Soviets were in the Party.[11]

Some interesting divergencies were revealed in the 'non-
production' intelligentsia. Whereas, for example, nearly half of
all candidates and doctors of science were Party members, only
about a quarter of the teachers and a fifth of the medical doctors
had joined.[12]

The saturation rate among deputies to local and higher soviets
and Trade Union officials was markedly above the average for
the intelligentsia as a whole; clearly, the Party has to be in a
position to exert strong influence on these organizations. The
figures for these categories afford a further example of the principle that the more responsible a post is, the more likely is its
holder to be in the Party. The relatively poor showing of low-

10. *Trud v SSSR*, Moscow, 1968, p. 29.
11. H. Rigby, op. cit., p. 433.
12. H. Rigby's study of these problems reveals some of the variations
amongst academics by seniority (p. 445). Until recently scholars in the middle
or lower grades seemed much more likely to be in the Party than those at the
top, though this imbalance is apparently being corrected. It may result from
changes in the pressure to join the Party at different periods in Soviet history,
or from the fact that really distinguished men have not found Party membership necessary for promotion.

standing Komsomol officials is probably to be explained by their youth and by the close ties which already bind the leadership of this organization to the Party.

According to Table 84, about one Soviet worker in eleven is a member of the Party. We have been at pains to show, however, that the Soviet working class is a very mixed body. The Party authorities have never concealed their desire to recruit into the CPSU its 'leading members', by which is meant (with reference to indices used elsewhere in these pages) the most opulent, skilled and educated. We would therefore expect different saturation rates for different layers of it. Official Party statistics give nothing away here, but O. I. Shkaratan's analysis of a sample of Leningrad toilers was very revealing.[13] Whereas 23.4 per cent of the highly skilled mental-cum-manual workers were communists, only 3.7 per cent of the unskilled labourers had achieved the distinction. As far as the unskilled mental workers (the low-grade 'employees') are concerned, the data in the 1967 Party report suggested that about 13 per cent of them were members; in other words they did far better than the 'workers', but lagged a long way behind the intelligentsia.

The collective farm community has its own very clear set of variations in Party membership, which seems to be distributed amongst the socio-occupational groups there as unequally as most other privileges. In 1959 93.5 per cent of all collective farm chairmen were in the Party; indeed, it seems not unusual for full-time *raikom* secretaries to be transferred to this post. At the other extreme the unskilled peasants registered in 1965 a figure of only about 5 per cent. The achievement of a reasonable level of saturation in the agricultural community has of course always been a major aim of the Party leadership. This is reflected in the relatively high rate of membership among agronomists and veterinary specialists.

If the Party authorities are concerned to cover the more influential occupation groups, they are no less anxious to extend their influence amongst the most educated. Table 85 shows

13. See Table 42. The same authors showed in their book *Ocherki istorii sotsialisticheskogo sorevnovania*, Leningrad, 1966, p. 228, that the shock-worker brigades in machine-building factories of Leningrad (1965) also tended to have a higher proportion of Party people in them.

Party saturation of four educational groups in Soviet society in
1967. Over a third of all people with higher education were
communists. At the other end of the scale we find that only 5 per
cent of those with less than complete general education had
joined. Thus it seems probable that the least favoured members
of this last group – those, say, with primary education or less –
were virtually excluded from the Party. It is a sobering thought
that at least a third of the adult population of the country was
still in this educational bracket.[14]

TABLE 85. *Party Saturation of Educational Groups, circa 1967*

Educational level	No. in society (millions)*	No. in Party (millions)†	Saturation (%)
Higher	6.4	2.2	35.5
Incomplete higher	2.8	0.3	12.0
Middle	26.4	4.2	16.0
Less than middle	124.4	6.5	5.2

*Persons aged sixteen and over.

†Party members must be aged eighteen or over. Note that for this reason
the saturation rates in the third column will be slightly understated. This does
not, however, appreciably affect the validity of the proportions.

Sources:

Figures for society: *Soviet Economic Performance, 1966–67*, U.S. Government
Printing Office, Washington, May 1968, p. 88.

Figures for Party (1 Jan. 1968): *Spravochnik partiinogo rabotnika*, Moscow,
1968, p. 540.

Although our main concern here is with the mass membership
of the Party, we may digress for a moment to consider data which
show that holders of even the meanest kinds of elective posts
have a much more strongly 'upper-class' background than the
Party membership as a whole. In 1969 there were 1.3 million
persons in the 'leading organs' of primary cells, which presumably meant the (elected) secretaries and members of the bureaux.

14. H. Rigby estimated that in 1959 only 0.3% of the over-twenties in this
category were in the Party. Education figures for our estimates from the
U.S. Joint Economic Committee print, *Soviet Economic Performance*, p. 88,
details from a study by A. S. Goodman and M. Feshbach.

Of these 16.7 per cent were workers and 13.3 per cent were collective farmers, so the remainder, 70 per cent, must have been employees.[15] If we turn these percentages back into figures (which is statistically a fairly safe procedure) and set them against the corresponding social groups (which is, admittedly, most precarious) we find an enormous difference in the election chances of worker, peasant and employee. It may even be that the proportions of the three groups holding elective posts in the Party varied by a factor of thirty or more (Table 86).

TABLE 86. *Proportion of Socio-occupational Groups in Elective Positions* (*Primary Party Cells, Hypothetical*)

Groups	% in elective positions
Employees	3.1
Workers	0.4
Peasants	0.1

Source:
Partiinaya Zhizn, No. 5, 1969, p. 9 (hypothesis, as indicated in the text).

At the same time the educational levels of Party officials are markedly above the average. In 1968 31.8 per cent of the secretaries of primary organizations had a degree, 6 per cent were studying for one and another 44 per cent had a complete general education. Only 2.5 per cent had not gone further than primary school. In 1967 91.1 per cent of the secretaries at the town and district level, and 97.6 per cent of those in higher committees had taken a degree.[16]

All this points to another slightly mathematical conclusion. We know that there is a high rate of turnover among Party secretaries of primary organizations. (In 1969 it was probably about 25 per cent per annum, though Khrushchev had wished to make a two-year term the maximum at this level.) If we presume that this rate is the same for all such secretaries, regardless of their social origin, and if the employees are evenly distributed

15. *Partiinaya zhizn*, No. 5, 1969, p. 5.
16. See sources as given on p. 216, footnote 3.

among primary organizations, then it seems that most, if not all, of them must occupy at least one elective position during their Party careers. But the 'elective' coverage of the other social categories is so low that chances of such a post are tiny.[17]

The marked increase in Party coverage from the less to the more favoured groups of Soviet society is in no way surprising. The fact that the Party operates as a kind of superior bureaucracy, spreading its influence through every enterprise, organization and farm in the country, and effectively controlling all forms of overt political activity, would lead one to expect no more. And, to judge on another plane, most political parties throughout the world have, or encourage, a class bias in their membership. But since 1959 the CPSU has claimed to be a party of the 'whole people': this slogan can evidently be justified only to a very restricted degree. It has been suggested that the rapid growth of the Party after the mid fifties is explicable primarily in terms of the growth of the Soviet intelligentsia. In order to maintain adequate saturation of this important social group, and yet keep a reasonable ratio between 'employees', 'workers' and 'peasants' in its ranks, the Party has been obliged to recruit large numbers of the last two categories. In a sense they may only be makeweights. The expansion of the mass membership has not, as far as we can gather, entailed any devolution of political power outside the professional Party apparatus, which is composed mostly of degree-holding 'employees'.

TO JOIN OR NOT TO JOIN

Membership of the CPSU is obviously associated with 'a better life' and the people who get on are more likely to be Party members. But that conclusion is rather academic. What are the real advantages from the point of view of a young individual who is trying to make up his (or her) mind whether to join or not?

No analysis of this most important matter ever seems to have been published by Soviet sociologists, though a few aspects of their work, as we shall see below, throw some indirect light on it.

17. While we may have some confidence in this generalization, the approximate character of the data to hand does not justify the adduction of figures. We leave that to a more intrepid analyst.

All we can offer here is a conceptual framework; perhaps, with the passage of time, statistical material in which it can be clothed will become available.

We may presume that most people join the Party in order to obtain certain tangible or intangible benefits. But they may be influenced by two factors which are not immediately apparent to outsiders. The first is that Party membership has important disadvantages as well as benefits. On a practical plane it involves a lot of tedious chores such as political meetings and unpaid 'social work' or 'commissions' (which we shall return to in the next section). As a consequence of these duties the Party member loses some of his time and personal independence. He is answerable to the general meeting of his primary cell (or its secretary) for the fulfilment of them. On another plane, he has to adopt attitudes and express opinions with which he might not always agree. Moreover, he lays any aspect of his conduct, public or private, open to criticism for being un-Party-like. Party standards of behaviour do not seem to be particularly high, but this vulnerability may be onerous to some. The decision about an erring member's future lies in the hands of professional officials who may not be sympathetic towards him.

The second factor is that the secretaries of primary Party cells are themselves usually under pressure from the local Party office to increase membership. Between 1953 and 1968, for example, the total Party membership grew from 6.8 million to 13.2 million, which, allowing for deaths and a small fall-out, must have meant an average intake of well over half a million a year. Thus many people who might not otherwise have bothered have to be persuaded to join. Refusal can require a good deal of stubbornness. Some people, therefore, find themselves in the Party without any very strong personal motivation.

The advantages to be gained from ordinary membership of the Party may be classed roughly as follows. Party members by virtue of their social involvement and minor responsibilities in the 'collective' are, in a way, meritorious. Like all would-be do-gooders, they have a justifiable claim to a larger share of any benefits going. First among these is the possibility of more rapid promotion at their place of work. The Party's concern with the 'foremost workers' means that the more responsible a person's job is, the greater will be the pressure on him to join. Conversely, other things being equal, Party members tend to have first call on any responsible jobs offered. For this reason, membership of the Party may compensate for an individual's personal short-comings (such as a lack of the necessary skills or formal training) and help him to get on despite them. The advantages for himself and his family which accrue from promotion may be manifold.

This bias leads to a kind of careerism which has been frequently criticized in the Soviet press. In the absence of more general data we may perhaps be excused for quoting one instance from the writer's personal experience. A certain teacher at the Faculty of Economics in Moscow University in the early sixties was known as a very mediocre academic, but was active as a secretary of the faculty Party Committee, or Partkom. In fact he practically ran the faculty with the help of some Party colleagues. His contribution to knowledge consisted of two or three very orthodox and unoriginal books on labour problems which may have been the work of his research students. By 1969, however, he was a member of the Partbureau of the University, and evidently in charge of Party work for the entire establishment. In that year we also find him writing an article about his work for the national daily *Sovetskaya Rossia*. He began with bitter criticism of an eminent scholar for purportedly unorthodox views on social structure. A year later he was listed as a member of the Moscow Party Committee.

The second major advantage which may be expected to stem from Party membership is an improvement in material status. Promotion at work means, of course, a rise in salary; but there are other advantages more directly associated with the Party. The key one which people quote most often is better housing. In 1968 nearly 70 per cent of all new living space was put up by state and cooperative enterprises and organizations themselves, for distribution among their staff. It is usual in such cases for the management to set up a Housing Commission which has the tricky task of deciding who gets what. In conditions of extreme shortage, such as exist in the USSR, the work of this Commission arouses keen interest. The presence on it of one or more representatives of the Party cell is almost taken for granted, and this generally means that the claims of Party members are put in the strongest possible manner. The actual outcome will depend on the balance of interests but, obviously, Party members have an advantage if they can put a forceful and senior spokesman in this position.

Another important fringe benefit is the possibility of travel abroad. Soviet citizens do not, of course, have the right to leave their country at will, and such foreign tourism as exists is subject to detailed control by the state authorities. It is in fact extremely difficult for the average Soviet citizen to get a place in a 'tourist delegation', especially to the capitalist West. Figures are very scarce, but a recent Komsomol handbook revealed that the 'Sputnik' travel organization, which is by far the most important source of foreign travel vouchers for young people, had issued a mere 55,800 in 1969. The majority were probably for East Europe anyway.[18] Members of the Party are in a much stronger position than others for obtaining the recommendations which are needed to support an application, especially if they have taken the precaution of not learning a foreign tongue. Passes to the better rest-homes in the USSR are also more easily available to Party members.

It would be wrong to underestimate the possible feedback of satisfaction which Party members get from knowing that they are an inner and favoured group. Party meetings for the discussion of current tasks, admissions, and other business are, under the terms of the statutes, in most cases held once a month. These gatherings are normally 'open' in the sense that the proceedings are not secret, and outsiders may attend. Closed Party meetings may, however, be called whenever it is necessary to distribute semi-confidential information from on high, such as a leader's unpublished speech, or discuss the personal affairs of members, particularly those who are in trouble. These meetings may satisfy a psychological need. Some less demanding people may enjoy the influence that participation in Party activities brings, quite apart from the occasional opportunity of a little say in running the enterprise where they work (this being a formal function of every Party cell). All the human responses which have been observed among inner groups in other communities are doubtless to be found in the CPSU, and such responses are consciously used to cement Party unity.

18. A. I. Kamshalov and others, *Ot S'ezda k S'ezdu*, Moscow, 1970, p. 85.

Like most closed organizations, the Party is prone to long domination by officials who cannot be removed. Khrushchev was aware of the danger, and attempted to lessen it by putting upper limits on the tenure of elective posts – at least for the lesser officials. As we know, this innovation was rejected by his successor. The USSR has its share of scoundrels; tragedy has frequently ensued when such people have captured important Party posts.

Finally, a word about the social standing of the ordinary Party member. This is a most difficult topic, as this standing is evaluated differently by people of different political views. The Party propagandists maintain that the Party accepts only the most worthy souls into its midst, and that membership itself is an honour. There are certainly idealists who try to measure up to these standards. As far as potential communists are concerned, local secretaries go to great lengths to exclude at least the ideologically unsound. Cases of older Party members refusing to give a recommendation because they considered the applicants to be unreliable are known to the writer. It may well be that the real selection of members is made at this point – which is no doubt a major aim of the Party's strict recommendation system.[19] In 1964 only 2.4 per cent of the people who had been accepted as candidates were actually refused full membership.

At the other extreme Soviet liberals and persons of oppositionist views claim that the quality of membership has deteriorated vastly since the Revolution, and that people join for material or other benefits, or because they are pushed into it. The truth probably lies somewhere in between. No doubt some Party members are honest and regard the Party as a channel for their efforts to improve the wellbeing of the people. Others may be sceptical about Party membership but join precisely to improve its quality and ideals. The importance of a careerist element is

19. According to the statutes approved at the Twenty-third Congress of the Party in April 1966, candidates under the age of twenty-three had to belong to the Komsomol and present three recommendations – one from the town or *raion* Komsomol Committee, and two from members of the CPSU of at least five years' standing who had known the candidate 'at production and social work' for at least a year. People aged over twenty-three had to submit three personal recommendations. The minimum age for joining was eighteen as before. These rules have changed frequently over the years.

not, however, to be doubted. The political acrobatics of the top
leadership, which have been so well documented, are hardly
compatible with the claim that there is a strong sense of honest
intention in the mass membership.

MASS PARTICIPATION–DEFINITIONS AND MEASUREMENT

The problem of the participation of the masses in running the
affairs of state is one which lies deep in Marxist philosophy. The
Soviet leaders have always claimed that their system of government has provided the answer, in so far as the Party, the soviets,
and a number of extra-governmental organizations, primarily the
Komsomol and trade unions, offer all the necessary opportunities for the public to involve itself in civic and social functions.

In practice, we know that all Soviet public organizations,
regardless of their size or nature, are ultimately subservient to
the central leadership. Sometimes they are used to channel the
surplus energies of the people into officially approved movements or campaigns; good examples of this technique are to be
found in the work of the Party in organizing the interminable
output competitions at state enterprises, or the Komsomol drive
to get young people to go to the Virgin Lands in the mid fifties.
Sometimes public organizations acquire para-civil functions, as
happens when trade union members have to administer social
insurance schemes, or when the Party organizes squads of young
people to keep order in the streets. In the field of artistic activities, hobbies and sport the authorities try and ensure that any
organization, national or local, is at least in the hands of good
Party members who are answerable to the local Party office for
the conduct of its affairs. Of course, every public body, from the
Party down, generates its own activities, with meetings, lectures,
outings, etc., which demand public effort and 'participation'.

These heterogeneous functions, which are part of the fabric
of Soviet life, are usually described by Soviet observers as 'socio-
political activity', 'social activity' or 'social work', without much
concern for possible distinctions between the terms. Since the
mid sixties the topic has been the subject of many sociological
investigations, some of which have been published. The Party

authorities have presumably authorized this work – and its partial publication – in the belief that it will help them gauge public reaction to their policies, and improve their methods of control. It is to some of these findings that we devote the following pages. But first a few comments on the material and the difficulties of interpreting it.

If the Party authorities permit, or encourage, studies of this kind it must be principally to secure results which appear to support their propaganda claims. This must entail preventing the study of 'negative' phenomena, limiting the questions which sociologists may ask, and even putting pressure on them to abandon academic rigour in the Party interests. Undoubtedly, investigation is narrowed and the presentation of results sometimes distorted by these pressures.

If we have ventured to use any of this material at all, it is because we adopt a basically positive attitude towards the people who have gathered it. We believe that Soviet sociologists belong, on the whole, to a liberal wing of the academic front; that those who undertake these studies are not necessarily Party hacks and may, at times, view the Party with scepticism or hostility; that most of them aspire to a respectable level of scholarship; and that it would be less than fair for outsiders merely to presume otherwise. In fact the results as published are, as often as not, ambiguous, and a good step removed from the ideals which the Party stipulates. If any of the results which we use here are false, then we can only conclude that they were falsified in a very unsatisfactory manner. We hope that our presumptions with regard to their basic veracity will one day be proved.

The second problem concerns the methodological treatment of the data by Soviet scholars – quite apart from its provenance. The main difficulty here is that of definition. Having decided what constitutes socio-political activities and what does not, the researcher has to determine both the amount of time which each instance of involvement takes up, and the frequency of these instances. In practice there are great variations between the 'participation' patterns of one person and another; this in itself requires investigation. Many people, of course, do not participate in any meaningful sense at all. For purposes of generalization over a whole sample, the sociologist may average out total time inputs per item for all the individuals included, thereby producing a sort of synthetic 'average participant' who devotes some of his time to every single item in the range chosen. This method is useful in comparing the weights of different kinds of activity, but can give, as we shall see, impossibly small quantities of time

TABLE 87. *Participation in Social Activities, Selected Survey Results (Approximate Chronological Order, as % of Sample)*

Source Number	Category of persons covered	Number in sample	Location	Year of study	Frequency of participation	Proportion of sample who participated %
1	Workers of instrument factory	528	Sverdlovsk	Jan. 1961	Constantly	46.1
	Workers of instrument factory	509	Sverdlovsk	Jan. 1962	Constantly	59.0
	Workers of mechanical factory	513	Sverdlovsk	Jan. 1961	—	28.7
2	Young workers	2665	Leningrad	1961–2	—	41.6
3	Workers	787	Leningrad	1963	Permanent commissions	50.0
					Temporary commissions	22.1
4	Workers	900	'Several towns'	early sixties	Few times a month	80.0
5	Workers (male)	500	Krasnodar *krai*	early sixties	Permanent commissions	45.0
					Periodic commissions	7.0
6	Young people,	2035	Leningrad	1963–4	Permanent social commissions	46.7
	'mainly workers'	2204	Leningrad	1966		44.4

TABLE 87 – *continued*

Source Number	Category of persons covered	Number in sample	Location	Year of study	Frequency of participation	Proportion of sample who participated %
7	Young workers	3433	Odessa, Nikolaev	mid sixties	Permanent social commissions	57.5
8	Students	3000 (?)	Sverdlovsk Pedagogical Institute	mid sixties	All the time Episodically No participation	33.4 38.0 28.6
9	Students	5000 (?)	Kharkov University (as a whole)	mid sixties	—	51.2
	—		By faculty	mid sixties	—	34.8
10	Students	3000 (?)	Kharkov Polytechnical Institute	mid sixties	—	54.7

Sources and Notes:

1. L. Kogan and P. Ivanova, article in G. K. Ashina & others, *Voprosy organisatsii i metodiki konkretno-sotsiologicheskikh issledovanii*, Rostov-on-Don, 1963, p. 176.

2. A. A. Kissel, in A. G. Zdravomyslov, *Trud i razvitie lichnosti*, Leningrad, 1965, pp. 112, 113, 121, calculated. No definition of participation is provided.

3. E. S. Kuzmin, *Osnovy sotsialnoi psikhologii*, Leningrad, 1967, p. 100 ff., calculated. Kuzmin examines, amongst other things, the relationship between involvement in the shockworker movement and involvement in social activities. He purports to show that members of brigades of Communist Labour are much more active. Later in this work he discusses the relationship between tendencies of workers to change jobs and their attitudes towards social activities. Not unexpectedly the attitudes of the more stable workers appear to be much more positive. Kuzmin's analysis, based on the work of other Soviet scholars, is worthy of more attention than can be given to it here.

4. V. G. Baikova, op. cit., p. 98. A figure of 36 per cent was given for involvement in political studies at least several times a month.

5. A. G. Pusep, in V. D. Patrushev (ed.), *Opyt ekonomiko-sotsiologicheskikh issledovanii v Sibiri*, Novosibirsk, 1966, p. 111.

6. S. I. Ikonnikova and V. T. Lisovski, *Molodezh o sebe, o svoikh sverstnikakh*, Moscow, 1968, p. 59.

7. A. S. Kapto, in Ts. S. Stepanyan, V. S. Semenov, and others, op. cit., p. 72.

8. A. F. Plyshevskaya and M. K. Syroeshkina, *Materialy mezhvuzovskoi konferentsii po probleme vozrastania aktivnosti obshchestvennogo soznaniya v period stroitelstva kommunizma*, Kursk, 1968, p. 483. Number of students hypothetical.

9. M. V. Kirillova, ibid., p. 477. Number of students estimated. In 1960 there were 4,192 in the full-time departments. No definition of participation given.

10. V. M. Kozhanchikov, ibid., p. 479. Number of students hypothetical, no definition of participation given.

per activity, and is for this reason unrealistic. These methodological weaknesses could be overcome by fuller mathematical analysis, but this to our knowledge is as yet lacking. Such gaps undoubtedly detract from the value of the information, but they are not, in our view, sufficient to justify the complete rejection of it, or invalidate any cautious conclusions which may be drawn from it.

Let us begin with a few of the more convincing analyses of the proportion of people in various survey samples who are said to participate. The data in Table 87 cover, in all, some 10,000 persons, and may be representative of large sectors of society. It will be noted that a third to a half of the people in most samples gave a positive reply; in some cases participation was described as 'constant' or 'systematic', though in others no definition was given. A few other samples not included in this table have shown much lower rates; in one of those discussed in a book by Yu. F. Bukhalov and E. A. Yakuba (to which we shall return below) the figure dropped to 10.5 per cent, while Zdravomyslov and Yadov claimed that only 12 per cent of the sample in their Leningrad study were so 'orientated'.[20] There are, as we have mentioned, good reasons for regarding the high figures with suspicion, but the sheer numerical strength of the mass organizations could at times ensure their attainment. By 1968 there were, after all, 24 million people in the Komsomol and over 80 million in the various trade unions.

A reasonably detailed breakdown of socio-political activities in the form in which they present themselves to the individual was provided by V. A. Artemov and a number of other sociologists in a recent book on time use in the USSR.[21] This is reproduced in Table 88. It will be noted that it is quite similar to breakdowns used by several other scholars to whom we refer below.

Artemov's table was composed primarily to illustrate the differences in time expenditure between shockworkers and other categories, but that is a point we will set aside for a moment. The

20. Yu. F. Bukhalov and E. A. Yakuba (eds.), *Rol' obshchestvennosti v upravlenii proizvodstvom*, Kharkov, 1968, p. 36, and *Chelovek i ego rabota*, p. 249.

21. V. A. Artemov and others, *Statistika byudzhetov vremeni trudyaschikhysa*, Moscow, 1966.

figures show that the average male worker who did not happen to be in the shockworker movement spent an hour a week in socio-political activities. The first six items in the time budget – those which were, incidentally, the most 'political' in character – took up 60 per cent of the fund of time available. No less than a third of the total was taken up by meetings and conferences. Elective functions, i.e. work which was consequent on election to one of

TABLE 88. *Time Spent on Socio-political Activities by Shockworkers and Others, Krasnoyarsk Krai Survey, 1963 (In Hours per Week, Decimals)*

| | Categories of persons | | | | | |
| | Shock-workers | | Competing for title★ | | Not competing | |
Items of time-use	Men	Women	Men	Women	Men	Women
Total	2.07	0.98	1.51	0.66	1.03	0.63
1. Preparations for lectures and reports	0.06	—	0.05	0.09	0.02	—
2. Giving lectures	0.02	—	—	—	—	—
3. Meetings, sessions, conferences, etc.	0.81	0.14	0.43	0.26	0.36	0.33
4. Elective functions	0.32	0.11	0.22	0.13	0.13	0.02
5. Work in Public Order squads	0.32	—	0.30	0.03	0.10	—
6. Carrying out commissions	0.14	0.09	0.11	0.01	0.06	—
7. Economic analysis groups†	0.02	—	—	0.01	0.01	—
8. Extra Sunday labour	0.13	0.20	0.07	—	0.10	0.02
9. Other social commissions	0.25	0.44	0.33	0.13	0.25	0.26

★ The title being 'Shockworker of Communist Labour'.

† Presumably a variety of production committee at the enterprise.

Source:

V. A. Artemov and others, *Statistika byudzhetov vremeni trudyashchikhsya,* Moscow, 1966, p. 189.

the numerous committees, together with work in the public order squads, averaged out at about a quarter of it. It will be noted that the table contains sizeable entries for 'commissions', and 'other social commissions' without explanation. These commissions, in the sense of duties or tasks, must have varied according to who allotted them; usually they involve such things as organizing meetings at the enterprise or elsewhere, youth work, visiting the sick, ensuring that work-mates and colleagues get social benefits they are entitled to, helping to conduct drives against litter, etc. More detailed accounts of what these activities mean for the individual may be found in Soviet and émigré literature.

The authorities have an interest in showing a growth in social activities over the years, but this is not easy in view of the short history of this variety of sociological investigation. V. G. Baikova and others claimed in a recent study that the amount of time devoted to them in the Krasnoyarsk *krai* grew considerably between 1959 and 1963; the figure for men rose from 17 minutes to nearly 2 hours, and for women from 27 minutes to 38 minutes.[22] (The more modest rise achieved by the latter may be due to the unrelievable burden of household chores.) Unfortunately we have no means of knowing what went on between the two surveys in the enterprises where these people worked, so it is risky to draw any conclusions. These were certainly years when Khrushchev, moved by the premises of the Third Party Programme, was endeavouring to increase the role of the social at the expense of the state organizations.

The scheme used by Yu. F. Bukhalov and E. A. Yakuba in their study of 1,302 workers, specialists and service personnel contained a broadly comparable spread of social activities, but it is particularly interesting in that the authors listed the items in order of popularity (Table 89). Work in the public order squads and labour discipline groups came first – perhaps because the former, at least, was out of doors and brought the chance of occasional horseplay. 'Political and mass work' came second; Bukhalov and Yakuba left the term unexplained but it probably covered the usual meetings, lectures, electoral campaigns, etc. 'Social control' came next, followed by the organization of artistic and sports events.[23] It is noteworthy that activities devoted to rationalization and invention, improving workers'

22. V. G. Baikova, A. S. Duchal', A. A. Zemtsov, *Svobodnoe vremya i vsestoronnoe razvitie lichnosti*, Moscow, 1965, p. 107.

23. Social control usually meant the verification, by selected groups of workers, of the functioning of enterprises, shops or offices, other than those in which they worked themselves, with the object of uncovering laxity, abuses, theft, etc. This was often organized within the system of the People's Control Committees.

TABLE 89. *Most Popular Forms of Social Work (Percentage Breakdown)**

Preservation of public order and struggle for labour discipline	20.3
Political and mass work	18.5
Social control	17.8
Cultural and mass work, amateur artistic activities	15.5
Rationalization and invention	11.0
Organization of living conditions, amenities	10.9
Perfecting the organization of labour and management	6.0

*Respondents were evidently distributed by their main preference. See Table 72, note.

Source:
Yu. F. Bukhalov and E. A. Yakuba (eds.), *Rol' obshchestvennosti v upravlenii proizvodstvom*, Kharkov, 1968, p. 40.

amenities, and the organization of labour and management were least popular. They may have been the most tedious and comparatively unrewarding. Not all of these pursuits, of course, were open to all workers in equal measure; each type required a different combination of skills and even physical abilities.

We have mentioned the difficulty of taking into account variations between individual patterns of participation. No systematic analysis of this has come to our notice, perhaps because figures would show official estimates to be generally inflated, but a few facts have been published. As far as the frequency of involvement is concerned, the Baikova study, based on a *Komsomolskaya pravda* survey of 782 workers, showed that of the 85 per cent of the sample who 'participated', 15 per cent fulfilled a duty every day, 22 per cent did so a few times a week, 43 per cent only a few times a month and the remaining 5 per cent even less frequently.[24] Artemov, in the study noted above, complained that social commissions were very unevenly distributed amongst those who took them on, and some people had as many as ten at a time. The main conclusion he drew from this, however, was

24. V. G. Baikova and others, op. cit., p. 108.

that these stalwarts could not use their free time effectively, and studied less as a result.[25]

Time inputs vary greatly between individuals. In the course of their study Bukhalov and Yakuba analysed the time budgets of 1,200 workers whom they categorized as 'social activists' and 'other members of the collective'. They did not explain how they delineated them, but it seems that the former devoted up to two and a half hours a week to social activities, while the rest of the sample averaged only about 25 minutes. The investigation showed, incidentally, that the activists performed, on average, 70 per cent of their duties in their free time, 17 per cent in their dinner hour and only 13 per cent in working time.[26] Press reports indicate that there has been an unwelcome tendency for people to get as much of this done in working hours as possible.

So much for the nature of social activities and general problem of participation. Despite the vagueness which surrounds so many key questions, we would probably be justified in saying that a large proportion of the able-bodied population is involved to some measurable degree. But what sections of society are most affected?

The evidence on participation by sex is confused. Some samples show that men are more likely to participate than women, but others show just the opposite. Age is different. Bukhalov and Yakuba's figures showed that people tended to get most involved in social work when they were under 25 years of age or over 30, the middle and late twenties being no doubt devoted to the more important business of home-making and child care (Table 90). The over-forties seemed to make most effort. At the same time there were significant changes in the type of activity taken on. Younger people spent more time in 'social-educational' functions, while the older ones were more involved in activities connected with the production process.

Education level seems to have some significance: surveys conducted in Leningrad in the mid sixties showed that the more education a person had the more likely was he to participate.[27]

25. Artemov, op. cit., p. 189.

26. Yu. F. Bukhalov and E. A. Yakuba, op. cit., p. 53.

27. Results set out in S. I. Ikonnikova and V. T. Lisovski, *Molodezh o sebe, o svoikh sverstnikakh*, Moscow, 1968, p. 64; A. A. Kissel, op. cit., p. 120.

G. S. Petrosyan and A. G. Pusep illustrated that the more educated activists devoted more time to these pursuits.[28] The Bukhalov–Yakuba analysis, however, suggested that the relationship might be more complicated: in that case the main division lay between persons with elementary education, who spent only 7.6 minutes a week on it, and the rest, who all seemed to spend

TABLE 90. *Time Devoted to Social Work (Breakdown by Item and Age-Groups, as a % of All Time-uses)*

Age groups (whole sample)	Type of social activity				
	Linked with the produc-tion process	Social educational	Cultural and mass	In place of residence	Total
18–25	2.1	2.6	—	1.6	6.3
26–30	1.5	0.7	—	0.3	2.5
31–40	3.6	2.1	1.0	—	6.7
over 40	11.8	1.3	—	1.0	14.1

Source:
Yu. V. Bukhalov and E. A. Yakuba, op. cit., p. 234. Figures were given for activists and the rest separately, but the time inputs for non-activists were small, and the pattern for activists alone closely approximates to that for the whole sample. This table well illustrates the methodological weakness of averaging out, as does Table 95.

around an hour and a half, regardless of educational achievement. Another reason which makes it difficult to generalize is that all the other factors which normally correlate with education – age, social background, etc. – may be more important. But it seems that on the whole the better-educated bear the main burden.

According to Bukhalov and Yakuba, activists tend to be people who live near their place of work (and are thus unconcerned about long commuter journeys), or people who have few family commitments. The average person in the sample spent no less than nineteen hours a week commuting. The same study showed

28. G. S. Petrosyan, *Vnerabochee vremya trudyashchikhsya v SSSR*, Moscow, 1965, p. 112; A. G. Pusep, in V. D. Patrushev (ed.), *Opyt ekonomiko-sotsiologicheskikh issledovanii v Sibiri*, Novosibirsk, 1966, p. 111.

that activists used the free time left to them rather differently from other people. They devoted much less of it to child care, visits to the theatre or watching television, and more to study, reading, sport and hobbies.

The figures published on the social status of participants seem to indicate, on the whole, a fairly even representation over the different groups. Just worthy of note are the data presented by A. A. Kostenko, of Sverdlovsk, at an enormous symposium on social participation organized in Kursk some time before 1968.[29] Kostenko's figures, like most of those reported at that gathering, were not backed by sufficient explanation of the sampling methods, and must be treated with considerable caution. Yet they again suggest that education was the overriding factor (Table 91). The peasants in most instances lagged far behind everyone else. Most active were the 'employees' who by definition had a superior educational background. Of course, the number of 'workers' with more than ten years of general school behind them must have been small.

Another commentator at the conference, V. V. Mostovoi, claimed, with the help of data from an undescribed Komsomol survey of 15,000 young people in 1966, that variations in participation between people of five major social groups (students, teachers and researchers, workers, ITR personnel, collective farmers and employees) were negligible (Table 92). Ikonnikova and Lisovski produced a comparison (Table 93) which seems at first sight to show marked differences, but these almost cancel one another out if the categories of people who actually participated are added to those who did not, but declared that they would like to. The relatively poor showing of the students, could, the writers held, be explained by the fact that most of them were in the last year of their studies and working hard for their degrees. The presentation of all these results may have been inhibited by the necessity of emphasizing social uniformity in this sphere.

29. *Materialy mezhvuzovskoi nauchnoi konferentsii* (as in source note 8, Table 87), Kursk, 1968, p. 473 (hereafter as *Materialy* . . ., Kursk, 1968). The published versions of the reports were, unfortunately, extremely brief, and very little was divulged about the samples or methodology on which they were based.

TABLE 91. *Participation in Socio-political Activities, by Social and Educational Groups, as % of Each Group**

	Education					
Social Position	Up to 4th class	5–6th classes	7–8th classes	9–11th classes	Middle special	Incomplete & complete higher
Workers	13.5	20.6	43.7	49.5	59.0	50.0
Peasants	6.2	10.8	25.6	34.0	60.0	—
Employees and ITR	—	20.0	41.1	53.7	68.7	76.4

*Mid sixties. No details of the sample or classifications available.
Source:
Report by A. A. Kostenko, *Materialy . . .*, Kursk, 1968, p. 473.

The data presented by N. E. Vorobiev for occupation groups in the collective farm indicated that here, at least, there were marked differences. A watershed ran between the administrative and managerial personnel on the one hand, and all other occupations on the other (Table 94). Within the farm community the

TABLE 92. *Participation in Socio-political Activities by Social Group**

Social group	% of group participating
Students, cultural, educational and research workers	over 70
Workers	68
ITR	66
Collective farmers	66
Employees & service workers	64

* Sample of 15,000, but no other details given.
Source:
V. V. Mostovoi, *Materialy . . .*, Kursk, 1968, p. 441.

TABLE 93. *Participation in Social Work by Social Group*
(as % of Each Group)

			Social position		
Do you participate?	*Students*	*Employees*	*Workers*	*Collective & state farmers*	*I T R*
Yes	29.6	39.5	38.6	47.1	53.9
No	31.2	26.1	33.1	30.4	33.2
Would like to, but none offered	9.0	7.2	8.4	8.9	2.4
No answer	30.2	27.2	19.9	13.6	10.5

Source:
S. I. Ikonnikova and V. T. Lisovski, op. cit., p. 64.

main burden of socio-political activities evidently fell on the management, though the high rates of participation registered for all groups do not inspire much confidence.

TABLE 94. *Social Activities and Occupation Groups in Agriculture*

Occupation group	*% of group participating*
Admin. & managerial personnel, employees	76.9
Mechanizers	42.4
Stock-rearers	41.6
Field workers	50.0
Workers in cultural, communal amenities, children's institutions	46.2

Source:
N. E. Vorobiev, *Materialy . . .*, Kursk, 1968, p. 496.

COMMUNISTS, KOMSOMOL MEMBERS AND
SHOCKWORKERS AS ACTIVISTS

A number of studies have been devoted to the more specific problem of how far members of the Party, Komsomol and shock-worker brigades are involved in them. The general aim is evidently to prove that the most exemplary members of society are very active in this sphere.

A survey of 1,353 workers conducted in two workshops of a glass-works in Saratov by the sociologist V. A. Osipov in the early sixties showed that whereas only 14.5 per cent of the non-Party people took part in social work, the figure rose to 39.1 per cent for members of the Komsomol and to 92.6 per cent for members of the Party.[30] Given the nature of Party membership, one would expect a high rate of involvement, but it may indeed be that this approaches 100 per cent. In addition, those Party members who participate apparently give more time to these duties than other activists. A. G. Pusep's data from the Krasno-yarsk *krai* study showed that whereas the Party members in his sample devoted nearly three hours a week to social work, Komsomol members gave up less than an hour and a half, and non-Party people just under an hour (Table 95).

There were also significant differences in the amounts of time which persons in these three categories devoted to the different items. The Party members spent more than six times as long as non-Party people at meetings and conferences, which took up well over 40 per cent of the time the former devoted to these activities. They spent ten times as long preparing lectures and talks or attending courses (though this was a comparatively minor item). By contrast they were less involved than non-Party people in the public order squads and amateur artistic activities. The Komsomol members also spent a great deal of time at meetings, but most of their other efforts went into squad work, amateur artistic activities, and 'working Sundays'. The table will yield a few other details of interest if the reader cares to peruse it.

The shockworkers are traditionally represented not only as the

30. V. A. Osipov, *Voprosy formirovania novogo tipa sovetskogo rabochego*, Saratov, 1965, p. 93.

TABLE 95. *Time Expenditures by Type of Socio-political Activity, Male Workers (Totals in Hours and Minutes per Week, Itemized as % of All Time Spent in These Activities)*

Item	% Time expenditure by		
	Party members	*Komsomol members*	*Non-Party people*
Total expenditure (hours and minutes)	2 hrs 56 mins	1 hr 25 mins	58 mins

% breakdown by item:

Item	Party members	Komsomol members	Non-Party people
Participation in meetings, sessions, conferences	43.3	33.3	20.8
Fulfilling other social commissions	23.9	9.2	10.4
Fulfilling elective functions (in Soviet, TU, Komsomol or Party committee)	11.3	5.7	22.8
Participation in commissions (Party, TU, Komsomol, NTO, etc.)	7.2	5.0	6.3
Participation in public order squads	6.5	18.4	10.4
Preparing for lectures, reports, in Party educ. system & various courses	3.4	3.5	1.1
Participation in working Sundays	2.1	11.4	10.4
Participation in artistic activities	1.7	13.5	15.6
Participation in economic analysis bureaux, construction bureaux, etc.	0.3	—	1.1
Giving lectures in the system of Party schools	0.3	—	1.1

Source:
A. G. Pusep, op. cit., p. 113.

best workers but also as the best all-rounders: they are purported
to take a greater interest in improving their educational levels and
technical skills, use their spare time more productively, and
contain a higher proportion of Party and Komsomol members
than the working class at large. It is not surprising if they are
supposed to play a leading part in social and political activities.

Although no meaningful figure for the proportion of the
activists who are also shockworkers has come to our notice, at
least two important studies provide data on the proportions of
shockworkers who undertake social work. A survey conducted
by N. B. Lebedev and O. I. Shkaratan of an unspecified number
of workers in Leningrad machine-building enterprises in the
spring of 1965 showed that 72.9 per cent of the shockworkers
were thus involved, whereas the figure for persons outside the
movement was only 39.6 per cent (Table 96). A survey of 789
Leningrad workers by E. F. Kuzmin gave substantially the same
differentials, though his figures for participation were in all cases
much lower.[31] The Lebedev–Shkaratan study also showed that
the shockworkers tended to take on more permanent commissions, and had more elective duties.

TABLE 96. *Participation in Socio-political Activities,*
Shockworkers and Others (% *of Each Group*)

	Type of socio-political activity						
	1	*2*	*3*	*4*			
			Perma-	*Tempo-*			
	Elective	*Elective*	*nent*	*rary*		*Do not*	
	work out-	*work in*	*social*	*social*	*Total,*	*partici-*	
Group of	*side the*	*the*	*com-*	*com-*	*items*	*pate in*	
workers	*factory*	*factory*	*mission*	*mission*	*1–4*	*socialwork*	%
Shockworkers	2.0	25.4	21.1	24.4	72.9	26.1	100
Competing for title	1.1	19.3	15.3	27.8	63.5	36.5	100
Not competing for title	1.3	7.6	10.5	20.2	39.6	60.4	100

Source:
N. B. Lebedev and O. I. Shkaratan, *Ocherk istorii sotsialisticheskogo sorevno-*
vania, Leningrad, 1966, p. 265.

31. See Table 87, Note 3.

The male shockworkers in Krasnoyarsk, according to Arte-mov's analysis, devoted on average twice as much time to socio-political activities as those who were outside the shockworker movement (Table 88). The distinctions between the women in each group were not so striking, but nevertheless significant. Most of the extra time went into attendances at meetings, elective functions, and work in the public order squads. Persons who were 'competing for the title' in most cases occupied an inter-mediate position. The small comparative study of 29 shock-workers and 33 ordinary workers in one of the shops of the Kirov factory, which is mentioned in the Baikova study, and Petro-syan's more elaborate survey of 44 work brigades in the towns of Erevan and Novosibirsk showed much bigger differentials. Shockworkers devoted 37 and 25 minutes per working day

TABLE 97. *Interest in Politics among Shockworkers and Others,*
(% of Each Group)

Group of workers	Engage in political self-education	Read political literature	Subscribe to newspapers
Shockworkers	47	67.5	89.5
Competing for title	30.1	61.5	no data
Not competing for title	22.3	59.5	74.4

Source:
N. B. Lebedev and O. I. Shkaratan, op. cit., p. 263

respectively to social activities, while others averaged only 8 and 5 minutes.[32] Lebedev and Shkaratan's results, incidentally, also implied that shockworkers had a stronger interest in orthodox politics – those in the sample engaged in 'political self-education' more frequently, read more political literature, and subscribed more frequently to newspapers (Table 97). This tendency has also been suggested by other surveys.

32. V. G. Baikova and others, op. cit., p. 108; G. S. Petrosyan, op. cit., p. 92.

ATTITUDES TOWARDS SOCIO-POLITICAL ACTIVITIES

Socio-political activities are not very popular. This fact is not, of course, emphasized in Soviet sources, but it may be easily inferred from the data we have already considered. It is also very evident from certain studies of attitudes. Thus a survey of some 2,000 workers in leading Gorki factories designed to show how people used the extra free day which they got as a result of the five-day working week revealed that social work was the least attractive pursuit out of ten suggested. In fact only 10.2 per cent of the sample mentioned it at all.[33] The Leningrad survey of 2,665 young workers which we considered in Chapter 4 also disclosed a lack of enthusiasm. When offered twenty-three ways of spending extra time off, 30.8 per cent of the workers in the sample listed it amongst their choices, and it was only thirteenth in order of popularity. Reading political literature was sixteenth. At the same time socio-political activities had more adherents than hiking, study in part-time general schools, hobbies like photography, radio or stamp collecting, participation in the arts, a second job, or just doing nothing at all.[34]

One would expect the pattern of motivation among people who participate to be rather complex, and this is indeed the case.

Let us begin with the results of an investigation which was referred to in the Bukhalov–Yakuba study. Table 98 gives their breakdown of some 400 activists by a kind of mixed index covering motivation and the type of social activity chosen. This treatment, in our view, leaves a great deal to be desired, as these elements could have been handled separately to greater effect. The whole structure of the analysis is very rickety. Nevertheless, it contains a few interesting details, and we present them for what they are worth.

The largest group of activists (the second) evidently avoided important commissions; this is most easily interpreted as a sign of coolness towards social work in general. Some people – an unknown part of group 3 and all of group 4 – participated because they had to. The people in group 5, and the remainder of group 3, thought of social activities as a means of furthering their

33. *Partiinaya Zhizn*, No. 11, 1969, p. 25.
34. A. G. Zdravomyslov and others, op. cit., p. 248.

TABLE 98. *Workers' Attitudes to Socio-political Activities
Breakdown of Sample of 400 Participants (by Interview)*

Group number and suggested characterization*	% of the sample	Type of social commission and reason for undertaking it
1 (Very enthusiastic)	24.9	Orientated to socially useful activities, commissions linked with the working collective, with the solution of the general, vitally important tasks of organizing and educating it
2 (Less enthusiastic, indifferent perhaps)	43.9	Take less important commissions
3 (Unwilling, moved by egotistic motives)	23.6	Fulfil exceptionally important commissions because they were obliged to (plus those who are endeavouring to develop their own personality with the help of less significant and temporary commissions)
4 (Unwilling, passive)	6.2	Fulfil less important commissions, and orientated to fulfilling social commissions, because they were given them, without any clear idea of their social usefulness
5 (Entirely egotistic)	1.4	Moved by egotistic, pecuniary motives in fulfilling different commissions

*The brief characterizations by degree of enthusiasm in the first column were added by us in an effort to make the distinctions between the groups a little clearer.
Source:
Yu. F. Bukhalov and E. A. Yakuba, op. cit., p. 26.

own wellbeing. The weight of 'egotistical' and negative attitude is, in our view, all the more striking in that the investigation was based not on anonymous questionnaires, but on interviews.

The same writers' analysis of replies to the question 'What prompts you to participate in social work?' also deserves attention

(Table 99). Three categories of people, Party members, workers and managerial staff were covered by separate surveys, and the published results have been brought together here for comparison. The questionnaire, which was of the type requiring each respondent to choose one of several standard replies, obviously could not give a complete picture, but the distribution of declared motives both within each sample and between them is intriguing.

Many people said they were mainly interested in 'educating' their fellow beings. This was the main motive among nearly a third of the Kharkov Tractor Works management. About a fifth of the samples of communists and workers were primarily concerned to improve working conditions – no figure was given for managers here. The next two reasons may be described as social; here we would expect to find people who are by nature sociable and primarily interested in being in company; it is a curious fact that nearly half the Party members put this down as their main reason for participation. Some 8 per cent of the communists and nearly 15 per cent of the workers believed that social activities 'promoted their general development'. This phrase is, to say the least, vague, but probably covered a 'positive' mixture of personal and ideological reasons. The seventh and eighth columns contain figures for those souls who put the *wrong* sort of reason first. The percentages covering those who admitted that they mainly wanted to improve their chances of promotion at work are tiny, and, given the size of the samples, suspect. A surprising number of people, however, between about 6.5 and 9 per cent according to the sample, indulged in social activities because they were obliged to. This may be an objective index of the extent of social pressure in these particular instances. Bukhalov and Yakuba approach a number of other topics which would normally deserve attention, but their treatment is too abstruse or faulty for the results to be credible.

Details of other investigations of motivation, though less detailed, are worth noting. Ikonnikova and Lisovski's study of 979 persons who participated in social activities indicated that the majority were apparently prompted by reasons acceptable to officialdom, though only 11.1 per cent took a narrowly orthodox stand and declared such activities to be a personal vocation

TABLE 99. *Answers to the Question 'What Prompts You To Participate in Social Work?'*

Sample*	Possibility of actively struggling for education of man	Desire to struggle with various deficiencies at enterprise	Desire to participate in improving conditions and organization of labour	Desire to be constantly in collective, participate in all its affairs	Desire to help people	Belief that social work promotes one's general development	Desire to improve one's position at work	Participate because commission was given, fulfilment obligatory	Other motives
				Motives (as a % of each sample)					
1. Party members	13.8	14.7	6.1	36.9	9.3	7.9	0.4	9.1	1.8
2. Workers of machine-building industry	17.7	18.0	5.4	26.8	10.9	14.7	0.7	5.8	—
3. Office & managerial staff	32.7	—	5.4	19.6	—	—	0.5	6.5	—

*Details as follows: (1) Approximately 400 Party members. (2) 1483 workers engaged in socio-political activities at four 'typical' Kharkov factories. (3) 717 representatives of shop and works administration at the Kharkov Tractor Works (data incomplete). Replies rearranged slightly in order of sequence, according to their nature.

Source:

Yu. F. Bukhalov and E. A. Yakuba, op. cit., p. 231.

(Table 100). At the other end of the scale 10.2 per cent said that they participated because they were obliged to, and 4.8 per cent

TABLE 100. *Reasons for Participation in Social Work*
(Incidence of Replies from a Sample of 979)

Motive	Number of persons	% of sample
Desire to be in the midst of life	592	60.5
Broadens social contacts	484	49.4
Serves as a good school of life	296	30.2
Helps to struggle more successfully against shortcomings round about	283	28.9
Because it is a duty	257	26.3
It makes it easier to defend personal convictions	149	15.2
Personal vocation	109	11.1
Because person was obliged to	100	10.2
Helps to get promotion	47	4.8
Other motives	57	5.8

Source:
S. N. Ikonnikova and V. T. Lisovski, op. cit., p. 60.

merely because it would help them to get promotion. The elaborate Komsomol survey to which V. V. Mostovoi referred at the Kursk Congress provided some additional information. Mostovoi declared that of those people who were engaged in socio-political activities, 50 per cent were both eager and satisfied: 20 per cent were not enthusiastic but participated because they thought it was their duty: and 5 per cent participated unwillingly or without interest. This left a residue of 25 per cent whose reactions were presumably not considered to be satisfactory enough for comment. Mostovoi claimed, not very convincingly to judge from these figures, that nearly all participants got involved for ideologically respectable reasons. Yet he also admitted that some 4 per cent (perhaps part of the residue) were concerned mainly to improve their position at work.

A few of the findings on attitudes towards participation which were presented by other speakers at the Kursk conference have the appearance of truth. The reports we have chosen for comment here covered the attitudes of two groups of students, some schoolchildren, and a number of young people in collective farm communities. In his study of students at the Kharkov

Polytechnical Institute V. M. Kozhanchikov revealed that no less than 38 per cent of the sample were 'dissatisfied with their social life', and 47 per cent were partially dissatisfied, leaving a residue of only 15 per cent who were presumably content. This is the highest figure for overt expression of dissatisfaction to come to our notice. Kozhanchikov showed that it was young people with military service behind them (i.e. the oldest and perhaps least academic types) who became the most active social workers at college. They were followed by the so-called production candidates,[35] while students straight from the general school lagged far behind. The latter would, of course, be younger and lacking in experience.

According to A. F. Plyshevskaya and M. K. Syroeshkina a third of the students graduating from an unnamed pedagogical institute expressed satisfaction with social activities, while only 3.2 per cent actively disliked them, and said that they were best ignored. P. V. Konanykhin's study of 630 senior pupils in the towns and villages of three widely scattered *oblasts* revealed that of those who engaged in social activities just over half had what he calls 'socially significant' motives (Table 101). Nearly one in ten participated for egotistical reasons. A study by N. E. Vorobiev of the young people in four collective farms, presumably in the Voronezh area, showed very mixed reactions to sociopolitical activities (Table 102). Just under 50 per cent of the sample were very satisfied or basically satisfied. At the same time 11.7 per cent were hardly satisfied and 6.8 per cent positively dissatisfied; a high proportion of those asked would not express an opinion.

It would be easy to prolong the list of investigations considerably, for many have been conducted. The material we have presented so far, however, gives a fair idea of the sort of facts available. We prefaced our discussion with an appraisal of its strengths and weaknesses, and stated why we believe that it has something more than curiosity value. The many divergences between results do not in themselves invalidate the conclusions – different sampling methods, real local or temporal variations would be sufficient to explain them.

If any conclusions at all may be hazarded, they are as follows.

35. For an explanation of this term see p. 292.

TABLE 101. *Motives for Participation in Fulfilling Social Commissions among Schoolchildren**

Type of motive	% which gave it
Socially significant	53.0
Practical	18.0
Egoistic	9.9
Residue	19.1

* Sample of 630 pupils of senior classes of urban and rural schools of the Kursk, Astrakhan and Kalinin *oblasts*.
Source:
P. V. Konanykhin, *Materialy . . .*, Kursk, 1968, p. 469.

It seems that a large proportion of the members of most collectives examined were engaged in social work regularly, although several low figures came to light. The distribution of the work burden and time inputs varied considerably between individuals, but many people spent a measurable amount of their free time at it. A small proportion of these were prompted by ideologically acceptable reasons; a fairly large number were carried along by the system, taking on duties which they would, on balance, have ignored were it not for outside pressures. The 'leading workers', especially Party members and shockworkers, seem to have borne the brunt of the burden. A few people objected or joined in for reasons of which the authorities disapproved.

It is difficult, on this evidence, to say whether the official aim

TABLE 102. *Attitudes to Participation in Socio-political Activities among kolkhoz youth*

Attitude	% of sample
Very satisfied	21.1
Basically satisfied	28.8
Not very satisfied	11.7
Dissatisfied	6.8
Indifferent	1.7
Difficult to say	3.4
No answer	20.5

Source:
N. E. Vorobiev, *Materialy . . .*, Kursk, 1968, p. 495.

of ensuring the participation of the masses in approved activities has been satisfactorily achieved or not. The authorities may claim that the levels here illustrated represent a massive involvement of the masses in the affairs of State. On the other hand critics of the régime could point to the shortcomings of the investigations and our ignorance of the sampling procedures. They might add that the most useful kinds of work could have been done by truly voluntary organizations (as in the West) if the State tolerated them.

The data we have reviewed may, however, improve our understanding of Soviet polity in another way. At the present almost the only statistical measures of political dissent in the Soviet system have been the results of the single-candidate elections to the Soviets. Yet the severity of the voting system strongly militates against open expression of opposition by ballot. This is why in the 1967 local elections we find that only 0.6 per cent of those eligible to vote did not do so. Comparatively small numbers of people voted against their candidates – less than a quarter of a million, or 0.25 per cent, at *oblast* level, for example. The analysis of these results is an intriguing exercise, but one which does not take us very far.[36] Two thousand or so 'oppositionists' are said to have signed protest documents in recent years, and there is evidence that several thousand persons have been imprisoned for 'anti-Soviet' activities. Statistically, if not morally, this is again meagre fare. It may be that the data on indifference or opposition to socio-political activities which most surveys disclose may be regarded as an extra guide to the levels of apathy and political opposition among ordinary people. Perhaps Soviet sociologists are, by this means, quietly providing an answer to a question which has never ceased to interest people in the West, and, for that matter, many Soviet citizens.

36. An analysis of dissent as measured by the 1957, 1961 and 1967 election results has been provided by J. M. Gilison in his article 'Soviet Elections as a Measure of Dissent: The Missing One Percent', in the *American Political Science Review*, Vol. 62, 1968, p. 814. Mr Gilison brings to light a number of interesting points, but does not give global estimates for the number of dissenters.

9
The Soviet School and Society

THE Soviet educational system is one of the most publicized institutions in the USSR. It has long been the pride of the Soviet authorities, and many studies have been devoted to it, both in the Soviet Union and abroad. That is not surprising in view of its great dimensions, rapid growth, and importance to the nation.

The relationship between any educational system and the society it serves is highly complex. The school will on the whole reflect the degree of development of society: thus the extent of industrialization, technological progress, the standard of living and cultural norms will all influence the forms and content of education. A theocracy, for example, must provide itself with priests, and train the young to respect priests: a highly industrialized society must have its engineers. But the school is not only the servant of society. It has a positive influence on social development, partly because it supplies the younger generation with knowledge and skills, and partly because its pupils have to find a place in the social hierarchy after they leave. Certain types of educational institution tend to serve specific groups in society, and in this sense the school may be regarded as a kind of social placement agency.[1] This is in fact the aspect of Soviet education which we have chosen for closer examination here (though we shall also give some descriptive notes on the main parts of the school structure). It is not a topic which is much illuminated by ordinary Soviet statistical data, so we shall have to rely heavily on the comments and studies of individual officials and scholars.

Superficially, the Soviet school system has much in common

1. I am indebted to Burton R. Clark, 'Sociology of Education' in *Handbook of Modern Sociology*, edited by R. E. L. Paris, Rand McNally & Co., Chicago, 1964, and William Taylor, 'The Sociology of Education', in *The Study of Education*, edited by J. W. Tibble, London, 1966, for their exposition of these concepts.

with those of West Europe; indeed many of its elements reflect long Western, and especially Franco–German, tradition. The young Soviet citizen may spend his early years at a nursery school or crèche, but this must be followed, from the age of seven, by attendance at a 'general' school for at least eight years. After that he may continue his general education for two years and acquire a school-leaving certificate (*attestat zrelosti*), switch to some low- or middle-grade technical course, or merely start work. Higher education (at a university or institute) is open to persons who have a full ten years of general schooling behind them. It lasts from four to six years, and culminates in a degree (or 'diploma', as it is called in Russian). This may be followed, after two years of further study, by a 'candidate' research degree. The Soviet doctorate, granted on the basis of a lengthy dissertation, takes many more. Nearly all formal education in the USSR is free. Highly developed extra-mural facilities exist at most levels, there are systems of boarding schools for deprived and handicapped children, and certain kinds of special schools for the more able. The enrolment figures for the main types of school in the USSR and their growth over selected years are shown in Table 103. There are political and military institutions as well, but these lie outside the main stream of schooling, and serve rather specific purposes, so we shall not deal with them here.

On closer investigation the system reveals features which may be collectively described as typically Soviet. The dominant one is an unusual combination of tight centralization and detailed government control. Most governments, it is true, regard education as one of their prime concerns, but few exercise such minute tutelage as the Soviet leadership.

The concept of local or institutional autonomy has always been completely foreign to the Soviet school. The principle of centralized control, which may be dated with the establishment of the People's Commissariat of Instruction in May 1918, is currently implemented through several types of administrative organ. Higher and 'middle special', i.e. technical, education is under the supervision of a Union Republican Ministry of that name. Low-grade training for manual trades is handled by the State Committee for Professional and Technical Education, while the

TABLE 103. *Numbers of Persons Engaged in All Kinds of Schooling and Training in the U S S R (Selected Years, in Millions)*

Type of institution	1953–4	1956–7	1959–60	1963–4	1968–9	1969–70
Pre-school institutions				6.30	8.82	
General school (all types)	32.16	30.13	33.36	44.68	49.19	49.43
Including:						
full-time	30.21	28.19	31.05	40.47	45.07	45.39
part-time	1.95	1.94	2.32	4.20	4.11	4.04
Trade & similar schools	1.03	1.37	1.00	1.47	2.29	2.44
Middle special educational institutions	1.65	2.01	1.91	2.98	4.29	4.30
Higher educational institutions	1.56	2.00	2.27	3.26	4.47	4.55
Training at work, raising qualifications	7.7*	8.02	9.76	11.29	15.36	17.92†

*Average 1951–5.
†A new definition used in the 1969 statistical handbook gives a positive discrepancy of about 2 millions.
Sources:
Narodnoe Khozyaistvo SSSR, relevant years.

general school is administered by a Ministry of Public Instruction in each republic and by departments of education at the local soviet level. Supreme authority is vested in the Department for Science and Education of the Central Committee of the Party, which is formally outside the state administration altogether. At the time of writing this department is headed by S. P. Trapeznikov, a staunch Soviet conservative and protégé of Leonid Brezhnev. It transmits the instructions of the top leadership to the government bodies concerned, coordinates their functions, and makes its own authoritative pronouncements on questions of theory and practice. It is also the prime source of the many meticulous decrees on the educational system, though they may be issued under the seal of other organs.

The high degree of centralization and control has always meant that the central authorities could introduce (if not fully

enforce) many changes at will. Thus though the main elements in
the Soviet educational scheme have remained essentially stable
since Stalin's death – one might even say since the early thirties –
post-Stalin leaderships have been able to attempt a number of
quick modifications, some of considerable social import. The
numbers of pupils and students have been greatly expanded in
response to the proclaimed need for more and better-trained
personnel, and the desire to improve the ideological temper of
Soviet youth. The government has decreed a variety of changes
in the curricula, the introduction of new courses and abolition of
old ones. The subject matter, particularly in the arts, has been
consistently modified so as to reflect current political campaigns
and shifts in the official party line. These are problems that we
shall consider with particular reference to general and higher
education, though we shall include most types of institution in
this summary.

NURSERY SCHOOLS AND KINDERGARTENS

The first element in the Soviet educational structure is the so-
called 'pre-school institutions' – crèches or nursery schools for
children aged from two months to three years, and kindergartens
for those aged from three to seven.

Now in a country where up to four fifths of all able-bodied
women are actually in full-time employment, and where children
start their general schooling comparatively late, one would
expect a well developed network of institutions for child care.[2]
In fact, facilities have always been inadequate. In 1968 there
were 8,822,000 places in all permanent crèches and kindergartens, which meant that at most a third of the children in the
relative age-groups were provided for. An extra four million or
so were, it is true, accommodated in temporary nurseries and
kindergartens in the summer. Perhaps not surprisingly, the geographical distribution of facilities is uneven: there are, for
example, big differences between the union republics. In 1969,
there were nearly twice as many places per thousand of the population in White Russia and Estonia as in Azerbaidzhan. The

2. In the USA in 1961 only a quarter or less of the adult women had full-
time jobs.

RSFSR came well up on the list.[3] Urban–rural discrepancies were also very evident: of the permanent places 7,103,000 were in the towns, and only 1,719,000 in the country.[4] Expansion is, however, being encouraged. The shortage of pre-school facilities is presumably compensated by the ministrations of the ubiquitous Soviet grandmother.

Another striking fact about pre-school institutions is that they are not free. Payments, fixed by a government decree of 1948 which is apparently still valid, depend on parents' income, the size of the family, and the number of hours the child spends in care. The basic rates vary from one and a half roubles a month for the poorest parents to fifteen for the most opulent, about fifteen shillings to seven pounds at the current rate of exchange.[5] These are more than nominal sums, and the wide range they cover indicates that the institutions are intended to cater for all income groups.

The absence of data in fact makes it very difficult to talk about their social complexion. According to popular opinion, the children who attend most of them are badly behaved, which implies that poorer families use them most. At the same time there is evidence that pre-school institutions vary in quality, and some, like that established for employees of the Council of Ministers in Moscow, are very good indeed. A few discreet private playgroups and nurseries charging very high rates are also known to exist.

GENERAL EDUCATION

The kindergarten is followed by the general school, or the 'middle general polytechnic labour school', as it was named after Khrushchev's educational reform of December 1958. This school is at present again in the process of reorganization, so comment on it must be somewhat provisional.

The general school was organized as a three-part structure, comprising classes 1–4, 5–7 and 8–10, in 1934. Later, in certain non-Russian areas like the Baltic republics, where Russian had to be learnt as a foreign language, an eleven-year course was

3. *Narodnoe khozyaistvo SSSR v 1968*, pp. 9 and 676.
4. ibid., p. 602.
5. N. T. Dodge, *Women in the Soviet Economy*, Baltimore, 1966, pp. 81, 86.

introduced. A school anywhere could contain the first four, seven or all ten classes: in the last instance it would be thought of as a 'complete' general school. The standardization of curricula meant that a child finishing the fourth or seventh class in one school could join the fifth or eighth in another without undue disruption. The streaming of pupils by ability was officially condemned and no formal allowance made for it. The structure of the curriculum was more or less taken for granted until the authorities began modifying it in 1954. Present plans envisage the reduction of the first, or primary part to three years, mainly to allow the pupils of tiny primary schools to move on to larger schools more quickly.[6] The seven-year course has been transformed into an eight-year one to match the rise in the school leaving age. The basic structure is thus becoming 3 + 5 + 2.

The coverage of the general school spread quickly after the war. Since about 1962, the authorities have claimed that practically all the children in the towns, and a majority in the country, have eight years of general schooling. By 1969 the figure was probably over 80 per cent for the USSR as a whole, which meant that the minimum school-leaving age had by and large gone up to fifteen. M. A. Prokofiev, the Minister of Education for the RSFSR, then declared that the coverage of the eight-year school varied from just under 70 per cent in Tadzhikistan to 98.6 per cent in the Ukraine.[7] This meant that the eight-year school could not play a major part in social selection.

As far as we are aware no specific study of the children who did not finish the eighth class has been published, so we can only guess at their social background. Most of them, no doubt, tended to come from poorer homes, or live in the more remote parts of the country where eight-year schools were fewer. Girls in the Moslem or backward minorities have, for example, tended to suffer from the reluctance of their parents to let them study.

One can distinguish a marked difference between the quality of the teaching and facilities offered in urban and rural areas.

The small scattered settlements so typical of Soviet rural areas often support only small schools which have to cater for children of all age groups. The average urban school in the RSFSR in

6. *Sovetskaya pedagogika*, No. 2, 1968, p. 12.
7. *Narodnoe obrazovanie*, No. 9, 1969, p. 11.

1967–8 had, for example, 605 pupils, while the rural school had only 120.[8] The Chelyabinsk *oblast* Party Secretary, writing in *Pravda* on 7 January 1968, complained that of the rural schools in his area (which numbered about 1,200) 150 had only one teacher and 480 only two. It is true that this defect is being countered by the closure of small, inefficient schools and the provision of transport to others for their pupils. But the acute shortages of equipment, the rapid turnover of staff and the general backwardness of the Soviet village exclude any easy solution. The overall result is, to quote one Soviet observer, that '. . . a significant number of children taught in rural eight- and ten-year schools, in their level of development, breadth of outlook, depth and quality of knowledge, are still behind urban school-leavers.' Comment of this kind is common.[9]

With the near-completion of coverage of eight-year schooling, the role of the general school as an agent of social selection was largely restricted to the last two (in some cases three) classes. We can single out three related reasons for this. Firstly, there is the purely numerical one. Places were available for only a proportion of the relevant age groups, yet a ten-year education was essential for admission to an institution of higher learning. Pupils who had to leave school without an *attestat zrelosti* forfeited, at least for the time being, their chance of getting into a VUZ.[10] The evidence shows that the last classes tended to be the preserve of the children of well-to-do families. Secondly, as the coverage of the last classes grew (in accordance, of course, with government policy) a certain amount of specialization was permitted between schools; the better ones obviously gave their pupils an advantage in the VUZ entrance exams. A law passed in November 1966 allowed schools to offer optional and special courses. (We have in mind here the ordinary ten-year schools, and not the 'special schools' which we shall treat separately.) Lastly, the channels of education which were open to pupils with only eight years of

8. Calculated from figures in *Narodnoe khozyaistvo RSFSR v 1967*, pp. 449–50.

9. Details from *Narodnoe obrazovanie*, No. 3, 1968, *Uchitelskaya gazeta*, 1 February 1968. For an account of other difficulties see *Pravda*, 7 January 1968. The problem of staff turnover is also dealt with in Chapter 12.

10. *Vysshee Uchebnoe Zavdenie*, or Institution of Higher Education.

general schooling behind them – the professional-technical (or low-grade trade) schools, and even the middle special educational institutions – made admission to a V U Z more, and not less, difficult, and were for this reason regarded as inferior.

(a) Coverage and Social Selection

Let us take the problem of the coverage of the last classes first. No convincing official estimate seems at present to be available, and the data published on the sizes of classes and age-groups is not sufficient for exact calculations. The number of graduations from the tenth (or eleventh) classes and the figures given for pupils in the eighth to eleventh classes would, however, suggest that by the late sixties something less than half of the corresponding age-groups were covered.[11] The seventh Five-Year Plan, approved in 1966, had envisaged the introduction of ten years of general education (or its equivalent) by 1970: however, it was announced in April 1969 that this goal would be 'basically' achieved only by 1972 or 1973.

There were, of course, considerable variations by locality. Some of the large centres achieved a ten-year education for virtually all children by the middle of the decade. Coverage of the last classes has been more extensive in the towns than in the villages. In the R S F S R in 1967 twice as many urban pupils as rural pupils went on to the ninth classes. In the school year 1967–8 over 55 per cent of the pupils who had started in the first classes of the urban schools of the Kazakh republic graduated from the tenth classes, while the comparable figure for rural schools was only 28 per cent. Fall-out of pupils between the eighth and tenth classes is probably much higher in the villages.[12]

Pupils who do graduate from rural schools (to jump ahead for

11. *Narodnoe khozyaistvo v 1969*, p. 667.

12. *Narodnoe obrazovanie*, No. 8, 1968, p. 7, No. 7, 1968, p. 33. The figures in the statistical handbooks suggest that the numbers of pupils in the ninth to eleventh classes were almost proportional to the population in both town and country. The explanation for this may lie in different definitions of 'urban' and 'rural'. The many schools which were in urban settlements located in rural areas could have been 'switched' to the rural category so as to even up the ratios. Qualitative distinctions between urban and rural schools, though a frequent subject of comment, are not easy to trace in the published statistical collections.

a moment) make much less adequate candidates for places in institutions of higher education. A survey conducted by the Soviet sociologist V. N. Shubkin showed that in the Novosibirsk *oblast* in 1963 only 28 per cent of the ten-year school-leavers from the village got into full-time VUZy whereas the figure for the towns was 46 per cent.[13] This suggests that the quality of instruction is also lower in the upper classes of rural schools.

A number of investigations conducted by Soviet sociologists in various parts of the country confirm the assertion that the last classes of the general school have a strong 'upper-class' bias. The surveys which we have chosen for discussion here show, in addition, that children from wealthier homes have higher educational aims and aspirations, and are more successful in getting into the tenth classes. They are thus better placed for advance up the social ladder afterwards.

Differences in educational aims between the children of different social groups were analysed by V. N. Shubkin in 1964.[14]

TABLE 104. *Career Intentions of Schoolchildren in the Novosibirsk Oblast, 1962–3, by Social Group*

	% of children intending to be			
Fathers' occupations	Specialists (intelligentsia)	Workers (industries & construction)	Workers (service industries)	Agricultural workers & peasants
Intelligentsia	71	25	3	1
Workers (industry & construction)	60	35	5	—
Workers (service industries)	36	56	4	4
Agricultural workers & peasants	—	88	—	12

The order of the figures has been rearranged slightly. It is not clear whether this table covers all children in the eighth to tenth classes, or those in the tenth classes only. See also the data in Table 108.
Source: Voprosy filosofii, No. 8, 1964, p. 24.

13. V. N. Shubkin, article in *Sotsialnye issledovania*, ed. N. V. Novikov, Moscow, 1965, pp. 127 ff. We would not, incidentally, wish to leave the reader with the impression that the USSR is unique in this respect.

14. *Voprosy filosofii*, No. 8, 1964.

This study was done on the basis of a questionnaire completed by pupils in all the schools of the Novosibirsk *oblast* in 1962–3. We present some of the published results in Table 104. Among the more striking points to emerge is that whereas 71 per cent of the children of the intelligentsia wanted to obtain specialized education, none of those with an agricultural worker or peasant background did so. They dreamt only of becoming workers in industry, or that, at least, is what they said. The offspring of industrial and construction workers appear to have aspired more frequently to higher education than those of the (lower-paid) workers in the service industries. Lack of aspiration on the part of poorer children is, of course, well recognized in many societies.

TABLE 105. *Career Intentions of Children in the Eighth Classes of General Schools in Nizhni Tagil, 1965*

Parents' occupations	Percentage of children intending to									
	Stay in gen. school		Attend middle tech. educ. institutions		Attend low-grade tech. educ. institutions		Work & part-time study		Don't know	
	B	G	B	G	B	G	B	G	B	G
Intelligentsia	55	78	41	13	5	—	—	—	—	4
Employees	28	57	36	31	28	4	4	6	4	2
Workers	28	48	33	34	31	7	6	7	3	6

B—boys, G—girls, in separate percentages. Minor discrepancies presumably due to rounding.
Source:
Molodoi kommunist, No. 6, 1966, p. 54.

Another study of pupils' aspirations, this time of those in the eighth classes of the schools in Nizhni Tagil (an industrial town of some 400,000 inhabitants in the Urals), was done by Yu. Petrov and F. Filipov in 1965. Some of their findings are shown in Table 105.[15] This investigation was, in its published form, much less scholarly than the Novosibirsk work (perhaps because it was directed at a popular readership), and no rural children

15. *Molodoi kommunist*, No. 6, 1966.

were included. Nevertheless, it revealed the same kind of picture. The children of the intelligentsia evidently desired to continue their education in the last classes much more frequently than those of the 'employees' (here evidently taken to mean service personnel) and the workers. There were interesting discrepancies between the sexes – girls seemed to be more interested in general schooling, and boys in technical courses. Low-grade technical training in trade schools also seemed to attract the latter more. We have omitted the figures for children whose mothers and fathers were of different social background because they were not adequately described. No proper analysis of the fulfilment of pupils' plans was given, but the authors did mention that 85.7 per cent of the sons of the intelligentsia were successful 'mainly in passing into the ninth class, which is what most of them wanted to do'.

TABLE 106. *Social Origins of Pupils in the Fourth and Last Classes of the General School, Gorki Oblast, 1964*

	% of all children	
Fathers' occupation	4th class	10th–11th classes
Specialist	25.8	42.8
Skilled labour	43.6	23.1
Unskilled labour	6.6	1.5
Pensioner, invalid	4.6	7.9
No father	13.4	16.6

Shortfalls of 6 per cent and 8.1 per cent in the percentage totals not explained.
Source:
G. V. Osipov, *Rabochi klass i tekhnicheski progress*, Moscow, 1965, p. 127.

Some data on the social origins of pupils who had reached the tenth or eleventh classes of schools in the Gorki *oblast* is to be found in a study which G. V. Osipov conducted in the early sixties.[16] Some of his figures are reproduced in Table 106. Nearly 43 per cent of these young people came from the intelligentsia,

16. *Rabochi klass i tekhnicheski progress*, Moscow, 1965, p. 127.

and another 23 per cent from families in the 'highly skilled' occupation bracket. Children who could be kept at school by pensioner or invalid parents must, it will be noted, also have come from the more opulent groups in society. At the other extreme only about one and a half per cent were of unskilled working-class origin. An equitable spread of pupils would have been more like that shown for the fourth class, since at that level virtually all children attended school. Osipov gives figures for the maternal background, but in the absence of full information these do not lend themselves to easy interpretation, and we have not adduced them. Two puzzling points about the Osipov figures are the tiny proportion of children of unskilled labourers, even in the fourth class, and shortfalls of 6.0 and 8.1 in the percentage totals. The first may be due to a very narrow definition of the term 'unskilled', such as we encountered in Chapter 5, the second to the omission of an 'others' category, a typographical error, or mere sloppiness.

TABLE 107. *Change of Social Status Among Ten-year School Leavers after Graduation (Novosibirsk Oblast, 1963)*

	Social position (%)			
Social groups	Fathers	Children		
		All	Sons	Daughters
Intelligentsia	62	73	68	79
Workers (industry)	10	18	22	13
Workers (service industries)	11	8	8	8
Agricultural workers and peasants	17	1	2	—

Source:
Voprosy filosofii, No. 8, 1964, p. 27, rearranged in roughly descending order of social status. Note that 41 per cent of the population of the *oblast* was rural at this time, *Narodnoe khozyaistvo SSSR v 1962*, p. 21.

Finally, let us consider some data which illustrate how the selective function of the last classes of the general school may affect social mobility, defined as the movement of the pupils with relation to their parents' social group after they left school.

These figures were provided by Shubkin on the basis of the above-mentioned Novosibirsk study (Table 107). Shubkin defines the new social position in terms of occupation, although he is not explicit about the intelligentsia. This category presumably contained those who were continuing their studies at a VUZ. It is evident from the table that completion of ten-year school meant social advance for most young people, as the 'intelligentsia' and 'industrial worker' categories are larger in the 'Children' than in the 'Fathers' columns. (When the children were still at school the distributions would have been identical.) Girls were more successful in moving into the intelligentsia than boys, who, perhaps because of social pressures, showed a greater proclivity for (manual) work in industry. Particularly mobile were the children of agricultural workers and peasants, since they nearly all changed their social group after graduation. We must not, of course, forget that there may have been some movements between categories which went against these general trends.

(b) Curricula, Course Differentiation and Special Schools

We have so far proceeded on the broad assumption that apart from a difference in the quality of education between urban and rural areas the Soviet general school was, in the mid sixties, a fairly standard institution providing all of its pupils (whatever their social origin) with a stereotyped education. The curriculum, as we noted, was fixed for the whole country, and the streaming of pupils of differing ability not officially tolerated.

We shall now turn to some important reservations on this score which should be kept in mind. Socially important revisions of the curriculum were made under Khrushchev, and new kinds of differentiation introduced after his fall. We shall also consider some of the 'special' general schools which have been allowed to grow and flourish alongside the ordinary ones. In any given locality Soviet schools, of course, vary in quality. The best institions are recognized as such; indeed they may serve the more favoured *microraiony*, or sub-districts. These relationships are an accepted fact of life for most Soviet citizens, but since they are difficult to prove by documentary evidence we must reluctantly leave them aside.

The curriculum of the general school has always been fairly

demanding. At present it embraces from 24 hours of classwork per week for the youngest pupils to 36 or 38 for the oldest. In the first classes the bulk of time has traditionally been spent on Russian language and mathematics. After this new subjects are gradually introduced until by the eighth class all those found in most European schools are present. The arts subjects have always borne the heavy imprint of the official ideology. This means they are made, when possible, to fit the Marxist–Leninist scheme, and conform with current official historiography. They are, on the whole, nationally introvert in character. Under Stalin, when the ten-year school was regarded as the pathway to a V U Z and little else, the course materials lacked any practical vocational element.

Khrushchev made a vigorous attempt to introduce a new and important element into this scheme by means of his so-called 'polytechnization' drive. The reasons for his policy were simple. With the spread of general education in the fifties more and more young people became eligible for higher education which could not be supplied quickly enough. A number of social problems, including youth unemployment, sprang up as a result.[17] The authorities – specifically Khrushchev – considered it desirable to change the *nature* of the general school, so as to make the courses less theoretical and less 'V U Z-orientated'. They should also include some training in low-grade manual skills. Pupils would not then look askance at manual labour in factory or farm, and their training would serve them in good stead if they dutifully decided not to go on to a full-time higher educational establishment.

The first moves in this direction began, it is true, just before Stalin died, but polytechnization was strongly promoted only after 1955, when Khrushchev was pretty well dominant in the Party. It was the central element in a major reform of education which he attempted in December 1958.[18] This is an event to which we shall return in some detail in later chapters. It had most impact on the last three classes of the general school, though it did not leave the eight-year curriculum unaffected.

17. See Chapters 10 and 11 below.

18. Such movements were of course by no means new in the history of Soviet education. Rather similar experiments had been organized soon after the Revolution, and in the twenties. Lenin favoured the earlier ones.

There were, in practice, three basic changes. Pupils were to spend part of their time at school learning simple manual skills, either in school workshops or directly at enterprises; their normal courses were, when possible, to be given a more practical bent; and everyone in the last three classes was to work for a few days a year at an industrial or agricultural enterprise. In its most advanced form polytechnization was intended to make pupils acquire a regular manual trade before they left the general school.

It is not improbable that the Soviet leader envisaged the eventual abolition of these classes anyway. The December 1958 reform stipulated that eight years of full-time schooling, rather than ten, would be the national norm. The implication was that most pupils would do the last two years in the various technical schools or maybe at part-time institutions. In the meantime the last classes were to be radically polytechnized, and were extended by a year to eleven years to make them a more time-consuming proposition. They may have been monopolized by the children of the intelligentsia (more so in the fifties than in the sixties) but Khrushchev wished to stop them from serving merely as a springboard to the VUZ.

The polytechnization drive, though superficially attractive to the proletarian mentality, was not really successful. The curriculum was indeed modified in the great majority of schools, and at the height of the campaign pupils in the last classes of many general schools were spending up to a day and a half weekly at local enterprises. By the school year 1963–4 four fifths of the pupils in the eighth to tenth classes of schools in the RSFSR were provided with working places at which they purportedly learnt some six hundred different trades.[19] Yet the necessary administrative arrangements, especially links between school and enterprise, proved too complicated to establish and maintain with any degree of efficiency. The numbers of schoolchildren trained in given trades rarely corresponded to the numbers needed by industry, agriculture, shops and offices in the same localities, and the school-leavers usually did not wish to take the jobs they had learned even when these were available.

There was concerted opposition from most of the parties

19. *Sovetskaya pedagogika*, No. 8, 1964, p. 53; *Pravda*, 28 May 1963.

involved. Pupils objected to having manual lessons thrust upon them, virtually without choice. (It would have been organizationally impossible for every pupil in a given school to be provided with the training he fancied, or found least obnoxious.) Parents thought the same way. Teachers objected to a lowering of standards, and sometimes extra duties. Managers, obliged to find places in their enterprises for groups of apathetic and perhaps frivolous schoolchildren, were unenthusiastic. A combination of these pressures slowed down the introduction of polytechnization very considerably, and by the early sixties the first signs of a retreat were visible. The central provisions on obligatory vocational and production training were finally rescinded in March 1966, leaving only a two-hour period for practical work in the curriculum for each class. By December of that year only a third of the schools in the RSFSR were still providing any production training at all at local enterprises.[20] Nothing seems to have been published specifically about the character of these schools, and we can only speculate on the background of children they attracted. The polytechnization episode, important while it lasted, may in retrospect be best regarded as an unsuccessful attempt to sever the well-established link between the upper general school and the more privileged groups in society.

In the autumn of 1966 the post-Khrushchev leadership introduced a new policy vis-à-vis the school curriculum which had, if anything, the opposite aim. It involved deliberate differentiation both between schools and between pupils of differing abilities. It may, as we have noted, been intended to balance the planned extension of ten-year schooling for everyone, since this would cause the ten-year school finally to shed its selective functions, as the eight-year school had done before. Perhaps the authorities now wished to ensure that some sector of the general educational system should still be recognized as the domain of the upper layers of Soviet society.

In November 1966 a decree entitled 'On Measures for the Further Improvement of the Work of the Middle General School' granted schools the right to offer '. . . optional lessons, starting from the seventh class, at the choice of the pupils, for

20. Details from *Sovetskaya Rossia*, 8 March 1966, *Pravda*, 12 December 1966, and *Sovetskaya pedagogika*, No. 2, 1966, p. 16.

deepening their knowledge in the natural sciences, including physics and mathematics, and the humanities, and also for developing their various interests and capabilities . . .' The implication here was that these lessons would be introduced in many schools throughout the country, and teachers would recruit the most able pupils for them. The decree then went on to mention a more specific type of specialization: 'Taking into account the positive results which schools have achieved, it is permitted to have a certain number of general schools and classes with more profound theoretical and practical study, in the ninth to tenth (or eleventh) classes, of mathematics, computer techniques, physics, radio electronics, chemistry and chemical technology, biology and agrobiology, and the humanities.'[21] The aim in practical terms was to encourage some specialization in the upper classes of most schools, while permitting a high degree of specialization for the really bright children in a few. Separating children by level of intelligence is still opposed by Soviet pedagogical science, but sifting by level of ability in a given subject is now legal and apparently desirable. The distinction must in fact be almost meaningless. In the Soviet context this kind of selection has very strong social overtones, since the more influential parents have every incentive, and perhaps better opportunities, to get their children into schools which offer better facilities for specialization.

The development of special facilities of both types has, it seems, been popular. Optional courses have been introduced in many places (though the quality of the teaching has sometimes left something to be desired). According to an article by M. I. Kashin, Deputy Minister of Education of the RSFSR, by 1968 some two hundred schools in the RSFSR had started special intensive classes. Some figures on the specialities offered are presented in Table 108. No less than 72 per cent of the schools involved were in Moscow.[22] Many of them apparently developed special relationships with local VUZy – which could only improve the career chances of their pupils, and raise the standing of the schools themselves. It does not, however, seem likely that Soviet sociologists will be permitted to analyse their social

21. *Sovetskaya pedagogika*, No. 12, 1966, p. 5.
22. *Sovetskaya pedagogika*, No. 2, 1968, p. 15.

TABLE 108. *Schools with Extra Theoretical Courses, R S F S R,*
1967–8

Course	No. of schools
Mathematics & computer technology	98
Physics & radio technology	40
Chemistry & chemical technology	41
Other subjects	over 21

Source:
Sovetskaya pedagogika, No. 2, 1968, p. 15.

composition, or compare them invidiously with less favoured institutions – that is, not unless someone in the leadership requires such material to attack this policy.

So far we have been concerned with the 'standard' curriculum and successive attempts to modify it. The Soviet educational system has, however, long contained an important, though little explored, set of 'special' general schools, or *spets-shkoly*, for children with special abilities. These institutions are also known to cater for the more privileged families. The standard curriculum is in this case supplemented by special classes, or partly modified in accordance with the needs of the pupils, at all stages.

One of the best sources of information about this sector, at least as far as Moscow is concerned, is the local telephone book, where they are (presumably all) listed.[23] According to this publi-

23. *Spisok abonentov*, Moscow, 1968, pp. 123 ff. The history of Soviet special schools is in general little known and needs investigation. A few details were collected by a delegation of observers who visited the U S S R under the auspices of the I I E P (U N E S C O) in 1965 (see *Educational Planning in the U S S R*, ed. K. G. Nozhko and others, Paris, 1968, p. 248). Special provision has long been made for children gifted in the arts, though this is not widely publicized. In the course of his campaign for the reform of education Khrushchev expressed his willingness to set aside some of the general schools for children who were gifted in the sciences, but this proposal was accepted

cation, in 1968 the capital's basic system of about eight hundred ten-year schools was supplemented by 87 musical schools, 70 schools where some of the normal curricula material was taught in a foreign language (English, French, German or Spanish), 19 sports schools, 4 schools for children gifted in the graphic arts, while two schools offered special instruction in mathematics. According to this count about 18 per cent of all Moscow general schools were in this category. Of the 202,000 general schools in the country, 3,000 were apparently for musically gifted children, and 500 were of the foreign language type. A few VUZy had their own mathematical schools, which were entered through all-union competitions or 'olympiads'.[24] It is not known what proportion of Soviet schoolchildren were in all these institutions.

Soviet boarding schools may be regarded as another sub-category. They cater mostly for orphans and children from poor homes, and in this sense are not comparable with boarding schools in the UK or America. Some of those located in the larger towns, however, may be attached to special schools and are said to be good enough for the more demanding parents. Khrushchev greatly favoured the expansion of boarding schools, mainly because he thought they would serve as a means of weakening traditional (and, in his view, retrograde) family ties. Thus, according to his plans, they were to expand and take some two and a half million pupils by 1965. But this idea, like so many others, was unpopular, and Khrushchev's target was abandoned after his fall. Since then the boarding schools have not received much mention in Soviet pedagogical literature. By the school year 1968–9 they catered for only 1.6 million children, less than four per cent of the general school contingent.[25]

Though they have remained, in general, institutions for children with less adequate family backgrounds, attendance in them is not, curiously enough, free: fees in 1956 ranged from six roubles a month for parents with an income of 35 roubles to 56 roubles for those with an income of two hundred a month. In

---

only as a subject for further consideration (De Witt, op. cit., p. 18). Perhaps the few mathematical schools listed in 1968 were established precisely as a consequence of this decision.

24. K. G. Nozhko, op. cit.

25. *Uchitelskaya gazeta*, 3 December 1968.

other words, the rate was heavy at all levels, much more so than for pre-school institutions. It appears, however, that in practice the children of very needy parents were either accepted without payment or subsidized.[26] In 1968–9 about 3.3 million children, or 7 per cent of all general school pupils, attended the extended day school with late classes and activities for children whose parents could not be home to receive them at normal hours. A third of a million children were in schools for the handicapped.

(c) The Part-time Sector

Part-time general educational facilities are an important supplement to the full-time school. They take the form of evening or part-time courses, and in 1969 catered for just over four million pupils (Table 103). There are three types of institution – schools for working youth, rural youth, and adults, some of which offer correspondence courses. The overwhelming majority of pupils are in the schools for working youth. Total enrolment of all types reached a peak of 4.8 million in the school year 1965–6, mainly as a result of Khrushchev's encouragement of all part-time education. Afterwards, however, the numbers fell off, especially in the fifth to eighth classes: the first four classes are now residual anyway. This trend must be a cause of unease to the authorities, who planned to increase enrolment to about seven million by 1970.[27] Nevertheless it is healthy in so far as it is due to the expansion of the corresponding classes in full-time schools. The increase in part-time facilities was planned to cater not only for young people who were leaving school early, but also for the fifteen million persons under thirty who, it was claimed in 1966, still did not have eight years of schooling behind them.[28]

The courses offered are modelled very closely on the full-time general school programme. The length of the school year is 36

26. A few figures are provided by N. Dodge, op. cit., p. 88. Thus he found that 25 per cent of the pupils in these schools in Leningrad were admitted free.

27. *Narodnoe obrazovanie*, No. 7, 1967, p. 75.

28. See N. Aitov, article in *Molodoi kommunist*, No. 7, 1966, p. 77. This is further discussed below.

weeks in the towns and 26 weeks in the countryside, though there is some variation according to level. The weekly study-load for evening students in the towns has been fixed at 20 hours, and for students in the countryside at 20–24 hours, exclusive of some 8 hours of homework.[29] The difference is presumably meant to balance the seasonality of work in the agricultural sector. Correspondence students have to manage with consultation periods (which may amount to six hours a week), submit written work and do tests.[30]

Part-time pupils are legally entitled to certain benefits at their place of work, including day-release at their average rate of pay during the school year, twenty days' paid holiday before their final examinations, and relief from shifts which interfere with their study.[31]

Part-time study has many well-recognized disadvantages. A work-load amounting ideally to a minimum of twenty-eight hours a week (in addition to a job) is an extremely heavy commitment and undoubtedly taxes the students' endurance to the limit. At the same time the facilities provided for them are often less than adequate. In 1967 only 20 per cent of the Schools of Rural Youth in the RSFSR had the use of physics laboratories, 12 per cent had chemistry laboratories, and only 5 per cent had biology laboratories, despite the emphasis on these subjects.[32] There appears to be a constant shortage of text-books (though full-time pupils also have this difficulty) and those in use are often not suitable for the more mature pupils. The teaching is poor, especially in rural areas. In 1967 92.1 per cent of all teachers in the Schools for Rural Youth had a full-time job in the day, which, in view of the long hours a Soviet teacher works, meant that they could hardly give of their best in the part-time

29. ibid., p. 72.

30. For these regulations see the Decree of the Minister of Education of the RSFSR, 31 May 1963, with appendices, in *Spravochnik po vechernei smennoi srednei obshcheobrazovatelnoi shkole RSFSR*, Moscow, 1963, p. 127 ff.

31. Decree of the Minister of Education of the RSFSR, 'On the Establishment of a Shortened Working Day . . .' of 16 November 1959, as modified by the decree of 7 August 1962, ibid., pp. 341, 345. This legislation is discussed in Chapter 11.

32. *Narodnoe obrazovanie*, No. 7, 1967, p. 76.

classes. There are the inevitable difficulties which arise from age discrepancies amongst the pupils, the gap between their leaving full-time school and starting part-time study, and the need for adults with families or responsible jobs to miss classes.[33] In addition, a steady stream of criticism over the years suggests that day-release and similar provisions are often ignored. Academic standards must suffer as a result of all these factors. N. Malakhov, head of the Schools Department of the Central Committee of the Komsomol, stated that the fall-out from part-time schools in urban areas of the RSFSR in the school year 1963–4 was 25 per cent, and in the rural areas 35 per cent. The figure for the USSR as a whole in 1969 was about a quarter. According to another source, in 1964 about one pupil in six repeated a course.[34]

The enormous shortfall in the 1970 enrolment plans may be attributed to these weaknesses. Indeed, by the end of 1969 the situation was so bad that the authorities were prompted to draw up a new set of regulations for part-time schools. The intention was to exclude the less serious students (and thereby reduce fall-out), introduce more flexibility into the courses, and improve teaching and consultation arrangements. Enterprises were asked to help by improving classroom accommodation. The changes, however, were unimaginative, and involved no radical departure from the established pattern of organization.[35]

Part-time general education may be the least satisfactory part of the Soviet general school system, but it is an important one. Who makes use of it? Some answer to this question may be gleaned from a study conducted by the sociologist N. Aitov in the Bashkir town of Ufa in 1965–6.[36] This was evidently a detailed piece of work, covering 1,955 part-time pupils in six evening schools. Unfortunately much of the important information it revealed was omitted when it was published as a popular magazine article which is the only part of it to have come to our notice.

33. *Narodnoe obrazovanie*, No. 3, 1968, p. 65.
34. *Pravda*, 2 December 1969, and *Sovetskaya pedagogika*, No. 5, 1964, p. 155.
35. *Pravda*, ibid.
36. *Molodoi kommunist*, No. 7, 1966, p. 77.

N. Aitov stated that 60.5 per cent of all the pupils in the sample were from the working class, 24.4 per cent were from the peasantry, 14.1 per cent were from employee families and 1 per cent consisted of 'representatives of other social groups'. His 'employee' group apparently contained both the intelligentsia and service personnel, but he did not state this explicitly. A comparable breakdown of the local population by social status is also lacking. He did claim, however, that the social composition of the pupils corresponded with that of the population, and that the evening schools were not merely 'schools for the poor'. Yet if the social mix of these institutions reflected that of the population, and 85 per cent of the pupils were of peasant or working class origin, the schools obviously had a much higher proportion of poor people in them than the last classes of the general school.

This was in fact the whole drift of his argument. He analysed, for example, the reasons for which the part-time pupils left full-time school, and found that virtually half of them wished to help their families financially, though the figure varied from 34 per cent in the employee, to 56 per cent in the peasant group (Table 109). Another 30 per cent wanted to be independent, and these must also have had their potential earnings in mind. The other motives were proportionally insignificant.[37]

Aitov revealed a number of other important elements in the pattern of recruitment. He claimed that the pupils could be divided into three groups by the reasons which prompted them to start part-time courses.[38] The largest group, comprising 58.4 per cent of the total, did so mainly in order to get into VUZy or middle special educational institutions. These were 'the least qualified (i.e. skilled) of the evening school pupils', who 'worked in the more dead-end and lower-paid jobs', as service personnel, especially in light industry, the trading network, and offices. These young people evidently came from those poorer sections of the community which happened to have rather high educational aspirations. It is not, however, excluded that their interest in study caused them to drop, or be pushed into less

37. There was one possible exception. A fifth of the peasant contingent would have stayed on at full-time schools had they existed in the village.

38. He evidently had each individual's principal reason in view; compare the note on Table 72.

TABLE 109. *Part-time Pupils' Reasons for Leaving Full-time General School*

Reasons for leaving full-time school	Average for the sample	As a percentage of social group		
		Workers	Peasants	Employees
Desire to help the family by earning	49.4	50.7	56.2	34.0
Desire to be independent	30.3	31.8	18.1	46.4
Resident in village and no middle school nearby	7.5	2.9	20.6	3.8
No desire to study	6.5	7.5	3.4	7.3
Illness	2.8	2.8	1.3	3.4
Difficulties at school: did not pass up: expelled: bad relations with teachers	3.5	4.3	0.4	5.1

Source:
Molodoi Kommunist, No. 7, 1966, p. 77.

attractive, work. They would no doubt have preferred to stay on in full-time schools, had they been able to do so. There were more girls than boys amongst them, though in the survey as a whole numbers were almost equal.

Some 34 per cent of the pupils, who made up the second group, had no clear motivation. They started evening school because their friends were going, because they felt they had not stayed at school long enough, or because they were generally interested in studying. Aitov stated that they had 'a reasonable material position' which probably meant that they come from more opulent homes.

The remainder, up to 7 per cent of the total, were already in relatively qualified positions, but required more formal schooling to get on. A third of these intended to keep the same jobs when they finished the part-time courses.

By and large Aitov's work supported his own contention that part-time schools were 'an important means for levelling out the opportunities for persons from different social strata to obtain a general education ...' They also fulfilled 'another important social function, being one of the main means of social movement (*peremeshchenia*), and for enabling workers and office personnel, and in particular the children of workers and peasants, to move into the ranks of the Soviet intelligentsia . . .'

INSTITUTIONS FOR TECHNICAL TRAINING

Up until the Khrushchev reform of December 1958 low-grade technical training of a formal, classroom type was conducted in many different kinds of schools, some under the Main Administration of State Labour Reserves and some under the ministries for which they trained workers. Courses generally lasted six months to a year, and graduates were directed to a place of work in an apparently planned manner. The average annual enrolment was around one million.

As a result of the reform, however, the system was expanded and regularized. All the schools were turned into so-called 'professional-technical schools', the term 'professional' being used merely to refer to artisan trades. Western observers sometimes call them 'trade schools' for this reason. In July 1959 they were placed under the jurisdiction of the State Committee for Professional and Technical Education, which replaced the old Main Administration of State Labour Reserves. The course was then fixed at from one to three years, and the schools were reorganized so as to take pupils from the eighth or tenth classes of the general schools, rather than from the fourth or seventh as before. By the beginning of 1968 there was even talk of amalgamating some of them with general schools, or modifying their curricula so that they could grant school-leaving certificates.[39] In April of that year *Pravda* announced that the professional-technical schools of the latter type would accept 50,000 young people, or 3.5 per cent of all newcomers, and that the figure would rise to 300,000 in 1975. All of these measures amounted to a strenuous exercise in upgrading.[40]

This sector of the educational system contained 2.4 million young people in the school year 1969–70. It was, however, still far from being the main source of new labour for the economy: about three quarters of the new entrants to the labour market

39. *Uchitelskaya gazeta*, 8 February 1968.
40. *Pravda*, 18 April 1969, and *Narodnoe khozyaistvo SSSR v 1968*, p. 564.

were general school-leavers who found their own jobs and were trained at work. These are included in the last item of Table 103.[41]

The reasons why an upgrading of the trade schools was necessary are not far to seek. Firstly, they had, by their very nature, a low social standing. In recent years about 60 per cent of the pupils have come from the village, presumably filling, in the first instance, the schools which train mechanizers. (The overwhelming majority of pupils are boys, anyway.) L. Mitrofanov, the headmaster of a provincial urban trade school, wrote in 1967 that 82 per cent of his pupils were the children of workers, and 93.7 per cent of these belonged to families in which per capita earnings did not exceed 25 roubles a month.[42]

Young people who go to these schools are, not surprisingly, below average in educational achievement. One third of the entrants to the trade schools of the R S F S R in 1966 had not even finished the eighth class. In the ten years 1956–66 only about 8 per cent of the pupils on average had ten years of schooling though by 1966 the number in this category had probably risen to about a quarter.[43] Even then they may have been amongst the weakest in their classes. Of the 40,000 trade school pupils who had eight years of general education in the Crimea in 1967, only 5 per cent had obtained a good mark in examinations taken before leaving school, and 55 per cent had obtained bare passes.[44]

The trade schools themselves are quite without academic pretensions. There are no entrance examinations, and the pupils

41. These schools have been given considerable prominence in discussions of labour training in the U S S R, and one may easily form the impression that they are the main source of new labour for the working-class and mechanizer group in collective farms. To make them so has long been the aim of a strong, and probably enlightened, lobby in Moscow. Training on production is usually limited to a few months, and is inferior to formal courses. The long apprenticeships favoured by trade unions in West Europe are unknown in the U S S R. Another noteworthy point is that the Soviet educational system has a not inconsiderable private sector which provides training, particularly in 'office' skills. Shorthand and typing, for example, are widely taught in this way, as small private notices testify.

42. *Komsomolskaya pravda*, 2 June 1967.

43. *Proftekhobrazovanie*, No. 3, 1966, p. 7. The estimates are ours. *Pravda*, 12 December 1966.

44. *Proftekhobrazovanie*, No. 1, 1966, p. 20.

receive, apart from their keep, payment on the sale of articles they produce in class, so in effect they earn as they learn. Living standards in the hostels are not good, and the number of buildings insufficient. This is important in view of the fact that a high proportion of pupils 'live in'.

These young people have a bad name with the public. 'Many of our pupils', wrote L. Mitrofanov, 'obstinately refuse to wear the school uniform. I began to ask why. The youngsters explained, "You get on an overcrowded bus or tram, and you grasp the handrail with both hands, or else some passenger will look askance at you and hold on to his pocket..." Most parents continue to regard professional-technical training as second-rate education. Many of them, and, still more unfortunately, the general school teachers, continue to impress on pupils that ending up in a professional-technical school is virtually equivalent to ruining one's life.' A poll conducted amongst 12,500 children in the eighth classes of the general school by the Research Institute of Professional and Technical Education in 1967–8 revealed that only 289, or 2.3 per cent of them, wanted to go to trade schools, while another survey of 5,000 pupils in them already showed that only 100 had entered them on their teachers' advice.[45]

The new emphasis on this system means that the authorities will have to try to alleviate, if not remove, these serious shortcomings. The problem is not a simple one. Apart from the fact that the schools offer only menial training and have by tradition accepted anyone, the system of planned placement to which the leavers are subject virtually prevents them from continuing their education, at least on a full-time basis. This practice, which dates from the establishment of the system, evoked a bitter comment from Mitrofanov in the above-mentioned article. There are, however, now signs of some modification of this rule: since 1966 pupils who graduated with distinction have been allowed to go directly to a full-time V U Z. This is only a small step, but it is in the right direction.

The last important type of school below university level is the middle special educational institutions. Some figures on the student body in them are given in Table 103.

45. *Komsomolskaya pravda*, 2 June 1968; no other details given.

It is not our intention to say much about them, partly because they are organized like, and run together with, the VUZy, to which we devote the next chapter, and partly because in our opinion they lack individuality. They do not appear to have been studied as closely as VUZy by Soviet scholars, and there is less information on them.

The following points are nevertheless worth noting. The middle special educational institutions offer two- to four-year courses, depending on the subject, and take both eight- and ten-year school-leavers who pass the entrance examinations. They have a similar list of specializations as the VUZy, but train to a lower level of competence; they turn out technicians rather than engineers, nurses rather than doctors, and nursery or primary school teachers rather than teachers of the upper school. Their graduates are directed to a place of work in the same way as VUZ graduates (or for that matter trade-school trainees) and they have to remain there for at least three years. This means that they too lose the opportunity of a full-time VUZ education in this period. The only exception to this rule concerns the top five per cent who can continue their formal education on a full-time basis, if they wish. The leaving certificate of a middle special educational institution is far less valuable than a degree, though it may take as long to come by. This is a major cause of their relative unpopularity.

No important studies of the relationship of the middle special educational institutions to the class structure, or their role in social mobility, have come to our notice. They offer advantages to young people who want some kind of specialized education, but who are, for one reason or another, unable to get into a university or institute. It may be that this type of candidate tends to come from the upper layers of the working class. The unpopularity of these institutions has led to a lack of middle-grade specialists in the economy – a phenomenon which has provoked regular complaint since the inauguration of the first Five-Year Plan in 1928.[46] But the pressure on places in the top classes of the general school and the VUZ is now, to judge from press reports, bringing about some improvement in their standing.

We have attempted in this chapter to do no more than indi-

46. *Narodnoe obrazovanie SSSR 1917–1967*, p. 291.

cate some of the principal relationships between the Soviet school system below VUZ level and society, and outline its development in recent years. This system, like any other well-developed one, has sectors to serve most layers of society. The upper classes of the full-time general school, and in particular the special schools, are largely the preserve of the privileged, while, at the other extreme, the part-time general school and trade schools cater for the poorer Soviet citizens. Other types of institution either cater for all groups or fall somewhere in between. If the authorities have, in the years under review, made considerable efforts to modify parts of the educational structure, it is because they have understood not only the economic, but also the social, factors involved.

10
Problems of Student Selection

DESPITE the impressive expansion of higher educational facilities in the USSR, professional training there is still a relatively scarce commodity. This is another way of saying that the demand for VUZ places exceeds supply, and that the authorities have to make a choice between applicants. It will come as no surprise to find that as a result young people from the more privileged sections of society have a better chance of going on to higher education than their less fortunate fellows. Our aim in this chapter is to outline the social problems involved in the process of selection and the government's attempts to solve them – for the Soviet authorities have traditionally taken a keen interest in the background of those who aspire to the ranks of the intelligentsia.

It will, however, be necessary for us to preface our study with a brief account of VUZ structure, and the administrative means by which the composition of the student body is controlled, since these matters are central to the argument. We shall also touch upon another topic which, though important, is rarely discussed in Soviet sources, and largely ignored by Western observers. This is the relative standing and attractiveness of different kinds of VUZy, for they vary considerably in this respect.

Otherwise the material seems to lend itself best to a chronological treatment, and this is the one we shall in principle adopt.

THE GOVERNMENT AND THE VUZY

The Soviet system of higher education is as centralized as the lower levels, the principle of university autonomy never having been acceptable to the Soviet leadership. Institutions of higher education were included in the important decrees of 1918, which in effect 'nationalized' the whole system, and the decades which followed have seen no significant departure from this rule. Since the late twenties the state authorities have exercised stringent control over the intake of students everywhere, and have also organized the direction of graduates to officially approved jobs. These practices were a very important element in the first Five-Year Plans – in fact a special Gosplan commission was established to regulate them in 1934.

The difficulties of planning intakes have always been enormous, and we shall have something to say about them in Chapter 12. Suffice it to note here that since 1956 the 'Department for Planning the Training and Distribution of Young Specialists' in the Ministry of Higher and Middle Special Education has been concerned with estimating, together with Gosplan, the desirable intakes of students for each of the three hundred and forty recognized specialities in all VUZy throughout the country. In practice this means approving the intake plans for each faculty and department individually.[1]

Students apply initially to one VUZ by submitting their *attestat zrelosti*, a recommendation and a medical certificate. If they do not pass the concourse exams there, they may apply to another, where there are still free places, later in the summer. But at this stage the process is much more haphazard. Second choices have become more difficult with the growth in demand for higher education; and there is no organized information about these vacancies anyway.

The actual selection of students is done on the basis of the VUZ entrance examination results and an interview conducted by an Admissions Commission which is appointed by the rector (or director in the case of an institute). Its choices are in principle supposed to depend on 'ability', and there is no indication that the intake plans sent out from the centre cover more than the numbers of places by specialization. But, obviously, to say this is not enough. Many references have been found to supplementary restrictions (perhaps issued as circular letters) on, for example, nationality quotas.[2] This type of instruction may in some cases

1. See *Vysshaya shkola*, 'Osnovnye postanovlenia', etc., Moscow, 1957, p. 18: M. A. Prokofiev, *Narodnoe obrazovanie v SSSR 1917–1967*, Moscow, 1967, p. 279.
2. N. De Witt, op. cit., p. 357.

be utilized to control the flow of students out of smaller, and less favoured republics. Stalin, we know, restricted the outflow of students from Georgia in order to raise that nation's student ratio. It is commonly accepted in Moscow that there is a tight limit on the admission of Jews; they certainly have difficulty in getting into the more popular faculties and institutes.

As far as social origin is concerned, this is presumably taken into account informally at the interview stage. It was formally excluded as a factor in selection in the mid thirties, perhaps because Stalin realized that by so doing he would automatically favour the new intelligentsia. Under the terms of the 1936 Constitution, which guaranteed an education to all Soviet citizens, favour or discrimination on this basis became in fact illegal.

The system of higher education in the USSR is officially held to be composed of equal units (i.e. VUZy) which serve all sections of the community in equal measure. There are good grounds for doubting the first part of this proposition as much as the second. Soviet VUZy in fact vary considerably in their quality and social prestige, and consequently in the kinds of students they attract. We may indicate a few of the main watersheds here.

There are two basic types of institution – universities and institutes, both of which may offer full-time and part-time facilities. Each of the forty-two universities offers training in a full complement of subjects, much as in the West, but the institutes are usually much smaller and embrace a few closely allied faculties in one field. Admission procedures are similar for both types. Generally the universities have a higher standing than the institutes, though some of the latter – like the Bauman Technical Institute or the Timiryazev Agricultural Institute in Moscow – are very much respected. Prestige presumably depends on factors familiar to us in the West: academic quality, the subjects taught, the kind of job that the training leads to, material facilities and even geographical location.

A survey of thirty Soviet VUZy conducted by the newspaper *Komsomolskaya pravda* in July 1966 revealed great differences in the number of applicants per place. The Kaunas Polytechnical Institute in Lithuania, for instance, attracted only 0.7, while the Kiev Aviation Institute and the Moscow Historical

Archives Institute had no less than 10 each. The average for the country was then about four. A similar survey in 1968 showed that the Faculty of Acting at the Lunacharski Institute of Theatrical Art in Moscow had received no less than 100 applications for each of its vacancies.

We can be sure that the relationship between the standing of VUZy and the social origins of the students in them is a highly complex one. There may, for instance, be important distinctions between faculties, or between similar kinds of VUZy in different parts of the country.[3] It is probably safe to generalize only for the ends of the spectrum. Institutions of considerable political importance, like the Institute for International Relations or the Institute for Foreign Trade, which train diplomats and responsible personnel for work abroad, are said to be the exclusive preserve of the children of the élite. Though not secret, they are not listed in the annually published handbooks for VUZ applicants.[4] Leading technical institutes also apparently tend to take the more privileged. On the other hand institutes which provide training in unpopular spheres like agriculture or internal trade, especially in the provinces, are bound to be a more realistic choice for the socially less fortunate.

There are evidently marked differences between the social character of the student bodies in full- and part-time higher education (on which the Soviet government has usually set great store). The size of the latter sector has varied, but in 1969 14 per cent of all graduates came from evening classes, and another

3. Among the more important influences one would expect to find: (a) the number of VUZy in a given region relative to the number of school-leavers, (b) the presence of a hostel for students who live far away (private accommodation being extremely expensive), (c) the prestige of the VUZ (which may, incidentally, inversely affect applications: a high-grade technical VUZ may be considered impregnable by average students, and thus attract only a few bright candidates, while a lesser institution, rumoured to be 'easy', may end up with a far greater demand for its places), (d) climatic and geographic factors, (e) the subjects offered, (f) 'fashion' and the changing tastes of the candidates.

4. See the *Spravochniki dlya postupayushchikh v vysshie uchebnye zavedenia* for recent years. Occasional references to these VUZy appear in publications such as the *Slovar sokrashchenii russkogo yazyka*, Moscow, 1963. The existence of secret or 'closed' VUZy – particularly military, defence and KGB institutes – is testified in private and by émigrés who have attended them.

34 per cent came from correspondence courses, making no less than 48 per cent in all. Part-time higher education is even more demanding than part-time general schooling. Whereas full-time institutions have four- to six-year courses (with 10 per cent of the lecture time devoted to ideological topics) the part-time courses, with basically the same syllabus, last only a year longer.

For these reasons part-time courses are traditionally un-attractive. In the past they have tended to serve poorer or less able people who had to stay in a full-time job. The state grants which the majority of full-time students are entitled to (on a means-test basis) are in themselves hardly sufficient to live on, and full-time students have to be in a position to get help from their relatives, or take on part-time work.[5]

The few data adduced below suggest, however, that the prestige of part-time courses has in recent years improved. The general pressure on full-time VUZ places and Khrushchev's admission policies evidently caused more people of wealthier background to register for them.

KHRUSHCHEV'S POLICIES ON STUDENT INTAKES

The Soviet Union has, by international standards, a very large student body. In the academic year 1969–70 there were over four and a half million students on full- and part-time VUZ courses, which according to a Soviet handbook gave the country a ratio of 187 students per 10,000 of the population, as opposed to 99 in Japan, 88 in France, and 63 in England. The only capitalist country listed as having a higher figure was the United States of America, with 226. This picture is probably not entirely accurate, but it indicates that the USSR was certainly well placed in student production.[6]

This success may be traced to government policies in the last

5. Grants were fixed by the Decree of Council of Ministers of 3 August 1956 at from a minimum of 140 roubles to a maximum of 315 roubles, depending on the VUZ speciality and the seniority of the student, *Vysshaya shkola, Osnovnye postanovlenia . . .*, Moscow, 1957, p. 429. See also S. M. Rosen, *Significant Aspects of Soviet Education*, U.S. Dept. of Health, 1965, and 'Vysshee obrazovanie v SSSR', *Statisticheski sbornik*, Moscow, 1961, p. 88. By the mid sixties the rate was 30–45 new roubles.

6. *Narodnoe khozyaistvo SSSR v 1968*, p. 174.

years of Stalin's rule, when both the number of possible candidates and the number of VUZ places rose. The two rates were, however, very different. Between 1946 and 1953 the number of pupils finishing full-time and part-time ten-year schools with a school-leaving certificate (which as we have indicated made them potential VUZ candidates) increased fourfold, from 137,000 to 579,000. The latter figure was about the pre-war level, and must have embraced about a sixth of the corresponding age-groups.[7] Intakes into full-time institutions of higher education rose correspondingly from 171,600 to 265,100 or by only 55 per cent, while the intakes onto part-time courses increased to 165,700, which meant a rise of about 45 per cent. Of course we cannot quite equate these sets of figures with the demand for and supply of VUZ places. Some ten-year school-leavers may not have wanted to continue their studies, while there was doubtless a fund of older war veterans who wanted VUZ places. Nevertheless it seems that by the time Stalin died there was a sharp increase in the demand for higher education which could not be met (see Figure 18).

Data on the social origins of the lucky candidates at that time is almost totally lacking, the last figures on the social composition of the student body having been published in 1938. Then, as may be seen from Table 110, the student body was heavily saturated by young people from the intelligentsia. It may indeed be that the table understates this phenomenon, since some VUZ applicants had an interest in declaring themselves 'workers' or 'peasants' rather than 'employees'. The reigning attitude seemed to favour duplicity here, rather as with entry to the Party. A curious feature is the remarkably good showing of the uncollectivized peasants.

Stalin's education policies certainly favoured students from better-off families. We have already referred to his contempt for 'harmful egalitarianism', expressed as early as 1931. While encouraging the expansion of educational facilities, he ensured that the new élite were first to benefit. In June 1940 fees were

7. The 1946 figure was estimated by N. De Witt, op. cit., p. 592. De Witt's table contains both estimates and figures published in the Soviet press which diverge somewhat from data given by S. L. Senyavski in *Rost rabochego klassa*, Moscow, 1966, p. 109.

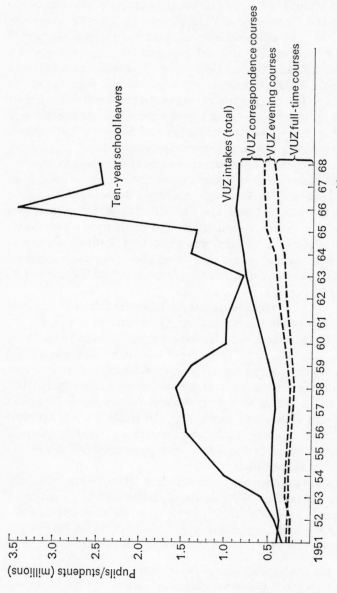

FIGURE 18. *Graduations from Ten-year Schools (All Types) and VUZ Intakes (All Types), 1951–68*

Ten-year school leavers

VUZ intakes (total)

VUZ correspondence courses

VUZ evening courses

VUZ full-time courses

Pupils/students (millions)

3.5 3.0 2.5 2.0 1.5 1.0 0.5

1951 52 53 54 55 56 57 58 59 60 61 62 63 64 65 66 67 68

Years

TABLE 110. *Social Groups and the VUZ Student Body, circa 1938*

Social groups	% of total population (1)	Students' social origins	% of total student body in VUZy (2)
Employees	17.7	Employees	42.2
Workers	32.5	Workers	33.9
Peasants (collectivized)	47.2	Peasants (collectivized)	16.1
Peasants (uncollectivized) & craftsmen	2.6	Peasants (uncollectivized)	5.6
Others	—	Craftsmen & others	2.2

Sources:

(1) Figures 1939 from *Itogi vsesoyuznoi perepisi naselenia 1959*, Moscow, 1962, p. 92; 'employees' in the sense of all workers of predominantly mental labour.

(2) Figures include part-time students, who were not listed separately; E. N. Medynski, *Narodnoe obrazovanie v SSSR*, Moscow, 1947, p. 168.

introduced for the last classes of the general school and (at a considerably higher rate), for middle special and higher educational institutions. It is true that these were offset by grants for students, and by the continued inflation of the rouble: but they

Sources for Figure 18:

VUZ intakes: *Narodnoe khozyaistvo SSSR*, relevant years. Graduations from the ten-year school:

1951–8:   S. L. Senyavski, *Rost rabochego klassa*, Moscow, 1966, p. 60.

1959,   N. De Witt, op. cit., p. 592, from *Pravda*, 14 July 1959 and 13
1960:   July 1960.

1961–4,   *Ezhegodnik bolshoi sovetskoi entsiklopedii*, section entitled
1968:   'Narodnoe obrazovanie i kulturno-prosvetitelnye uchrezh-
          denia', relevant years.

1965:   *Pravda*, 26 July 1965.
1966:   *Ekonomicheskaya gazeta*, July 1966.
1967:   *Izvestia*, 16 July 1967.

must have remained a barrier to the poor student. The rich were not appreciably affected. In June 1944 school-leaving certificates (an old tsarist institution) were reintroduced for school-leavers, and admission to a VUZ without one became impossible. This signified a final rejection of the proletarian informalism of the early thirties. At the same time a new system of gold and silver medals ensured preferential treatment for the best pupils in VUZ entrance procedures. This again strengthened the position of the socially favoured pupils, if only because they had better conditions for studying. A decline in the proportion of part-time (as opposed to full-time) VUZ courses meant relatively fewer opportunities for the poor.

In 1954 the post-war policy of expanding the general school reached fruition, and the number of young people reaching the last class of the ten-year school suddenly almost doubled. The great excess of ten-year school-leavers over full-time VUZ places now posed the question of selection in a very acute form. Under the terms of the 1950–55 Five-Year Plan the Soviet leadership was committed to extend ten-year schooling to all young people, but a lightning expansion of full-time higher educational facilities to accommodate all the possible candidates so produced was impracticable. The unsatisfied demand for places raised new social problems; in particular it encouraged bribery of VUZ officials and voluntary, pre-college unemployment amongst the unsuccessful applicants. It is interesting to speculate what the government reaction to this situation would have been had Stalin been alive. As it was, the more relaxed political atmosphere meant that it could not be ignored.[8]

The remedies adopted reversed some long-established educational practices. The most important was the polytechnization drive – an attempt, as we have seen, to encourage general school-leavers to start work immediately, and put off their entry to a full-time VUZ for a couple of years at least. The most energetic were expected to work and continue their education on a part-time basis. In 1955 the full-time VUZ entrance rules were changed so that people who had been employed for two years or more in factory, office or farm – the so-called 'production candidates' – would automatically have a fixed quota of VUZ places

8. We shall return to the problem of unemployment in Chapter 11.

set aside for them. This helped them in so far as they would not have to compete directly with candidates fresh from school. The quota was to be decided for each VUZ separately, but it was supposed to be generous. On the 6 June 1956 the old system of fees was abolished. There was a new emphasis on the expansion of part-time VUZ facilities, coupled with a slight reduction of the intakes onto full-time courses. An attempt was made to improve the conditions of employment of part-time students: in September 1954 an order of the Ministry of Higher Education granted them the right to extra time off at the expense of the enterprise.[9]

These measures did not have an overtly 'class' character, but they undoubtedly affected the selection of VUZ students to the advantage of children from less privileged homes. The new entrance rules and the restriction on the growth of full-time courses in VUZy were real obstacles to children who had hoped to go straight from school to college. The lower classes gained relatively from this, and the removal of fees was also of greater benefit to them.

The reversal of Stalin's 'élitist' policies in the field of higher education was, like the polytechnization drive, almost certainly due to Khrushchev's own efforts. The Soviet leader heartily disliked the so-called 'white-handed' school-leavers who, he thought, were too remote from the tasks of communist construction, and were potential troublemakers.[10] The fact that the great majority of budding students were in the Komsomol was no guarantee of the contrary. Being of humble origin himself, and having studied as a part-time student, Khrushchev was quite convinced that Soviet society had much to gain from drawing more young workers and peasants into the intelligentsia. He frowned on the efforts of rich parents to get their children into VUZy by bribery or *blat* – at least, many examples of this evil were criticized in the press of his day. (This did not, of course,

9. *Sbornik zakonodatelnykh aktov o trude*, Moscow, 1956, p. 459; *Pravda*, 5 January 1955, *Spravochnik sekretarya pervichnoi komsomolskoi organizatsii*, Moscow, 1958, p. 335. See also Chapter 11.

10. See, for example, his speeches before youthful audiences on 11 April 1956 and 18 April 1958, and his notes to the Presidium of the CC CPSU, 21 September 1958, N. S. Khrushchev, *O kommunisticheskom vospitanii*, Moscow, 1964, pp. 8, 40, 46.

mean that the privileges enjoyed by the topmost layers of society, to which Khrushchev himself belonged, were at any time threatened. There are no reports that any of the 'prestige' VUZy were downgraded in these years.)

By 1958 it became evident that Khrushchev's first measures had not achieved the desired results. Young people leaving the ten-year school (and they numbered over a million and a half in that year) had only one chance in seven of a place in a full-time VUZ; they still did not want to work, and voluntary unemployment amongst them was apparently getting worse than ever. It is true that the 'war dent' could be expected to reduce the number of ten-year school-leavers drastically, and, as our figure shows, it did. The authorities could, however, safely assume that the backlog of disappointed candidates would maintain the old pressures on VUZ places.

In September of that year, moreover, Khrushchev admitted that the proportion of workers' and peasants' children in the student body had not risen as he had hoped. He then went on to give the first official figures on students' social origins for two decades:

It is impossible not to see that there are still few children of workers and peasants in the higher educational institutions. In the Moscow VUZy, for example, only 30–40 per cent of the students are the children of workers and collective farmers. The remaining students are the children of white-collared workers and the intelligentsia. Of course, this situation is clearly abnormal. Not to mention the fact that workers and collective farmers who are themselves studying full-time at VUZy can be numbered literally in ones and twos.[11]

The situation may well have been about the same everywhere; Moscow, though a cultural centre with a high proportion of rich inhabitants, presumably had much in common with many large towns. The solution Khrushchev proposed at this stage was contained in some of the provisions of his December 1958 reform. The relevant ones require brief mention.

Firstly, the government's retreat to an eight-year general school was intended to restrict the number of pupils obtaining their *attestat zrelosti* at seventeen. The VUZ entry rules, on the

11. *Komsomolskaya pravda*, 21 September 1958.

other hand, still required the submission of this document. Eight-year school-leavers who went on to a trade school or middle special educational institution would in general miss the VUZ, as before. Most young people, he hoped, would take a regular job and this, coupled with attendance at a part-time general school, would bring them to the VUZ portals in the same way as workers or peasants. Only a minority, he implied, would finish their general education on a full-time basis. It was obvious that this last channel, which Khrushchev certainly favoured least, would appeal most to the more elevated in the community, as it would provide them with an opportunity for keeping their children at school. Khrushchev's answer to this was the provisions for extending the full-time course by an irritating extra year, and introducing a much stronger manual and technical bias into the last three full-time classes.

Secondly, the Soviet leader extended the policy of giving preference to the production candidates in VUZ entrance procedures, with the result that by the autumn of 1964, when he was dismissed, 62 per cent of all VUZ entrants were in this category. The proportion reached 80 per cent in some institutions. A law passed on 18 September 1959 was another step in the same direction. This permitted state enterprises and collective farms to propose deserving young toilers for places in universities and institutes, and pay for their subsistence, on the understanding that these people would return to their old place of employment after graduating.[12] By 1964 about 14 per cent of the VUZ acceptances were of this type. Poorer candidates again stood to gain most from this provision, though it seems that many young people of good family started taking jobs merely to benefit from it. The participation of local Komsomol organizations in the scheme may have meant that it favoured the more orthodox-minded.

Thirdly, evening and correspondence courses were greatly expanded: of the 1.4 million increase in the student body between 1958 and 1964, 1.1 million was attributable to the expansion of part-time study. This again was mainly to the advantage of those young people who had to work to keep themselves,

12. Decree in *Sbornik zakonodatelnykh aktov o trude*, Moscow, 1965, p. 146.

though, as we shall see, there is evidence that candidates who could not get into a full-time VUZ sometimes took these courses as a *pis aller*. Benefits for part-time students, in the form of extra time off and release from night-work, were extended.[13]

Lastly, the law on educational reform stipulated that many technical VUZ courses were to be initially part-time, or split up sandwich fashion, so that all their students, regardless of social background, would spend some of their time doing non-professional work at an enterprise. This was intended to compensate for the fact that technical VUZy were allowed to take a larger proportion of their students straight from school.

STUDENTS' SOCIAL ORIGINS IN THE SIXTIES

Khrushchev was anxious that his innovations should be far-reaching and effective, but it is doubtful whether they produced any profound changes in the social composition of the Soviet student body in the end. This was strongly élitist when he came to power; the effort which he put into changing it alone suggests that he encountered major difficulties. Official reticence on the results was another sign of malaise.

In 1966 the mystery was to some extent solved when the Soviet economist E. L. Manevich provided some figures on the social composition of students for the whole of the USSR in 1963–4. They are reproduced in Table 111. They show that in the final year of Khrushchev's tenure of office the children of 'employees' were still three and a half times as numerous as their social group would warrant in the full-time, i.e. most desirable, VUZy. The children of 'workers' were under-represented by about a third, and the peasants by a fifth.

A comparison of these figures with the 1938 data suggests some interesting conclusions. The 'employees' as a social group grew proportionately little but continued to provide the majority of students for full-time VUZy.[14] The peasants gained consider-

13. Provisions of Decree of 2 July 1959, ibid., p. 171.

14. The slow rise in the proportion of employees is not as surprising as might at first appear. The population grew greatly over these years and the main educational effort resulted in a raising of general educational standards, rather than of changes in the ratio of mental as opposed to other occupations.

ably. The main losers in relative terms were the working class, in whose name education was promoted.

E. L. Manevich also provided some data on part-time students. As may be seen from the table, the peasants almost dropped out of the picture altogether in this respect: both evening classes and correspondence courses seem to have been largely the preserve of the children of workers and employees. There was, however, a big difference between the two channels, in so far as workers (or their children) were in a majority in the evening classes, while the employee group provided over two thirds of the participants in correspondence courses. In some of the union republics, Manevich added, the figure went up to over 85 per cent. A student body of élitist configuration as late as 1963–4 could only denote the failure of Khrushchev's policies.

TABLE III. *Social Groups and the V UZ Student Body, Circa 1964*

Social groups (*1*)	% of total population	% of V UZ student body (*2*)		
		Full-time courses	Evening courses	Correspondence courses
Employees	21	41.0	47.1	67.3
Workers	54.1	39.4	50.6	25.7
Peasants	24.8	19.6	2.3	7.0

Sources:
(1) *Narodnoe khozyaistvo SSSR v 1964*, p. 33. The figure for 'employees' is an approximation for all workers of predominantly mental labour. Private peasants and craftsmen now comprised only 0.1 per cent of the population.
(2) E. L. Manevich, *Problemy obshchestvennogo truda v SSSR*, Moscow, 1966, p. 63.

Another indication of their lack of impact may be gleaned from the figures available on the urban–rural composition of new entrants to agricultural institutes (Table 112). These institutes were always unpopular for obvious reasons. One would expect that the great majority of students in them would be from the countryside, if not from peasant families, and the authorities certainly aimed at this. In fact, in 1960 over a quarter of the new entrants to them were townspeople. This proportion fell steadily to 17 per cent in 1964, but in the two years after Khrushchev's fall it rose again. It seems, incidentally, that students of true peasant origin were a very small minority. S. P. Pavlov, first secretary of the Komsomol, complained in March 1962 that of all agricultural VUZ students who came from rural areas, only one third were from peasant families.[15] That would have meant a

TABLE 112. *Urban–Rural Origin of New Entrants to the Agricultural Institutes of the USSR, 1960–66*

| Year | % of New students | | Sources |
	Urban origin	Rural origin	
1960	27	73	V. T. Petrov, article in *Iz istorii sovetskoi intelligentsii*, ed. M. P. Kim, Moscow, 1966, p. 141
1961	25	75	*Vestnik Vysshei Shkoly*, No. 5, 1962, p. 50
1963	20	80	*V.V.Shk.*, No. 1, 1964, p. 20
1964	17	83	V. T. Petrov, op. cit.
1965	18	82	*V.V.Shk.*, No. 2, 1966, p. 12
1966	20	80	*V.V.Shk.*, No. 12, 1966. p. 7

little over 20 per cent of the student body in these institutions at that time. Pavlov avoided the term 'collective farmer', presumably to exclude the collective farm élite. The rural 'non-peasants' were evidently the children of collective farm chairmen and specialists, or workers and employees in the state farm and rural-industrial sectors.

The social composition of the student body as a whole must depend on the social composition of the successive batches of ten-year school-leavers who go into it. We noted the preponderance of the children of the intelligentsia in the tenth classes in the last chapter. Figures from the Novosibirsk *oblast* survey done in 1963 show that these young people were also far more successful than their less privileged classmates in actually getting a VUZ place (Table 113). Thus whereas 93 per cent of them wished to continue their studies after school (in most cases, one presumes, at a VUZ), 82 per cent of them were able to do this. At the other end of the scale, 76 per cent of the children of agricultural workers entertained this desire, but only 10 per cent

15. *Komsomolskaya pravda*, 6 March 1962,

were successful. The other two groups came in between. The consistently ambitious plans of all social groups was due to the fact that only children who got as far as the tenth class were included in the sample.

TABLE 113. *Career Intentions of Ten-year School-leavers (by Social Group) and Their Realization, Novosibirsk Oblast, 1963*

| | Percentage of children: | | | |
| | Wishing to | | Actually going to | |
Parents' occupations	Work with or without part-time study	Study only	Work with or without part-time study	Study only
Urban intelligentsia	7	93	18	82
Rural intelligentsia	24	76	42	58
Workers (industry & construction)	17	83	39	61
Workers (transport & communication)	18	82	55	45
Workers (service industries)	24	76	41	59
Agricultural workers/peasants	24	76	90	10
Other occupations	50	50	75	25
Average for the sample	17	83	39	61

Source:
V. N. Shubkin, *Voprosy filosofii*, No. 5, 1965, p. 65 (slightly simplified).

There is one further consideration which should not be forgotten. This is that the under-representation of the peasants and poorer workers in the student body may well be exacerbated by the fall-out which is inevitable from all courses. The weaker and less secure students tend to go first. In the mid sixties the fall-out was running at 22 per cent for full-time courses, and must have been higher on part-time ones.[16] A fall-out rate of this

16. *Vestnik vysshei shkoly*, No. 3, 1966, p. 19, and ibid., No. 9, 1965, p. 16. This is a post-Khrushchev figure. The rate in the early sixties, as we note below, was much higher.

magnitude *could* mean the virtual elimination of less privileged children from the graduation classes – and thus from the new ranks of the intelligentsia. A well-known expert in Soviet affairs once stated that one should make sure that Soviet phenomena exist before analyzing them. With this in mind we may hazard the proposition that the Soviet intelligentsia maintained and even consolidated its position in higher education over the twenty-five years between the end of the Second World War and the beginning of this decade.

KHRUSHCHEV'S SCHEMES CRITICIZED

Khrushchev's policies for proletarizing the student body had some very undesirable secondary effects on Soviet higher education. A few unmistakable warnings were made in the early sixties. In November 1961, for example, no less a figure than A. D. Aleksandrov, Rector of Leningrad University, wrote a long article for the youth newspaper *Komsomolskaya pravda*, in which he criticized the university Komsomol organization for over-praising physical labour, the presumption being that this was at the expense of study. There were, he said, 'grey, faceless people' in the student body, by which he clearly meant the production candidates. The fact that *Komsomolskaya pravda* carried this article at all suggests that he had support in high places.

The most revealing attacks on Khrushchev's innovations, appeared, however, when he was safely out of the way. A particularly devastating one was contained in an article on the working of the system of higher education in the September 1965 number of the journal *Vestnik vysshei shkoly*. The writer, one T. D. Samilova, did not disclose her official position, but may have been a deputy minister or Central Committee official. She demonstrated that all types of part-time higher education (which had been so favoured by Khrushchev) gave considerably worse results than full-time courses. She claimed that at the time of writing nearly 60 per cent of the students on evening courses, and 70 per cent of those on correspondence courses, failed to complete their studies on time. The fall-out rates were nearly 30 and 40 per cent respectively. Part-time students had only a quarter as much time available for study anyway, and the great majority of them had to use their free days and holidays for this purpose. They had, said Samilova, two and a half times less sleep than was required to meet physiological norms. As a result of this they fell ill more often, or at least took a lot of time off on medical grounds. And, despite all their laudable efforts, they were promoted much more slowly at work. This was, perhaps, the most damning criticism of all.

The article also contained a number of unpleasant generalizations about the fall in standards in full-time VUZy during the Khrushchev period. The fall-out rate between the intakes of 1953–4 and 1959–60 (which, significantly, spanned these years) had risen from about 20 to 40 per cent: the number of persons repeating a course increased 2.4 times, and the number of people switching courses, or VUZy, rose by 70 per cent. These facts were not readily explicable in terms of an increase in the size of the full-time student body, because, as we have seen, there was hardly any. Samilova implied that most of the blame should be placed on the method of selecting students – in other words, the privileges accorded to the production candidates. Up to 60 per cent of these, she claimed, tended to drop out in the first year; by 1964–5 61 per cent of them were in jobs which had no relation to the subjects they wished to study at their VUZ. A third of them had studied in part-time general schools, where standards were known to be lower. They were a much more heterogeneous group, in age and experience, than young people straight from school, and this made them more difficult to teach. Their presence had caused the average age of the student body in full-time institutions to go up by two years. We may add that, notwithstanding all these pungently expressed drawbacks, it is doubtful whether Khrushchev's educational innovations ever achieved the other aims he had in view: to encourage school-leavers with an *attestat zrelosti* to go into industry or agriculture, and cure the youth employment problem.

The turmoil which Khrushchev's ideas caused in Soviet education at nearly every level was widely resented. Some of the young workers and peasants whom he helped to 'go to college' may have been aglow with gratitude, but it seems that hardly anyone else was. In fact his VUZ reforms evoked the same sort of opposition as had polytechnization. Richer parents objected to the new impediments which their children had to face in their attempts to gain a higher education; the children themselves bemoaned their fate; managers of enterprises disliked the stream of part-time students and short-term production candidates who caused more trouble than they were worth; while the academic community, like rector Aleksandrov, lamented the fall in standards.

In the end, of course, the opposition won, and Khrushchev's attempts to get a better deal for the poorer students at any cost were officially relegated to the category of hare-brained schemes. In April 1965 M. A. Prokofiev, Deputy Minister of Middle Special and Higher Education of the USSR, indicated that in accordance with a law passed on 18 March the *proizvodstvenniki* could expect to have a harder time in entrance examinations. Heads of VUZy were now authorized to share the places available between them and applicants straight from school, in proportion to the size of each category.[17] This was tantamount to removing the Khrushchev advantages, and it resulted in the numbers of production candidates falling dramatically to 30 per cent of the VUZ intake by 1967.[18] A little later an official declared that the proportion of students on part-time courses would be cut down from 59 per cent, where it stood in October 1965, to 47 per cent by 1970. By 1969, however, it was still 53 per cent so there may have been some resistance from those who benefited.[19]

A slackening in the drive towards equality of opportunity in this particular sphere was evident. The new policy implied a better-trained but more élite student body, and consequently more difficult access to the intelligentsia by outsiders.

A NEW APPROACH

A year or so later there were, however, signs of yet another shift of emphasis. In January 1967 M. A. Prokofiev, in a speech remarkable for its clarity and objectivity, called upon the rectors

17. *Vestnik vysshei shkoly*, No. 4, 1965, p. 16.
18. S. P. Pavlov's speech to the Central Committee of the Komsomol, *Komsomolskaya pravda*, 27 December 1967.
19. *Narodnoe khozyaistvo SSSR v 1969*, p. 675.

of pedagogical institutes to reserve 60–70 per cent of their places not for production candidates, but for young people from the villages. Fifty per cent of the student body of the pedagogical institutes of the RSFSR were in this category at that time. The appeal could have been interpreted merely as another attempt to cut down the turnover of teachers in village schools, as this was an important aspect of the flight of the intelligentsia from the countryside. But Prokofiev's proposals were soon extended. In January 1968 V. P. Elyutin, Minister of Higher and Middle Special Education of the USSR, made a strong appeal for increased representation of both working-class and rural youth in the student body.[20] In the course of the next two years, this theme was taken up by well-known sociologists like M. N. Rutkevich, Yu. V. Arutyunyan, and N. Aitov, who had already devoted much time and effort to investigations of the social aspects of education. They produced a series of articles in which they expressed concern at the degree of inequality which still existed.[21] Many professional journalists also turned their attention to it, usually proposing some modification of VUZ entrance procedures so as to favour young people from the country. Yu. Arutyunyan suggested that all rural candidates should be admitted without any concourse exam at all; N. Goncharov thought that they should be given extra credits; while A. Agranovsky and A. Yemelyanov proposed resorting to a long-standing Soviet solution in such cases – the establishment of preparatory courses for the less successful categories of candidates.[22]

This was, in fact, the policy which the authorities adopted. On 6 September 1969 *Pravda* published a decree entitled 'On Organizing Preparatory Sections Attached to VUZy'. This envisaged the creation of preparatory sections with eight to ten month courses at institutions of higher learning, in which instruction was to be organized on a full-time, part-time, or

20. *Narodnoe obrazovanie*, No. 1, 1967 and *Uchitelskaya gazeta*, 13 January 1968.

21. M. N. Rutkevich, *Pravda*, 21 June 1969; Yu. V. Arutyunyan, *Uchitelskaya gazeta*, 4 July 1968; N. Aitov, *Molodoi kommunist*, No. 3, 1968.

22. N. Goncharov, *Sovetskaya Rossia*, 31 May 1968; A. Agranovsky, *Izvestia*, 14 November 1968; A. Yemelyanov, *Sovetskaya Rossia*, 1 July 1969. I am indebted to Mr D. Pospielovsky for these references.

correspondence basis. The courses were to be restricted to people with complete general education from among the best workers, collective farmers and demobilized soldiers. 'Young people starting these courses', the decree stated, 'must have at least one year of work on production behind them. The selection and direction of youth to these sections will be carried out by industrial enterprises, construction sites, transport and communication organizations, state and collective farms, commanding officers in military units, on the recommendation of Party, Komsomol, and trade union organizations.'

It is not easy to judge the full significance of this measure at the time of writing, and it will probably be necessary to wait a year or two until its action becomes clear. It may be explained as a real attempt to help talented people in the lower strata of society; concern had been expressed that a fund of ability was being wasted here. It may again have been intended to counterbalance the new trend towards specialization in the general school system which we discussed in the last chapter. Slightly conflicting policies are, of course, not uncommon in Soviet, or for that matter any other government. Preparatory courses are a well-tried Soviet remedy usually implying state intervention in the selection process. This particular measure was rather like the Khrushchev law of September 1959, which allowed the social organizations in state enterprises and collective farms to put up their own candidates. We noted the possibility of an inbuilt political bias there, in so far as organizations would tend to pick not only the more needy, but also the more politically reliable, youngsters. There is no reason to believe that the 1969 law does not have the same purpose.

There are signs that this new attempt at popularization has encountered opposition in academic circles. In October 1969 none other than V. N. Stoletov, Minister of Higher and Middle Special Education of the RSFSR, wrote that education should be designed not only to fit a person for a job, but also to broaden his horizons; and that graduates should not worry if they are not immediately given work commensurate with their skills.[23] This does not easily accord with assumptions underlying so much official legislation, for example, that young people should be

23. *Komsomolskaya pravda*, 9 October 1969.

chosen for higher education on the basis of their performance at work, or that the education system should be trimmed to serve current production needs.

Over the last decade and a half the Soviet authorities have gone to considerable lengths to alter the social composition of the student body. Khrushchev made a significant departure from Stalin's policies and tried to ensure that the less privileged social groups should provide most of the new entrants to the intelligentsia. On the whole these efforts were not successful. The period after 1964 saw a rejection of them and a return towards more élitist trends. But by the end of the decade there were new signs of hesitation. The post-Khrushchev leadership evidently found that active intervention in this important social process was needed in order to counteract the marked élitism which Soviet institutions of higher education, like those of many other lands, seem to engender.

11

From School to Work – Problems of Youth Employment

THE transition from school to work, from a largely passive role in society to an active one, is an important stage in the lives of most young people. The social problems involved have, however, been recognized on a national level only comparatively recently. The first agencies dealing specifically with the problems of youth employment (in the sense of placement) began to appear in the most industrialized societies in the twenties; but even then these bodies tended to have rather limited aims, and did little more than provide information on vacancies. Generally they bothered neither to elucidate the inclinations of young applicants nor to steer them to places suited to their tastes – procedures which came to be known as 'vocational guidance'.

The post-war years have seen notable advances, both in vocational guidance techniques and the provision of comprehensive placement services. Official or semi-official organizations have been developed in many industrialized countries, including Great Britain and the USA, for just this purpose. The object is, ideally, to tell young people as much as possible about careers open to them while still in school, and attempt to elucidate, by tests or interviews, their desires and aptitudes. They may then be provided with information about jobs actually available, and sent up for interviews with prospective employers. In some cases youth employment services maintain contact with the employers afterwards. In 'capitalist' societies the youth employment services form a bridge between school and work, but attempt nothing in the way of overt persuasion. Although the needs of society may not be ignored completely, any attempt to influence a young person without the most careful regard for his own interests would be regarded as highly improper.

In the Soviet Union the authorities incline to a basically

different view of the matter. Article 12 of the Constitution describes labour as an obligation and matter of honour for every Soviet citizen. In practice the government exhibits a marked tendency to regard placement as a form of labour direction, which implies that the individual, be he an experienced toiler or a mere beginner, should be employed in a manner most suited to apparent national needs. Personal aptitudes and desires may be satisfied only in so far as they accord with state plans. This approach is partly a reflection of the traditional paternalistic attitude of the Russian government towards its citizens, and partly a consequence of the Bolshevik drive rapidly to transform an agricultural society into an industrial one.

The Soviet authorities have attempted to control the various sectors of their labour market over the years by a variety of means and with varying degrees of success. A study of all of these aspects would be too vast an undertaking for these pages. In the remaining chapters we shall confine ourselves to the two basic means for the placement of young people which were well established by the mid fifties and were still paramount in the late sixties. (We shall explicitly exclude placement within the collective farm, because this, as we have seen, was supposed to be largely automatic.)

The first may be termed 'controlled' or 'directed', and thought of as typically Soviet. It was devised for those young people who had been trained at technical institutions of all types. These graduates themselves fall into two distinct categories: those who are from the low-grade 'trade' schools, originally the state labour reserve system, and those who finish middle special or higher educational institutions. This part of the system antedated the First Five-Year Plan in 1928. Antecedents of all kinds of labour direction may, of course, be traced to the Civil War period, in particular to Trotsky's notorious labour armies. It is official practice to direct graduates of both these categories to a place of work for periods of three or four years, with their consent or without it. We shall devote Chapter 12 to the placement of VUZ graduates, as their fate is, perhaps, the most widely commented upon and interesting.

The second kind of placement which concerns us here is for school-leavers who come onto the labour market without any special training. They are under no obligation to take a specific job, and may be thought of as making up the 'free' sector of the youth labour market. As far as we can tell they tend to come from the least privileged sections of Soviet society – though with the spread of ten-year schooling and the increase of pressure on VUZ places these contingents have been joined by young people well placed enough to want, but not able enough to obtain, a more advanced education. No proper analysis of the social composition of these, the main body of young work-seekers, has ever been published by Soviet scholars, but some clues to their social origin may be extracted from a recent investigation into their motives for starting work.[1] Thirty-nine per cent of the sample thought they were too weak to get into a VUZ, 17 per cent were from families which could not keep them, 15.7 per cent wanted to achieve material independence, and 19 per cent had no desire to study. The last three motives, mentioned *in toto* by nearly 52 per cent of the sample, strongly suggest a low social status.[2]

Some of the most revealing information on the social problems involved in placement in the free sector has been published as a result of the rather complicated juvenile unemployment problem which arose in the mid fifties and was still there a decade later. This prompted the authorities to take a number of counter-measures, and even introduce an element of state control where there had been virtually none before. This took the form of a peculiarly Soviet youth employment service. We shall approach the problem, therefore, from the standpoint of unemployment. Unfortunately we shall find ourselves as much concerned with state administration as with the more sociological problems, but this is inevitable. This topic, too, is best treated chronologically.

SOME LABOUR-MARKET MYSTERIES

The ease with which young people can negotiate the passage from school to work depends in the first instance on the ratio of work-seekers to vacancies; problems of training, aptitude and even placement itself are to this extent secondary.

1. Article by L. Kogan and S. Artemov in *Komsomolskaya pravda*, 24 January 1968.
2. See Table 72, note.

It is unfortunate that the Soviet authorities publish such unsatisfactory data on new entrants to the labour market, and virtually none on the work places available for them. Obviously, over several years, the number of work-seekers in the free sector must equal the sum of the relevant age cohorts, minus the young · people who continue their education. Lack of data, however,

TABLE 114. *Influx of New Workers into the Economy*

Year	No. trained on production (in thousands)	No. trained in trade schools (in thousands)	% trained on production
1950	2326	493	83.0
1958	2605	653	80.0
1960	2807	689	80.3
1962	2875	888	76.4
1963	3159	915	77.5
1964	3332	941	78.0
1965	3407	1042	76.6
1966	3713	1063	77.7
1967	3922	1111	78.0
1968	4058	1229	76.7

Source:
Narodnoe khozyaistvo SSSR for relevant years, with modifications introduced by Yu. Novgorodski and N. Khaikin, article in *Planovoe khozyaistvo*, No. 1, 1970, p. 21. We have made the presumption that they are improvements on the *Narodnoe khozyaistvo* figures.
The last column is calculated.
The categorization used in the first column is in effect 'numbers taught new trades and specialities'. These are presumably new entrants to the non-peasant labour force, but we have not found this stated explicitly. Further training may be termed 'raising qualifications'. Some 'employees' were also taught new trades and specialities; these, however, only numbered 200,000 in 1968.

makes it impossible to fix the age distribution of those who start work in any given year, or to establish their average age.

The annual flow of young people into the non-agricultural sector of the economy rose substantially between 1950 and 1968, mainly as a result of the post-war baby boom and the flight from the land (Table 114). It seems unlikely, however, that this trend can continue long into the seventies, and indeed the falling birthrate makes a reduction inevitable in the long run. Of course, the age-mix must have changed over the eighteen years in question – there was undoubtedly a steady fall in the number of work-seekers under seventeen years of age as the coverage of the general school increased. By 1972–3, if the government's plans for complete coverage of the ten-year school are implemented, the 'free' youth labour market will consist of people between seventeen and eighteen years old, with an admixture of nineteen-year-olds who were late finishing school.

The demand for juvenile labour is another puzzle. It is clear that any slackening in general labour requirements must complicate the task of job-finding for young people, who are naturally inexperienced and often amongst the least desirable applicants for work. It seems that at least until the last years of the sixties (when signs of a preponderant labour shortage began to appear) the supply of labour was on the whole sufficient to satisfy national demand at the existing level of mechanization, but that certain kinds of labour shortage coexisted with pockets of unemployment. There are fairly standard, global arguments to support these contentions. Thus on the labour shortage side one may point to data which show that from the mid fifties up to the end of the sixties the rate of growth of the Soviet economy, though declining, was much in excess of the growth of the labour force. Productivity was not high. Many branches of the economy were, by West European standards, undermechanized, and continued to require big inputs of labour. Successive Soviet leaderships endeavoured to inaugurate crash programmes for agricultural, and to some extent industrial, development in comparatively uninhabited parts of the country, and this policy also demanded great numbers of workers. References to labour shortages are frequent in Soviet publications.

Other factors, however, suggest that considerable surpluses of labour occurred in certain localities. The large towns have always attracted outsiders (despite all residence restrictions) and it has long been recognized that there is a relative shortage of decent jobs in them. State investment in the small, less accessible towns, which in 1969 contained up to a quarter of the population, has not been sufficient to ensure their healthy growth, and they have had well-recognized surpluses of labour. A third of the Soviet labour force is still employed in agriculture, which is highly seasonal in nature; the same may be said of certain branches of industry and construction. Automation is making some progress, especially in heavy industry, and this eventually means redundancy. The so-called Shchekino experiment, a method of enterprise organization designed partly to ensure a more rational use of manpower, may have had the same effect. Veiled references to labour surpluses have also, since the mid sixties, been finding a place in Soviet press reports. And finally, it is obvious that any society must put up with a flow of labour from one job to another, and hesitation on the part of individual work-seekers, even when vacancies exist locally. In a word, there is no doubt that the Soviet economy possessed, for most of the years within our purview, many of the conditions needed for local or more general unemployment.

TWO KINDS OF YOUTH UNEMPLOYMENT

The existence of youth unemployment as a serious social pheno-menon was first publicly admitted by A. N. Shelepin, first secre-tary of the Komsomol, in April 1954. This fact did not prevent the Soviet authorities from adhering rigidly to the proposition, in their plan fulfilment returns, that unemployment was un-known in the land. But in the course of the next three years a spate of major articles in the central press threw quite a lot of light on it. The types of settlement where it seemed most preva-lent were precisely those where unemployment might have been expected, namely the largest towns of republican standing with a probable surplus population problem, and the smaller, more neglected towns of the provinces.[3]

The most common type of youth unemployment to be men-tioned may be loosely termed 'involuntary'. This term would fit most kinds of unemployment, since this is generally regarded as an unpleasant condition. But we use it here with a rather special connotation. The immediate cause of this involuntary unemploy-ment may be traced to certain labour laws enacted in the mid fifties. The Bolshevik government, it will be remembered, had

3. Press references and decrees mentioned below may be found in my articles in *Soviet Affairs*, St Antony's Papers, No. 12 (3), London, 1962; *Osteuropa*, No. 7, 1962.

introduced fairly sweeping benefits and protective provisions for juvenile workers (i.e. those under the age of eighteen) in 1918, and reaffirmed them in the Labour Code of 1922. These provisions were largely ignored in the thirties and more or less forgotten as the labour market was militarized in 1940.

The situation changed radically in the summer of 1955 and spring of 1956, when a series of important decrees largely re-established the former safeguards. Under the new provisions the hiring of young people under fifteen years of age was normally forbidden, the only exception being that fourteen-year-olds could be taken on 'with trade union approval'. Juveniles aged between fourteen and sixteen were limited to a four-hour working day, and those aged sixteen to eighteen had a six-hour day, as opposed to the standard eight hours for adults. But at the same time juveniles were to be paid as for a full day. The presumption was that they would in any case earn less, since they were usually involved in training schemes, or at the lower end of the wage scale. In addition, they were not to be employed for overtime or night work, and were guaranteed one month's holiday with pay instead of the standard two weeks. They could not do many jobs listed as dangerous or unhealthy.

This very liberal shift in policy can best be regarded as part of the 'de-Stalinization' of labour relations. It sprang, no doubt, from the desire of the leadership to make some palpable concession to the workers after two decades of very oppressive rule. It was in April 1956, after all, that workers regained the right to change their jobs on their own initiative. This was also the time when Khrushchev was beginning to understand the fundamental discrepancy between the career intentions of ten-year school-leavers and the welter of uninspiring jobs available to them. The changes in labour law were, like polytechnization, an attempt to make manual jobs more attractive.

However this may be, the changes certainly made juvenile labour much *less* attractive to employers. The under-eighteens not only did less work, but were more difficult to fit into the production process. As far as we can tell, managers were expected to carry this extra burden without any reduction in their production commitments. If there had been extensive shortages of labour they may have put up with it. But it seems that usually there was no need for them to do so. Frequent reports in the papers criticized individual managers for refusing to employ young people, or, if they did employ them, ignoring the new limitations on juvenile labour. 'An excellent law is passed on shortening the working day for minors, yet it brings but cold comfort to many of them,' a correspondent of the newspaper *Trud* wrote in November, 1956. 'Bureaucrats and officials have interpreted the laws to suit themselves, and thereby deprive young men and women of their great happiness [i.e. employment]. How have they managed it? In the spring, as soon as the laws had been announced, these smart alecs began to think up ways of getting rid of their six-hour workers . . .'[4]

An allied difficulty was caused by the new conditions of employment for persons engaged in part-time study, which, as we have seen, the leadership was by then anxious to encourage. An order of September 1954 obliged enterprises to give all evening students twenty days extra paid holiday a year to take their examinations and tests, while correspondence students were given an extra thirty days. All part-time students in the last year of study were entitled to a full four months off, one of them with pay, to do the obligatory dissertation. The 1955 law was extended in scope in July and November 1959, when the Council of Ministers of the USSR authorized managers to grant other minor concessions, including day release, to people still studying in the upper classes of the part-time general schools.[5] Some managers were quick to develop an aversion for applicants straight from school who seemed likely to enrol for part-time courses. 'Some managers', wrote a *Pravda* correspondent in July 1957, 'do not employ young people because they consider that part-time education is a lot of bother. "Just look at how many part-time students we've got already," they say; "you do nothing but write out leave passes for them to take examinations. That's not much use, is it?"'[6]

A third major source of trouble was the fact that many young

4. *Trud*, 16 November 1956.
5. *Spravochnik po vechernei srednei obshcheobrazovatelnoi shkole, RSFSR*, Moscow, 1963, p. 341, and *Sbornik zakonodatelnykh aktov o trude*, Moscow, 1965, p. 171, ff.
6. *Pravda*, 19 July 1957.

people, especially those with ten classes of general schooling behind them, had no intention of working for very long anyway. They were much more interested in getting into a full-time VUZ, and went to work either to pass the time until the next set of entrance exams came along, to earn some money, or to get a certificate proving they had actually been 'on production', and were thus genuine production candidates. Managers with enterprise plans to fulfil naturally took exception to this attitude and refused to employ them. The result was that whenever there was a slackening in the demand for labour in a given locality juveniles and part-time students were the first to suffer.

The youth unemployment of these years was not, however, only of an involuntary kind. Dozens of newspaper articles reflected the existence of a 'voluntary' variety, in other words, a refusal on the part of young people to take jobs when they were available. The culprits here were the increasing numbers of ten-year school-leavers who, despite Khrushchev's efforts to the contrary, still dreamed of going straight into college, and could not be induced to do manual labour for love nor money. This was an attitude which Khrushchev himself commented upon with considerable scorn. He called the young people involved 'white hands', and they became a constant object of press criticism during his tenure of office.

Yet it is evident that this important social phenomenon could hardly be explained only in terms of a dislike for physical labour. Young people in Great Britain, for instance, are hardly less sophisticated than their fellows in Russia, and their chances of getting a higher education have been much smaller. But although the desire for a higher education is very palpable, we do not observe amongst them either a 'college fixation' of the Soviet type, or a mass aversion to unskilled or semi-skilled jobs.

Several explanations suggest themselves. The problem may, of course, be partly one of presentation by the mass media. Refusal to work is a recognized political misdemeanour in the USSR; in the West it is hardly newsworthy, especially if the individuals concerned have other means of support. Another answer may lie in the nature of the comparison. The last classes of Soviet general school were for many decades 'élitist' in character, and in some ways more comparable to private rather than state schools in the West. The products of English 'public' schools, for instance, would not readily become fitters' mates. On the Soviet side there is the long-standing cultural gulf between the Russian/Soviet intelligentsia and the masses which has only recently begun to narrow. Persons who could claim membership of the intelligentsia would have little to gain and much to lose by deserting it. As mentioned above, managements of nationalized or State-controlled enterprises in the U S S R may put more emphasis on the possession of a degree than the heads of private firms in other countries, so that a higher education becomes more necessary for upward social mobility. And it may be that the distinctions in living standards between the upper and lower layers of Soviet society are more keenly felt than material differences in richer societies. The Soviet working class has to suffer many more immediate shortages than its counterparts in more fortunate lands, and the desire of individuals to rise above them may be correspondingly greater.

The principal explanation, however, is probably to be found in the 'shape' of the Soviet income and employment structure, which we discussed in Chapter 5. The low level of mechanization and high proportion of relatively poorly paid manual jobs in many branches of the economy, together with the comparative neglect of the service and light industries, has meant a shortage of desirable jobs for young people who benefited from a full ten years of general schooling. Even in the late sixties up to half of the jobs offered were unmechanized and probably required no more than eight years of general studies. In 1969 37 per cent of all young people under eighteen employed in the national economy had not, apparently, needed any special training for their jobs. On the other hand three quarters or more of the ten-year school-leavers wished to go on to *higher* education.[7] It is not difficult to detect a major imbalance here.

The discrepancy between the general direction of official policy and the realities of the labour market has become a common topic for discussion among Soviet sociologists. One finds reference to it in the works of V. Shubkin, N. Aitov and V. Kantorovich, to mention but three scholars. 'A premature

7. Review article by A. Soloviev in *Ekonomicheskie nauki*, No. 2, 1968, p. 33. M. Makhankova, article in *Planovoe khozyaistvo*, No. 1, 1970, p. 86.

TABLE 115. *Reported Youth Unemployment in the USSR, 1955–7*

	Place	Year of graduation from school	Numbers unemployed	% of graduates unemployed	Type of unemployment	Minimum length of unemployment	Source
Republics	White Russia	1956	5,400	10(?)	Voluntary	12 months	*Pravda* 28/6/57
	Kazakhstan	1956	'Thousands'	+ 7	Involuntary	10 months	*Koms. pr.* 27/4/57
	Georgia	1956	6,000	18	Voluntary	6 months	*Koms. pr.* 8/1/56
	Moscow	1955	6,000	22	Voluntary	1–2 years	Supreme Soviet report p. 306*
	Yaroslavl'	1955	+1,000	+16	Voluntary	1 year	*Izvestia* 1/7/56
	Yaroslavl'	1957	+1,500	+14	Voluntary	1 year	*Uchit. gaz.* 8/5/58
Oblasts	Kemerovo	1955	+2,000	+10	'Mainly' voluntary	9 months	N. N. Zabelin, p. 149†
	Mogilev	1957	+1,000	10		6 months	*Uchit. gaz.* 13/3/58

Stalino	1955	5,047	18	—	6 months	T. S. Ponomarenko, pp. 8–9‡
Stalino	1956	3,000	12(?)	—	6 months	Uchit. gaz. 17/12/57
Kuibyshev	1957	420	10	—	11 months	Uchit. gaz. 15/5/58
Rostov-on-Don	1955	759	17(?)	—	27 months	Uchit. gaz.
Rostov-on-Don	1956	437	10(?)	—	15 months	26/9/57
Rostov-on-Don	1957	700	17	Involuntary	3 months	
Taganrog	1956	—	25	—	'Several months'	Uchit. gaz. 3/1/57
Towns — Gorki	1956	+2,000	+20	Involuntary	5 months	Uchit. gaz. 5/1/57
Tbilisi	1955	2,000	30(?)	—	14 months	Zarya Vostoka 23/8/56
Kiev	1955 or 1956	2,000	20(?)	Voluntary	—	Koms. pr. 10/7/56
Kalinin	1956	200	—10	Involuntary	6 months	Uchit. gaz. 1/5/57

Further sources:

* *Zasedanie verkhovnogo soveta SSSR, December, 1958. Stenographic report. Moscow, 1959,*

†N. N. Zabelin, *Narodno-khozyaistvennoe znachenie gosudarstvennykh trudovykh rezervov*, Moscow, 1959.

‡T. S. Ponomarenko, *O vybore professii vypusknikami desyatiletki*, Stalino, 1956.

switch to forms of education which are not brought to life by the real requirements of the national economy', wrote Shubkin, 'only leads to our deferring the attainment by young people of an independent status, giving them knowledge which is not needed, and evoking requirements which society is in no position to satisfy.'[8] No convincing answer to this problem seems to be in sight.

A WIDESPREAD PHENOMENON

There is every reason to believe that youth employment of the types described became very widespread. The data presented in Tables 115 and 116 are fragmentary, but they are sufficient to give some impression of its proportions and extensive geographical distribution.

It will be noted that they have been grouped for two periods, 1955–7 and 1964–7, separately. This is because little was written about the problem in the years between. It may have eased as a result of the fall in the size of the age cohorts (i.e. the war dent), but it is unlikely that it disappeared altogether. There is an excellent reason why journalists should have stopped writing about it. This was the time when Khrushchev was trying to implement his polytechnization plans, and any reports suggesting that they were ineffective would presumably not have done the authors any good.

The problem re-entered the realm of discussion in 1966 when the retreat from Khrushchev's policies was in full swing. (Some of the references were retrospective.) Youth unemployment became particularly acute in that year as a result of the final abolition of the eleventh class, for this meant that the youth labour market had to absorb school-leavers from both the tenth and eleventh classes together.

We may well ask how serious the Soviet youth unemployment problem was in comparison with that of other countries. The answer depends, of course, on the choice of economy. Unemployment among young people often reaches catastrophic

8. V. Kantorovich, 'Sotsiologia i literatura', *Novy Mir*, No. 12, 1967, p. 152, V. Shubkin, *Sotsiologicheskie Opyty*, Moscow, 1970, Chapter 4, N. Aitov, article in *Molodoi Kommunist*, No. 3, 1968, etc.

proportions in underdeveloped lands, but industrialized societies usually manage to control it. In Great Britain, where the statistical returns are reasonably accurate, unemployment amongst school-leavers showed seasonal variations of from 1.2 to 6.1 per cent over the three-year period 1965–7.[9] Variation by region, however, was much greater: while a low rate of 1 per cent was recorded in London and the South-east in October 1965, the figure for Wales in February 1967 was as high as 13 per cent. Against the UK national averages the occasional figures for European Russia shown in the tables seem to be high or extremely high. But those available for the Transcaucasian republics are probably not untypical of less industrialized societies.

KHRUSHCHEV'S PALLIATIVES

The youth unemployment of the mid fifties caught the authorities unaware. The problem was made worse by the fact that Stalin's policies, while increasing state direction of labour and extending the controlled sector, had all but suppressed information on jobs and removed most administrative machinery for placement in the free one. Let us pause to consider the facilities still available at the time of Stalin's death.

The old Soviet labour exchanges had disappeared soon after 1931, when unemployment was declared not to exist and employment benefits were stopped. The People's Commissariat of Labour was abolished in 1933. After that some of the larger towns gave details of local demands for more skilled categories of workers through general information kiosks (*gorodskie spravochnye buro*). Yet these were a poor substitute for the exchanges. Most people looking for work in their own locality had to rely on occasional notices in the local press, at factory gates, or in shop windows. Sometimes, of course, they would find out about jobs through friends or relations working at places where vacancies occurred.

The only placement agency in existence was the so-called Orgnabor, or the Administration for the Organized Recruitment of Labour. This administration ran a network of recruiting

9. *Youth Employment Service in Great Britain*, the National Youth Employment Council triennial report, 1965–7, p. 58.

TABLE 116. *Reported Youth Unemployment in the USSR, 1964–7*

Place	Date Reported	Percentage/ numbers unemployed	Persons involved & other information	Source
USSR	March 1967	5%	10–11-year school leavers	*Trud,* 26/3/67
		1%	8-year school leavers	
Union Republics				
Ukraine	March 1967	−1%	Residual figure	*Uchit. gaz.,* 2/3/67
Armenia	Oct. 1966	50%	Residual figure	*Koms. pr.,* 22/10/66
Armenia	Oct. 1966	16% ⎫	10–11-year school leavers	⎫ *Trud,* 26/3/67
Azerbaidzhan	Oct. 1966	18% ⎬		⎬
Georgia	Oct. 1966	12% ⎭		⎭
Oblasts				
Arkhangelsk	Sept. 1966	12,000	10–11-year school leavers	*Koms. pr.,* 28/9/66
Kemerovo	Oct. 1966	7%	10–11-year school leavers	*Trud,* 26/3/67
Kemerovo	Sept. 1967	25%	10–11-year school leavers	*Izvestia,* 22/6/68
Magadan	1965	2.6%	10–11-year school leavers	M. S. Shcher- bavskikh, see below
Tula	Oct. 1966	13%	10–11-year school leavers	*Trud,* 26/3/67
Towns				
Irkutsk	1967	3,000	—	*Izvestia,* 16/4/68
Chelyabinsk	Jan. 1964	0.1– 0.6%	Age-groups 17–14	L. E. Epshtein, see below

offices in the villages and large urban centres for drawing up labour contracts with peasants or workers wishing to take jobs on building sites or in industrial enterprises in Siberia and the Far East. Orgnabor placements were proverbially unattractive, but in any case contracts could not be made with anyone under the age of eighteen.[10] By 1953 the Orgnabor offices were said to be handling less than a million placements a year (as compared with over three million after their establishment in the thirties) and five years later this had fallen to half a million. According to another specialist, the proportion had fallen to four per cent of all placements, that is, not only first placements, by 1962.[11] Orgnabor itself was, incidentally, subject to many minor re-organizations, but was never extended to provide anything approaching a general placement service.

Another method of placement which, though devoid of any permanent organization, requires mention, was the so-called 'social call-up', or *obshchestvenny prizyv*. This dated at least from the thirties, but it was used by Khrushchev for his virgin land campaigns from the spring of 1954 on, and for some of the building site campaigns after 1955. The technique here was for work to be advertised by local Komsomol officials at meetings and in the local press, and young people persuaded to apply. Those who were selected would then be sent off to their destination in a merry group, perhaps after a ceremony at the station. No comprehensive account of the numbers involved ever seems to have been made available: all we have is a tangle of vague and partially contradictory estimates. It seems, however, that during the Khrushchev era 'placements' of this kind numbered from

Further sources to Table 116:
M. S. Shcherbavskikh, in D. I. Valentei, *Naselenie i trudovye resursy severo-vostoka SSSR*, Moscow, 1968, p. 57. Fate of 8.1% of this sample was unknown. L. E. Epshtein, *Ekonomicheskie faktory kommunisticheskogo vospitania*, Chelyabinsk, 1966, p. 243. Overall figure given by the author is methodologically suspect.

10. K. P. Urzhinski, *Trudoustroistvo grazhdan v SSSR*, Moscow, 1967, p. 90.
11. M. Sonin, *Vosproizvodstvo rabochei sily v SSSR*, Moscow, 1959, pp. 182 and 186, and S. L. Senyavski, *Rost rabochego klassa*, Moscow, 1966, p. 109.

about 50,000 to 150,000 a year, and were therefore only a very tiny proportion of all new labour.[12] Many of those involved in this soon returned home, and there was no significant reactivization of this method in the latter part of the sixties.

The Soviet labour market was thus, before Khrushchev started to reform it, arranged in a very lopsided fashion. In the controlled sector, covering persons who had received vocational or specialist training at an educational institution, placement was determined by highly detailed, though sometimes ineffective, plans and regulations. Most other work-seekers, including ordinary school-leavers, were in a kind of limbo. But once they had taken a job they could not, under the onerous law of June 1940, leave it without the permission of the management.[13]

When juvenile unemployment of the kinds we have described first began to make its appearance, the Soviet leadership's principal reaction was to modify the educational system in the manner described in Chapters 9 and 10. The polytechnized curricula were supposed to help school-leavers to find work by turning them into trained (or partially trained) workers who would be more acceptable to harassed managers. The direct school–enterprise links were supposed to be all-important in this process. The first reports of headmasters trying to arrange for their pupils to be taught trades in the last classes, and go to work in local enterprises afterwards, began to appear about 1956. The general school course in the Ukraine was actually lengthened by a year to allow for this.

At the same time, however, the government took the first timid steps towards setting up vocational guidance and placement services. The decree of August 1954, which stated that the State Labour Reserve system should establish trade schools specially adapted for ten-year school-leavers, contained an instruction ensuring 'the widespread participation of soviets in

12. M. Sonin, op. cit., Moscow, 1959, p. 234; A. S. Pashkov, *Pravovye osnovy nauchnoi organizatsii truda*, Moscow, 1967, p. 84; P. A. Gureev, *Lgoty pri orgnabore i obshchestvennom prizyve*, Moscow, 1968, p. 77.

13. We have in mind employment for normal, able-bodied people. Local Soviets had long been empowered to make *ad hoc* arrangements for the placement of orphans (who usually went to trade schools), invalids, delinquents and former prisoners.

affording all possible help to young people from the ten-year schools to choose a suitable trade and obtain work'.[14]

In the two or three years which followed some local soviets did indeed set up permanent commissions to gather information about vacancies for young people and assist the latter in obtaining employment. We know that Moscow City Council gave a good deal of attention to the problem, and there were reports of place-ment commissions, *kommissii po trudoustroistvu molodezhi*, appearing in about a dozen other large towns, including Lenin-grad. It seems, however, that the commissions' activities did not, on the whole, attract much support or interest, and an article in *Pravda* on 19 June 1957 stated in so many words that they did not work.

Meanwhile the placement aspect of the polytechnization drive was going badly: in the Ukraine, for example, in 1956, despite the most strenuous efforts, only about 13 per cent of all ten-year school-leavers acquired a trade, and it is probable that only a tiny proportion of these found jobs which accorded with it. It was no doubt the relative failure of polytechnization which prompted the authorities to try and improve the functions of the placement commissions. They did so, however, in an unusual manner.

In September 1957 an important decree entitled 'On the Placement of Ten-year School-leavers in Industrial and Agri-cultural Production' was published. This stipulated that authorities from Republican Councils of Ministers down to local soviets were to cooperate with the Administration for State Labour Reserves and the planning offices of Khrushchev's new regional economic councils in fixing 'for all enterprises, con-struction sites and organizations, within the confines of their labour plans, a quota for hiring and training ten-year school-leavers and juveniles'. Gosplan departments at all levels were ordered to cooperate with other interested bodies in compiling annual and long-term quota plans, by economic region and branch of the economy, so as to control the flow of juveniles into production. The local soviets would, in accordance with Gosplan instructions, direct school-leavers to local managers who would

14. *Direktivy KPSS i Sovietskogo pravitelstva po khozyaistvennym vopro-sam*, Vol. 4, Moscow, 1958, p. 250.

be obliged to accept them. The actual business of deciding who went where was to remain in the hands of the soviets' *ad hoc* placement commissions.

The quota, or *bronya,* system was in effect an attempt to integrate the general school and the free sector of the youth labour market, in the sense that most pupils would learn to be workers while at school and join a local enterprise by prior arrangement when they left. These quotas may have helped to ease juvenile unemployment to some small degree, but the fact that Khrushchev decided to go ahead with such an extensive reorganization of the general school system in the autumn of 1958 suggests very strongly that the improvement was marginal.

The economic and social implications of the *bronya* system were, by contrast, breathtaking. It involved a vast amount of planning: ideally, even in 1958, something like a million and a half initial placements should have been effected by the State. The provision of technical training for young people still at the general school entailed the widespread construction of school workshop facilities and finding hundreds of thousands of temporary work places at local enterprises. The scheme inevitably meant a severe restriction on the individual's choice of training, quite apart from that imposed by the complexion of the local labour market. Each pupil in any given tenth class might be expected to have his own ideas about the trade he wanted to learn (or found least repugnant). And except in areas where there were long-established trades or jobs, there would normally be almost as many choices as pupils.

It was obviously impracticable, within the bounds of the school programme, to allow each and every pupil to arrange his own production practice where he pleased. What usually happened was that headmasters came to an agreement with one or two enterprises to take all of their pupils, and teach them one or two standard trades, regardless of individual taste, not to mention local requirements. Indeed, the administrative problems of other arrangements became so great that as early as 30 May 1961 a law was passed limiting the choice of trades in any given class to two. This in turn must have further complicated the task of aligning the supply of properly trained school-leavers with the needs of industry. An example of the hopeless discrepancies which arose in the Chelyabinsk *oblast* in the early sixties is illustrated in Table 117.

As may have been expected, young people often refused to work at trades they disliked. E. L. Manevich, commenting on

TABLE 117. *Nature of Special Training in the General Schools of the Chelyabinsk oblast, 1961–4*

| | Of Pupils in 9–11th classes | |
Trade acquired	As a % of pupils	As a % of needs of the oblast
Fitters	28.3	52
Turners	24.1	62
Other operatives	6.0	48
Lab. assistants & chemists	8.0	1600
Seamstresses	16.4	420
Draughtsmen	2.2	740
Automized line operators	5.1	19
Other trades	9.9	184

Source:
L. E. Epshtein, *Ekonomicheskie faktory kommunisticheskogo vospitania*, Chelyabinsk, 1966, p. 234. Data from the Chelyabinsk *oblast* education and planning office.

this fact, states that despite polytechnization and intensive efforts to teach trades in the last classes of schools in Moscow, Kiev, Sverdlovsk and a number of other towns, in 1960 only about 17 per cent of the young people from the tenth classes actually started work, and these 'as a rule' chose jobs which did not correspond to the skills they had acquired.[15] The quota system raised a new voluntary unemployment problem without solving the old one.

The last major effort at amelioration which was made under Khrushchev's leadership took the form of the law of 4 December 1963 entitled 'On Improving the Placement of Juveniles'. This noted the continued existence of youth unemployment, and fixed the enterprises' quotas for juveniles at between three and five

15. E. L. Manevich, *Problemy obshchestvennogo truda v SSSR*, Moscow, 1966, p. 42.

per cent of their labour intakes. Local authorities were now to compile statistical reports on the youth employment situation in their areas, the term used for the jobless being 'juveniles who are not studying in educational institutions and not engaged in production'. This was probably the first reference to a distinct category of able-bodied unemployed in a legal document since the early thirties. The law itself can be regarded only as a belated attempt to strengthen a system which was failing badly. Khrushchev had pinned his faith on polytechnization, and thought that other measures were needed only to supplement it.

SOVIET YOUTH EMPLOYMENT SERVICES APPEAR

The years which followed Khrushchev's removal were marked by a new realism in the sphere of placement, perhaps as a reaction to the former leader's 'hare-brained' approach, perhaps as a consequence of the labour shortage which received more and more attention in published sources in the late sixties.[16] We can in fact trace three main developments.

The first affected the labour market as a whole. Early in 1967 a union-republican State Committee on the Use of Labour Reserves was established, and on 27 May the Council of Ministers of the RSFSR approved the statutes of the Committee for the Russian Republic. It was evident from these that the authorities had taken the first steps towards the re-establishment of something approaching a general labour exchange system. The functions of the committees included

the placement of members of the public in employment, and also the provision of information on the requirements of enterprises, building sites and organizations for workers and office staff: the analysis of the able-bodied public not engaged in social labour, and the elaboration of proposals, together with the planning and economic organs, for the rational use of these labour resources . . .

In addition the committee was empowered to organize retraining and resettlement, provide employment by the encouragement of

16. A series of articles and books on the location and nature of 'labour surpluses', and the need to employ them, was followed in the autumn of 1969 by a campaign against slacking, and by attempts to tighten labour discipline.

new industry, and fulfil the diminished recruiting functions formerly performed by Orgnabor (which it in effect absorbed). Thus labour planning which had hitherto been shared by bodies such as Gosplan and the Central Statistical Administration, not to mention the local soviets, was to be done by a body specifically created for that purpose. The State Committee for Labour and Wages (established in May 1955) had been concerned only with labour legislation and wage rates.

Progress in this sphere was steady, if not rapid. By 1969 the union republican committees had established a network of over thirty Bureaux for Placement and Information, presumably in the largest towns. Those in the R S F S R received 243,000 applications for jobs in 1967, and 600,000 in 1968, when they advertised no less than 900,000 vacancies. It was intended at that time to open bureaux in towns with a population of over 100,000 – which would have meant a network of 174 units.[17]

We have no means of knowing what proportion of the applications were from school-leavers, but there is every reason to suppose that some of these used the service. In any case 'organized placements' of young people either through the bureaux or through placement commissions now assumed very considerable proportions. Thus N. Novikov claimed that in 1967 in the R S F S R alone no less than 790,000 young people were placed 'in an organized manner', while in the following year the number rose to 927,000. This may have been as much as a third of all newcomers to the labour market in the republic outside the collective farm sector.

The second development involved precisely a massive upgrading of the placement commissions. The decree of 2 February 1966 on the placement of school-leavers established them as a coherent, country-wide organization, with a recognized place in the soviets from republican level down.[18] They were to be headed by a deputy chairman of the Council of Ministers at the top and a deputy chairman of the corresponding soviets at all

17. K. Novikov, article in *Kommunist*, No. 13, 1969, p. 107. This, admittedly, was a modest target for a country with a labour force of over 100 million.

18. Details from *Kommentarii k zakonodatelstvu o trude*, ed. A. N. Mishutin, Moscow, 1966, p. 23, and *Trudovoe pravo*, ed. S. A. Ivanov, Moscow, 1969, p. 197.

lower levels. Other members were to be drawn from 'representatives of Party, trade union, Komsomol and economic organizations, educational offices and the professional-technical training system'. Representatives of the State Committee for the Use of Labour Resources were to take part in their work and coordinate their activities. The fact that they were to have a small full-time office staff also indicated that the venture was a serious one. The first meeting of the republican Placement Commission for the RSFSR was held in Moscow in March 1966. It was followed, a few days later, by a conference of the chairmen of subordinate commissions throughout the country.[19]

The commissions had two main functions. On the one hand they were to administer the old quota system, which meant helping to draw up placement plans for the body of school-leavers every year, and passing these plans on to managers of the enterprises who still, in theory, had to accept them. The quota system was, however, now made a little more flexible, in that enterprises could allot between 0.5 and 10 per cent of their jobs to young people, as the management thought expedient. Apprentices and learners were placed outside the general labour and wage structures, so that enterprises would not suffer any financial loss in taking them on, and output norms for young workers were somewhat reduced. This gave managers much more latitude in the handling of juvenile workers, and may have removed some of the frictions which had built up a decade before.

On the other hand the commissions were to issue, to school-leavers or any other young people under eighteen who were looking for work, vouchers for jobs in the enterprises, institutions, and organizations of the locality, within the quota limits. The voucher was ideally to be handed to the school-leaver together with his school-leaving certificate.

At the time of writing it is difficult to gauge how well the scheme has been working. The emphasis on planning, state control and sheer organization has not ensured the successful solution of social problems in the past; and it is doubtful whether a local commission of this type can do much with a manager who does not want to take young people, or young people who do not want the jobs offered them. It may be that the scheme works only

19. *Pravda*, 18 March 1966.

when the economic and social conditions are favourable, i.e. when placement would have been easy anyway.

The third development was no less serious in intent. This was the setting up of a kind of vocational guidance service, or to use the Soviet term, a 'professional orientation' service, to advise young people while they were still at school.

Professional orientation, like so many other things, had enjoyed a shadowy existence in the Soviet Union in the twenties, but was considerably restricted after the abolition of the People's Commissariat of Labour and suppressed completely in 1936.[20] The need for some system of this kind was again recognized in the law of 2 August 1954, in so far as it ordered ministries and administrations to organize extensive 'explanatory work' amongst the pupils of general schools with regard to manual skills. The law of 12 September 1957 also contained a clause to this effect, but progress was again hampered by Khrushchev's evident belief that polytechnization would make a separate service unnecessary. The Soviet authorities' claim in a United Nations handbook of 1963 that a vocational service already existed in the USSR was very much of an overstatement.[21]

There was a rapid growth of interest, however, as Khrushchev's educational policies were abandoned. The juvenile unemployment problem, not to mention the findings of important sociological surveys, underlined the gap between the aspirations of many young people and the real possibilities of employment. Several Soviet scholars now frankly denied that polytechnization alone could be expected to bring young people's attitudes into line with current needs.[22]

After 1965 certain institutes began to investigate the question from the psychological and pedagogical angles, and in 1967 a

---

20. V. A. Drozhzhin, article in the *Vestnik Leningradskogo Universiteta*, No. 11, 1967, vypusk 2.

21. 'The Organization of Educational and Vocational Guidance', publication No. 254 of the International Bureau of Education and UNESCO, Geneva, 1963.

22. References to some of these criticisms may be found in *Berufslenkung, Berufswahl und Berufsberatung in der UdSSR*, by Thomas Kussmann, *Osteuropa Wirtschaft*, No. 4, 1968, p. 303. See also L. E. Epshtein, *Ekonomicheskie faktory kommunisticheskogo vospitania*, Chelyabinsk, 1966, p. 236.

number of important all-union conferences were devoted to it.[23] On a more practical plane, some progress was reported from the localities. It was announced in June 1968 that 'Councils for Professional Orientation' had been set up in all towns and districts of the RSFSR, though there is evidence that in some districts individual consultants did the job.[24] We may presume that these councils or consultants were attached to the local soviet and worked together with such bodies as the education department, the placement commission, and older bodies called the administrative commission and the commission for juvenile affairs (which was concerned with the care and employment of delinquents).

A highly favourable description of vocational guidance in the Sheksninski *raion*, Vologda *oblast*, in 1968, was published in the journal *Kommunist*. It appears that up to the sixth class local youth were educated in a spirit of respect for labour, and 'acquainted with agricultural production'. (One wonders exactly what this meant, since most of them, from their earliest years, would have helped their parents in the fields anyway.) Excursions and meetings with outstanding agricultural workers were arranged. In the seventh and subsequent classes there were optional hours for the study of agricultural machinery, meetings with agricultural specialists and collective farm chairmen, together with film shows and talks. Seminars, lectures, and study groups were organized in some of the ninth and tenth classes. Superficially, this seems to have amounted to a very concentrated programme of persuasion.

Vocational guidance in the Soviet Union, as these details show, acquired a distinctly Soviet colouring. The UNESCO recommendations on the aims of placement services, approved in December 1962, covered the five problems of collecting statistics, providing information on work available, advising the individual on his choice of a career, helping him to find work, and keeping in contact with him afterwards. A recent Soviet formulation, on the other hand, included the provision that such services should 'ensure the proportional distribution of labour with regard to the

23. T. Kussmann, op. cit., p. 303; *Voprosy psikhologii*, No. 5, 1967; *Shkola i proizvodstvo*, No. 9, 1967.

24. Article by T. Afanasieva in *Molodoi kommunist*, No. 8, 1969, p. 78.

interests of society'.[25] This seems to imply the introduction of an element of state direction.

How successful have all these measures been? Sociological investigations conducted in the late sixties showed that both the school and the formal vocational guidance services still had little influence on school-leavers' decisions regarding their careers. Thus a survey of about a third of the pupils in the eighth classes and ten-year school-leavers of the Sheksninski *raion*, organized in 1968, showed that nearly three quarters of them got their information about jobs from adverts in local papers or radio programmes. Advice from teachers was significant for only about 4.5 per cent. Hardly anyone, incidentally, was helped by the Komsomol. An investigation of 750 pupils of the eighth and tenth classes of schools in the Ural town of Nizhni Tagil, together with 400 of the teachers there, also gave disappointing results (Table 118). Though 81 and 85 per cent of the pupils in the respective classes had apparently made up their minds what

TABLE 118. *The Influence of Various Factors on the Choice of Profession among Pupils of the Eighth to Tenth Classes of Nizhni Tagil* (%)

Factors	Pupils of the 8th classes*	Pupils of the 10th classes*
Teachers' advice	6	5
School vocational guidance measures	4	4
Parents' advice	41	39
Cinema and books	21	27
Friends' and acquaintances' advice	8	10
No advice from anyone	20	15

*As a percentage of all those answering.
Source:
A. F. Belikov, L. V. Kuznetsov, *Zakreplenie kadrov na predpriatii*, Moscow, 1971, p. 26.

25. V. A. Drozhzhin, op. cit., p. 140.

they wanted to do, less than a tenth of them had been influenced by their teachers or by formal vocational guidance procedures.

There can, of course, be no question of 'solving' the general problem of placing young Soviet citizens – predominantly the less privileged ones – in jobs which they like or which the authorities regard as desirable. As in other societies, it will always be a complicated and rather untidy process. Even so young people in the USSR were until recently very inadequately provided for in this respect. It is difficult to judge the degree of improvement registered in the years since Khrushchev's dismissal, as most of the social and economic aspects are still beyond the reach of objective research. The authorities do, however, seem to be making an effort to free themselves from the opaque ideological arguments which blocked progress for decades. Stalin's denial that frictions or difficulties of this kind were possible in Soviet society, and Khrushchev's bland assertion that they could be removed simply by applying the right pressures from above, appear to have been jettisoned in favour of a more healthy, if somewhat bureaucratic, pragmatism.

12
Jobs for the Intelligentsia

UNIVERSITY graduates are, by definition, people who have acquired advanced skills, and in most instances these skills can be usefully applied only in a comparatively limited number of jobs. The placement of these young people in work which is satisfactory from an economic or social point of view, and suits them personally, tends to be rather an intricate business. Most governments now recognize this, and do not actively interfere – even when they have paid for, or subsidized, the training involved. Even the governments of underdeveloped lands who send their youth to study abroad usually do no more than insist that they return after graduation to apply their knowledge in their homeland.

The Soviet authorities, however, and the governments of certain Soviet-type states, adopt a different approach. They attempt nothing less than the planning of initial placements for all graduates of higher and middle special educational institutions throughout the country. This is possible (at least in theory) because, as a part of their centralist educational policies, the state authorities control all student admissions, and have since the early thirties had the legal and administrative machinery necessary to retain graduates at their place of work for three years after graduation. The use of administrative order transcends such market forces as exist in this sphere, not to mention the wishes and desires of the graduates themselves.[1]

1. Market forces are excluded from graduate placement in the USSR to the extent that there is a high degree of standardization of wage rates and prices. Obviously, different careers offer different pay and other prospects, and graduates may take this into account when choosing their course and VUZ. There are recognized pay differentials between branches of industry and zones of the country. Pay is higher in heavy industry and coal mining, for instance, or in the Far North and equated regions, though in this case the better rates are somewhat offset by higher prices. At the same time standardization means that the graduate is deprived of an opportunity to haggle over

We have just made a parenthetical reference to theory. In practice totally planned placement sets a massive administrative problem for the Soviet authorities. In 1969, for example some 907,000 young people graduated from the full-time courses and 676,400 from part-time courses of higher and middle special educational institutions.[2] All of the full-time graduates and (under a recent law) many of the part-time graduates had to be directed into suitable jobs; a task of this magnitude, undertaken annually, is a daunting prospect. Graduations can, moreover, be expected to rise. The sociological implications are profound, for the government is attempting nothing less than to fix the employment and residence patterns of all newcomers to the ranks of the intelligentsia for the first years of their working lives.

The process of placement has thus several interesting facets. It is another example of government indulgence in social engineering, as a kind of supplement to the higher educational system. The young people involved are destined one day to occupy responsible positions in Soviet society. The data available, though scattered, allow us to gauge, in some measure, the effectiveness of government control over this aspect of their careers. And this obviously has a certain political significance.

Our treatment of the topic will be as follows. First we shall review, albeit briefly, the administrative procedures of graduate placement. Then we shall go on to consider the organizational problems which arise and illustrate them with the few figures to hand. Finally we will endeavour to examine the response of the young specialists themselves. The graduates of middle special institutions are covered by the same legislation as those of the VUZy; in order to render the problem a little more manageable, we shall concern ourselves principally with the latter. The placement procedures for certain categories of specialists, such as army, militia, or KGB officers and persons directed to closed, i.e. secret, organizations are not publicly discussed and must remain largely a matter for conjecture.

---

his starting salary or find a similar job with completely different basic rates.

2. *Narodnoe khozyaistvo SSSR v 1968*, p. 688.

THE SYSTEM OF PLANNING

The planning of graduate placement is, in its early stages, an integral part of admission planning, and it likewise dates from the first Five-Year-Plan period. The first steps in the process with regard to the graduates of any given year must in fact take place a decade or more earlier, since all the admissions have to be planned, in principle, in five-year blocks (corresponding to the national Five-Year Plans), and graduations come four to six years after admission. It is clear that such long-term projections can only be approximate, and that they will require refinement as each stage in the planning procedure passes. Although Soviet publications, therefore, stress the Five-Year Plan principle, this must in practice be modified by what the economists term a 'rolling' plan. The numerous reports on placement suggest that this is indeed so.[3]

Some five to seven years before graduation Gosplan, the state planning authority, has to make its final decision on how many students to admit to each specialization at every VUZ in the country. Planning at this stage entails finding out from the cadres departments of a large number of ministries, administrations, and local soviets the number of specialists of all types who will eventually be required for their enterprises and organizations. Estimates are worked out within each administrative hierarchy separately, and then transmitted to Gosplan where they are co-ordinated with demands from other sources, and trimmed to fit the number of student places actually or potentially available. This last piece of information presumably comes from the Ministry of Higher and Middle Special Education. Educational facilities cannot, of course, be expanded instantly to suit the whims of managements. Gosplan then passes the revised estimates to the Department for Planning the Training and Distribution of Young Specialists of this Ministry which finally determines the intake of students for each faculty of all institutions within its jurisdiction.

3. For Soviet statements see V. E. Komarov, *Ekonomicheskie osnovy podgo-tovki spetsialistov dlya narodnogo khozyaistva*, Moscow, 1959, Chapter II (3), and K. G. Nozhko and others, *Educational Planning in the USSR*, IIEP, Paris, 1968, p. 127.

The second step in the process takes place about a year before the students are due to graduate. This entails the collection by Gosplan of firm orders for specialists from factories, shops, offices and farms through the usual ministerial channels. At the same time the above-mentioned department of the Ministry of Higher and Middle Special Education requires all educational institutions to submit data on the people they expect to graduate, for the number may well be different from the original intake several years before. VUZ administrations naturally try to keep the numbers on their courses steady, but fall-out and course-switching inevitably cause modifications, which may cumulatively be great.

The orders for specialists must now be brought into alignment with the number of graduates about to come onto the market. Orders which are finally approved by Gosplan are forwarded to the same department of the Ministry of Higher and Middle Special Education, where they are divided between all the VUZy in the country, according to capacity, as logically as circumstances permit. All of these plans and orders may be checked by the regional offices of ministries destined to receive the graduates, republican councils of ministers and the regional officers of Gosplan. The extent to which the process is centralized in Moscow is not known.[4]

The next part of the process, known as the personal distribution of graduates, takes place within the VUZ itself. This is the point at which the state plans have to be presented to the individual. When the list of jobs available comes through, the learned council of these establishments sets up one or more 'Commissions for Personal Distribution' – the number of commissions depending on the size of the VUZ. This Commission is composed of the head or deputy head of the VUZ, the dean of the

4. Most details of this very complicated process as it functioned in the late sixties may be found in the statutes of the Ministry of Higher Education of the USSR, 2 November 1955, the decree 'On Measures for Improving the Training of Specialists and Perfecting the Management of Higher and Middle Special Education in the Country', of 3 September 1966, and Statues for the Personal Distribution of Young Specialists approved in April 1968, published in the *Byulleten Ministerstvo Vysshego i Srednego Obrazovania*. The system has been subject to repeated modification and there is a large body of legislation on it.

faculty, representatives of the Ministry of Higher and Middle Special Education, and representatives of the ministries and administrations to which the students are to be sent. Officials of the local Komsomol or trade union organizations sometimes attend. The enterprises and organizations to which graduates are to be directed may also send their own officials to express their preferences for individuals. This horizontal link between the supplier and receiver can introduce a useful element of flexibility into the system. The make-up of the commission has varied from time to time, as we shall see in a moment, but it has always been designed to include officials most interested in the placement of graduates.

When it meets the commission examines materials on the academic progress, health and family circumstances of the students in their last year of study, so as to decide what places to offer whom. Then it interviews each student in turn, preferably, as the statutes put it, in a 'solemn and business-like atmosphere', and offers him a place. The Commission may examine any request for employment which a student himself makes, and come to a decision on it; but the fulfilment of the state plan, which is the basis for its work, is of paramount importance. The failure of a young specialist to agree with the decision of the Commission does not free him from his obligation to take up the post allotted to him.

The last stage of the process is, ideally, the registration of the graduate at his new place of work, that is, after the month's holiday to which he is legally entitled.

PLAN AND REALITY

A bare statement of the steps involved in graduate placement tends, however, to leave a false impression. In practice multiple difficulties arise, and cause all too frequent distortion of the plans. The planning, moreover, varies considerably in accuracy. The authorities can estimate, with a fair degree of exactness, the number of specialists who will be required in fields like education, accounting, medicine, and law, since these needs are dependent either on fairly stable demographic factors, or on deliberate government policy. In 1968 about half of the country's 510,000 graduates fell into these 'easy' categories.

The long-term demand for specialists in the fields of material production has on the other hand always presented a knotty, and at times insoluble, problem. Efforts by planners to develop some kind of scientific method for determining an enterprise's requirements of production specialists on the basis of its output and general labour force have not, apparently, been very successful. There has been continuing trouble in working out the basic ratio between high- and middle-grade specialists (or technicians). In practice rule-of-thumb methods seem to be common, so that long-term orders are often based on little more than guesswork. In addition, managers have a propensity to overstate considerably their need for this human commodity (as for so many others), in the expectation that they will get only a proportion of what they request.

Prognostication has been further complicated by the comparatively rapid growth of the economy and the many sharp, unheralded changes in government priorities. Khrushchev's campaign for agricultural development which was launched in September 1953, and his drive to increase the output of plastics in May 1958 and fertilizers in February 1964, are good examples. Both demanded large numbers of specialists who had not been trained. Long-term planning, then, can be very much of a hit-or-miss affair.

Planning the placement of students in their last year raises another set of problems. Discrepancies between the planned and actual numbers of students on VUZ courses may build up over the years, and come to light at this juncture. On the other hand, the immediate demand for the young specialists available may turn out to be greater or less than expected. The selection of figures covering graduations for the years 1946 to 1950 and 1962, given in Tables 119 and 120, show huge variations in plan fulfilment for these reasons; indeed, they recall the disproportions in the polytechnical and placement schemes for school-leavers which were so hurriedly introduced and executed under Khrushchev. The decades of administrative experience with graduates seems to have counted for little. When errors such as these occur the authorities either have to try and transfer students from one course to another for retraining, or direct the students into the jobs that seem least unsuitable for them in the circumstances.

TABLE 119. *Discrepancies between Plans and Selected Student Graduations, 1946–50*

Speciality	No. of orders (thousands)	No. of grads. (thousands)	Surplus or deficit, %
Engineers-mechanics	40.3	33.1	−17.9
Electrical specialists	11.1	17.0	+54.0
Metallurgists	7.0	7.0	—
Mining engineers	9.7	13.0	+34.0
Chemical technologists	13.2	11.0	−17.0
Food processing engineers	5.0	10.8	+116.0
Light industry & textile engineers	4.5	4.3	−4.0
Economists*	13.6	4.8	−66.0
Other specialists	15.6	9.2	−41.0
Total	120.0	110.2	−8.4†

*Economists from non-technical VUZy excluded.
†This figure covers a surplus of 15,000 graduates in some fields and a shortage of 25,200 in others.
Source:
I. A. Lyasnikov, *Planirovanie potrebnosti narodnogo khozyaistva v spetsialistakh,* unpublished candidate dissertation, Moscow, 1954, p. 204.

TABLE 120. *Discrepancies between Plans and Student Graduations in Agricultural Specializations, for 1962*

Speciality	Surplus or deficit, %
Agronomists, field	+10
Agronomists, fruit & vegetables	+18
Agronomists, pesticides	+62
Engineers-mechanics	−36
Electrical engineers	−53
Veterinary surgeons	−33

Source:
Kommunist, No. 4, 1968, p. 53.

The tendency for Soviet managers to exaggerate their real requirements is felt at this late stage also. Two highly placed officials wrote in August 1965 that over the preceding two years the VUZy of the RSFSR had been able to satisfy only *one third* of the stated requirements for specialists in all branches of the national economy, precisely because 'the country's requirement for new engineers and a number of other types of specialists [were] artificially overstated'.[5] Numerous references to the same problem have been made in open or veiled terms.[6] As a consequence, the task of the central planning bodies in deciding which orders are to be met is greatly complicated.

The fact that such discrepancies are common means extra headaches for the VUZ commissions. They must fulfil the distribution plans received from above as adequately as possible, but if the plans do not fit their assortment of graduates this cannot be easy. Moreover, the Ministry of Higher and Middle Special Education does not include many 'spare' places in the distribution plans it sends out, even when such places are available. (This is a point which has never, apparently, been elucidated in published sources, but 'planned' placement cannot but imply a limitation of choice at the lowest level.) If planning is to mean anything at all, the number of vacancies received by any given VUZ must tend to equal the number of students graduating. Differences in the quality of jobs of a given type raise another difficulty. It is not just a matter of giving the best places to the most able contenders.

It seems that no satisfactory answer has been found to the problem of how the places of varying quality should be allotted among students of varying ability. There will always be a tendency for the demand for 'top jobs' to exceed supply, so they

5. I. Shakhov, Chief of the Russian Republic State Planning Committee's Department of Higher Schools, and I. Vlasenko, Chief of the Sub-Department of Technical Colleges, in *Pravda*, 9 August 1965.

6. Some examples: 'At least 2,500 teachers are needed for the present academic year. Where are they to be found? . . . The Ministry of Education of the Bashkir Republic decided that the local education authorities had overstated their requirements, so it sent them 1,877 [graduates] instead of the 2,500 they had asked for.' (*Uchitelskaya gazeta*, 16 February 1967.) 'Certain ministries and administrations have fallen into the bad habit of refusing specialists at the last moment, even though they had requested them. That is why it was necessary to change the placement plans of nearly a thousand graduates of VUZy and 425 graduates of middle special technical schools. Miscalculations such as these in planning impede the distribution of young specialists in the national economy.' (*Pravda*, 6 August 1967.) See also the article by L. Tulchinski in *Komsomolskaya pravda*, 10 June 1967.

may become the focus of all kinds of pressures from interested parties. Some VUZy try to allot jobs primarily on a geographical basis (sending students to work as near home as possible). More ambitious devices include the use of a point system which awards students marks for all their activities – social and political as well as academic. The graduates with the highest ratings then have first choice of jobs. This is an attempt to introduce a 'political' element into the process and obviate difficulties arising from the fact that the employment decision has to be made before the diploma is issued. In any case, it records only pass or excellence.[7]

The dilemmas which arise at this point absorb much of the time and energy of the country's best students. The sort of tangle which can develop was well illustrated by an article describing the solution attempted in the VUZy of Vladivostok in 1961. It involved including in the general assessment a mark for Komsomol activities, but was unsatisfactory enough to involve the ire of the editors of *Komsomolskaya pravda*.

The fact is that before the personnel direction begins in the Vladivostok VUZy [wrote the correspondent] the institute administrations work out, with the help of Komsomol activists, a rota to determine which graduates get their postings first and who will come last. All the marks of five, four and three [out of five – WMM] which the student obtained during his five years of study are added up, the sum is divided by the number of subjects, and then his fate is decided down to two decimal places. If you get a good mark, your choice is a rich one: if your mark is poor you have to take what's left. Recently they decided to perfect this system. Now they add to the success ratings a mark for Komsomol activities. Why?

'To make it fair,' answered Vladimir Shalatov, secretary of the Komsomol Bureau of the Construction Faculty. 'Let's suppose that Ivanov spent five years doing the donkey work in the Institute's Trade Union branch, while Petrov did nothing but swot. Why should Petrov get a good post and Ivanov a bad one?'

I asked [continued the correspondent] how the distribution of the students of the faculty had gone off this year.

7. It has recently been suggested, partly in an effort to solve this problem, that diplomas of different classes should be introduced, as in Great Britain or the USA. This gradation could include an assessment of the student's involvement in social activities, etc., and a higher grade could give the right to better pay. (*Pravda*, 20 January 1970.)

'The places were mainly in Vladivostok, Sverdlovsk and Birobidzhan . . .'

'And who went to Birobidzhan?'

'The people who studied badly and who were too lazy to take on Komsomol commissions,' answered Shalatov, with a note of triumph in his voice.[8]

Even after the distribution process has been completed there are snags. There is a tendency, often criticized, for employers to give young specialists jobs in offices, rather than on production, and, in some of the less popular branches of the economy, to release them from their posting completely.

The most striking and measurable examples of these evils are to be found in agriculture. Thus of the 320,000 specialists trained for the Ministry of Agriculture in the years 1946–53, only 19 per cent were still actively engaged in agricultural production on the farms by the end of the period. Some 21 per cent were working in the offices of the Ministry, while the rest had left agriculture altogether.[9] The Soviet statistical handbooks show that over the eleven years 1958–68, 361,800 young people took degrees in agriculture and forestry, yet the number of specialists employed in these branches of the economy rose by only 111,100, from 130,900 to 242,000. Retirements would have accounted for 30,000 at most, so about two thirds of the newcomers must have deserted over the period.

The efficiency of the planning also varies according to whether the jobs are in the town or in the country; all the evidence suggests that placement in rural areas is the less effective. The village has, of course, long suffered from the unwillingness of the authorities to introduce a comprehensive system of higher pay and better conditions of service to compensate for uncongenial or primitive surroundings.

A glimpse of the sort of situation which can arise in a rural area as a result of desertion is afforded by two chance reports on the Omsk *oblast*. It appears that by 1962 90 per cent of the agricultural specialists sent there in the preceding years had no contact with the farms, and over two thirds of the new teachers had

8. *Komsomolskaya pravda*, 17 August 1961.

9. See Khrushchev's speech at the September 1953 plenum of the Central Committee.

left their jobs.[10] Planned placement of the intelligentsia there had evidently in large measure broken down.

The existence of major loopholes in the administration of graduate placement in the USSR such as we have reviewed here suggests that the end result must be, in a significant proportion of cases, a travesty of the ideal which the planners set themselves. Of course, the apparatus is not run by loons, and some of the problems are undoubtedly solved by timely modification of plans and directives. In some instances it may prove possible to use the graduates of part-time courses to fill gaps, though (at least until 1968) these graduates were not legally subject to direction. One is, however, justified in asking whether a procedure so frequently inefficient is worth the time, effort and financial resources which are required to run it.

THE SOCIAL RESPONSE

Graduates, naturally, have their own ideas about where they want to work. The question of how individuals react to state orders is no less important than the transmission and nature of these orders.

The sociological aspect of graduate placement has not so far received much attention from Soviet scholars, perhaps because the confrontation between the individual and the State in this matter can be unpleasantly stark. Soviet students have, however, benefited from the rebirth of sociological investigation in so far as their attitudes towards their chosen specialities and professions have become a subject of research.[11] These studies are closely relevant to the problem of placement because students' attitudes may so easily affect their readiness to accept the jobs allotted to them.

A detailed survey of this kind was recently conducted on the basis of a sample of 2,403 full-time students (some 66 per cent of the total), at Lvov University. The questionnaires were

10. *Komsomolskaya pravda*, 9 March 1962, and *Uchitelskaya gazeta*, 25 July 1962.

11. See the articles by G. V. Osipov in L. A. Volovik (ed.), *Sotsiologia i ideologia*, Moscow, 1969, p. 306, and Yu. I. Leonavichus in *Vestnik Vysshei Shkoly*, No. 11, 1969.

anonymous, and may thus have given quite a true picture of what the young people thought.[12] It transpired that a significant number of them were dissatisfied with their choice of speciality: 27 per cent of the sample declared that if they had to start again they would not choose the same subject, another 16 per cent said they would still like to change it. These last were presumably people whose dissatisfaction was active rather than passive. It is also significant that the number of students anxious to change their specialities rose from 8 per cent on the first course to 26 per cent on the fourth. The figure was down to 17 per cent on the fifth and sixth courses, but only, perhaps, because these students had resigned themselves to their academic fate. Significantly, whereas 18 per cent of the arts students wanted to switch, only 2 per cent of the science students did so. The most appealing professions for these were doctor and engineer. These figures were not, perhaps, higher than one would expect, given the volatile quality of youth. But they would be amplè to wreck planning arrangements.

The authors did not give a comprehensive analysis of why students discontented with their subjects wanted to change. They did, however, reveal that some 18 per cent were moved by the desire to avoid work in a village or a distant region. The figure varied from 25 per cent for the children of employees to 14 per cent for those of collective farm origin. Another 15 per cent had decided that the prospects in their chosen profession were not good. It appears that many people were unwilling to work as teachers, even though this is usually a major outlet for university graduates. Thus 10–12 per cent of the first- and second-year students, 16 per cent of those on the third and fourth courses, and no less than 22 per cent of those on the fifth and sixth courses had this prejudice. Among the physicists 39 per cent declared that they wished to find a job 'on production', 38 per cent wanted to go into research and only 6 per cent had reconciled themselves to schoolteaching.

Dissatisfaction of this kind is in part a consequence of young people choosing their VUZ and field of study in a sloppy and haphazard manner. A study of 59 per cent of the graduates of

12. L. V. Sokhan', *Sotsiologia na Ukraine*, Kiev, 1968, p. 43, article by D. D. Nizovi and L. O. Olesnevich.

full-time courses at the faculty of political economy at the Saratov Economic Institute, conducted about 1966, indicated, for example, that only 38 per cent of the sample had chosen the institute because they thought it suited them. Thirty-one per cent acted on the advice of friends, and 17 per cent went there because they couldn't get into another institution. (No comment was made on the residue of 14 per cent.) As far as the choice of a faculty was concerned, 47 per cent had been guided by their interests: 26 per cent could not obtain places at another faculty and 26 per cent didn't care what faculty they went into. It is not surprising if, in these circumstances, up to 20 per cent of the students graduating in 1967 did not intend to work in the speciality that they acquired.[13]

Occasional figures of a similar nature are not hard to come by. Sixty-two per cent of the people on the first course of the Pedagogical Institute of the Urals in 1969–70 did not, apparently, believe that the subject they were studying would really interest them, and some 20 per cent actually wanted to become doctors, journalists, geologists or agronomists. Two per cent of them had no professional interests whatever. Of those who had specifically chosen the Pedagogical Institute most wanted to do research or indulge their interest in the subjects taught, rather than become teachers. No less than 49 per cent of a sample of students at the Arkhangelsk Medical Institute thought they had no vocation for medicine.[14] These aberrations must be a major source of trouble for the Soviet planners, who have to reckon with potential opposition from students predisposed against their chosen professions.

An appearance before the Commission for the Personal Direction of Graduates is a real challenge for most students, whether they are happy with their choice of subject or not. The first concern of nearly everyone must be to avoid the bad jobs. Students who have reason to believe that they will be landed with one, or who wish to get around an official posting anyway, have several possible escape routes. They can approach the manager

13. *Ekonomicheskie nauki*, No. 1, 1968, article by K. Babaitsev and others. The slight discrepancy in the second set of figures is due to rounding of percentages.

14. *VVShk*, No. 1, 1970, and *VVShk*, No. 6, 1969.

of an enterprise beforehand and request him to send an order in for them personally. No figures seem to have been published on this practice, but it is common. Some students make use of provisions in the distribution statutes which release persons with bad health or onerous family responsibilities from planned postings. It is not uncommon for girl students to choose, just before they graduate, conveniently located and suitably employed husbands, and then to claim that they cannot leave them. According to occasional press reports, students sometimes actually go so far as to refuse their postings in front of the Commission, but since by so doing they lay themselves open to unpleasant pressures from the Komsomol and VUZ authorities they are few in number.

The best indications we have of the overall efficiency of the placement system at this particular stage were provided by K. P. Savichev, an official at the Personnel Distribution Department of the RSFSR Ministry of Higher and Middle Special Education in July 1965.[15] Savichev said that under-fulfilment of the distribution plans in 1962, 1963 and 1964 throughout the Republic was *at least* 18–20 per cent. He presumably had legal or pseudo-legal avoidance of planned postings in mind. Local reports of discrepancies of various kinds are quite common. Two officials of Moscow University stated in August 1967 that the Commissions up and down the country had to change up to 50 per cent of placements after they had been made because these no longer corresponded to the enterprises' needs.[16] This, they claimed, was a consequence of holding the distribution procedure a year before graduation, a practice initiated by Khrushchev. In the past it had been as little as three months. The main cause of the difficulties, as we have seen, lay much deeper.

The planners' tribulations do not end when the commission completes its work. There is massive evidence to show that many students do not turn up at the jobs allotted to them, even though they agreed to do so. Occasional figures indicate that the proportion of non-arrivals may in exceptional cases reach 90 per cent. The ministries which suffer most from this ill are, again, those which offer jobs in rural areas, particularly the Ministries

15. *VVShk*, No. 7, 1965, p. 30.
16. *Komsomolskaya pravda*, 15 August 1967.

of Agriculture, Public Instruction, and Health. Thus the story of what happened to a contingent of graduate teachers in Armenia in 1964 is evidently by no means untypical.[17] According to the head of the Cadres Department of the (republican) Ministry of Public Instruction, it was planned to place 683 graduates from the local pedagogical faculties in schools throughout the Republic. Of these graduates 201 refused their placements on various pretexts and 132 more failed to turn up. This meant that nearly half of the contingent did not conform to the placement plan. And, of course, we do not know how many of those who did stayed on. Of the 85,000 or so graduates of pedagogical institues in the USSR in 1961 nearly 13,000, or about 15 per cent, did not take up their appointments.[18] Many other examples may be found.[19]

We have already noted the regrettable desertion rates in the Omsk *oblast* in the early sixties. Other regions where living conditions are bad evidently have the same problem. Between 1958 and 1962 schools in the Novosibirsk *oblast* received 1,670 teachers, and lost 1,500; in the school year 1960–61 comparable figures for the Brest *oblast* were 357 arrivals and 552 departures.[20]

An analysis of the reasons for desertion amongst agricultural specialists in the Novosibirsk *oblast* was recently made by the Soviet scholar V. N. Ladenkov.[21] Unfortunately, his presentation of the data was vague, but what he said seemed plausible and ties in with what we know about migration from the village in general. He claimed that 28 per cent of the specialists who moved to the towns, and 18.5 per cent of those who did not, were in fact dissatisfied with their profession. The causes for discontent among the whole sample (apart from having chosen to train for farm work in the first place) were poor organization of labour, a working day which averaged out at thirteen hours, extremely inadequate transport arrangements, low pay (though improvements effected after the March 1965 Plenum of the Party were

17. *Uchitelskaya gazeta*, 23 June 1964.

18. *Uchitelskaya gazeta*, 30 October 1962.

19. M. P. Kim, *Iz istorii sovetskoi intelligentsii*, Moscow, 1966, p. 161; *Kommunist*, No. 4, 1968, p. 56.

20. *Uchitelskaya gazeta*, 30 October 1962 and 20 December 1962.

21. Article in T. I. Zaslavskaya, op. cit., p. 192.

welcomed), inferior living conditions and cultural amenities, and personal reasons. These last were, however, sometimes used as a cover for the other motives which, Ladenkov claimed, were 'open to social control', i.e. removable by proper organization. In addition, a fifth of the specialists complained of an inattentive or 'variable' attitude towards them on the part of their managers.

SOME LEGAL ASPECTS

The authorities have been acutely aware of failings in the placement system at least since the mid thirties, and have made numerous efforts to correct them. At least eight sets of modifications of the published instructions on graduate planning and distribution may be traced, sometimes in response to shortcomings in the system itself, sometimes as a result of wider changes in the structure of economic planning. Between 1948 and 1969 five new versions of the statutes on the personal distribution of graduates appeared. The story of all these changes is long and boring; fortunately, it need not be recounted here, for it contains no changes of principle. Perhaps the most interesting aspect is the variation in the legal and social pressures exerted on graduates to conform with state plans. These are worth looking at a little more closely.

The commissions for the personal distribution of graduates, like so many governmental organs, were affected by the growing rigidity of Stalin and by 1953 had lost all power to depart from the state plans. One of the lesser benefits of the post-Stalin thaw in labour relations was to increase their authority. In December 1955 they were given, for the first time, the right to grant 'free diplomas', that is, diplomas which allowed their holders to find their own work if nothing suitable could be offered to them in the context of the plans received. At the same time the medical and family grounds on which graduates could refuse a posting were extended. The statutes of November 1957 and October 1963 were progressively more liberal. Graduates were to be supplied with much more information on their rights, responsibilities and future working conditions. The commissions were given a freer hand in redirecting the graduates if it transpired, while they were still in session, that proper employment was not available. The heads of educational institutions were supposed to take an active part in helping graduates to find their own jobs when the commissions did not have any suitable ones to offer. On the other hand ministries, Khrushchev's local economic councils, and local soviets were given the right to redirect young specialists to other jobs within their own systems if, despite their orders, there was no work for them.

The most recent version of the statutes, approved in April 1968, permitted yet more flexibility. The commission could now 'critically examine' orders for specialists, and depart from the distribution plans if these orders did not correspond with the graduates' specialities, or if the enterprises or organizations concerned could not guarantee living space. This has always been a major cause of desertion. At the same time young specialists acquired the right to request the ministry for which they worked to move them to another enterprise if the management refused to give them the post promised. Stronger direct links between VUZ and enterprise were to be encouraged, and managers were expressly forbidden to employ young specialists in office duties.

A new clause brought the graduates of part-time and evening courses into the scheme for the first time, and specifically granted them the right to change their jobs before the end of the three-year term if they could not obtain a responsible post in the enterprise where they worked during their years of study. These modifications were evidently designed to make the practice of distribution a little more reasonable and humane, though it is doubtful whether they have effected any real improvement in its efficiency.

The post-Stalin period has also seen some interesting changes in the legal controls over both the young specialist and the manager who hires him. Penalties for avoidance of posting were imposed in February 1934 when Stalin was tightening up on the labour market. Persons who refused to accept their posting then became liable to a minimum of six months' imprisonment, with partial or complete confiscation of property. In September 1940 this was changed to imprisonment for a period of from two to four months, in accordance with the labour mobilization law of 26 June 1940. This easement was made possibly because specialist labour was in greater demand at that moment, or perhaps because judges were reluctant to pass the harsher sentence. The 1955 statutes altered the term once again, and imposed penalties set out in the law of 26 October 1951, but this has apparently never been published. The beginning of liberalization in this sphere was formally registered in the statutes of 1957 which stipulated the removal of this penalty. Thereafter the graduate had to face only social pressures if he refused to conform. Managers were still forbidden to employ graduates who did not have the necessary documentation, i.e. a direction order, but this was now apparently defined as an administrative and not a criminal misdemeanour.[22]

The failure of the liberal provisions of the late fifties and early sixties to bring about an improvement in the functioning of the placement mechanism is perhaps what prompted the authorities to try a new type of restriction. Under the terms of the 1963 statutes graduates were to be handed their diplomas not when they actually graduated, but a year later, and then only if they were still at the jobs to which the commission had directed them. This was a typical Khrushchev measure, crude, but without the vicious overtones of Stalinism. Others in the leadership, however, must have wished to pursue a strong line, for on 5 November 1964, shortly after Khrushchev's removal, the Ministry of Higher and Middle Special Education acquired the right to *deprive* graduates of their diplomas if they did not take up their posts. This move had been actively canvassed by S. P. Pavlov, First Secretary of the Komsomol, a few months before. The Komsomol, incidentally, always seems to have associated itself with demands for more rigorous sanctions; a call to allow the so-called Comrades' Courts to deprive agricultural specialists of their diplomas if they refused to work in agriculture was made by a Secretary of the Kostroma Oblast Komsomol organization in the summer of 1962.[23]

Yet 'de-Khrushchevization' has been evident here as well. A

22. For comment on these points see K. P. Urzhinski, op. cit., p. 116. The last reference to criminal responsibility which we have been able to trace was in a law of the Ministry of Higher Education of 18 May 1956. The legal position with regard to this matter is not, as far as we can see, very clear; most legislation concerns the young specialists.

23. *Komsomolskaya pravda*, 30 June 1962.

law of 3 September 1966 stated that graduates were to get their diplomas immediately on graduation, as before, and the relevant clause of the October 1963 Statutes, together with the law of November 1964, were repealed. There is no evidence at the time of writing that this more moderate policy has led to any radical improvement in the system.

We have tried to illustrate in this chapter the main strengths and weaknesses of that part of the Soviet system of placement which covers an extremely important category of job-seekers. A few general conclusions emerge. The Soviet government has not been particularly successful in its bid to control this aspect of social behaviour. It makes the two characteristically Soviet mistakes of aiming at complete administrative control, and giving state requirements a clear priority over the wishes and desires of individuals. Naturally, those people who are shunted into the less agreeable jobs resist as best they can, thereby distorting carefully laid plans. It is doubtful whether any administrative system could be made flexible enough to control, to any degree of efficiency, such a massive and intricate process.

Satisfactory placement in the Soviet Union, both from the point of the individual and the State, is further complicated by the nature of the Soviet economy. A salary structure which does not adequately reward specialists for the disadvantages of employment in certain branches of the economy or geographical locations, the sharp differences in the standard of living between town and country, or capital and province, not to mention the erratic nature of government employment policy, create very specific difficulties. Our own feeling is that anything up to half of the placements effected are not economically satisfactory, are rejected before the end of the term required by law, or simply do not accord with state plans.

The authorities have, however, given no indication that they intend to abandon the old positions. The introduction of computers may permit some improvements in planning procedures, but there seems little possibility that individuals will react differently to the same state pressures. The growth in the number of graduates which is promised can, in the circumstances, only exacerbate this social problem.

Note on Bibliography

The two bibliographies which follow contain the most important books and articles referred to in the text. The bibliographies are in this sense only selective. Works which were needed for background reading or which were marginally relevant have not been included. The many articles from Soviet newspapers and journals which have been mentioned are not listed here either.

Bibliography of Soviet Publications

Aganbegyan, A. G. and Maier, V. F., *Zarabotnaya plata v SSSR*, Moscow, 1959

Artemov, V. A. and others, *Statistika byudzhetov vremeni trudyashchikhsya*, Moscow, 1966

Arutyunyan, Yu. V., *Opyt sotsiologicheskogo izuchenia sela*, Moscow, 1968

Baikova, V. G., Duchal', A. S. and Zemtsov, A. A., *Svobodnoe vremya i vsestoronnee razvitie lichnosti*, Moscow, 1965

Baranov, M. M., *Novye progressivnye formy oplaty truda v kolkhozakh*, Moscow, 1967

Belikov, A. F. and Kuznetsov, L. V. *Zakreplenie kadrov na predpriatii*, Moscow, 1971

Bolgov, V. I., *Rabochee vremya i uroven' zhizni trudyashchikhsya*, Novosibirsk, 1964

Bolshaya Sovetskaya Entsiklopedia, 2nd edn, Moscow, 1950–58

Bukhalov, Yu. F. and Yakuba, E. A. (eds.), *Rol' obshchestvennosti v upravlenii proizvodstvom*, Kharkov, 1968

Churakov, V. Ya. and Suvorova, L. I., *Ispolzovanie trudovykh resursov v kolkhozakh i sovkhozakh*, Moscow, 1967

Davykin, R. P., *Rabochi klass SSSR na sovremennom etape*, Leningrad, 1968

Direktivy KPSS i sovetskogo pravitelstva po khozyaistvennym voprosam, Moscow, 1958

Dmitrashko, I. I., *Vnutrikolkhoznye ekonomicheskie otnoshenia*, Moscow, 1966

Ezhov, A. I., *Istoria sovetskoi gosudarstvennoi statistiki*, Moscow, 1969

Ezhov, A. I., *Organizatsia statistiki v SSSR*, Moscow, 1968

Ezhov, A. I., *Statistika i metodologia pokazatelei sovetskoi statistiki*, Moscow, 1965

Figurnov, S. P., *Stroitelstvo kommunizma i rost blagosostoyania naroda*, Moscow, 1962

Glezerman, G. E. and Afanasiev, V. G. (eds)., *Opyt i metodika konkretnykh sotsiologicheskikh issledovanii*, Moscow, 1965
Grigoriev, V. K., *Kolkhoznoe provo*, Moscow, 1970
Gureev, P. A., *L'goty pri orgnabore i obshchestvennom prizyve*, Moscow, 1968
Gurianov, S. T., *Sotsializm v SSSR*, Moscow, 1965

Ikonnikova, S. I. and Lisovski, V. T., *Molodezh o sebe, o svoikh sverstnikakh*, Moscow, 1968
Itogi vsesoyuznoi perepisi naselenia 1959, svodny tom, Moscow, 1962
Ivanov, S. A. (ed.), *Trudovoe pravo*, Moscow, 1969

Kamshalov, A. I. and others, *Ot s'ezda k s'ezdu*, Moscow, 1970
Karnaukhov, E. S. and Kozlov, M. I., *Puti povyshenia proizvoditelnosti truda v selskom khozyaistve*, Moscow, 1964
Khodzhaev, D. G., *Puti razvitia malykh i srednikh gorodov*, Moscow, 1967
Kim, M. P., *Iz istorii sovetskoi intelligentsii*, Moscow, 1966
Kniga kolkhoznika, Moscow, 1953
Komarov, V. E., *Stroitelstvo kommunizma i professionalnaya struktura rabotnikov proizvodstva*, Moscow, 1965
Komarov, V. E., *Ekonomicheskie osnovy podgotovki spetsialistov dlya narodnogo khozyaistva*, Moscow, 1959
Konstantinov, F. V. (ed.), *Stroitelstvo kommunizma i razvitie obshchestvennykh otnoshenii*, Moscow, 1966
Kryazhev, V. G., *Vnerabochee vremya i sfera obsluzhivania*, Moscow, 1966
Kukushkin, M. S., *Narodny dokhod*, Leningrad, 1965
Kurylev, A. K. and Kopylov, I. Ya., *Formirovanie kommunisticheskikh obshchestvennykh otnoshenii*, Moscow, 1965
Kuzmin, E. S., *Osnovy sotsialnoi psikhologii*, Leningrad, 1967
'KPSS v tsifrakh', in *Partiinaya Zhizn*, No. 10, 1965; No. 15, 1967

Laptiev, I. D., *Nakoplenie i potreblenie v kolkhozakh*, Moscow, 1967
Lebedev, N. B. and Shkaratan, O. I., *Ocherk istorii sotsialisticheskogo sorevnovania*, Leningrad, 1966
Lotukhina, E. A., *Realny dokhod i zhizenny uroven' trudyashchikhsya*, M. Z. Bora (ed.), Minsk, 1966
Loznevaya, M., 'Matematicheskie metody v planirovanii zarabotnoi platy', *Sotsialisticheski trud*, No. 10, 1968

Maier, V. F. and Krylov, P. N., *Planirovanie narodnogo potreblenia v SSSR*, Moscow, 1964

Manevich, E. L., *Problemy obshchestvennogo truda v SSSR*, Moscow, 1966

Materialy Mezhvuzovskoi Nauchnoi Konferentsii po probleme vozrastania aktivnosti, Kursk, 1968

Matyukha, I. Ya., *Statistika byudzhetov naselenia*, Moscow, 1967

Mishutin, A. N. (ed.), *Kommentarii k zakonodatelstvu o trude*, Moscow, 1966

Morozov, D. A., *Trudoden, dengi i torgovlia na sele*, Moscow, 1965

Narodnoe khozyaistvo SSSR, various years

Nozhko, K. G. and others, *Educational Planning in the USSR*, IIEP Publication, Paris, 1968

Osipov, G. V. and others, *Rabochi klass i tekhnicheski progress*, Moscow, 1965

Osipov, G. V. (ed.), *Sotsiologia v SSSR*, Moscow, 1966

Osipov, G. V. and Szczepański, J. (eds.), *Sotsialnye problemy truda i proizvodstva*, Moscow and Warsaw, 1969

Osipov, V. A., *Voprosy formirovania novogo tipa sovetskogo rabochego v usloviakh avtomatizatsii*, Saratov, 1965

O soblyudenii obshchestvennogo poryadka i pravil blagoustroistva v Moskve, Moscow, 1958

Pankratov, I. F., *Osnovnye prava i obyazannosti rukovodyashchikh kadrov kolkhoza*, Moscow, 1957

Pashkov, A. S., *Pravovye osnovy nauchnoi organizatsii truda*, Moscow, 1967

Patrushev, V. D. (ed.), *Opyt ekonomiko-sotsiologicheskikh issledovanii v Sibiri*, Novosibirsk, 1966

Petrosyan, G. S., *Vnerabochee vremya trudyashchikhsya v SSSR*, Moscow, 1965

Platonov, K. K., *Lichnost i trud*, Moscow, 1965

Pod'yachikh, P. G., *Naselenie SSSR*, Moscow, 1961

Preobrazhenski, E. and Bukharin, N., *Azbuka kommunizma*, Moscow, 1921

Programma Kommunisticheskoi Partii Sovetskogo Soyuza, XXII s'ezd, stenograficheski otchet, tom III, Moscow, 1962, p. 229

Prokofiev, M. A., *Narodnoe obrazovanie v SSSR 1917–1967*, Moscow, 1967

Pyatnitsky, P. P. and others, *Denezhnaya oplata truda v kolkhozakh*, Moscow, 1960

Ryvkina, R. V. (ed.), *Sotsiologicheskie issledovania*, Novosibirsk, 1967

Sarkisyan, G. S. and Kuznetsova, N. P., *Potrebnosti i dokhod semi*, Moscow, 1967
Sbornik zakonodatelnykh aktov o trude, Moscow, 1956
Sbornik zakonodatelnykh aktov o trude, Moscow, 1965
Selskoe khozyaistvo SSSR, Moscow, 1960
Senyavski, S. L., *Rost rabochego klassa*, Moscow, 1966
Shaibekov, K. A., *Pravovye formy oplaty truda v kolkhozakh*, Moscow, 1963
Shunkov, A. M., *Organizatsia truda sluzhashchikh*, Moscow, 1965
Sidorova, M. I., *Obshchestvennye fondy potreblenia i dokhody kolkhozni-kov*, Moscow, 1969
Slovar' pravovykh znanii, Moscow, 1965
Slovar' sokrashchenii russkogo yazyka, Moscow, 1963
Sokhan', L. V., *Sotsiologia na Ukraine*, Kiev, 1968
Sonin, M.,*Vosproizvodstvo rabochei sily v SSSR*, Moscow, 1959
Sovetskoe trudovoe pravo, Moscow, 1966
Spisok abonentov moskovskoi gorodskoi telefonnoi seti. Organizatsii, uchrezhdenia, predpriyatia, 1968
Spravochniki dlya postupayushchikh v vysshie uchebnye zavedenia, various years
Spravochnik partiinogo rabotnika, 1968
Spravochnik po nalogam i sboram s naselenia, Moscow, 1968
Spravochnik po selskokhozyaistvennomu zakonodatelstvu dlya predse-datelya kolkhoza, Moscow, 1962
Spravochnik po vechernei srednei obshcheobrazovatelnoi shkole RSFSR, Moscow, 1963
Spravochnik sekretaria pervichnoi komsomolskoi organizatsii, Moscow, 1958
Stalin, I.,*Ekonomicheskie problemy sotsializma v SSSR*, Moscow, 1952
Stalin, I.,*Voprosy leninizma*, Moscow, 1953
Statisticheski slovar', Moscow, 1966
Stepanyan, Ts. A., Semenov, V. S. and others (eds.), *Klassy, sotsialnye sloi i gruppy v SSSR*, Moscow, 1968
Stepanyan, Ts. A., Semenov, V. S. and others (eds.), *Problemy izme-nenia sotsialnoi struktury sovetskogo obshchestva*, Moscow, 1968

Trudovoe pravo, entsiklopedicheski slovar', Moscow, 1969
Trud v SSSR, Moscow, 1968

Uledov, A. K., *Obshchestvennoe mnenie sovetskogo obshchestva*, Mos-cow, 1963

Urlanis, B. Ts., *Rozhdaemost' i prodolzhitelnost' zhizni v SSSR*, Moscow, 1963
Urzhinski, K. P., *Trudoustroistvo grazhdan v SSSR*, Moscow, 1967

Valentei, D. I. and others (eds.), *Voprosy teorii narodonaselenia pri sotsializme*, Moscow, 1967
Veinberg, G. P. and Fainburg, Z. I.,*Vlianie tekhnicheskogo progressa na kharakter truda*, Moscow, 1964
Volkov, A. P. and others, *Trud i zarabotnaya plata v SSSR*, Moscow, 1962
Volovik, L. A. (ed.), *Sotsiologia i ideologia*, Moscow, 1969
Vorozheikin, I. E. and others, *Sovetskaya intelligentsia*, Moscow, 1968
Vysshaya shkola, osnovnye postanovlenia, etc., Moscow, 1957

Yovchuk, M. T. and others, *Pod'yem kulturno-tekhnicheskogo urovnya sovetskogo rabochego klassa*, Moscow, 1961

Zabelin, N. and Sundetov, S., *Ispolsovanie trudovykh resursov v voprosakh balansa truda*, Alma-Ata, 1966
Zaslavskaya, T. I., *Raspredelenie po trudu v kolkhozakh*, Moscow, 1966
Zaslavskaya, T. I. and Ladenkov, V. N., 'Sotsialno-ekonomicheskie uslovia sozdania postoyannykh kadrov v selskom khozyaistve Sibiri', *Izvestia Sibirskogo otdelenia A.N. SSSR*, seria obshchestvennykh nauk, No. 11, 1967
Zdravomyslov, A. G. and Yadov, V. A., *Trud i razvitie lichnosti*, Leningrad, 1965
Zdravomyslov, A. G., Yadov, V. A. and Rozhin, V. P., *Chelovek i ego rabota*, Moscow, 1967
Zvorykin, A. A., *Nauka, proizvodstvo, trud*, Moscow, 1965

Bibliography of Non-Soviet Publications

Ammassari, Paolo, 'Ideologia e Sociologia nell'Unione Sovietica', *Rassegna Italiana di Sociologia*, Jan.–March 1964

Brackett, J. W., 'The Human Resources', *New Directions in the Soviet Economy*, U S Congress Report, Washington, 1962, p. 611

Broderson, Arvid, *Soviet Labour*, New York, 1966

Brown, E. C., *Soviet Trade Unions and Labour Relations*, Cambridge (Mass.), 1966

Bukharin (Boukharine), N., *La Théorie du Matérialisme Historique*, Paris, 1927

Chambre, H., 'Urbanisation et Croissance Économique en URSS', in *Économie Appliquée*, No. 1, Jan.–March 1964

Clark, Burton R., 'Sociology of Education', in *Handbook of Modern Sociology*, ed. R. E. L. Faris, Chicago, 1964

Dewar, M., 'Labour and Wage Reforms in the USSR', in *The Soviet Economy*, ed. H. G. Shaffer, London, 1961

De Witt, N., *Education and Professional Employment in the USSR*, Washington, 1961

Dodge, N. T., *Women in the Soviet Economy*, Baltimore, 1966

Durham, F. G., *Use of Free Time by Young People in Soviet Society*, Center for International Studies, Massachusetts Institute of Technology, mimeograph, Jan. 1966

Eason, W. W., *The Population of the USSR*, Report to the Judiciary Commission of the House of Representatives, US Congress, Washington, 1964

Fainsod, M., *Smolensk under Soviet Rule*, London, 1958

Florinsky, M. I., *Encyclopedia of the Soviet Union*, New York, 1963

Florinsky, M. I., *Russia, a History and an Interpretation*, New York, 1964

Gilison, J. M., 'Soviet Elections as a Measure of Dissent: The Missing One Percent', *American Political Science Review*, Vol. 62, 1968

Goodman, A. S. and Feshbach, M., 'Estimates and Projections of Educational Attainment in the USSR, 1950–1985', quoted in *Soviet Economic Performance 1966–67*, Joint Economic Committee report to US Congress, Washington, 1968, p. 79

Gunther, John, *Inside Russia Today*, London, 1962

Inkeles, A., *Social Change in Soviet Russia*, Harvard, 1968

Inkeles, A. and Bauer, R., *The Soviet Citizen*, Harvard, 1959

International Bureau of Education and UNESCO, publication No. 254, *The Organization of Educational and Vocational Guidance*, Geneva, 1963

Johnson, E. L., *An Introduction to the Soviet Legal System*, London, 1969

Kaser, M., 'Soviet Statistics of Wages and Prices', *Soviet Studies*, Vol. VII, Glasgow, July 1955

Kussmann, Thomas, 'Berufslenkung, Berufswahl und Berufsberatung in der UdSSR', *Osteuropa Wirtschaft*, No. 4, 1968

Lewin, M., *Russian Peasants and Soviet Power*, London, 1968

Lewis, Robert A. and Rowland, R. H., 'Urbanisation in Russia and the USSR, 1897–1966', *Annals of the Association of American Geographers*, Vol. 59. No. 4, Dec. 1969

Lorimer, Frank, *The Population of the Soviet Union*, Geneva, 1946

Madison, B. Q., *Social Welfare in the Soviet Union*, Standford, 1968

Matthews, Mervyn, articles on youth employment in *Soviet Affairs*, St Antony's Papers, No. 12 (3), London, 1962, *Osteuropa*, No. 7, 1962

Meissner, B., *Sowjet Gesellschaft im Wandel*, W. Kohlhammer Verlag, 1966

National Youth Employment Council, triennial report, *Youth Employment Services in Great Britain*, 1965–7

Newth, J. A., 'Income Distribution in the USSR', *Soviet Studies*, Vol. XII, Oct. 1960

Nicolaevsky, B. I. and Dallin, D., *Forced Labour in Soviet Russia*, London, 1947

Nove, Alec, *An Economic History of the USSR*, London, 1969

Ossowski, S., *Class Structure in the Social Consciousness*, London, 1963

Prokopovicz, S. N., *Histoire Économique de l'URSS*, Paris, 1952

Rigby, H., *Communist Party Membership in the USSR, 1919–1967*, Princetown, 1968

Roof, M. K. and Leedy, F. A., 'Population Redistribution in the Soviet Union, 1939–56', *The Geographical Review*, Vol. XLIX, No. 2, April 1959

Rosen, S. M., *Significant Aspects of Soviet Education*, U.S. Dept. of Health, Education and Welfare, Washington, 1965

Schwarz, Solomon, *Labor in the Soviet Union*, London, 1953

Taylor, William, 'The Sociology of Education', in *The Study of Education*, ed. J. W. Tibble, London, 1966

United States Govt Dept of Health, Education and Welfare, *Digest of Educational Statistics*, Washington, 1966

United States Govt Dept of Health, Education and Welfare, *Social Security Bulletin*, Jan. 1965

United States Govt Dept of Health, Education and Welfare, *Statistical Abstract of the U.S.*, Washington, 1968

Utechin, S. V., *Russian Political Thought*, London, 1964

Wädekin, K. E., *Privatproduzenten in der sowjetischen Landwirtschaft*, Köln, 1967

Wädekin, K. E., 'Zur Sozialschichtung der Sowjetgesellschaft', *Osteuropa*, Heft 5, 1965

Wädekin, K. E., 'Landwirtschaftliche Bevölkerung und Arbeitskräfte der Sowjetunion in Zahlen', *Osteuropa Wirtschaft*, No. 1, 1967

Yanowitch, M., 'The Soviet Income Revolution', *Slavic Review*, Dec. 1963

Index